Blood on the Street

The Sensational Inside Story of How Wall Street Analysts Duped a Generation of Investors

Charles Gasparino

Free Press
NEW YORK · LONDON · TORONTO · SYDNEY

Free Press
Rockefeller Center
1230 Avenue of the Americas
New York, NY 10020

For information regarding special discounts for bulk purchases,
please contact Simon & Schuster Special Sales at 1-800-456-6798
or business@simonandschuster.com

Manufactured in the United States of America

5   7   9   10   8   6   4

Library of Congress Cataloging-in-Publication Data is available.

ISBN 0-7432-5023-0

To my wife and my love, forever and ever, Amen
For Mom and Dad, if you could only see me now

Contents

Blood on the Street

Prologue

In January 2000, Jack Grubman was at the top of his game as hundreds of his admirers, men and women he helped make rich, took their seats under the desert stars, at the exclusive La Quinta resort in Palm Springs, California. It was the final day of his popular telecommunications investment conference, where the gospel according to Grubman—summed up in his unwavering belief that investors could make a bundle investing in a handful of new, high-tech telephone companies—was celebrated in all its glory.

As the top telecommunications analyst at Salomon Smith Barney, the prestigious investment-banking arm of the massive Citigroup financial empire, Grubman had one of Wall Street's best platforms from which to spread his theory. For the past five years, he had pumped out dozens upon dozens of reports on his top stocks—companies like WorldCom, Global Crossing, Qwest Communications, and Winstar—that soared to new highs with every one of his "buy" recommendations.

But Grubman's real power was not just as an analyst who recommended what stocks investors should buy. He was a deal maker, who used the power of his research to re-create the modern telecommunications business through a series of mergers and huge financings. It was this dual role that helped Grubman earn page one treatment in *The Wall Street Journal* as "The Jack of All Trades." And it was this dual role that made him one of the highest paid executives on Wall Street, earning as much as $25 million in 1999 alone.

As Grubman would tell anyone who listened, his was a true rags-to-riches story. He said his journey to Wall Street began in the working-class neighborhood of South Philly, the fictional home of Rocky Balboa, where he took a double major in boxing and mathematics. His parents, Izzy and Mildred, worked hard so he would have a life outside the old neighborhood, pushing him to get a top-notch education, first at MIT and then at Columbia University, where he studied for a Ph.D. in math. That was all before he landed a job at the nation's largest telephone company, AT&T, and his career took a prophetic turn. Grubman saw the coming changes that would revolutionize the way people communicate and started thinking about how to apply them to make money on Wall Street.

His theory, which he spread like a televangelist during the 1990s market boom, was almost too simple to be true: An endless demand for products, everything from cell phones to high-speed Internet lines, had changed the shape of a once stodgy industry dominated by AT&T. Companies that followed his advice by laying down miles upon miles of high-speed cable lines and offering multitudes of new products not only earned Grubman's coveted "buy" rating but also the support of investors who hung on his every word.

With Grubman's stock picks doing better than ever, the conference had become one of the most popular events on Wall Street. More than one hundred companies and over one thousand people representing the best and brightest on Wall Street would make the trek to Palm Springs, much as they had done in the previous years Grubman hosted the event. The festivities included slide shows, presentations, and speeches. Ted Turner, now the vice chairman of TimeWarner, announced during one session that his company's recent merger with AOL (a deal completed by Grubman's mentor, investment banker Eduardo Mestre), had increased his net worth by another $2.5 billion—a feeling he compared to having sex for the first time.

It's unclear what Turner did after his speech, but those who stayed to the end of the conference were treated to an elegant dinner at the five-star resort, wines from Napa Valley, and entertainment that one attendee described as a knockoff of Broadway's popular *Riverdance* Irish dance act. Despite a busy schedule, former Treasury Secretary Robert Rubin, now a top Citigroup executive, had agreed to give a much-anticipated dinner speech on Wall Street's role in the nation's current prosperity.

As Grubman worked his way around the room, shaking hands and hugging admirers, he had all the confidence of a man at the height of his power. He was lean, over six feet in height, with a body, he claimed, honed by one hundred push-ups and one hundred sit-ups every day before work, though he wasn't averse to throwing back a shot of bourbon, and, in his early days, a line of coke.

Even his detractors, most of them rival analysts who lost deal after deal to Grubman, would concede that his rise to fame certainly was amazing. In 1997, he took credit for approaching WorldCom's chief financial officer Scott Sullivan with the idea of teaming up with another industry giant, MCI, then the second-largest long-distance player after AT&T. After the deal was announced, he switched hats, urging investors to "load up the truck" and buy more WorldCom, even though the new company was socked with billions of dollars in new debt.

And they did. Shares of WorldCom rose from $30 in mid-1995 to its peak of just over $64 a year after the transaction was announced. Everyone, it appeared, was happy. Investors were earning big bucks, the company's balance sheet appeared fine, and Salomon Smith Barney walked away with one of its biggest paydays ever, earning more than $32 million in fees for advising WorldCom on the $35 billion merger, and an additional $15 million on a related bond deal. A year later, the transaction helped Grubman win a lucrative contract from his notoriously tight-fisted boss, Sandy Weill, the head of the Citigroup financial empire, that made him among the top-paid people in the profession.

"Jack was like God," recalled one rival analyst. "And the conference was like being in the center of the universe."

Grubman seemed to live a charmed life. Along with Mary Meeker, of Morgan Stanley, and Merrill Lynch's Henry Blodget, he was one of a handful of stock analysts who achieved rock-star status during the stock market boom by combining stock picking with deal making. In some ways, Grubman tried to keep a lower profile than his counterparts, avoiding CNBC, the daily blow-horn of Internet and technology stocks that pumped up the careers of Blodget, Meeker, and a slew of lesser-known analysts. But he adroitly courted the print media, which detailed every inch of his life story and market theory, and never failed to hype his research calls with "blast voicemails" sent to hundreds of money managers around the globe. Regulators, meanwhile, looked beyond numerous news reports of his conflicted relationship with his banking clients, apparently buying into Grubman's rationale that rather than hurting his research, such conflicts made him more informed about the companies.

By early 2000, Grubman's argument was selling better than ever. In addition to executives from all the top money management firms, outfits like Fidelity, T. Rowe Price, Putnam, and the new masters of Corporate America all paid homage to the man who put them on the map. Global

Crossing CEO Bob Annunziata was given a special invitation by Grubman to provide a "keynote presentation" on the third day of the conference. "We look forward to your positive response and will call you shortly to follow up on this invitation," Grubman wrote. It was an offer Annunziata could hardly refuse; after all, Grubman was said to have recommended that Global Crossing's chairman, former Drexel Burnham Lambert junk-bond salesman Gary Winnick, appoint Annunziata as the CEO of Global a year earlier.

Others like Joe Nacchio, the gruff CEO of Qwest Communications, came for similar reasons. Like Annunziata, Grubman recommended Nacchio for the post thanks to his close relationship with another one of his followers, Qwest founder Phil Anschutz. AT&T CEO Michael Armstrong felt as though he didn't owe Grubman anything, but he, too, couldn't miss the event. Indeed, Armstrong despised Grubman for his constant criticism of how he ran AT&T. But just a few weeks before the conference, Grubman had shocked the markets with a dazzling about-face, turning bullish on the stock and Armstrong after years of negativity. The reason appeared evident when AT&T announced it was preparing to spin off its wireless unit, worth tens of millions of dollars in underwriting fees. Grubman made sure that he featured the deal during one of his many presentations, as it became clear that Salomon Smith Barney would earn a chunk of that money.

But the event's biggest star (after Grubman, of course) was Bernie Ebbers, the CEO of WorldCom. Like Grubman, Ebbers had come a long way from his days as a high-school basketball coach and owner of a chain of motels in Mississippi. Ebbers arrived in a black limo, dressed smartly in a dark suit, and was immediately surrounded by a throng of supporters as he made his way around the conference. It's easy to see why—WorldCom was among the market's hottest stocks, thanks significantly to Grubman's never-ending support, and Ebbers had become one of the nation's richest men, worth more than $1 billion.

More riches would follow, Grubman predicted. "The state of the union" as Grubman used to call his vision of the telecom business, was never better, as attendees heard again and again during the course of the day. Grubman and his staff went to great lengths to arrange panel discussions that featured upcoming deals that he thought would change the scope of the telecom business—and in the process, make them more money. Several veteran investors said the event reminded them of the old "Predator's Ball," a big conference held by former junk-bond king Michael Milken. Like Milken, Grubman understood one-stop shopping, bringing together the biggest investors and money managers with the new masters of Corporate America he helped create.

As the day came to an end, and Grubman prepared for the dinner activities, his guests assembled underneath a large white tent, guzzling expensive wines and gossiping about the stock market boom that Grubman helped perpetuate. Even more than his stock picks, what money managers appeared to appreciate the most about Grubman were his deal tips—the mergers and acquisitions that could move stocks. Knowing what stocks would be bought before the deal was announced was like money in the bank for portfolio managers, and Grubman appeared more than willing to talk up any deal that came across his radar screen.

Grubman, meanwhile, sat at the front table with several of his best customers, waiting for the night's special guest to begin his speech. Now a top executive at Citigroup, Robert Rubin made his fortune as a savvy bond trader and later rose to the position of chairman of the prestigious Goldman Sachs & Company investment bank. In the early 1990s, as treasury secretary in the Clinton administration, he prodded President Clinton to cut a ballooning budget deficit during a recession by raising taxes. It was widely believed that Rubin helped spur the endless stock-market expansion, due largely to the resulting low interest rates that provided cheap credit to many of the companies Grubman had championed, and advised to expand.

Rubin walked quickly to the podium dressed in his dark suit, and looking a little too serious for the occasion. One money manager in the audience immediately sniped, "It's Darth Vader." Rubin's speech was even darker than his appearance. "I went through this with Sandy," Mr. Rubin said, referring to Citigroup's CEO Sanford I. Weill, "and Sandy told me not to make this speech."

Although he didn't mention Grubman by name, what followed was a not-so-subtle attack on his philosophy that the stock market would never stop booming. "My comments may seem a bit dour," he added, but "there is a paradox that accompanies our prosperity." That paradox, simply stated, was that the market couldn't sustain the lofty stock prices found among many of the New Economy stocks issued by the high-tech

Internet and telecommunications companies so popular among investors. People in the room, he said, had a moral obligation to prepare the country for the inevitable burst of the stock market bubble.

"I agree with the view that this is a time of great opportunity and enormous constructive change. But I profoundly disagree with the notion that there is a new economy that is not susceptible to severe and prolonged reversals," he said, "Technological developments, globalization, the move to market-based economies, and improved understanding of how economies work are powerful positive forces," he added. "But some see it as more than that. They see a new paradigm that renders irrelevant so many traditional concerns about downturns, risk, and sound policy."

Simply put, the never-ending growth advocated by Grubman "would be contrary to all of human history with respect to markets and economies, and that should be a sobering caution."

It was a message many in the audience chose to ignore, including the host himself. About halfway through Rubin's speech, people began to leave their seats; some were heard muttering how bored they were with all the gloom and doom. Those who left were spared another obvious insult when Rubin zinged Grubman once again, attacking the financiers in "New York where all aspects of financial life are pervaded by the assumption that all will always be well, and that any interruptions will be temporary and mild at worst."

The speech was lengthy, about forty minutes, but at least Rubin ended on what he considered a positive note. "There will be ups and downs and much will depend on how well the private and public sectors meet the challenges of promoting competitiveness and maintaining constructive economic policy around the globe," he said. "I've enjoyed being with you, and now you can go from my somewhat dour, or at least mixed, perspective, to the dynamic prospects of your companies. Thank you."

There was a brief round of applause. Rubin shook hands with Grubman before heading off, possibly to seal another banking deal for Citigroup. Grubman stood near the dais, shaking hands and seemingly unfazed by whatever Rubin may have directed toward him and his fans.

But not everyone ignored Rubin's warning. Susan Kalla, an independent telecom analyst who at the time was looking for a job on Wall Street, broke out in a cold sweat halfway through Rubin's remarks. Kalla's husband had worked with Grubman at AT&T, and as a competitor she kept tabs on Grubman's rise to power. Unlike Grubman, Kalla had already started to question the valuations of telecom stocks by keeping track of the supply of broadband, the cable lines that were used to connect computers and other telecom products to the Internet. For the past six months, broadband prices were in a free fall, which, according to Kalla's analysis, meant that companies like WorldCom, Global Crossing, Qwest Communications, and Winstar would have to cut prices to attract new customers.

That's when it dawned on her that for years Grubman had advocated rapid expansion through the issuance of debt, which his top picks had followed religiously by issuing billions of dollars in bonds, much of it through Citigroup. But if prices kept falling, how were they going to pay their bills?

Kalla surveyed the room for reactions. Attendees huddled under heating lamps sipping drinks and planning their schedule for the remainder of the conference. "But what about the speech?" she asked. She heard the same answer again and again: *Who cares.* After all, how many times in the past five years had they heard the market was about to crash only to watch it rise higher on Jack's every word?

Then Kalla walked up to Grubman, who was holding court with several followers. "So, Jack, what did you think of the speech?" Like the others, Grubman appeared unmoved. "Markets go up and markets go down," he said, shrugging his shoulders, before resuming his conversation.

Kalla left the party and went straight to her hotel room. The next day, she called her broker and began unloading technology stocks from her personal account. It turned out to be the best trade she ever made.

Looking back, Jack Grubman's comments to Susan Kalla may have been the most prescient of his controversial career. Within two months, the market for the high-technology stocks that made Grubman and the other celebrity analysts, namely Mary Meeker and Henry Blodget, into superstars for their persistent bullishness on Internet and telecom companies would reach its peak. On March 10, 2000, the NASDAQ Stock Market, the broadest measurement of the value of technology stocks, rose above the 5,000 level, nearly double what it was just a year earlier, before dropping almost 4,000 points during the next three years and draining trillions of dollars from the American economy. WorldCom, Grubman's most touted stock, already coming off its highs during the conference, would suffer a similar fate despite Grubman's unwavering support. In mid 2002, WorldCom traded at just a few dollars a share, and soon fell into bankruptcy amid a massive accounting scandal that would lead to the indictment of CEO Bernie Ebbers and other high-ranking officials. All of this occurred largely without a peep from the Wall Street analysts like Grubman, who claimed throughout the boom to have such grand insight into the company's finances.

Arguably there were many reasons for the stock market bubble of the 1990s. There was a broad "democratization" of the markets, as a new generation of investors armed with the ability to snap up stocks using their computers decided to jump into the markets without much thought of the consequences if the averages should fall. During the 1990s, as companies began to eliminate old corporate pension plans, employees were for the first time forced to save for retirement themselves through 401(k) and Keogh plans. Low interest rates on bonds and other fixed income investments gave investors little choice but to buy stocks, particularly those in the high-flying technology sectors, which investors were led to believe would offer the greatest return by the time they were ready to retire.

But the biased research pumped out by the Wall Street analysts may have been the most significant factor in pushing the markets to their unsustainable highs during the bubble years. Ostensibly, the job of the analysts was to recommend what stocks investors should purchase. But throughout the 1990s, they gave credibility to the overvalued markets to millions of new investors, who were largely unaware that the analysts had taken on a more conflicted role of recommending stocks and helping their firms win the lucrative investment banking deals from the same companies that helped pay their own outsized salaries. This book is about the choice analysts had to make when the interests of small investors "conflicted" with their own self-interest. As I plan to show, investors lost out almost every time as analysts chose to promote and hype rather than analyze and critique when faced with a choice that would make them less rich.

Several of the people profiled here were more culpable in this duplicity than others. Of the three analysts featured in this book, only Mary Meeker chose to address all the questions surrounding her research in a series of on-the-record conversations after surviving a two-year investigation into her research practices. Blodget, who has since been banned from the business because of his allegedly fraudulent research, declined to comment about his Merrill Lynch days because of confidentiality restrictions. Grubman, also banned from the securities industry, referred questions to a spokesman. Despite her reputation as "Queen of the Net," Meeker was in many ways a reluctant bull. She refused to recommend and underwrite many speculative stock deals that ultimately moved to competitors. She also provided ample evidence that she warned investors of the coming doom. "I told anyone who would listen that there was risk," she says. "Where's the individual responsibility?"

Good question, and in the coming pages, I have attempted to depict the people "duped" by the faulty research as complex individuals who were victimized not only by the Wall Street hypsters, but also by their own greed to make a fast buck. But it's also a question that Meeker and her employer, the Morgan Stanley investment bank, should be answering as well. Meeker may not be guilty of outright fraud, but she embraced an utterly fraudulent system, where she was expected to help her company make hundreds of millions of dollars underwriting stocks, and then issue "objective" research on the same companies just a short time later.

One excuse I've heard repeatedly was that research ratings really didn't matter, particularly to sophisticated mutual fund managers and other sophisticated investors who handle the vast majority of investor wealth. This book will in fact show how not only small investors used research to make investment decisions, but that the supposedly sophisticated "institutional investors" closely followed what Grubman, Meeker, and Blodget had to say about the markets and the stocks they covered. The so-called market professionals packed into the trio's conferences as if they were going to a rock concert. They demanded face time with the superstar analysts to get an inside track on the industry they were covering. One analyst for a large pension fund so idolized Jack Grubman that she professed her love and desire to have sex with him on a daily basis (more on that later). And based on numerous interviews with market participants, I have found that many sophisticated money managers wouldn't think twice about receiving an inside tip on a stock before analysts released such news to the public.

In the end, one thing is certain. This is a story where there are few heroes, and even fewer people willing to provide an honest account of what went wrong. The research scandals were unraveled by New York Attorney General Eliot Spitzer, who did great work exposing the corrupt process, but ultimately gave a pass to one of Wall Street's biggest and most politically powerful players. Regulators at the SEC say they continue to investigate biased research and its impact on the investing public thanks to the leadership of SEC chairman William Donaldson, one of the founders of the first "independent" research firm, Donaldson, Lufkin & Jenrette Securities. But the SEC chief is getting a late start. Under various SEC chairmen, Wall Street's top regulatory agency largely ignored the issue. Donaldson, himself, said very little about the problem when it became clear that his old firm, DLJ, embraced the system of conflicts throughout the 1990s market boom.

Perhaps the most honest account of Wall Street research I could find came from a man named Gerry Rothstein, a veteran analyst near the end of his career. In an interview, Rothstein recalled a telephone call from his son, Mike, who had just completed his MBA from Duke University, one of the premier business schools in the country. The year was 1997, Grubman, Blodget, and Meeker were stars of the brokerage business, and Wall Street research seemed like the place to be. Mike wondered whether he should follow in his dad's footsteps and become a stock analyst, preferably at one of Wall Street's most prestigious firms.

His father's answer was short and to the point. "Don't do it," he said. "Unless you want to be a servant for investment banking."

CHAPTER ONE

The Seeds of the Scandal

By the start of the great stock market bubble of the 1990s, Jeff Liddle had built a reputation as one of the meanest and toughest lawyers on Wall Street. Balding, with broad shoulders, a bad temper, and a passing resemblance to Mr. Clean, Liddle's specialty was getting the big Wall Street firms to cough up large settlements to brokers and other Wall Street executives who claimed they were "wrongfully dismissed" from their firms.

There was no one better at getting Wall Street to pay than Liddle, and opponents point to his hardball tactics as the secret of his success. Liddle has sued at least one opposing lawyer on behalf of a client for slander. Several times he has been criticized by arbitration panels over belligerent behavior. Maybe most telling, Liddle openly brags that the best time he ever had in a courtroom was the eight days he spent grilling an executive, who also happened to be his ex-wife.

But what ultimately gave Liddle his edge was an inside knowledge of the inner workings of Wall Street. He was an attorney for the infamous Drexel Burnham Lambert, and knew the seedier side of the brokerage business better than the vast majority of his peers, from the ass grabbing that women regularly endure on trading desks to the boardroom power plays that leave a trail of firings and potential clients in their wake. "Most of the firms on Wall Street are so poorly managed that almost anything goes," he once said.

Liddle believed that Wall Street research easily fit within his worldview. By the mid-1990s, Wall Street research had strayed far from practices employed by Donaldson Lufkin & Jenrette Securities, the first "independent" research firm. DLJ, as it was known on the street, built a business model based on issuing research to money managers who were more than willing to pay for honest stock tips and business analysis. The payment came through stock trading commissions, which covered analysts' salaries.

DLJ's first research report, titled "Common Stock and Common Sense," argued that the only thing holding investors back was a "lack of knowledge" about the markets, and by the end of the 1960s founders Bill Donaldson, Dan Lufkin, and Dick Jenrette had become millionaires several times over thanks to their success in selling investor-focused research. Donaldson ultimately sought out a career in politics and would become chairman of the New York Stock Exchange, while Jenrette and Lufkin became some of the key players on Wall Street.

But DLJ's high-minded business model wouldn't fare as well. The turning point came in May 1975, when Congress approved a major change in Wall Street trading practices. No longer would trading commissions be "fixed" by the NYSE. Instead, a new floating-rate system was installed, allowing market forces to control commissions.

Almost immediately, trading commissions floated lower. DLJ, like the rest of Wall Street, was forced to remake itself into an investment banking firm and pay analysts from revenues gleaned from investment banking deals. Now that the gravy train was over, it didn't take long for analysts to become de facto investment bankers, attending road shows and hyping their assessments of banking prospects in an attempt to win business and earn their keep.

As the investment banking booms of the 1980s and 1990s accelerated the commingling of these activities, DLJ seemed to embody everything its founders were against. "We used to joke that the house that research built was turning into the house that investment banking runs," says Tom Brown, a former DLJ analyst who claims he was fired from the firm after criticizing an important investment banking client. Brown wasn't the only analyst to notice the change. During much of the 1990s, analysts at DLJ openly complained about being pressured to hype ratings to win deals. (A DLJ contract offered to a prospective analyst guaranteed "banking related compensation of at least $1,500,000 during the calendar years covered by [the agreement].") One afternoon, a DLJ analyst and eventual stock research chief, Mark Manson, had some words of wisdom for analysts at the firm under pressure to hype ratings to win banking business, recalls Brown. "The key to working with investment banking," Brown says Manson told the group, "is learning how to say 'Forgive me, father, for I have sinned.' " (Manson doesn't recall making the statement.)

Others at DLJ were even more direct. During a management meeting, one executive was given a list of candidates for a stock research job. "Which one is the least offensive, we have a big banking calendar," the executive quipped, according to one of the other participants. Many former DLJ executives say that the firm maintained its traditionally high research standards. But inside DLJ, the decline of research was obvious. In the 1990s, both Dick Jenrette and Bill Donaldson were working as DLJ consultants with offices at the company. One afternoon, Jenrette burst into Donaldson's office and asked his old partner to look at a recent research report published by a DLJ analyst. "Isn't this one of the worst things you've ever seen?" Jenrette said. Donaldson agreed.

By the summer of 1995, Liddle was ready to show that Merrill Lynch practices weren't much different. He had filed an arbitration case on behalf of a former Merrill oil and energy stock analyst named Suzanne Cook, who said that she was fired from the firm even though she excelled at the single most important part of her job as an analyst: winning investment banking business. Cook sought back pay and an unspecified amount of damages, charging that her supervisors at Merrill gave her the boot to make room for a male less qualified at snaring banking deals.

Liddle loved the case for several reasons. First, he considered gender discrimination fertile ground for big settlements since men outnumber women across all the Wall Street job classifications (except secretary). Meanwhile, Liddle believed that Wall Street locker-room behavior was still alive and well at most of the big brokerage firms, with fancy strip clubs like Scores in New York becoming hubs of deal-making activity. Merrill stock research chief Andrew Melnick also made a particularly inviting target, Liddle believed. Melnick had fired Cook in 1992 just a few months after she and other top analysts received an invitation to dine with company CEO Dan Tully as part of a special program to advance the firm's top analysts. Cook claimed that Melnick at one point reminded her that working for a Wall Street firm is a "man's job." Melnick denied making the remark, but Liddle couldn't wait to get Melnick on the stand. Melnick's monotone voice and thick glasses made him seem like an odd duck rather than a top research executive. During the early days of the case, Liddle even came up with a nickname for Melnick: "The Creature," for the way he ate a tuna fish sandwich one afternoon during a break in the proceedings.

But even more promising for Liddle was the fact that Cook came ready to expose some controversial practices inside Merrill's research department. Analysts at Merrill were far from the green-eyeshade types the company had portrayed to small investors who bought stocks through its massive brokerage network. After reading thousands of documents, Liddle believed that the final product—the Merrill Lynch research report with its stock recommendations targeted for unsophisticated small investors—was nothing more than a tool used by the firm's bankers to win lucrative stock deals.

Melnick, Liddle believed, was a key player in this conflicted process. He kept detailed records of how many deals each analyst worked on, the bankers involved in the transaction, and how they rated the analysts' work. Liddle hit pay dirt when he found one memo from Melnick titled "IBK Impact" (shorthand for investment banking impact) in which analysts were asked to fill out a form listing their contributions to the firm's investment banking efforts "in order to properly credit your efforts." Maybe more telling, each month Melnick prepared a separate report for his boss Jack Lavery that helped senior management determine bonuses for their analysts. These reports, known as Monthly Executive Operating Reports, or MEORs (pronounced *meeors*) listed all the deals his team of analysts worked on, in addition to other factors that went into the bonus calculation. As Liddle would discover, Melnick loved to trumpet analysts' role in winning business when lobbying for higher compensation for his people. One MEOR dated September 1992 was particularly telling: "With the growing sense that IBK [investment banking] requires research to do business, or that our investment bankers are not of the quality to win investment banking business without research, the balance of compensation at year-end should be tilted toward research," he wrote.

Melnick added that "it is important that the firm should adjust to the fact that our best analysts should be compensated, considering their increasing importance to the firm, to what we and other firms are willing to pay to attract good commercial analysts. Our budget process should take this into account."

Liddle found evidence that top officials at Merrill were well aware of these practices. Lavery, Melnick's supervisor, wrote his own memo touting analysts' contribution to the firm's banking work that each month was passed on to top executives, including Merrill's chairman and CEO. Both Melnick and Lavery, of course, were supporting their employees, but they were also underscoring the inherent conflicts in Merrill's research operations. They weren't pleading for more money just because their analysts had a good record for picking stocks, or claiming that picking stocks was even a priority for analysts at Merrill. Instead, both Melnick and Lavery revealed just how much time Merrill analysts spent on a bigger priority at the firm, namely, winning banking deals.

That said, Merrill wasn't ready to concede defeat just yet. In addition to defending its research policies, Merrill was prepared to argue that Cook was nothing more than a second-rate analyst by directing attention to what they said was her own poor record. Bolstering their case was the fact that in April 1995, an administrative law judge found Cook guilty of securities fraud, a decision that was later reversed. The decision stemmed from a civil case in which the SEC alleged that Cook had helped prepare an upbeat press release for a small energy service outfit that contained both false and misleading financial information. The SEC said Cook prepared the report *knowing* that the company was "almost certain to sustain a loss." (Cook maintained that she had no idea that the company was misleading investors.) The reasons the SEC asserted for Cook's actions appeared even more damaging. Her husband won a consulting contract from the company around the time his wife began meeting with officials as part of her work with Merrill. There were other conflicts as well; the SEC said Cook's husband was introduced to the company's CEO through his wife's contacts within the outfit, and that he later became one of the highest-paid employees there. Cook herself stood to benefit from this relationship; she conceded to the SEC that she was working several deals involving the company, including a proposal to merge it with another Merrill client.

The case, *Cook v. Merrill Lynch,* was filed with the National Association of Securities Dealers, Wall Street's self-regulatory organization in August 1995. Wall Street, it should be noted, has a peculiar way of settling disputes. Outside of the brokerage business, courts have become the final word on everything from employment disputes to claims of improper business dealings. But on Wall Street, brokerage clients and employees waive the right to go to court, opting for a system of arbitration, where a panel of supposedly independent people make the rulings.

Each year, arbitration panels award tens of millions of dollars in damages to disgruntled employees, investors, and countless others who maintain they were wronged by the brokerage industry in one way or another. Investor advocates, meanwhile, claim that many of the panels often side with the big firms and that investors would fare better in the courts. One thing is certain: The process is conducted in secrecy, meaning that unless a decision is reached, much of the damaging evidence is never made public.

Liddle seemed to luck out from the beginning, though. The arbitrators, two men and a woman, granted nearly every request Liddle made, ensuring the disclosure of thousands of pages of confidential documents, and the testimony of several top Merrill officials including Melnick, the man who developed the firm's research strategy. The proceedings took place in Dallas; according to NASD rules, arbitration panels conduct proceedings in the city where the employee last worked. (Cook had worked in Merrill's Dallas office.) For the next two years, some of Merrill's top officials, such as Jerome Kenney, who reported to the firm's CEO, Daniel Tully and later David Komansky, were forced to take time out of their busy schedules to appear before the panel. Melnick's testimony came on a hot July morning in 1997. Dressed in a dark suit and wearing the thick, horn-rimmed glasses that had become his trademark, Melnick appeared haggard as he walked into a large conference room at the Adolphus Hotel for his deposition. He complained of a bad cold, but as it turned out, that was the least of his problems.

When the proceedings began, Liddle was primed for action. He asked Melnick to describe his academic and professional experience, how many people he supervised in the past, his fields of expertise, and how he paid his employees. Wall Street executives receive a relatively nominal salary, a six-figure number that varies from firm to firm. Most of their compensation comes in the form of a bonus, usually doled out toward the end of the year, and often many times larger than their annual salary. What Liddle believed he discovered from the memos was that investment banking work was given more weight than other factors, such as the accuracy of research, when Melnick handed out bonus checks.

Liddle addressed the compensation issue head-on. "When did you learn what your responsibilities would be regarding bonuses?" he asked.

Melnick pointed out that he inherited the bonus system when he joined Merrill in 1988. The "dominating factor" in analyst's compensation, he explained, was the size of the firm's bonus pool. The larger the pool the more money he had to parcel out. Unlike many firms, analysts at Merrill were paid not specifically for banking work. "What we're trying to avoid is that the analyst will do a deal just because (he or she) would be paid for a deal," Melnick said.

But Liddle wasn't buying the explanation. He pressed Melnick on how he made bonus decisions on specific analysts. Melnick said such decisions were made on a case-by-case basis, based on how well the individual analyst worked as part of the Merrill Lynch research team, and the accuracy of their research calls. But toward the end of his answer, Melnick cited another consideration—"The sense from investment banking." It was the answer Liddle was waiting for. "The third thing you said was that you wanted to get a sense of how the investment bankers viewed the value of the analyst," Liddle asked.

"That's correct," Melnick responded.

"What do you mean, get a sense of it?" Liddle pressed. "Was it like you call them up anonymously and ask them what their thoughts were, or did you formally ask them for their opinion?"

Melnick's answer surprised Liddle in its honesty. Certainly, he said, Merrill practiced quality control. Analysts must sign off on any deal that the firm chooses to underwrite, meaning that if they are not comfortable with a company's finances, the firm can't underwrite the stock. But Melnick said he got his "sense" of how well analysts fared with investment bankers through a detailed process of record keeping, interviews, and cross evaluations that allowed senior management at Merrill to understand just how much each analyst contributed to the firm's investment banking business.

The process began early each year, he explained. In January or February analysts were ordered to submit forms that listed all the deals they worked on, what services they contributed to getting the deal, and what bankers they worked with. Liddle pressed for more details on how Melnick kept track of all the banking work analysts completed. As it turned out, while Merrill didn't pay analysts on a per deal basis, Melnick created the next best thing, an "index based on the amount of money involved and the sense of the contribution of the analyst."

In fact, Melnick was so concerned about how analysts performed on banking deals that bankers themselves actually evaluated the analysts' performance. Cook had issued several reports that predicted a decline in energy prices, often a prelude to energy stocks falling as well. Many of those were Merrill investment banking clients, and Melnick said he reprimanded her for the reports, saying she needed to get his approval before issuing an opinion contrary to that of the firm's upbeat assessment. For Cook, the implication was simple: Don't mess with investment banking clients. That point was driven home after several bankers complained to Melnick about her work. Several, he said, "were not comfortable with what she did." Cook had apparently crossed swords with the most powerful banker at Merrill, Barry Friedberg, who complained to Melnick that Cook didn't issue a report on the stock of one company that was an investment banking client. Liddle argued that Friedberg had basically conceded that at Merrill, companies received coverage if they were investment banking clients.

As the arbitration continued, Liddle's accusations became more and more sensational. At one point, he boasted that he was "willing to bet" that Melnick put a "check mark next to every female's name at Merrill Lynch," as part of a method to pay women like Cook less than men. At another point, Liddle argued that Melnick's discrimination may have been a subconscious act. Melnick, Liddle said, "never satisfied himself that in some subliminal way or some other way, that female employees were being undercompensated in relation to their male counterparts."

While it was unclear if Liddle had been able to prove that his client was the victim of sex discrimination, as the case dragged on, Merrill's vaunted Chinese Wall separating research and banking looked less and less solid. During one presentation to the arbitration panel, Liddle contended that Cook's problem was not only that she was a woman, but also she was not willing to shade her opinions to win business. He mentioned one situation involving a "road show" presentation to clients. Analysts were often required to work with investment bankers to market new stock deals to investors. These "road show" presentations were not just common to Merrill Lynch, but to all of Wall Street, as a way of drumming up interest from investors for deals in the pipeline. Cook wasn't always willing to play along. During one such presentation before large investors in the natural gas industry, Cook broke from the script and said that natural gas prices would fall, meaning shares of companies, many of them banking clients, would fall as well. It was not exactly the kind of message Merrill wanted to be sending investors, and according to Liddle, Cook paid for it. When the presentation was over, Liddle charged, Cook was "treated shabbily" by her male counterparts at Merrill Lynch. Liddle claimed that executives at Merrill "refused to take cabs with her from the airport to the hotel . . . refused to eat with her . . . refused to give her an opportunity to speak" at other presentations "until the very end when there was a minute or two left." Liddle said Melnick gave Cook ninety days to prove her call to be accurate.

"Shockingly enough," Liddle charged during the proceeding, at the end of the ninety days, natural gas prices fell to the levels predicted by Cook.

What Cook didn't know, Liddle alleged, was that she had stumbled upon a broader scheme at Merrill Lynch. "The reason this is an important issue is because natural gas prices are directly related in some shape, manner, or form, to the price of the stocks in this area . . . making a call like this is an important warning to investors." Liddle charged that he believed that Merrill's trading desk took advantage of Cook's research by *shorting* stocks of natural gas companies, a practice known as front running. (A short sale allows an investor to profit when stocks decline in value; traders front run stocks when they trade on information not available to the public.) "You will see in the compendium of rules and regulations regarding how research analysts should do their jobs at Merrill Lynch," Liddle added. "There is an entire section devoted to the impropriety of what Mr. Andrew Melnick supervised in this particular situation, and that is you should not front run your clients, you should not take the position that is contrary to the position you are recommending for your clients."

Merrill spent two years denying the bulk of Liddle's charges. There was no "scheme" by Melnick to single out women, just Cook, who had not fared well at the firm based on various objective measurements and was warned numerous times about her work quality, the company argued. In terms of Cook's call on natural gas prices, she was way out of bounds, Merrill's attorney Stuart Bompey said, because she wasn't qualified to make statements about the broad market, just the specific companies she covered. In terms of Liddle's charges that the firm's research was somehow biased, witnesses pointed to the firm's record in the industry (it was considered among the best research outfits, according to the prestigious *Institutional Investor* magazine survey), and unlike other firms, refused to pay analysts to snare *specific* deals.

"What happened to Suzanne Cook?" Bompey asked during the proceedings. "She was terminated because . . . Suzanne Cook ended up the lowest rated of all—of all—not just the research analysts in oil, of all research analysts of Merrill Lynch."

Thanks to Liddle, however, it was Merrill's research process that was receiving the low ratings. Liddle continued to attack every conflicted practice he could find. He called top executives to testify about how the firm commingled research and banking. He cited internal company memos listing Cook's contributions to the firm's bottom line through her relentless pursuit of deals above and beyond the effort put in by her male colleagues. It didn't matter if some of the information had little if anything to do with the underlying charge of sex discrimination. Liddle was looking for dirt wherever he could find it, and the firm's research department was a dirty place. Liddle found additional evidence to bolster his suspicion that research played an integral part in the firm's banking activities. At issue: a 1992 memo titled "Issues and Concerns." In it, Melnick listed his "prime concern" that "analysts who have truly helped produce business for Merrill Lynch be properly rewarded in their year-end compensation."

It was a startling piece of evidence, but certainly not the only piece as Melnick took the stand for a second time in the summer of 1997, nearly two years after the case was first filed. Armed with the document, Liddle went on the attack, looking for a way to get Melnick to admit the link between investment banking and research. Melnick said he couldn't recall Cook's specific contribution to banking, but conceded that analysts under his watch were obsessed with deal making. One exchange stood out: Liddle referred to a memo Melnick wrote in 1988, informing his immediate supervisor, Lavery, that analysts believe they "don't get paid when no transaction takes place." The statement seemed to contradict the firm's policy of not paying analysts based on specific deals. Melnick tried to spin it differently, saying he was merely campaigning to get his people paid more money during bonus time.

But Liddle rejected the argument. "Ultimately what you did do . . . is request a larger amount of money allocated to the pool from investment banking so you could then allocate it among research analysts based on their investment banking activity among other things, is that correct?" Melnick replied that he "wanted more from the firm" for his analysts' banking efforts "because the competition was doing it that way. So in order to retain our analysts in hiring, I needed more money." Melnick had all but admitted the obvious: The Chinese Wall at Merrill was an illusion.

Later in the month, Liddle was seated in yet another conference room with Frederick Brown, Merrill's new lawyer, preparing to cross-examine Jerome Kenney, one of the firm's top executives, who oversaw research from his perch on Merrill's powerful executive committee. As they watched Kenney walking toward the conference center, Liddle turned to Brown with a peace offering. "Fred, it's now or never." He urged Brown to come up with a settlement offer that would make both sides happy. It hadn't been a good year for Merrill. Whatever headway Liddle may have made toward proving that Merrill had discriminated against Cook, he found substantial evidence that the firm had been mixing its research and banking functions for years, without regard for the impact conflicted research would have on small investors. The last thing Merrill needed was for the messy details of the case to leak to the press. Meanwhile, Cook herself had received a jolt of good news: The SEC's board of commissioners reversed the action by the administrative law judge, who had ruled she was guilty of securities fraud.

Now, armed with Liddle's offer, Brown left the room, huddled with several of his associates, and then called company headquarters in New York City for some advice. Within fifteen minutes, he came back with a deal. Liddle won a settlement worth around $800,000 for Suzanne Cook. There was just one condition: The case would have to be sealed from the public. Liddle agreed. At least for now, Merrill's research practices would remain a secret.

CHAPTER TWO

"This Guy's Going to Be Trouble"

In early 2000, at the height of the market's euphoria, Henry Blodget was given an assignment that spoke volumes about his celebrity on Wall Street. Affectionately known as "King Henry," Blodget was a confident, handsome thirty-four-year-old managing director at Merrill Lynch on his way to earning an annual salary of close to $10 million, thanks largely to his prediction that technology stocks, particularly those involving the Internet, would make investors rich for years to come.

And now the king was about to hold court. Blodget was asked to make a presentation to Merrill's board of directors about the Internet and the future of tech investing. It was hard to imagine that Henry Blodget, a young man who couldn't get a job in journalism just a few short years before, was now lecturing some of the most powerful people on Wall Street about technology stocks and how Merrill could become a leader in the field.

But Blodget had always lived a somewhat charmed life. After his failure to break into journalism, Blodget's career path led him to the stock research department at Oppenheimer & Company, a midsized firm, which hired him to work as a junior analyst just as the stock market mania began to build steam. At first, Blodget impressed his supervisors as hardworking and diligent, if not slightly boring. But that all changed two years later with a single, ballsy call—his prediction that Amazon .com, an online bookseller, would trade at an astounding $400 a share. When it actually did, Blodget became a star. He was recruited by Merrill Lynch to head up its Internet research department, a huge responsibility for someone with a little more than five years of Wall Street experience under his belt.

As tech stocks continued to soar throughout the late 1990s and into 2000, so did Blodget's career. He didn't create the mania that caused many investors to put their life savings into tech stocks, but he did his best to spur the craze to greater and greater heights with his upbeat assessments of some of the era's most speculative companies, many of them, of course, paying back millions of dollars in investment banking fees to the big Wall Street firm. However, this conflict of interest, and its effect on small investors who were using Blodget's "objective" research to buy stocks, appeared to go unnoticed by Merrill's legal department, one of the largest on Wall Street. Blodget, after all, had satisfied Wall Street's single most important criteria for survival: He was making Merrill money.

Today was no different. Board members quietly took their seats in dining room J on the thirty-third floor in Merrill's downtown Manhattan corporate headquarters to hear the company's boy wonder explain his magic touch. It was an elegant setting, with waiters serving lunch prepared by the company's in-house chef. The room itself, overlooking New York Harbor and the Statue of Liberty, was reserved for special occasions, such as visits by foreign dignitaries and high-powered clients. What better way to celebrate the Internet stock boom than to hear from one of the people who helped make it happen?

Dressed in a dark suit, Blodget spoke for forty-five minutes, using a PowerPoint slide show to demonstrate how the Internet would change the economy. He sprinkled his sentences with New Economy jargon; how the Internet had created a "new paradigm" that would disrupt "old economy" businesses, forcing them to embrace technology or face extinction. Blodget had given this speech many times before. He gave his standard warning that many companies in the Internet "space" would fail, though "industry leaders" like his top stocks, Pets.com, Internet Capital Group, Infospace, AOL, and Amazon.com—all of them Merrill Lynch banking clients—would weather the storm and make investors rich.

While Blodget's audience listened intently, Merrill CEO David Komansky beamed. Komansky had been under pressure by these same board members to capitalize on the technology-banking boom. They had been watching untold profits fall to competitors Morgan Stanley, with its high profile analyst Mary Meeker, and Credit Suisse First Boston, where banking superstar Frank Quattrone had just set up shop. But in the year he had been with the firm, Blodget had already made his mark, capturing a string of deals that would have been snapped up elsewhere were it not for Blodget's presence.

And today the board seemed to agree. When his presentation was complete, Blodget received a warm, generous reception. To the casual observer, the speech was a big hit, another stepping-stone in the improbable rise of an improbable market guru. But not everyone was happy. At sixty-eight years of age, John Phelan had been an investor, head of a venerable "specialist" firm on the New York Stock Exchange, and finally the Big Board chairman during the bull market of the 1980s before taking a job on Merrill's board of directors. Phelan thought that he had seen and heard it all during his long career. But after listening to Blodget, Phelan was surprised at how someone who knew so little had gotten so far.

He raised his concerns with Komansky. First, Phelan said he objected to the idea of a "superstar" analyst. What Merrill needed were "team players," and Blodget, he said, was a "salesman, not an analyst." But more than anything, Phelan seemed bothered by Blodget's unwavering confidence, his unfaltering belief that the New Economy would translate into higher stock prices for years to come. Phelan warned Komansky to keep in mind that "New paradigms come and go." In other words, the last thing Merrill needed was to be associated with a fad.

Komansky, for his part, says he doesn't recall the conversation, but he wasn't the only senior Merrill executive who received Phelan's warning. Later, Phelan approached Paul Critchlow, Merrill's public relations chief, whose job it was to make sure Merrill stayed out of the newspapers as much as possible.

This time, Phelan was more emphatic. "Watch this guy," Phelan said. "He's going to be trouble."

The oldest of three children, Henry Blodget grew up on the Upper East Side of Manhattan in a socially mobile world of cocktail parties and weekend tennis games. He often mixed with his father's colleagues discussing politics and, of course, the markets. His dad, a mid-level commercial banker for Citicorp, made a comfortable living helping Wall Street firms obtain bank loans (his wife often complained about the elder Blodget's lack of ambition).

Young Henry, though, wanted none of what Wall Street had to offer.

He attended the exclusive Phillips Exeter Academy, showed an early acumen for writing and eyed a career in journalism. But he seemed to take after his father in at least one respect: Like his dad, Blodget appeared to lack the ambition needed to make it big in the financial world, despite constant pressure from his mother. "She was the ambitious one," Blodget would later remark.

Blodget certainly wasn't a total wipeout. He was a good athlete, excelling at tennis, and a good student. Blodget applied and was accepted to Yale, where he majored in history. He was politically liberal, almost socialist in his beliefs about the economy. "I believed capitalism was evil," he later said. While many of his college chums sought financially lucrative careers on Wall Street, Blodget held firm to his antiestablishment values, and after graduating from Yale in 1989 he pursued a master's degree in creative writing at New York University. Writing may have been in Blodget's blood—he tried his hand at some freelance journalism—but his only published work during these years appears to be a letter to the editor of *The New York Times* attacking former vice president candidate Dan Quayle, who had come under scrutiny for his lightweight résumé. "It is a good thing that Dan Quayle is only forty-two years old," Blodget wrote. "This way when he finishes his world leadership courses and schmoozes his way through the Presidency, he will still have time for the Professional Golf Association tour."

Blodget certainly could have used some of Quayle's schmoozing skills. Blodget took a job in Japan teaching English, but about a year later, he returned to the United States to work for a nonprofit environmental group in San Francisco and moonlight as a tennis pro. It wasn't long before he came back to the East Coast, eyeing a career as a journalist, and began taking classes at NYU in hopes of earning a master's degree in creative writing. At one point, he applied for a position as a copy editor for *The Wall Street Journal*'s Asian edition, which he didn't get. With few alternatives, Blodget worked briefly as a fact checker for *Harper's Magazine*. Life as a wannabe writer was certainly challenging, but Blodget wasn't ready to trade his flexible hours for the daily grind of a nine-to-five job. "I was exploring the world," he would later say.

Then two things happened. First Blodget's mom died tragically during a fire in the family's Connecticut home. Blodget says the death of his mother made him reevaluate his life and decide to do something that his mom would have appreciated—get a steady job. "I came to the conclusion that life isn't a dress rehearsal," he said. "You only get one shot here, so let's get things going." With that, Blodget's career as a writer was put on indefinite hold when he was offered a full-time job as a production assistant for CNN's financial news show, *CNN FN*. At that time, television financial news was still in its infancy, and the job itself was hardly interesting. His main responsibility was to locate data concerning the market's fluctuations for charts and graphs.

Blodget found the CNN job tedious and boring; the closest he got to writing news copy was feeding scripts through the teleprompter. But Blodget grew fascinated with the markets. Though he never traded in his credentials as a socially conscious liberal, Blodget became so obsessed with the culture of Wall Street—the huge egos and the big salaries—that he began pondering the notion of a career as an investment banker. After reading *Liar's Poker*, which chronicled both the insanity and the oversize salaries among executives at the Salomon Brothers investment bank, Blodget was hooked.

On the advice of his father, Blodget sent out dozens of résumés to various Wall Street firms. But his big break came in early 1994. Blodget reached out to one of his former tennis students who knew someone who worked for Prudential Securities, a large brokerage firm. Her connections led to a sit-down interview with an investment banker who was impressed enough with Blodget's broad understanding of the markets and his ability to communicate them that he offered him a slot in Prudential's corporate-finance training program, an apprenticeship for aspiring investment bankers.

The two-year program began in 1994, not the best time to launch a Wall Street career. The crash of 1987 was still fresh in people's minds, and the markets themselves were sputtering as the Federal Reserve raised interest rates several times over the course of the year. The Dow Jones Industrial Average fell for the first time in three years to 3,834, almost a 3.6 percent drop. The NASDAQ stock market, which measured the stocks of technology companies, fell 6 percent to finish the year at a paltry 752. While Wall Street slumped, Blodget worked twelve- to eighteen-hour days, largely as a gofer for investment bankers. He considered quitting several times and thought about returning to his first love, writing, or trying something completely new. But in the end, he decided to stay with the program. "I really wanted to make an honest try."

Soon enough, Blodget found himself in the right place at the right time. By mid 1995, the markets began to rally. The driving force was the new technology that began to capture the popular imagination as Microsoft prepared to unveil its new Windows 95 program and computer companies burst onto the scene. Meanwhile, traffic on something called the Internet—once a little-known government project designed to transmit information over computers—began to soar as people began "surfing the Web" for all kinds of information. Wall Street wasted little time seeing gold in the expansion of the tech business. A slew of new companies that offered tools to transmit data over the Internet quickly received financing, which in the past would have taken years to obtain. By August 1995, the NASDAQ breached an important milestone, passing the 1,000 level amid increasing demand from investors for these New Economy companies, many of them headquartered in Silicon Valley, the northern California communities of Palo Alto and Menlo Park where the modern technology economy was born.

Then came the Netscape IPO. Netscape was a company that produced a "browser," an innovation that allowed people to search the Internet with speed and efficiency. Its founders, Jim Clark, a former mathematics professor, and Marc Andreessen, were already stars in the high-tech world. Clark founded Silicon Graphics; Andreessen helped created the ground-breaking Mosaic browser. The Netscape IPO was handled by the best tech team on Wall Street—Morgan Stanley star investment banker Frank Quattrone and the firm's Internet analyst Mary Meeker.

The deal was an instant success. The Internet was still in its early days and companies like Netscape weren't even making money, but judging by the demand, investors believed they were buying gold. Amid the frenzy, shares jumped nearly 108 percent during the course of one day. When it was all over, Clark, who held the largest stake of any investor, was worth more than $600 million. Quattrone and Meeker became the most sought-after financing team in the tech world as the success of the Netscape deal spawned a wave of financings from other companies looking to cash in.

Wall Street geared up to meet the demand that it had helped create. Firms expanded their ranks of bankers to bring these companies public. Maybe the biggest change involved the job of research analysts, which became a focal point of the hiring. In the past, bankers had driven investor demand for deals and analysts provided a valuable support function, a remnant of the old Chinese Wall separating investment banking and research functions. There was no Chinese Wall on Netscape. Meeker worked hand in hand with Quattrone to win the deal and later to drum up demand from investors, digging into her knowledge of the markets and her deep relationship with tech investors to make the offering a success. Now other firms were ready to follow the Morgan model.

Blodget, for his part, was toiling away in Prudential's investment banking department. He had always been fascinated by technology, and the Netscape deal inspired him to take it further. He obtained a copy of Netscape's famous "browser," allowing him to search the Web, and he began to read voraciously about technology and the Internet, from its beginnings as a government project known as the Arpanet to the founding fathers of the tech business, such as Jeff Bezos at Amazon.com and Jim Clark. Many of the blue-chip deals were going to the established leaders in the Wall Street technology business, but Prudential angled for a sliver of the action, and Blodget was thrown right into the competition. One of his first assignments was to cold-call five hundred companies on a list of potential banking clients. Blodget focused on a company called Connectsoft, one of the early pioneers in email technology.

With Blodget's help, Prudential won the assignment to underwrite an IPO for the company, although later the deal was pulled. But what impressed executives at Pru the most about Blodget was his ability to describe concepts like email—then a little known product—to bankers who had a limited knowledge of the finer points of Internet technology. Prudential soon gave him the assignment of writing a sixty-page report for America Online, one of the biggest Internet outfits. The report not only enhanced Blodget's reputation as someone who understood the tech business, but also as someone who could communicate its value as well.

By the end of 1995, the Prudential training program was ending, and Blodget was ready for the next step in his career. Benefiting from Wall Street's post-Netscape hiring spree, he was offered positions as an investment banker at several boutique outfits, and a job with an Internet startup. Then he interviewed with Scott Ehrens, the lead technology analyst with Oppenheimer & Company for a job as a junior analyst covering tech stocks at the firm. Ehrens and Blodget had crossed paths at Phillips Exeter, and came from similar backgrounds; while Blodget was working as a writer, Ehrens pursued a career as an artist. Over a bottle of wine, Ehrens made his pitch to Blodget: The market was primed to take off, and he needed someone to help put Oppenheimer on the map in the Internet field. Blodget couldn't wait to get started.

Blodget took the job, earning an annual salary of $70,000 a year, with the prospect of more depending, of course, on the market. Though he was a relative unknown on Wall Street, his first few weeks at the firm showcased his drive and determination to make it big. He met with scores of large, sophisticated investors, experts on the New Economy who snapped up tech shares for pension funds and mutual funds. He began making inroads with the financial media, calling the top tech writers of major publications.

Blodget loved his job, but almost immediately he paid a price for his enthusiasm. After just a few weeks, he learned that Ehrens wanted an assistant more than a partner. Ehrens complained to at least one journalist that Blodget was going behind his back to members of the press that were his contacts. Blodget, unprepared for a turf war with his boss, began looking for another job. He sent his résumé to dozens of Wall Street firms, even interviewing for a job as a research assistant for Mary Meeker at Morgan Stanley.

He also decided to roll the dice. "Look, I know I have no experience as a research analyst, but I can write and I know the industry," he told Chris Kotowski, Oppenheimer's cohead of research. His proposal: to split up the tech research position and make him an analyst. Blodget thought he was about to be fired, but instead he got a promotion. As it turned out, top officials at Oppenheimer liked what they saw in Blodget. In 1996, only a year after the Netscape IPO, few institutional investors had a firm grasp of the various businesses that made up the Web, and even fewer Wall Street executives had a clue to what was going on. Blodget filled that void. In just a few years, he had developed an encyclopedic knowledge of the Internet's various sectors, and a knack for being able to reduce the Internet craze to understandable soundbites, which not only impressed investors who were looking for guidance, but also his Web illiterate supervisors, who needed a translator. "We were looking for a guy who was a good communicator and had an interest in the Internet area," said Lee Tawes, Kotowski's cohead of research at the time. "Henry met those qualifications." Kotowski told Ehrens the Internet was big enough for two analysts and Blodget would be given a chance.

Ehrens wasn't happy, but Blodget was ecstatic. He was given a handful of stocks in the electronic commerce sector, nothing sexy, but it was a start. Meanwhile, the NASDAQ marched on. The success of the Netscape deal signaled that technology and the Internet could play a role in people's lives. Wall Street wanted in on the action as small investors jumped into the market, buying shares of the money-losing tech outfits in the hopes of finding the next Microsoft. Over the next five years, firms continued to bulk up departments dedicated to bringing new technology companies public and hired teams of brokers to sell these new stocks to investors.

It should have been the best of both worlds—an influx of new investors willing to pay for advice, and Wall Street expanding to meet this demand. But by the mid 1990s, the interests of Wall Street and Main Street were hardly aligned. As Blodget walked into Oppenheimer's offices in the World Financial Center in downtown New York, the role of the research analyst was totally unlike the traditional model of earlier decades. Analysts no longer offered objective assessments to help investors pick stocks. They were now part of the banking "team" that helped their firms pitch and win deals. Writing research reports became a secondary function, something that analysts completed after paying for their keep, which meant helping their firm win the next big banking deal. Some firms, Oppenheimer included, even paid their analysts based on how much banking revenues they helped generate. The issuance of "positive" research was part of the deal; companies demanded it as a condition of selecting underwriters, while large institutional investors accepted it because they wanted nothing to interfere with the performance of their portfolios. Brokerage firms, meanwhile, guaranteed it after they received their investment fees.

That's not to suggest that everyone at Oppenheimer welcomed Blodget. Several complained about his lack of experience. Former Oppenheimer broker Peter Wagner recalls the first time he worked with Blodget. A wealthy client had asked Wagner to see if Oppenheimer could take a small Internet company public. Wagner immediately approached the young analyst, but Blodget's financial shortcomings were obvious from the start. He described Internet stocks through concepts like website "hits" and "clicks" of a computer mouse instead of through share prices and earnings. Wagner was shocked. He had finally found a stock "analyst" who appeared to know even less about finance than he did.

Blodget, by all accounts, took it all in stride. He moved forward with his first research report, a sixty-page tome titled "Electronic Commerce," but not before rewriting it five times. The report was issued in March 1997, just as the dot.com engine was revving into high gear. For the most part, Blodget wrote the piece in a sober, almost journalistic fashion, nothing like the hype that would be associated with his work in the not so distant future. Though his plug for a company called Sterling Commerce is worth noting. Blodget called Sterling "the dominant independent back-office software and network vendor for the Fortune 500," slapping an outperform rating on the stock even as shares were falling. Why the enthusiasm? Blodget would tell you he loved the stock. Still, in a few weeks, Sterling announced that it signed "a letter of intent to acquire Wayne, Pa.–based Automated Catalogue Services," a harbinger of more investment banking deals to come.

It's unclear how much of an impression the report made on Wall Street; there's no record of Oppenheimer winning banking business from Sterling. But Blodget didn't wait for potential clients to come to him. He stepped up his contact with reporters who would quote him in their stories about the Internet revolution. Ehrens complained to one reporter that Blodget was trying to upstage him. Closer to home, Blodget became even more assertive when pitching his ideas to Oppenheimer's sales force. Gerald Rothstein, a former analyst who was running a private equity fund at Oppenheimer, remembers the first time he heard Blodget discuss the concept of "eyeballs" in measuring the financial health of Internet stocks during his morning research call. Rothstein just shook his head. When he looked around the room, Rothstein noticed that others seemed similarly unimpressed.

But history was on Blodget's side. While some people at Oppenheimer groused that Blodget was still unqualified to crunch numbers and make sophisticated research calls, the old rules now seemed obsolete. Internet stocks could double overnight as new investors flooded into a sector where the supply was scarce. Stocks were no longer being assessed on traditional measures of value like share price and company earnings, but on an amorphous concept known as "momentum," an investing theory that focuses on where the money is heading.

Blodget may not have had the financial background to rip apart balance sheets, but when it came to momentum investing, he had found his calling. Tech investors, meanwhile, loved Blodget's enthusiasm for the

New Economy, and his ability to discuss broad investing trends sparked by a flood of new money that hit the tech markets. While more seasoned analysts scoffed at his style, Blodget's promise that the Internet and technology would remake civilization struck a nerve with investors, particularly younger money managers who, like Blodget, believed they were taking part in a revolution. One former investment banker at Merrill recalls the first time he heard Blodget's name. It came from an experienced venture capitalist that brought many Net companies public. "Henry gets it," the VC said. During the boom years of the late 1990s, there was no higher praise.

So in early 1998, when Ehrens left the firm, there was little discussion about who would take his place as the firm's senior technology analyst. To some observers, Blodget was dangerous, an analyst without a deep understanding of finance and all too willing to dive into any deal. But Oppenheimer had created a system that rewarded such eagerness. As the market mania helped fuel a massive expansion of investment banking opportunities, Rothstein noticed how normally skeptical analysts began molding their ratings to support those companies that could spread the wealth. Blodget, he recalls, was right in the mix. "It didn't matter that Henry wasn't financially sophisticated," he said in an interview. "When it came to banking, he was cooperative."

Ehrens's departure was certainly beneficial for Blodget. His salary was rising faster than the markets; his annual pay jumped to $300,000 a year, a 400 percent increase in a little more than four years. Internet companies were going public by the day, and people like Blodget were in demand. Ehrens, after leaving Oppenheimer, landed a job as the Internet analyst at Bear Stearns, where he helped the firm win an IPO for Globe.com, which jumped nearly 600 percent in its first day of trading. Globe.com recorded the best performance of any IPO that year, and Ehrens was jubilant, telling one newspaper that he was fulfilling his mandate of putting Bear Stearns on the radar screen for tech banking.

Blodget wasn't complaining either. Over the past year, he had clearly come into his own. A tireless worker, Blodget constantly met with potential banking clients and investors. Even his reports were growing more sophisticated. Blodget might not have been an expert at crunching numbers, but he brought a journalist's investigative eye and a writer's flair to the job. At one point, he bashed Excite after uncovering some suspicious accounting he said distorted the company's future earnings. But the line that caught everyone's eye was Blodget's description of the move as a "vanishing overpayment." (Blodget believed the accounting gimmick, which temporarily boosted earnings, would disappear over time.) Meanwhile, he said, executives at Excite should be given credit for their "creativity and chutzpah" in coming up with the gimmick. The report seemed to establish Blodget's bona fides as a top Internet analyst; he wasn't in Meeker's league just yet, but he was a rising star. "I'll be honest with you, Henry was accessible and sensitive to the needs of the press—and not as arrogant as Mary Meeker," said one financial reporter. Blodget knew his success was in building a "brand name" for himself. He told *Brill's Content* magazine that his goal was to become a guru, someone who commanded the respect of all players in the markets, from the venture capitalists to the sophisticated investors and officials who ran the big tech companies. In other words, he was looking to move the markets. Blodget was certainly a hot commodity, so hot in fact that in mid-1998, he was approached by a dot-com outfit, offered a job, and asked to name his price. "I want $1 million," Blodget said, spitting out the first number that came to mind. Without blinking, the CEO of the firm agreed. Blodget was blown away, but what really surprised him was Oppenheimer's response. They were ready to match.

It was money well spent. That year he earned a ninth-place finish in *Institutional Investor* magazine's beauty contest of Wall Street analysts. The voting was telling; it didn't measure quality of stock research, but it did measure an analyst's name recognition. Still, one challenge remained: how to break into the ranks of the elite Internet analysts, people like Mary Meeker of Morgan Stanley, who not only scored well in the *II* rankings, but more important, ruled when it came to the most important and lucrative part of their job—winning investment banking business.

Up until now, Blodget had been considered a bull on Internet stocks, but a sober one, and certainly no match for the over-the-top enthusiasm embodied in reports published by Meeker and some other pundits that the market seemed to love. (Meeker's July 1998 report on Yahoo!, titled "Yahoo, Yippee, Cowabunga," suggests what Blodget was up against.) Blodget decided the time was right to play hardball. He set his sights on Amazon.com, the online bookseller. For Blodget, it was an easy choice. The company embodied the essence of the New Economy, offering customers a cheap and easy way to purchase an Old Economy product. Maybe even more enticing, Blodget now had a chance to one-up his principal rival, Mary Meeker, who was still smarting over her firm's decision not to participate in Amazon's 1997 IPO because of a banking "conflict." (Meeker had openly complained that she couldn't compete because of Morgan's long-standing relationship with Amazon rival Barnes & Noble.)

In his report, titled "Amazon.com; Initiating Coverage," Blodget called Amazon "one of the most controversial stocks in our universe," and cautioned investors about the stock's volatility, given the high level of "short interest" from professional investors who were betting shares would decline. But what Blodget thought would set the market on fire was his prediction about Amazon's stock price. Despite his official $90 price target on Amazon and his cautious wording, under the right circumstances, Blodget wrote, Amazon "could be worth more than $400 a share."

When there was no fire, Blodget began asking some colleagues where he went wrong. That's when a veteran Oppenheimer stock salesman offered him some advice: "Henry, if you really believe people should own these stocks, speak your mind." In other words, the market wants less analysis and more red meat.

On the afternoon of December 15, flying back from a client meeting in Houston, Blodget made his move. As Blodget remembers it, he was traveling coach, near the back of the plane, when he started playing around with some concepts. Amazon, Blodget noted, was among the most controversial stocks on Wall Street. New Economy types loved the stock and its swashbuckling CEO Jeff Bezos, but professional short sellers, people who make money betting shares will decline, believed shares were overvalued based on the company's balance sheet, which underscored the precarious nature of its business model. The company was losing money and would do so for years to come.

But Blodget believed that "momentum" was on Amazon's side. Internet mania had blinded investors to profits and losses. There was also a scarcity value to Amazon; so many people had shorted the stock (in a short sale, an investor profits by borrowing shares of stock and selling them immediately, and making money by replacing the borrowed shares at a lower price) that any bit of good news could result in a huge pop.

For Blodget, the question wasn't whether Amazon would start trading higher, but how much higher. He developed two scenarios, one in which only moderate revenue growth would push the price up to $300 a share. Under another more aggressive revenue estimate, shares would trade at $500. In coming up with a $400 price target, Blodget later said, "I just split the difference."

He got to the office early the next day so he could publish the rating change before the markets opened. "Amazon.com: Rising Price Target to $400." In it, Blodget cautioned investors that Amazon was still "a long way from proving that it will ever make money." But he added that given the company's revenue growth rate, particularly after the Christmas sales season, $400 a share was an achievable target. Blodget was sitting in his office at around 5:30 A.M., when research chief Chris Kotowski poked his head in to say hello. "Four hundred dollars a share?" he asked. "You read the report, that's what I said," Blodget answered. "Okay, fine," Kotowski replied before going back to work.

Michelle Caruso-Cabrera was a rookie reporter for CNBC, the most popular financial news outlet during the bubble, who had the thankless task of getting to work at around 5 A.M. to report from the trading floor of Instinet, a service that allowed investors to trade stocks before the 9:30 A.M. opening bell. Most days passed uneventfully. Even as the Internet mania began to accelerate, pre-market trading was practiced by only a few. But this morning, something had changed. Caruso noticed a strange surge in the trading of Amazon.com. "Honestly, there wasn't usually a lot of early activity at that point, just some holdovers from London," Caruso now recalls. "Then I noticed that Amazon was active, noticeably active." Shares of the stock, trading at around $240 per share, had started to jump in huge increments. One possibility: Amazon, like many companies during the 1990s market boom, was "in play," the target of a takeover.

It wasn't. Somehow word seemed to have leaked about Blodget's call. His phone was already beginning to light up when he began his morning call over Oppenheimer's "squawk box," an internal broadcast where analysts discuss their top stock recommendations for the day. Actually, Blodget didn't even start with Amazon, but with America Online and some development that he believed would bode well for the stock. Then he turned to Amazon almost as an aside. "By the way, we are maintaining our Buy rating for strong-stomached long-term investors and raising our one-year price target to $400 a share," he recalls saying. Blodget's rationale was simple. He said the company was "knocking the cover off the ball," adding that it was in the "early stages of building a global electronic-retailing franchise," according to an account of the conference call published in *Brill's Content*. Taken together, Blodget said, $400 is easily achievable in the coming year.

Blodget certainly hit a nerve. One stock salesman demanded "a little more color on this." Another wanted Blodget to explain such a radical move. Blodget explained the call wasn't so radical after all; he was predicting "only" a 67 percent annual appreciation in an era when some stocks spiked that much almost overnight. As news spread, traders around the street were divided. Oppenheimer's capital markets chief Tom Ortwein was sitting on the trading desk when he heard the call. Ortwein thought it was a joke, but soon the betting on the trading desk was that Blodget's prediction would move not just shares of Amazon, but the markets as well once it hit the newswires. "There was tremendous buzz around the trading desk, ranging from 'can you believe it' to 'this is nuts,' " Ortwein recalls.

Rothstein, now in the firm's asset management department, recalled thinking "This is the biggest joke going." The markets, however, weren't laughing with him. By 9:14 A.M., word had spread on Bloomberg News, a wire service used by every trader on Wall Street. A few minutes later, Maria Bartiromo, the glamorous CNBC reporter, chimed in as well. Bartiromo had made a name for herself scooping the competition by giving viewers previews of analyst calls before they became public.

"I've got a huge call to tell you about," Bartiromo said, according to an account of her broadcast in *Brill's Content*. "Amazon.com, as we speak, is up ten dollars . . . Oppenheimer is talking about the stock. They're lifting their price target to an unbelievable level."

David Faber, CNBC's markets reporter, was the first out with a comprehensive report describing Blodget's prediction. Normally, research was considered "proprietary" and firms handed reports only to their high-end clients before making their analyses available for commentary to reporters later in the day. But Faber received a leak that provided a blow-by-blow account of the report. "The key to this move is Blodget's belief that Amazon is only beginning to build what in his words will be an 'electronic retailing franchise,' " Faber said. Amazon's "franchise" would generate $10 billion in revenue in five years, justifying, according to

Blodget, a multiple that would equate to a $400 price. All this for a company that had yet to turn a profit.

Wagner remembers sitting at his desk watching the tape, shaking his head as shares jumped in $10 increments throughout the course of the day. "This is mindboggling," he told a coworker. Faber later discussed what people had to say in the online chat rooms, the popularity of which grew wildly during the late 1990s as investors scouted the Internet for tips and gossip on stocks. "Thank you, Oppenheimer," one investor wrote. "I'm a zillionaire . . . first Yahoo options, then AOL, and now this . . . Yes." Blodget was as suprised by the reaction as anyone. Despite his bullishness on the sector, he had always preached a mixed message: Internet stocks aren't for everyone even if they were going to change the world. People close to Blodget said he often fretted about how so many small investors were blowing their life savings in stocks known for their wild zigzags. Sure enough, Blodget soon came under attack, as competitors labeled him as irresponsible. When word came back about the market's reaction, Blodget issued a "clarification." The $400 price target, he said, was a long-term projection, not a trigger to immediately start buying. But no one seemed to notice. At one point during the day, shares of Amazon rose more than $51.

Blodget's Amazon call not only jolted the markets, but his competitors as well. Mary Meeker, the nation's top ranked Internet analyst, couldn't believe the commotion. "What the hell is going on," she asked an assistant. Later, she placed a call to Amazon's investor relations department to get their reaction, but top company officials were in a state of panic as well. Contrary to popular belief, companies distrust one-day price swings because they can be reversed just as quickly. After hearing from Meeker, Russ Grandinetti put in a call to Blodget to let him know the company wasn't happy, but he couldn't get through; Blodget's voice mail was past its limit. Meanwhile, newspapers across the country demanded interviews; CNBC offered a live shot. Most important, the large investors who could make or break an analyst's career by trading off their stock picks started putting Blodget into their Rolodexes.

Jonathan Cohen, Merrill Lynch's top Internet researcher, got into the act as well, this time playing the anti-Blodget. Cohen, a bald, somewhat nebbishy fellow, lacked Blodget's good looks and gift for sound bite quotes, but he was a sharp financial analyst who had been skeptical about Internet stocks, Amazon in particular, as the markets zoomed to new, seemingly absurd heights. Later in the day, Cohen fired off a competing research note on Amazon designed to calm the hysteria Blodget had started. The company, he explained was expensive at its current stock price; Blodget's financial analysis was faulty and the stock was worth closer to $50 a share.

He kept up the attack for a few more weeks, but for Cohen, it was a losing strategy. Shares of Amazon closed $46.25 higher during the day, a 19.1 percent jump to $289 a share, well on its way to Blodget's price target. Uncharacteristically, Blodget declined several additional requests by CNBC for an interview. That night, Blodget didn't leave the office until midnight, returning dozens of messages, his last to Grandinetti and Amazon CFO Joy Covey, who loudly complained that such wild calls hurt the stock in the long run. Blodget, however, stuck to his analysis. The call, he said, was well reasoned and the market would prove him right.

The market reaction to Blodget's price target did more than cement his place in history; it signaled that the Internet revolution was real and average Americans could profit from it by listening to the superstar analysts. Small investors flocked to online trading outfits like Ameritrade, E*trade, and Charles Schwab, where they could buy and sell their favorite Internet stocks quickly and easily using Wall Street research as their guide. Many of the market's traditional experts now appeared out of touch. In early 1998, Foster Friess was considered one of the world's best investors known for his formidable skills in understanding industries and their finances. Sensing a market correction as shares rose to insane heights, he promptly sold nearly all the stocks in his Brandywine mutual fund, converting nearly the entire portfolio into cash. Although he based his call on research tools that served him well for years, he only succeeded in crashing his career as tech stocks continued to move higher.

Cohen, who received his MBA from Columbia University's business school, suffered a similar fate as some bankers and salesmen at the firm began demanding someone new who understood the "new paradigm" as the Internet stock craze was called. Scott Ryles, Merrill's tech banking chief, had been reporting back to senior management that venture capitalists, Internet company executives, and some large institutional investors had formed an opinion that Cohen was out of touch with the market. Your analyst, Ryles was told, "just doesn't get it."

The last straw for Ryles occurred some time in late 1998, when Merrill lost a high-profile IPO to Morgan Stanley and the bullish Mary Meeker. Ryles asked a venture capitalist on the company's board for a postmortem. "Listen," he said, "we love Merrill Lynch, we want Merrill Lynch to succeed here, but given the chance to choose between you guys and Mary Meeker, we're going to hire Mary Meeker every time."

What Cohen, Friess, and others didn't recognize was that stocks during the Net bubble were driven by something that couldn't be measured by conventional analysis. The driving force was emotion. People wanted to believe that the Internet could make them rich. Mary Meeker, and now Henry Blodget, merely led the way.

Blodget, meanwhile, was reaping the rewards of fame. Oppenheimer, now part of a Canadian bank, CIBC, became a household name on Wall Street as word spread about the firm's Internet guru. Blodget himself became one of the most recognizable experts on the technology market. Reporters clamored for his quotes, CNBC made him a regular guest. Job offers flooded in.

One morning a few days after Blodget released his $400 price target, Nate Gantcher, the longtime CEO of Oppenheimer, was eating breakfast at the Regency Hotel in Manhattan. That's when he was approached by Larry Tisch, the head of Loews Corporation, a massive financial conglomerate and one of the nation's leading investors. Tisch was a legendary bear on the New Economy Internet and technology stocks, but even he couldn't ignore Blodget's famous call. "Nate," Tisch said, "I got a bone to pick with you."

"What's that, Larry?" Gantcher replied.

"Your analyst said Amazon is going to $400 a share. If he said it was going to six hundred dollars, I would have bought some," Tisch said with a laugh. Gantcher just shook his head in disbelief. For a moment, he wasn't sure if Tisch was joking.

Merrill Lynch didn't think Blodget was a joke. On January 6, 1999, shares of Amazon traded at about Blodget's price target. The NASDAQ rose to close to 2,500. Blodget wasn't the sole reason for the frenzy, but his dead-on call certainly lent credibility that the Internet was a place to make money. The surge in prices created an atmosphere in which thousands of new companies were looking to come public and expand through the sale of stock. But these "underwriting" opportunities weren't heading Merrill's way. After all, why would a new Internet company select Merrill as its lead investment banker when Jonathan Cohen, its lead analyst, was likely to trash not just the deal but also the company's prospects for survival.

It was around this time that Blodget received a telephone call from a headhunter representing Andrew Melnick, Merrill's research chief. Sensing the growing discontent from within the firm, Cohen resigned to take a job at Witt Capital and Merrill needed a replacement. Melnick asked Cohen who he thought might be a good choice to take his place. His answer was Henry Blodget.

Melnick's offer to Blodget was startling. He was not yet thirty-five years of age and Blodget would serve as the firm's top Web analyst, commanding an entire research department that was attempting to make Merrill a player both in technology research and, more important, technology banking. With salary and bonus, Blodget would earn around $3 million during his first year, multiples above what he was currently making at Oppenheimer, with the promise of much more down the road. When his supervisors at Oppenheimer heard the news, they were prepared to match Merrill's bid.

After several days of discussions, Blodget's career at Oppenheimer came down to a short meeting with Kotowski, Tawes, and several other senior officials. Blodget was reminded of all the good will he had built up at the firm, and a simple fact of life at a mid-sized company like theirs, namely that he was in a position of near total control. At Merrill, they argued, he would be a mere foot soldier in the firm's efforts to catch up to Goldman Sachs and Morgan Stanley in the race to win tech banking deals.

Blodget listened, but in the end, the decision was easy. Oppenheimer, he conceded, was a great place to work, but at Merrill, with its massive banking department and fifteen thousand brokers, he would be in the thick of the revolution that he had been predicting. Maybe more important, the timing was right. Like all revolutions, Internet mania wouldn't last forever. He had a small window to make his mark.

Despite its reputation as a brokerage house that specialized in selling stocks to small investors through its massive "retail" brokerage network, Merrill had grander visions for the future. By the mid to late 1990s, underwriting stock and bonds for corporate America had become Wall Street's most lucrative business. In "underwriting" a stock or bond deal, Wall Street acts as the middleman, buying shares from companies in need of cash for expansion, and immediately selling the stock to sophisticated "institutional investors"—pension and mutual funds and small investors, through Merrill's "retail" brokerage network.

It was easy money. Firms developed a system whereby they would "pre-market" deals before the actual underwriting began to make sure investor demand would meet supply. Although fees varied depending on the size and complexity of the deal, firms typically charged anywhere from a few million dollars to more than $60 million for a complex stock transaction.

By the early to mid 1990s, Merrill wanted a bigger piece of the action. It had beefed up its underwriting ranks by luring away top-notch talent from other firms, helping it move up in the "league table," or the yearly ranking of the top Wall Street underwriters. But one area of underwriting the company was never quite able to crack was the booming technology and Internet sector, where long-standing relationships such as Mary Meeker's ties to various Silicon Valley entrepreneurs and Frank Quattrone's reputation as Wall Street's top investment banker had given them a huge advantage over anyone Merrill Lynch could offer.

When Blodget joined Merrill in February 1999, top officials at the firm were obsessed with making Merrill competitive in the lucrative technology banking business. Merrill soon increased Blodget's profile even more, assigning a full-time public relations person to get him more television time, while using his research as enticement for firms to turn to Merrill for investment banking business.

For a kid who just a few years earlier thought capitalism was evil, Blodget fully embraced Merrill's moneymaking strategy. Merrill bankers quickly began their process of dangling the prospect of positive research when pitching its investment banking credentials to tech companies looking for firms to underwrite their stocks and bonds. Analysts were told to keep track of their deal making so they could be compensated for it at the end of the year, and Blodget began working closely with Merrill's investment bankers. In August 1999, Merrill was the lead underwriter for Internet Capital Group's lucrative IPO, and later an additional "follow-on" offering, which combined helped Merrill generate $33 million in fees. Blodget soon issued a glowing report on the company, an Internet "incubator" that invested in start-up technology companies. For investors, it was the riskiest of both worlds; not only would investors be throwing their money at something with no track record, no profits, and a thin business plan, but as an "incubator" of forty-seven smaller Web companies, ICG's underlying assets were conceivably even more risky.

Blodget didn't see it that way. The stock had a great run "since August IPO and is undeniably expensive," he wrote. But, he added, the outlook for the company's niche of the Internet, "business-to-business" commerce, or B2B, was "excellent and ICGE is one of the best ways to play B2B." Within a few weeks, the stock soared to $164 from its $12 IPO price.

Blodget's recommendations continued to generate excitement as the market for Internet stocks rose throughout 1999 and into 2000. He was working harder than ever, getting little sleep, and constantly traveling. "I'm going to have to work like crazy for the next few months,' he emailed a friend. But Merrill was willing to compensate Blodget for all his hard work. At the end of 1999, he was paid nearly $5 million in salary and bonus, $2 million more than originally promised. Merrill's message to Blodget: Keep up the good work. Blodget's message to investors was somewhat different. He said 75 percent of all Internet companies were destined for failure (and designated stocks as high risk), but added that investors would find the long-term winners from the remaining 25 percent. More often than not, these winners turned out to be Merrill Lynch investment banking clients.

Top Merrill officials, including CEO David Komansky, became winners as well. In 1998, Merrill found itself mired in a messy public spat with its competitors that offered online trading (Merrill is a traditional brokerage, where investors buy stock through a broker or "financial adviser") when brokerage chief, John "Launny" Steffens, called Internet stock trading a "serious threat to American financial lives." Steffens, himself a former stockbroker, never quite warmed up to Internet investing, but as shares of Net stocks continued to rise, his comments became a rallying cry for the New Economy. At one point, so many investors defected to Schwab that in early 1999, Schwab had overtaken Merrill in terms of its stock market value. Worse for Merrill, bankers found themselves shut out of the technology deals in Wall Street's hottest sectors because Internet companies believed the firm was hostile to the New Economy. It was about this time that Komansky received a stern warning from the company's board of directors to start turning things around or look for another job.

Blodget's hiring was a decisive step in that new direction. He was assigned to help the firm develop a system to compete with Schwab, where investors could trade cheaply using their computer without ever having to rely on one of its brokers. Merrill's strategy to increase Blodget's airtime on television helped the firm lure investors into Merrill's brokerage offices located in almost every major city in the country. In an era that emphasized investment advice reduced to sound bites on CNBC, Blodget's smooth delivery was better than any advertisement Merrill could air. *The Wall Street Journal* mentioned him nearly one hundred times during the three years since his Amazon call, while *The New York Times* cited him around sixty times and *The Washington Post* a little more than fifty. In 1999, Blodget appeared on television nearly eighty times, an average of once every three workdays. He was looking for more in 2000.

According to *Money* magazine, his team of seven Internet analysts now covered as many as thirty companies and Blodget continued to support other areas of the firm's banking business. He was in such hot demand at Merrill that Scott Ryles, the firm's technology banking chief, lodged a strongly worded complaint to Merrill management that he needed more of Blodget's time. "I was trying to get the tech banking group going and I couldn't get Henry on the phone," he said. Blodget himself complained about his tremendous workload. "Life is totally grueling, totally unsustainable," he wrote to one colleague.

But he kept moving. Merrill's top executives were so infatuated that they rarely passed up an opportunity to showcase Blodget's talents. When he wasn't meeting with bankers, Blodget was lecturing Merrill clients and executives about the Internet. One afternoon, he would be in San Francisco talking to a group of brokers, and the next day, he would find himself at the swanky Villa D'Est resort on Lake Como in Italy, addressing top brokerage clients whose individual net worth totaled $100 million or more.

Where was his research? Blodget just couldn't find the time. "(We) are now up to 11–12 internet banking transactions in the pipeline by the technology group and at least 2–3 more from the telecom side (including a couple that we have not yet been able to peruse at all)," he wrote Ryles, and his supervisor, Margo Vignola, on March 21, 1999. But he added that his current schedule called for 85 percent of his time dedicated to bank-

ing and only 15 percent was reserved for research. "It is clearly impera-
tive that we don't shoot ourselves in the foot by failing to allocate at least
50 percent of my time and the overall research team's time to research
and institutional marketing," he wrote. "Without the reputation among
the institutions, we will quickly have nothing to sell."

It's unlikely that Merrill's senior management took Blodget's warning
too seriously. The deal flow continued to build and Blodget considered
creating two, possibly three subsectors of Internet coverage that reflected the growing diversity of what the Web had to offer. But with the
new business, the conflicts would grow, as Blodget was quick to concede.
"There's certainly a tendency to give the company the benefit of the
doubt," he told *The Washington Post*, not long after joining Merrill Lynch in
February 1999. "The best analysts find a way of balancing the needs and
wants of their constituencies. It's like being a good politician."

Blodget's biggest political victory, however, may have come in converting
Merrill's old guard to the religion of the New Economy. The most significant convert was Komansky, the firm's CEO. Komansky was a Bronx-
born son of a postal worker, who worked his way up the Merrill food
chain starting as a broker in Forest Hills, Queens. But Komansky had little use for computers; he never used email and he first discovered online
shopping after he noticed that his teenage daughters had bought flowers
for his wife over the Internet. But with Blodget on board, it didn't take
Komansky long to catch Internet fever. Just a few months after Blodget
started at the firm, Merrill offered the ML Direct platform, where investors could buy and sell stocks on their computers for $29.95, the same
rate charged by online rival Charles Schwab & Company.

Soon the old broker was hooked. He ordered a special mailing of
Blodget's research reports to one thousand top Merrill Lynch customers
and CEOs. The response was huge. "These people couldn't get enough of
Blodget," he said. Komansky made Internet fever a firm-wide effort. He
gave Ryles the green light to hire bankers and analysts to help Blodget
snare a bigger share of the deals from companies offering Web-based services. Komansky even started dressing differently. Gone were the dark
suits as Komansky began showing up to the office in khakis and polo
shirts, as if Blodget's advice extended to his wardrobe.

As it turns out, Blodget was giving him other tips. Occasionally, Blodget could be spotted in Komansky's opulent office, lounging on his couch giving advice to the boss about the future of the Internet, its impact on Wall Street and Komansky's own stock portfolio. According to company insiders, Blodget had become Komansky's de facto financial adviser for Net stocks that both he and his wife traded on. Why Komansky would turn to Blodget was an indication of the frenzy that had the nation mesmerized. As CEO, Komansky had access to the best research money could buy. And with more than thirty years of Wall Street experience under his belt, he had certainly witnessed his share of manias, enough to know that markets that rise to wild heights always crash.

Yet over time, both Blodget and his message became increasingly persuasive. In fact, the two grew so close that Komansky came up with a catchy nickname for his firm's star. It occurred to him after inviting Blodget to a Giants football game where he could schmooze clients in the firm's private box. The dress code was business casual. Blodget, Komansky recalls, arrived in sandals, a sweater, and a baseball hat.

At the time, one of the most popular commercials on television featured a crazy office clerk named "Stuart" with long red hair, who helped his boss, a befuddled fifty-ish middle manager named "Mr. P," buy stocks over the Internet. "For some reason, he reminded me of that kid in the Ameritrade commercial," Komansky would later say. "That's when I started calling him Stuart." And the name stuck. At meetings, presentations, even at one gathering where Blodget was set to address Merrill's board of directors, Komansky rarely passed up the opportunity to introduce "our very own Stuart."

Merrill executives still talk about the time in March 2000 when Komansky hosted a dinner for three hundred of its top brokers. The markets were booming, and Merrill was honoring some of the men and women who helped boost the firm's earnings to record levels. The Dow Jones Industrial Average had been hovering between 10,000 and 11,000 for much of the past year. But the real action was in the NASDAQ. On March 2, the index of tech stocks closed at 4,754.51, nearly double what it was just twelve months earlier, and many multiples above its level when Blodget took his first job on Wall Street in 1994. There were several reasons for the mania that pushed the NASDAQ to such levels, and one of them, Komansky pointed out, worked right at Mother Merrill.

As such, it was only fitting that the event's special guest speaker was Henry Blodget. The audience was scheduled to hear one of Blodget's standard speeches about the prospects of Internet investing and how technology was changing everyone's life, before Komansky interrupted with a slight change of plans.

Komansky told the audience that he had obtained "a surreptitious video" of his first encounter with Blodget, which he was now ready to play. He ordered the lights dimmed as the Stuart commercial appeared on a large screen television. Stuart's red hair was longer than Blodget's, but many of the most seasoned brokers in the audience couldn't help but see the similarities in their skill sets. Bald and fat, "Mr. P" even had an uncanny resemblance to Komansky.

The place went wild. Komansky could barely control his own laughter. Blodget, the target of the bizarre gesture, even cracked a smile. But Komansky wasn't finished. "When Henry—alias Stuart—came to Merrill he had to get a haircut," Komansky noted. "Henry, to make you feel more at home, we have something for you," he added, whipping out a wig with long red hair. "And to remind you to keep your courage when the markets move against you, here's a little something else," he said, handing a smiling Blodget a rubber chicken. It was a tough act to follow.

The crowd, drunk on wine and the bull market, cheered Komansky's performance. Blodget himself burst out laughing, overlooking the obvious irony of being compared to an office clerk who didn't know much more about tech investing than point-and-click.

By now, Blodget had his Internet speechifying down to a science. His standard speech went something like this: He would lecture the audience on diversification, the risk associated with Internet investing, and then caution that "volatility," the Wall Street way of saying stocks that go up also go down, is also part of the Internet equation. But finally, that the Internet was creating huge opportunities for investors for those ready to take the plunge.

Blodget appeared to win over the crowd, which applauded warmly. He was, after all, the man who made them rich. Over the next week, the NASDAQ index rocketed past the 5,000 level. But as Wall Street would soon discover, times were changing, and Blodget, the whiz kid who helped start it all with an unbelievable $400 price tag on a money-losing company, would need all the courage he could muster.

CHAPTER THREE

"Aren't You the Internet Lady?"

In late 1998, Mary Meeker was on top of the world. She was credited with ushering in the era of high-tech investments by helping, just three years earlier, to bring public Netscape, the now famous browser company. Since then, she had become one of the most prominent spokespeople for the new breed of companies that hoped to capitalize on the euphoria, outfits like eBay, the online auction house, Yahoo!, a popular search engine, and countless others. Hollywood stars, Hall of Fame baseball players, even a billionaire Saudi prince, Alwaleed Bin Talal, sought her counsel. As Internet fever spread to the masses, Meeker's popularity grew. *Institutional Investor*, publisher of a widely watched ranking of Wall Street analysts, created a special category, "The Internet Analyst," largely on the basis of the Mary Meeker phenomenon. The magazine's first choice? Who else but Mary Meeker, naturally.

But trouble was brewing. Despite Meeker's reputation as one of the founders of the 1990s tech craze, she was a reluctant warrior for the cause. She believed in the Internet, or to be more precise, the promise of the Internet, but she also feared that far too many companies would fail to deliver on their high expectations. Her doubts manifested themselves in her reluctance to bring public dozens of high-tech outfits that clamored for her blessing, which put her at odds with some of the firm's most powerful people. (Meeker often boasted that she helped the firm turn down more than $1 billion in banking fees.)

Now, in late 1998, she was gearing up for another battle. Her immediate supervisor at Morgan Stanley, Dennis Shea, had recently asked Meeker to make what he believed was a small concession. Shea had been an analyst himself, covering bank stocks in the early 1990s, and understood all too well the pressure analysts faced to sell out. Most, he knew, succumbed to the pressure. Meeker held her ground. "A banker couldn't get her to cross the street if he asked her," he once said. But for months he had seen the incredible buzz caused by analysts who placed these incredible price targets on Net stocks, and now he wanted Meeker to follow suit. The market loved it, he argued, as did many of the firm's clients. Morgan's massive brokerage network, which marketed hot stocks to small investors, needed the guidance as well. And just think of all the publicity. Why let the competition have all the fun?

But Meeker wouldn't give in. Meeker believed that stock prices seemed propelled by emotion, rather than reality. Even many of her favorite stocks, the core stocks that she believed would survive any correction, were still unprofitable. "How can you measure something that can't be measured?" she responded.

Shea backed off, but then came Blodget's Amazon call. Sitting in her office overlooking Times Square, Meeker received an urgent message from an assistant. "Henry Blodget placed a four-hundred-dollar price target on Amazon!" and shares were starting to soar. Meeker didn't know Blodget personally, but she knew his reputation as an analyst hungry for recognition and as far as Meeker was concerned, extremely dangerous. "He has no one watching out for him," she told one colleague. Meeker believed Blodget was more than willing to compete by lowering standards, and his $400 price target was clearly one giant step in that direction.

Now she had a more immediate fear. Shea had been asking her for price targets. She knew he would soon be demanding them once he saw Blodget's call.

Sure enough, Shea burst into her office. but before Meeker could put up a fight, Shea told her to relax.

"Okay, you win," he said. "Four hundred dollars for Amazon . . . This is fucking crazy." Meeker's response was a mixture of relief and frustration. "Well it took you long enough."

If Henry Blodget was the ultimate salesman of the New Economy, the woman who was called "Queen of the Net" by *Barron's,* was the era's ultimate weapon. Petite, Midwestern, and famously hardworking, Meeker looked more like a high-school librarian than one of the most powerful players on Wall Street.

But for much of the 1990s, Meeker was the Internet's touchstone, the first stop for companies looking to go public, the guru sought by investors looking for advice about the market for New Economy stocks. Her record of picking winning stocks during the bubble years was amazing. What truly set Meeker apart was that she was a star even beyond the world of Wall Street. People would stop her on sidewalks to ask her for a stock tip. Meeker would just smile, nervous that she was losing control of the mania she helped propel. "Aren't you the Internet lady?" a cabdriver once asked.

"That's what I hear," is all she said.

Mary Meeker grew up in the small town of Portland, Indiana, about one hundred miles outside Indianapolis, but far from the Wall Street money machine. Her father, J. Gordon Meeker, was the No. 2 executive at a small steel company, which he helped sell to Teledyne Incorporated in the late 1960s. Her mother, Catherine, was a housewife. Mary was the younger of two children, and her parents were well into their forties when she was born. Her older brother was a twenty-one-year-old senior in college. "Growing up, I always felt like an only child," she later recalled.

But being an only child also has its benefits. J. Gordon Meeker was an intense and driven man who would push his daughter into his twin passions: golf (he had a putting range in his backyard) and playing the market. While at Jay County High School, Meeker became the captain of the golf team, often rising as early as 5:30 in the morning to practice her swing. At her father's insistence, she also became a regular reader of *Barron's* and *The Wall Street Journal*, took a class in investing, and made her first stock recommendation, an oil refinery headquartered in Minneapolis and trading at around $1 a share. Three months later, the stock doubled, and Meeker was hooked.

After high school, Meeker attended a liberal arts college, DePauw University, as an economics major, but soon switched over to psychology after being impressed by one of her psychology professors. At one point, she joined the student newspaper working as a photographer and spent her junior year studying in Europe. Still, she couldn't get the markets out of her system. As an undergraduate, Meeker kept her subscription to *The Wall Street Journal,* and continued to follow the markets. "How many college students at a liberal arts school in the early 1980s subscribed to *The Wall Street Journal?*" she said. By her junior year, she switched her minor to business administration and began looking toward a career on Wall Street.

As she began her senior year, a friend told her about his internship with a stockbroker in Chicago, a man by the name of George Yared who worked at Dean Witter Reynolds. "I think you might enjoy it," he said. He was right. Meeker spent about a month at the firm. "I wasn't adding much value," she says, but Yared gave her an interesting assignment. He asked her to read through a stack of about four dozen research reports and pick a stock she liked. Meeker came up with MCI, one of the new long-distance companies that were trying to go toe-to-toe with industry giant AT&T. Meeker wrote up a report, detailing her likes and dislikes about the stock and why the investors should buy shares of the company. Meeker doesn't remember what Yared did with the information, but Meeker knew she had found her calling.

The following year, Meeker applied and was accepted to Cornell University's MBA program. Cornell, located in an isolated section of upstate New York, is known for two things: its strong academic programs and its brutally cold winters. Between her first and second year, Meeker suffered a near fatal accident—a car hit her during a blizzard, leaving her wheelchair bound for about a month. It was clear then that Meeker had inherited some of her father's tenacity. Though she suffered a severe concussion and a fractured pelvis, Meeker made the best of a bad situation, reading some of the classic books about finance, including Burton Malkiel's *A Random Walk Down Wall Street*.

While Henry Blodget was fantasizing about writing the great American novel, Meeker dreamt about a future investing in stocks. That summer, healthy enough to walk, Meeker interned as a broker for a few months, and later as a gofer for a popular market newsletter run by a man named Kiril Sokoloff. Meeker says she got the job at Sokoloff's company, located in a small office in Mt. Kisco, New York, by "agreeing to sweep the floor" for a small salary and no benefits. It wasn't long before Meeker was doing real work, tracking regulatory filings for companies targeted for takeover by corporate raiders. Under securities laws, big investors must alert the markets to their activities by registering with the SEC when they purchase 5 percent or more of a company's stock. Sokoloff used the filings as a benchmark, steering his newsletter clients into the stocks that the big takeover artists of the 1980s, T. Boone Pickens and Henry Kravis, were driving higher. Meeker was fascinated, not just by the investment process, but also in the larger picture of how Wall Street worked. Behind the numbers there were larger-than-life figures, and tremendous risk. Little did Meeker know that within a few years, she would come to symbolize both.

After she graduated from Cornell, Meeker joined Salomon Brothers' analyst-training program in 1986, where she covered a variety of industries and hoped to develop the necessary skills to be a money manager. One of her first projects was writing a report on a textile manufacturer. Later she wrote one on Coca-Cola's international operations, which won praise from the company's then CEO, Roberto Goizueta, who sent a letter to Salomon calling Meeker's work some of "the best" he'd seen. But Meeker wanted more. She took a job covering photo and imaging companies like Pitney Bowes, Kodak, and Polaroid. She made the transition into technology in 1989, when Salomon's tech analyst, Michele Preston, approached her with an offer to work as her No. 2 covering computer companies. Meeker had little more than a passing interest in technology; the sum total of her experience was taking an introductory computer-programming class and later buying an IBM personal computer, which she used while attending business school at Cornell. But Meeker viewed the new post as another stepping-stone to her ultimate career in money management. "I just thought I would do it for a while and then move on," she later said.

Meeker didn't realize it at the time, but she was on the ground floor of something very big. Silicon Valley began pumping out a steady stream of high-tech IPOs and Meeker became fascinated by the swashbuckling entrepreneurs that dominated the tech sector, people like Microsoft CEO Bill Gates; John Chambers, the chief executive of Cisco Systems, Inc.; and Jim Clark, the founder of Silicon Graphics and later Netscape. She threw herself into her work, displaying the competitive fire that would be her trademark for years to come, working long hours and traveling to Silicon Valley to develop relationships that would serve her well.

To colleagues, Meeker seemed one-dimensional, an enigma even early in her career. Work seemed to be her world; she rarely talked about her personal life. She was single and living alone in New York City, although she did apparently have one outside interest. When she wasn't working, Meeker played "Ultimate Frisbee," a grueling sport that resembles rugby, only with a Frisbee. Meeker joined a local league, which held tournaments on the weekend. The game, she says, fueled her competitive streak, and Meeker trained to win. After work, she ran wind sprints to stay in shape. Meeker says she was hooked on what devotees of the sport call "The Spirit of the Game," a credo that embraces fair but brutal competition.

Salomon should have been a perfect place for someone with Meeker's drive and ambition. In the late 1980s, the firm was dominated by swaggering bond traders, people like John Merriwether, who was immortalized in Michael Lewis's classic *Liar's Poker*. But the firm was less interested in the technology companies Meeker and her boss, Preston, found interesting. So in 1990, when Preston took a job at Cowen & Company, a mid-sized brokerage firm that specialized in tech stocks, Meeker followed. That's where she caught the attention of Frank Quattrone, who was in the early stages of building his technology banking empire at Morgan Stanley, one of Wall Street's premier investment houses.

Quattrone was already a legend. Five years earlier, he was one of the first bankers to set up shop in Silicon Valley, convincing Morgan Stanley to open up an office in Menlo Park, California. His proximity to the tech sector's major players gave him a tremendous advantage when these companies needed Wall Street's help to finance their expansion through the issuance of stocks and bonds. Already, he had helped take public such technology leaders as Cisco and Apple, and now he wanted more.

Quattrone viewed research as a double-edged sword. An independent analyst, issuing downgrades and criticizing a company's strategy, can be an investment banker's worst nightmare, particularly when business is on the line. In fact, Quattrone had for years tried to convince Morgan's management to have tech analysts report directly to him, rather than the head of research, because he wanted more control of their ratings. But he also knew that those analysts who understood how to be "team players" with bankers could make the difference between winning and losing a lucrative underwriting. As Quattrone and his team began scouring the brokerage business for the right fit, Meeker's name came up again and again. She was smart, hardworking, and green enough to mold in his own image.

At first Meeker said no. It was a job that most ambitious thirty-year-olds would die for, but Meeker wasn't sure she was ready for the big leagues. Meanwhile, a career as a money manager was still an option. But Quattrone was persistent. He came back a second and a third time. His second in command, Bill Brady, turned on the charm, inviting Meeker to the West Coast to discuss her career goals. Like any true believers, Quattrone and his team held fast to his theory that a technology revolution was looming as more and more people used computers. More computers meant more financing opportunities for Wall Street, and no firm was better positioned to take advantage of this wealth than Morgan Stanley. Join us, Brady told Meeker, and you'll be part of something that's going to change the world.

The hard sell, however, didn't work, that is until Meeker turned to one of her closest advisers in the business, a money manager named Bob Corman. Corman worked for Jennison Associates, which specialized in managing money for rich people who wanted to invest in up-and-coming technology companies. Corman knew all the players in the market, from the venture capitalists who provided seed money that financed companies like Yahoo! and Amazon.com to the Wall Street bankers now looking to make money in the business. Quattrone, he said, was a visionary, the markets were about to explode, and Morgan was a great platform. "A job like this comes around once every five years," he said. Meeker finally knew what to do.

Meeker's initial reluctance didn't prevent her from trying to make a splash early on. In January 1991, the technology stocks that listed on the NASDAQ had yet to capture the imagination of mainstream investors, but Meeker believed the mood was changing. In her first report, she launched coverage on ten tech stocks, placing "buys" on eight of them, and included in her report something she billed as her "Ten Commandments for Investing in Tech Stocks." In the report, she warned investors to "Buy [stocks] when no one is interested in them," but sell them "when everyone is interested in technology." In words that would prove prophetic years later, she told investors "not to fall in love with technology companies," and "Remember to view them as investments." For seasoned pros in Morgan's research department, the report seemed overly simplistic, and cliché ridden. "What idiot doesn't know to view these companies as investments," said one former analyst. And when Meeker's stock picks bombed (the bad calls damaged her stock-picking average for the first two years), so did her reputation. For Meeker, this was the most difficult time in her young career. Fellow Morgan analyst Andy Kessler gleefully began spreading juicy tidbits he heard about Meeker from the firm's powerful institutional sales force, which had lost money following her stock calls. Meeker wasn't crazy about Kessler either; she made a point of telling people that she believed Kessler was "weird" after noticing that he never carried a suitcase when traveling, but instead kept a fresh pair of underwear in a cardboard legal folder.

But inside the firm, Kessler's comments resonated, and Meeker soon felt the sting. Some executives began referring to Meeker as the "Heat Seeker." The message was: If you listen to Meeker's research, you'll get burned. When an assistant told Meeker about the name, she was devastated. Having a bad year is one thing, but another misstep and she would be looking for a job. Meeker knew she would have to turn things around quickly.

During the months that followed, Meeker did a lot of soul searching, even considered quitting, albeit briefly. The firm's sales force openly mocked her during morning meetings where analysts present their picks of the day. Meeker felt alone; a young woman getting off on the wrong foot at one of Wall Street's premier firms. Back then, there were few female role models on Wall Street, and even fewer who were willing to lend Meeker a hand. One afternoon, she was reading an annual report of a company she was covering that explained the outfit's triumphs over the past years, and a few of its missteps, when it dawned on her that maybe she should do the same. Over a period of days, Meeker wrote a long self-evaluation—a personal annual report—about what she did right, but mostly what she did wrong during the past twelve months.

Meeker would later credit the exercise with helping her rebound from her dismal first-year performance. But she had something else backing her as well. Frank Quattrone had played a key role in recruiting Meeker, and he wasn't about to let a star pupil fail. He was also motivated by self-interest. Over the next two years, former colleagues say, Quattrone took Meeker under his wing, while using her research expertise to help snare banking deals. This would prove a major turning point in Meeker's career. In the world of investment banking, Quattrone was a purist. He believed no Chinese Wall should ever exist between the two functions that were intrinsically linked, and continued to push for control of tech research. Quattrone was unsuccessful at getting the control he wanted, but that didn't stop him and Meeker from working closely on helping the firm snare deals that would soon make Morgan the premier technology banking firm.

The team made a mark almost immediately. America Online, the giant user-friendly online service that offered everything from email to searches of the Web, had been public for about a year when Meeker began to cover the outfit. Morgan Stanley didn't get the assignment; in fact, Morgan executives claim they passed on the IPO because AOL was losing money. But a year later, Morgan's relationship with AOL changed. Quattrone made sure he led the company's next stock deal, and Meeker initiated coverage with an "outperform." For a time, it was one of Meeker's best calls. AOL continued to attract customers—"eyeballs" and "clicks" as Meeker referred to them in her reports—and with it, increased revenues and stock prices. Quattrone's tutelage helped Meeker's early disasters fade into the distance as tech stocks began to rebound, and Meeker became a vital cog in the firm's technology banking efforts. Even critics within the firm began to take notice as she worked longer and harder than anyone, with increasing success. Kessler recalls being awoken from a deep sleep one night by his wife, saying, "Mary Meeker has a question for you." Kessler, who was recovering from a long business trip, was astounded. "Does this woman ever stop working?"

Meeker later said that her AOL report was a defining moment of her career, but true superstardom was still a few months away. In 1994, Meeker came across an article in *The New York Times* about a new company, Mosaic Communications, and how it had developed something called a "browser," which allowed consumers to easily and quickly search the Web. The article said the company was run by a couple of super-smart entrepreneurs, one named Jim Clark, a former math teacher who founded Silicon Graphics, and the other, Marc Andreessen, a computer whiz, who were pushing technology in a dynamic new direction. The moment she read the article, Meeker says she called Quattrone with the following message: "I know you know Jim Clark, and this could be innovative." Accounts as to who made the first call vary. (People close to Quattrone say Mosaic was already on his radar screen.) But one thing is certain: No one was arguing with the results. By now, Mosaic had been renamed Netscape Communications, and Quattrone found a group of top-notch investors to put money into the outfit, including Times Mirror, in preparation for an upcoming IPO.

The idea of an IPO for a company like Netscape was certainly radical even by Wall Street's loose standards. In the past, companies had to churn out four consecutive profitable quarters before they went public. Netscape barely had one. But it had Quattrone and Meeker. They worked tirelessly lining up investor interest on the transaction. Their sales pitch:

Netscape was going to revolutionize the online world, come and be a part of it. Quattrone used his muscle inside the firm to snare Morgan's well-respected CEO Richard Fisher to give opening remarks during the deal's investor conference at the Pierre Hotel in New York. The Fisher speech was a coup for the Quattrone-Meeker team. Morgan Stanley had built its reputation as the investment banker for America's top companies, outfits like AT&T, General Electric, and General Motors. Fisher's interest signaled that the premier investment bank believed the nascent tech sector was for real.

And it worked. The meeting room was packed with money managers from the top mutual fund companies, but Meeker had little time to bask in Fisher's presence. Regulatory rules prevented Meeker from issuing a formal report until the end of a required "quiet period," no less than thirty days after the IPO date. Not content to sit on the sidelines, Meeker became a de facto investment banker, noticeably handing out deal "prospectuses," a legal document that provides valuable information about the sale, and explaining terms of the offering to investors during the "road show" that introduced the deal.

In the end, Meeker's hard work paid off. On August 9, 1995, the Netscape IPO hit the street to tremendous demand. Shares jumped 108 percent from its issuance price, the largest first-day pop ever. Morgan could barely keep up with the demand from its own brokerage network, not to mention the demand coming from outside firms. But what made the deal so successful was what it said about the new climate for issuing stocks. Netscape had yet to turn a profit and was basically giving away its famous browser. Yet investors ignored this fact and bought the deal based on a concept, sold to them by an analyst working like a banker, who all but promised to support the stock through a buy rating down the road. Meeker and her cohorts would continue to use the sales pitch with great success for years to come.

The success of Netscape erased any doubt surrounding Mary Meeker. Netscape opened at $28 a share, but with Meeker's relentless support in her research reports, shares traded as high as $171 by the end of the year. Other tech stocks began to take off as well, following the momentum Meeker started. The NASDAQ stock market had risen nearly 135 percent to 1059 since her debut in 1991. No longer overshadowed by Quattrone, Meeker now developed her own identity. John Doerr, the Valley's leading venture capitalist, started returning Meeker's calls as fast as Quattrone's.

The Valley's top entrepreneurs sought out Meeker for advice, as did other major players in the technology world. She was a Queen in the making.

Netscape was not just a milestone for Meeker, but for Wall Street research as well. The deal's success proved that the market could digest the New Economy companies that seemed dubious by traditional standards. Maybe more important, Meeker proved the research analyst wasn't just a value-added component of winning deals, but the most important element in snaring them.

Meeker, though, wasn't content to take a victory lap. She followed up her Netscape success four months later with a three-hundred-page research report named "The Internet Report," that sought to acutely define the craze she helped set in motion. The book-length report, written largely by Meeker and fellow analyst Chris DePuy, included charts, graphs, and descriptions of the major Internet companies, as well as testimonials from Internet luminaries like Netscape cofounder Andreessen and Steve Case, CEO of America Online.

Meeker billed the "Internet Report" as required reading, the first report of its kind to describe the Internet and its various players. "There were only a few public Internet companies, so this created a huge buzz," said one rival analyst. Others were less kind. "It was totally macro," said one. "There was very little deep financial analysis." Speculation spread that the report was actually Quattrone's creation, an effort to drum up investment banking business. They weren't far off. Many of the companies featured in the report were still losing money, and Quattrone played a major role in reviewing the document before it was released, and of course, the firm's top banking clients had been prominently featured.

Despite the carping, "The Internet Report" was a huge hit. As news spread about Meeker's "cutting edge" research, *The Wall Street Journal* featured the report in a prominent news article on its widely read Money & Investing page. Morgan's phone lines were soon jammed with people looking for a copy. Someone in Japan ordered fifty thousand reports. Meeker received emails from as far away as New Zealand. Morgan simply couldn't keep pace with all the demand. Meeker's solution was to post a copy on the Internet and let people download theirs free of charge. Research chief Mayree Clark suggested the company charge for copies. "What are we going to do, ask people to mail us a check?" Meeker shot back. In the end, the firm began charging ten cents a page, its standard rate for copies of its research reports but later found a way to make a larger profit off Meeker's growing reputation by selling the commercial rights to HarperBusiness, which published the *Internet Report* in soft cover, charging $20 a copy. (Meeker received part of the royalties.)

Meeker's star was certainly rising. Newspapers and television and radio stations in need of an expert to explain the New Economy turned to her for help. For years, television financial news had a minuscule following, mainly businessmen and hardcore market junkies. But with the bull market reaching a larger demographic, Meeker became a natural spokeswoman for the masses. At conferences, Meeker found herself surrounded by money managers, small investors, and anyone looking for insight into the Internet market. A friend once remarked that Meeker was being "pecked to death" because of the constant frenzy when she walked into the room. In her stock picks, Meeker sought out what she called "ten baggers." These were stocks she believed would increase in value ten times over the course of five years. Her basket would change from time to time, but the core group included outfits like AOL, Netscape, Compaq, and Dell, some of the hottest stocks in the markets.

Meeker's career trajectory was moving to greater heights, but no one could have predicted how far she would go in April 1996. Even with his success in the high-tech world, Quattrone was growing restless at Morgan. For years he had demanded almost complete autonomy over his people, and total control over research, which Morgan denied. Deutsche Morgan Grenfell, the U.S. brokerage subsidiary of Deutsche Bank, was looking to make a mark in the booming tech sector, and officials held back nothing in recruiting Quattrone. The deal included a yearly salary of as much as $120 million, and some control over technology research.

Perhaps more important, they gave him the resources to bring over whomever he wanted. Quattrone just couldn't resist. He convinced several top members of his team, including Brady and George Boutros, to join him. Now all he needed to complete the coup was Meeker.

Sensing the threat, top officials at Morgan, led by John Mack, Morgan's second in command, swung into action. Terry Meguid, one of Morgan's top bankers, was dispatched to Silicon Valley, to prevent Quattrone from poaching the West Coast staff even further. Meeker was in the

Hamptons, only available by pager, weighing whether to stay or go. Quattrone made Meeker what seemed to be the offer of a lifetime: a huge salary increase, possibly as much as $10 million—a high-paid analyst at the time would make around $2 million—and the promise of additional riches down the road, including a cut of the revenues generated by the tech group. Morgan countered with a package that included stock and a sizable increase in pay, though not nearly what Quattrone had offered.

Meeker was torn. Quattrone had been a mentor and a friend. But she loved Morgan's corporate culture, and its reputation. Meeker spoke to many people in weighing her move, including several veteran analysts who knew how much Quattrone wanted to control what they did. But for Meeker the decisive moment came after a meeting with the firm's top investment banker, Joseph Perella. Perella had experienced his share of booms and busts on Wall Street. He and his partner, Bruce Wasserstein, created one of Wall Street's great investment banking franchises at First Boston and later at their own firm, Wasserstein Perella. His advice to Meeker was direct. "One of the great things about Morgan Stanley is that it's a big organization." With Quattrone gone, Meeker would have the largest platform on Wall Street all to herself.

Morgan lived up to Perella's promise, boosting Meeker's salary and promising to give her near total autonomy, not just over Internet research but also banking. It was certainly a radical move. At most brokerage houses the functions remained clearly separated as the firms kept at least some semblance of a Chinese Wall. But Morgan, which for years prevented a banker from heading research, now gave an analyst control over banking.

Any doubt Meeker had that she made the right move vanished one afternoon, not long after Quattrone had left. Meeker received a telephone call from John Doerr, the famed Silicon Valley venture capitalist. Because he invested in many of the marquee start-ups, Doerr had a strong voice in what firms would underwrite IPOs and other deals. Doerr and Quattrone were close, and with Frank gone, Meeker expected to lose a valuable contact.

But Doerr relayed a different message. "Bankers may facilitate the business, but research analysts have a face and a name," Doerr said. "And we *pay attention* to research analysts." Meeker knew she could hold her own. (Doerr says he doesn't remember the conversation.)

• • •

Quattrone soon discovered what he was up against. Meeker's competitive juices flowed in overdrive in 1997, when a key decision was handed down from Morgan's executive suites to pass on Amazon.com's initial public offering. Amazon was still losing money, but Meeker loved the concept of buying books over the Net, and considered company founder Jeff Bezos one of the smartest guys in the New Economy. There was just one problem. Morgan's long-standing relationship with competitor Barnes & Noble, which had launched its own online bookseller, created a conflict. The relationship could be traced to the top of the investment bank; Morgan's chairman Richard Fisher was the primary banker for the company due to his relationship with B&N's CEO Len Riggio.

But Meeker wouldn't give up. She explained to her supervisors that Amazon was a high-profile offering, a "franchise deal" that would bolster Morgan's rep as the premier tech banking outfit. When that failed, she asked for a private meeting with Fisher. If Morgan passed, Amazon would likely appoint Quattrone and his Deutsche Bank investment bankers to run the issue. "This would put him on the map," she said. Fisher was impressed with Meeker's feistiness, but in the end, he wasn't persuaded by her argument. Morgan passed and Amazon went with Quattrone. Not long after the IPO, Meeker initiated coverage on the company with a "buy" rating, the first of a long line of positive research reports Meeker produced on Amazon.

Quattrone's supporters on Wall Street have a different view of how the deal was won, namely, that Morgan's relationship with Barnes & Noble had nothing to do with Meeker losing the assignment. Quattrone and his analyst, Bill Gurley, they say, simply "outbanked" the Meeker team. Regardless, Meeker made up for the loss in a big way. Thanks to her enthusiastic research (in one report, she summed up her support for AOL in just two words, "bull market"), Morgan became one of Amazon's top investment bankers, handling deal after deal, and reaping tens of millions of dollars in fees over the next five years. Quattrone couldn't have played it better.

And he didn't. In the summer of 1997, about a year after Quattrone had moved his team to Deutsche Bank, a man named Jay Walker had an idea to create a business for buying airline tickets and hotel rooms over the Internet. He believed he could sell these products cheaper and faster over the Internet by purchasing the excess capacity that often went to waste and then creating an online "auction" for consumers. He soon convinced a handful of venture capitalists to finance his dream, and in April 1998, he launched his website, known as Priceline.com.

Priceline seemed like New Economy heaven. Walker, an entrepreneur from Connecticut, teamed up with Richard Braddock, a former Citicorp executive, to create the type of seasoned management team missing from most Internet start-ups. The product immediately caught the eye of Web-savvy consumers who believed the Internet would make life easier and cheaper. The next step for the company was to find an underwriter for an IPO to provide further financing and make the initial investors rich. Meeker got one of the first calls.

The company's primary financial backer, General Atlantic Partners, made the contact. Bill Ford, a former Morgan Stanley investment banker now with General Atlantic, understood just how much the line between research and banking had blurred. He called Meeker directly about setting up a meeting with Walker. Meeker, familiar with the company's progress, was immediately impressed with Walker's knowledge of his product and his vision for the future. Priceline was losing money, but the losses stemmed in part from an expensive ad campaign featuring actor William Shatner. The company's core business—selling tickets—was increasing dramatically.

It wasn't long before Meeker plunged into the deal from both ends, serving as Morgan's primary banker on the transaction and preparing a research report once the deal was complete. The competition was fierce. Archrival Goldman was vying for the deal as well, as was her old friend, Quattrone.

By now Meeker had assembled her own team to snare deals and go toe-to-toe with Frank Quattrone and the nerds at Goldman Sachs. Ruth Porat, a straitlaced veteran investment banker known as one of the smartest people at the firm, and Andre de Baubigny, one of Meeker's assistants, were key players in the Meeker entourage. The trio made a good team for several reasons. They all believed in the Internet, they were hungry to beat the competition, but they also had a healthy skepticism about the current market environment.

The Priceline IPO would be an interesting test case for this seemingly contradictory approach. In the spring of 1998, the NASDAQ market was on fire; shares were rising fast and the index moved steadily higher to-

ward the 2,000 level. Internet IPOs soon became the hottest products offered on the street. Investor demand was so heavy that as soon as an IPO
was ready to begin trading in the market—after the underwriters allotted
stocks to their favorite customers—investors would often bid up shares
well beyond their issuance price, causing the stock to spike two, three,
sometimes four times higher. In fact, the business of selling IPOs to investors had become so lucrative that firms came up with an interesting
way to profit from the excitement. Credit Suisse First Boston, as would
later be exposed, charged large investors higher commissions on their
stock trades if they wanted a healthy allocation of a hot public offering.
But Meeker's team believed there was also a distinct downside to all the
hype. Even the best Internet companies weren't worth the money investors were willing to pay at the opening bell, Priceline included. Ruth
Porat, a capital markets expert on Meeker's team, did some research. She
believed Priceline could pop to $100 a share during its first day of trading.

The trick was to convince management that Morgan should price the
IPO much closer to reality. During the presentation, Porat laid out how
the markets would price the deal. "Based on all the feedback, we're seeing
the market trade north of $100," she said, to the delight of Priceline's
board of directors, "but that's insane." She emphasized that when the
current mania was over—and it would be at some point—shares would
trade significantly lower. The trick was to manage expectations, not cash
in on the hype. After all, how would it reflect on the company if Morgan
priced the deal at the market, only to watch share prices fall dramatically
in the face of a market correction. "We think you should price this close
to $16 a share," Porat added. "It's the right thing." Braddock, the
company's CEO, responded matter-of-factly: "Let's do the right thing."

When the sale was complete, Porat's prediction was on the money.
Shares of the company spiked to $69, not the $100 price she said would
happen, but not far off. Meeker explained that the low offering price
showed the company didn't buy into the Internet hype, but company officials simply believed they left money on the table. Bankers at Morgan
Stanley started wondering if Meeker understood the market.

As with almost anything, success brought additional pressure. Historically low interest rates helped fuel enormous confidence in the U.S. economy. A surge in the stock markets and lower credit standards opened the

financing spigots to tens of thousands of new companies. Combining that with the public's absolute mania to get their hands on New Economy stocks, a "bubble" was created as thousands of new Internet companies found Wall Street receptive to their plans to issue stock and go public to enormous investor demand.

As 1998 drew to a close, there was another term for Meeker's exalted status. She was known as the "Ax," the market's most important analyst who could cut down a stock in a single stroke. It wasn't just that *Institutional Investor* had rated her the nation's No. 1 Internet analyst for three years in a row. Meeker's power was larger, more potent. She could underwrite any Internet deal she wanted.

The implications of this power were enormous, not just for Meeker, but for Morgan as well. Being the most powerful Internet analyst meant that Meeker's stamp of approval was now coveted by nearly every tech company looking to turn public. Morgan recognized this immediately as clients began demanding her presence in deal meetings. As a result, Meeker became not just a key part of the banking team, but the team leader.

Now she had the first peek at hundreds of new deals that were coming to market, and by most accounts she considered every one of them. It was grueling work, which would ultimately test the limits of her high standards. Her day began at around 6 A.M. and lasted well into the night, sometimes as late as midnight. Nearly half her time was spent weeding through the various proposals piled on her desk, trying to determine which companies would meet the standards that companies like Netscape and Priceline had met with great success. Things got so bad that one night, she slept under her desk, covering herself with her Perry Ellis coat. Dennis Shea, who ran U.S. stock research, stopped by Meeker's office and noticed Meeker's legs sticking out from under her desk. "Mary, are you all right?" he asked. Meeker's response was blunt: "Are you fucking kidding?"

Mostly, however, Meeker seemed to thrive on the pressure. She took a perverse pride in her "endurance," bragging about her dad, who was well into his nineties, and her mom, who gave birth to Meeker at forty-five. But Porat became so concerned that her colleague's life was so one-dimensional that she took Meeker aside one afternoon and told her to lighten up. "All you do is work," she told Meeker. "You got to get out a little." Meeker just shrugged.

For Meeker, there weren't enough hours in a day. She brought a fax machine along with her during a skiing vacation so she could work on deals when she wasn't on the slopes. During Thanksgiving dinner, her mother noticed that between courses she paused to send an email on her Blackberry about an upcoming IPO.

Always competitive, Meeker now became absolutely rabid about maintaining her place as the Net's top analyst and deal maker. "If you didn't work with Mary you were now the enemy," said one colleague. Lise Buyer, a money manager who had grown close to Meeker in the mid 1990s when she was a high-tech portfolio manager for mutual fund company T. Rowe Price Associates, remembers the first time she ran into Meeker at a conference after Buyer joined Quattrone's team sometime in 1998. Buyer tried to strike up a conversation with her old friend, but Meeker barely uttered hello.

Morgan Stanley's competition in the tech-underwriting race wasn't just Quattrone, but also the bankers at Goldman Sachs. On one level, Goldman's Internet analyst, Anthony Noto, was no match for Meeker in terms of star status, but the firm had another advantage when competing with Morgan for banking deals. At Morgan, Meeker's position as the firm's quality control expert gave her tremendous power to kill deals, something she did with too much regularity as far as Morgan's bankers were concerned. By the late 1990s, Morgan bankers were still smarting over a 1996 decision involving the IPO of Yahoo!, now one of the linchpins of the Internet. Meeker initially had her doubts about the company's long-term survival. "I just don't get all the fuss," she said at the time, using her "sign off" to keep Morgan out of the deal, handing the top underwriting spot to, of course, Goldman Sachs.

It was a big mistake. As shares of Yahoo! exploded, Morgan's bankers pointed to the call as further evidence that the Internet Queen was missing parts of the market. Meeker sought advice on how to bounce back from the disastrous call from one of the old sages of the Internet market, Jim Barksdale, the former CEO of Netscape. His solution was simple. "When you see a parade," Barksdale said, "get in front of it." And Meeker did. In July 1998 she recommended shares of Yahoo!. Despite her initial misgivings about the stock, Meeker had converted into a true believer as demonstrated in her report, titled "Yahoo, Yippee, Cowabunga."

Meeker wrote: "Forty million unique sets of eyeballs and growing in time should be worth nicely more than Yahoo's current market value of $10 billion." Yahoo! had yet to turn a profit, but as shares continued to rise, Meeker's rating seemed right on the money. Morgan soon became one of Yahoo!'s primary underwriters for future deals.

Meeker found herself in a similar position a short time later. Given her experience with Priceline, Meeker thought she was a shoo-in for the honors of "lead manager" for another company with a similar business model, online auction house eBay. It didn't quite happen that way. EBay CEO Meg Whitman was annoyed early in the process when a call to Meeker about the upcoming IPO went unreturned. During the "bake-off meeting" where bankers pitched their expertise to eBay's board of directors, one from Morgan received a call on his pager, excused himself, and abruptly left the room never to return. EBay officials interpreted the move as Morgan giving the company the short end of the stick. Their doubts were further compounded when, during the process, Meeker seemed distracted to the point where she seemed not to care whether or not she won the bid.

But eBay would soon have Morgan and Meeker's undivided attention. Within a few days, Meeker received the bad news; eBay was prepared to go with Goldman for the IPO. Meeker was devastated. Still smarting over her Yahoo! disaster, Meeker decided drastic action was needed.

She postponed a ski trip in Colorado, rented a hotel room near the Denver airport, and began plotting strategy with Porat and de Baubigny. Once again, Meeker said she was fighting for a "franchise" deal, meaning that its combination of strong management and potential to turn a profit fit neatly inside her model for the perfect Internet company. Her plan was to write a glowing report on the company and personally present it to Whitman, eBay's CEO, during a hastily arranged meeting at Logan Airport. If all else failed, she would beg.

During the meeting at the American Airlines club, Whitman liked what she read and heard from Meeker. The report, Whitman noted, was everything that had been missing from Morgan and Meeker's presentation, filled with enthusiasm for the stock and the company's future. Whitman liked what she read, but not enough to change her mind. "We already made a commitment to go with Goldman Sachs," Whitman said.

Meeker took another stab at winning Whitman over by playing off one drawback Goldman faced as the deal's lead underwriter. Securities regulations prevented Goldman from issuing research until sometime after the IPO was completed. These "quiet period" restrictions only applied to analysts who were brought "over the Chinese Wall" and into the turf of investment banking. Nothing prevented Meeker from scoring some points with eBay with a positive research report while Goldman was sidelined with deal responsibilities.

On the day after the deal was brought public, Meeker made her move. She approached Morgan's sales force during the 7:30 A.M. meeting with the following comments: "We are initiating coverage with an outperform rating," she said, adding that while the move was unusual since Morgan had been rejected as a banker, special companies deserve special treatment. "This is the first time we've ever done this and it will be our last." In effect, Meeker vowed never to lose a deal of this magnitude again. In her research report released later that morning, Meeker laid the groundwork for a long and lucrative relationship with eBay. The report hit the tape with an "outperform rating" and these words of wisdom: "Another Internet company? Not! Check it out for yourself," Meeker said, providing the company's Web address, before adding, "We think chances are you'll get hooked."

As shares continued to rise after initial trading, the report allowed Meeker and Morgan to claim credit for one of the most successful IPOs during the Web boom, and ultimately one of the most successful Internet companies. There was, predictably, lots of grousing from competitors. "This was unprecedented," complained one rival analyst, who believed Meeker had just shilled her way into eBay's next deal. Others were impressed with Meeker's ballsy tactics. "Now that is aggressive," said Henry Blodget when he heard the news, "but it's a nice move."

Meanwhile, Morgan's payback was almost immediate. EBay awarded two banking deals to Morgan, one in 1999 and another in 2001, in which the firm grossed $13.8 million in fees. Meeker would later write about her eBay experience, noting that "When we miss a winning IPO, we should work like crazy (with tons of ideas) to secure a spot as . . . book running manager on follow-on offerings."

By the end of 1998, Mary Meeker was making more than $10 million, an almost unheard-of sum for a research analyst, but not as much as she could have earned elsewhere. A prominent CEO of an Internet outfit tried to woo her with a pay package worth around $400 million in stock and options. Meeker couldn't believe how anyone, herself included, was worth that much money. "I'm not taking it," she told Shea. "Good," he said, "because we can't come close to matching that one." Quattrone persisted with offers if she would join him in his new gig at Credit Suisse First Boston. One person with knowledge of Quattrone's offer says the Internet banking king offered Meeker a salary, stock, and options worth $50 million in one year, less than half his yearly take of his tech group's draw but still a sizable sum. Again Meeker refused. As much as she admired Quattrone, no amount of money seemed worth giving up her regal status inside Morgan. Around the same time, several executives at Goldman made a similar offer, and Meeker gave the same response.

Meeker had become star material. She was front-page news in every major newspaper and magazine; the *Barron's* December 21, 1998, cover featured a beaming Meeker, seating at her desk in her trademark black suit and short cropped hair, under the headline "Queen of the Net." The article pointed out what everyone on Wall Street already knew: "An Internet stock hasn't arrived until it gets a stamp of approval from Morgan Stanley's Mary Meeker." But it also raised an important point: Is she too optimistic, given the risks involved with start-up companies operating in an untested business? Meeker said there were risks, many risks, but added: "Nothing has happened like this before. It just hasn't. TV and radio took years to develop. This has taken virtually months." Internet mania had become such a big moneymaker for Morgan, the story said, that Meeker was "one of the best paid analysts at the firm with a compensation package of perhaps several million dollars a year."

Despite the news coverage, Meeker tried to keep a low profile, ignoring many requests to appear on television business shows, including the increasingly popular CNBC. But as the lure of Internet stocks spread to Middle America, so did Meeker's celebrity among the masses. Average people, not just Wall Street types, began approaching her in airports and stopping her on the street. After one encounter, a former colleague recalls how Meeker returned to her office in a cold sweat. "She couldn't believe what was happening," the former colleague said. Though she reveled in her power at Morgan Stanley, often chewing out subordinates for the slightest infraction, Meeker found it hard to accept all the wider public adulation and the sometimes bizarre life of a celebrity. During a photo shoot with *The New Yorker* magazine, which was planning a long story on the Internet Queen, Meeker showed up at the studio in her usual dark pantsuit (people inside Morgan swear she had more than one) But the photographer had other ideas. He wanted Meeker dressed in an orange jacket, wrapped in electrical wires, and speaking on her cell phone. Meeker's response: "You got to be kidding." In the end, they compromised; Meeker wore the jacket, and an artist drew in the wires. The article itself proclaimed Meeker's lofty position as "The Woman in the Bubble," calling her "the most influential Internet analyst on Wall Street."

Still, life wasn't easy at the top. Around this time, Meeker says she began examining the performance of every technology stock deal that had come public since 1980. What she found was somewhat shocking. Meeker added up the market values of all the tech stocks that she could find. Despite the obvious success of Microsoft, Cisco, and several others, the New Economy actually produced far more losers than winners. In fact, only 5 percent of the technology companies that were brought public over the previous fifteen years created nearly all of the wealth.

The exercise formed the basis of Meeker's investment thesis: "Take the best Internet companies public and help build the leading companies of the future." Indeed, Meeker often took a perverse pride in how many times she exercised her "analyst veto" on those companies she believed couldn't make the cut. Several Morgan bankers even kept a running tally of how many deals Meeker refused to approve—and how much it cost the firm. Contrary to popular opinion, the Queen of the Net was losing her place as the market's top deal maker. Since 1995, Meeker had rejected more than two hundred IPOs. One banker showed that if Morgan had done just 50 percent of the deals Meeker rejected, banking revenue would have increased 300 percent. The talk around the office was that Meeker was costing Morgan a lot of money, possibly $1 billion in revenues over the course of four years.

The rejects weren't always big names like Yahoo!, but also scores of smaller companies that were more than willing to look elsewhere if the Queen said no. In late 1999, Meeker and Porat spent a fair amount of time with the people at Pets.com, the online pet supply company. As Meeker and Porat began interviewing company officials about its prospects, someone placed the company's popular sock puppet on the table as a symbol of the strength of its brand. Meeker, however, wasn't impressed. "The losses are staggering and the market isn't big enough," she told Porat after laughing about the puppet and examining the company's financials. But after Morgan turned Pets.com down, management moved to the next best thing, Merrill and Blodget, handing the firm several million in fees for a deal that could have easily gone to Morgan.

When Meeker turned down iVillage, a website focused on women, Goldman stepped in and shares tripled during the first day of trading. Nearly the same, she claims, happened with the TheStreet.com, an online business newspaper created by columnist and investor James Cramer. This one particularly stung because Morgan appeared to have the inside track on the company's stock deal. TheStreet.com's then CEO Kevin English was the brother of a top Morgan Stanley investment banker, and Morgan bankers had used the family connection in their deal pitch. But Meeker believed the money-losing outfit needed more time before going public and passed. Too bad the market disagreed. After Goldman handled the company's IPO (Cramer says Goldman was always his first choice), shares of TheStreet.com soared.

At one point, Meeker asked Shea for some advice. Shea had been an analyst for fifteen years before going into management in the mid 1990s, and Meeker considered him a friend and someone she could confide in. "What are we missing?" she asked. Shea, who had been intermediating complaints from investment bankers, didn't mince words. "The market is telling us that there's something to these companies."

By 1999, Morgan's market share of Internet banking deals began slipping; internal Morgan Stanley data showed Credit Suisse First Boston and Quattrone winning bragging rights as the Net's biggest deal maker, taking down nearly 19 percent of all deals, compared to Morgan's 9 percent market share. Goldman had surpassed Morgan as well, underwriting 11 percent of all deals that year. Having someone like Meeker turned out to be a double-edged sword. Meeker was the Internet main attraction, but picky about whom she let into the show, and rival bankers wasted little time using Meeker's high standards against Morgan. Goldman became the first choice for the Meeker rejects, and who could blame them? While Meeker was demanding that Morgan's deal makers cultivate only the best the Internet could offer, analysts at Goldman were no match for the firm's powerful investment bankers. In fact, one former banker there said he and his colleagues could personally edit research reports and soften or remove negative comments about potential clients.

At Morgan, Meeker was the star reporter and no one dared to touch her copy even when banking business was on the line. Shea began getting emails from across the firm second-guessing Meeker's banking decisions. One top executive pulled Shea aside and asked outright, "Are you sure you guys are doing the right thing?" Shea said he was, but he, too, had questions. The stocks Meeker kept turning down seemed to keep going up, particularly, it seemed, those underwritten by Goldman. Every major firm on the street rejected TheGlobe.com, but Bear Stearns stepped in and underwrote the deal, which spiked 600 percent in its first day of trading. Goldman Sachs partners invested in an online grocer named Webvan, and brought the company public in November 1999. Shares spiked 66 percent.

It wasn't just individual bankers who were getting antsy. Joseph Perella, Morgan's investment banking chief, wanted answers as well. What concerned Perella even more than losing business to Goldman was Morgan's lackluster performance in underwriting stocks of companies headquartered in New York's "Silicon Alley," a section of lower Manhattan that housed a growing number of Internet companies, such as TheStreet.com, iVillage, and TheGlobe.com. "He wanted to know why we weren't doing New York deals," said one banker with knowledge of the matter.

Meeker decided to set the record straight. She called Perella to set up a meeting to explain her investment philosophy. It was yet another indication of just how little was left of the Chinese Wall, but Meeker was looking for allies and this was the best she could do. The meeting lasted around two hours. Accompanied by Porat, Meeker calmly explained the reason behind the group's recent decisions. TheGlobe.com, Meeker said, was a stupid idea. TheStreet.com was coming to the market "too early." As for Webvan, Meeker said "We fundamentally don't believe in this; it's *Waterworld.*"

Perella and his second in command, Terry Meguid, sat and listened. Meeker had made a convincing case. The year was ending, and even with the recent doubt over her judgment, Meeker was still the authority on Wall Street's hottest market. Since the beginning of the year, Meeker was personally responsible for fifty-three underwriting assignments, including seventeen IPOs, worth a total of $180 million to Morgan's bottom line. Netscape had certainly seen better days as its stock sank when Microsoft entered the browser business. But Meeker's "buy" rating turned out to be the right call for investors, as AOL bought the company for $4.2

billion. Morgan, naturally, handled the transaction, earning $16.2 million in fees.

Despite the missed business opportunities, it was hard to argue with her overall results. In his evaluation of Meeker's 1999 banking performance, Shea could barely control himself. "What a year it was!" he wrote. "Phenomenal year in banking." Meeker was so hot, Shea wrote, that the "entire research department and IBD [investment banking department] leverage off [her] Internet franchise."

At Morgan, analysts are graded not just by their supervisors, but also by their peers, including investment bankers who had every incentive to attack those who didn't play the game. But with the market soaring, and with her deal flow rising, even her biggest critics had to rejoice. She's a "commercial animal," one banker wrote, who had built "the premier Internet franchise on the street."

Meeker, herself, couldn't pass up the opportunity to tout her own success. For several years now, she had continued her year-end task of writing a self-evaluation of her work, an "annual report" submitted to management when they were debating her performance and year-end bonus. It was a trying year, she pointed out. Competition from Quattrone was still formidable, and new players were coming onto the scene every day. Big banks "acquired and destroyed the Silicon Valley" banking boutiques; Alex.Brown, Montgomery Securities, and Robertson Stephens were all snapped up by players with larger clout and capital, players that could give Morgan a run for its money. To meet these challenges, "It is critical for [Morgan] to compensate its Internet research/IBD team appropriately," she wrote. Meeker issued another warning, this one on behalf of her overworked team. "When folks in MSDW tech group depart," she added, one major reason they cite for leaving is "I was burned out and saw no end in sight."

Meeker wasn't speaking just for herself. Her team of bankers, led by Ruth Porat and Andre de Baubigny, needed "the appropriate level of support to succeed." But if Morgan stepped up to the plate, Meeker added, the future held great promise. "As expected the impact of the Internet on business has been and will continue to be unprecedented," she wrote. Just as AT&T and General Motors "were important to Morgan Stanley's past, America Online, Amazon.com etc., are important to MSDW's future," Meeker predicted.

Just how important? The increase in technology banking revenue had exploded from $8 million when she got to Morgan in 1991 to $505 million by the end of 1999. And she predicted this was just the beginning. "Bottom line, my highest and best use is to help MSDW win the best Internet IPO mandates."

The eight-page single-spaced report was jam-packed with data and statistics underscoring Meeker's power and prestige. It was a wonderful sales job. There was barely a trace of self-doubt in the document, which was written in the breezy, carefree style of the New Economy. It was much like her research reports, where she described the "rocking addition of newcomers" to her Internet group, who contributed to the record year in snaring investment banking deals. Though much of the report focused on her record in bringing home deals, she made sure management understood that she had the stock research to back up her work. "YTD Stock Picks . . . up 172%," she wrote, adding ". . . IPO gains up 69%." And it worked. A few months later, Meeker received her biggest paycheck ever, a combined salary and year-end bonus worth about $15 million.

CHAPTER FOUR

The Bloviator

In late 1997, the great financier Sanford I. Weill had just purchased Salomon Brothers, a key element in building his financial empire, eventually known as Citigroup. After completing the transaction, Weill invited about a dozen of Salomon's top research analysts for drinks and hors d'oeuvres, a chance to meet and greet some of the company's best and brightest people. He was speaking with Michelle Applebaum, a highly regarded and widely quoted analyst who covered the steel companies, when he noticed a well-dressed man out of the corner of his eye. It didn't take Weill long to connect the face with the reputation. It was Jack Grubman, the single most important analyst covering one of Wall Street's hottest businesses, the fast-growing telecommunications industry.

In a flash, Weill pushed his way past Applebaum to shake hands with one of his company's new and most valuable assets. "He basically knocked me over to get to Grubman," Applebaum recalled in an interview.

Applebaum didn't speak with Weill for the rest of the meeting, but Weill made sure to spend enough time with Grubman. And with good reason. By the time Weill took the reins at Salomon, Grubman had made a name for himself as one of the most successful of a handful of analysts in the United States who broke tradition by straddling—some would say obliterating—the Chinese Wall making Salomon the leading banker for telecom outfits who were looking to grow.

For a time, everything seemed to run smoothly. By the late 1990s, the mania infecting Internet stocks had spread well into the telecom sector, particularly those companies favored by Grubman—outfits like World-Com, Global Crossing, and Qwest Communications, companies that followed his advice and expanded rapidly to meet the increased demand Grubman predicted for New Economy telecom services, everything from broadband, which helped to connect people to the Internet, to cell phones. Grubman's power to win deals was clearly enhanced by his role as an analyst who regularly published his opinions in lengthy reports on the same companies that kicked back lucrative investment banking fees to his firm, and padded his own massive salary.

Grubman had clearly perfected the conflicted system. He didn't just support his favorite stocks, he fought for them, bashing competitors who disagreed with his research and attacking journalists who refused to take his theories at face value. For years, he bloviated about the shortcomings of AT&T, that is, until the company was preparing to pick underwriters on a massive stock deal. Then Grubman did one of the most amazing about-faces during the bubble years, suddenly recommending the stock and predicting better days ahead for the stumbling telecom giant.

But that was nothing compared to Grubman's endless support of WorldCom, a company that kicked back nearly $100 million in fees to Salomon over a five-year stretch, becoming its largest investment-banking client. "Load up the truck" and buy as much WorldCom stock as possible, Grubman blared in one research report as the company became one of Wall Street's biggest investment banking clients.

For the competition, it was difficult, almost impossible, to match Grubman's combination of hype and connections to top officials in the telecom business. "Don't even bother," was the order from one of Morgan Stanley's top investment bankers, Terry Meguid, after hearing that his staff was going head-to-head on one major banking assignment. Others, like Merrill, studied his every move to determine how he was able to keep the fastest growing telecommunication companies under his control. Goldman, meanwhile, went a different route. The investment bank attempted to lure Grubman away, offering him a multimillion-dollar contract despite the opposition of its well-respected director of research, Steve Einhorn, who disagreed with Grubman's style. In the end, Grubman stayed with Salomon, using the Goldman offer and the implicit threat of all those profits fleeing to a competitor, to extort one of the largest pay deals in the history of Wall Street research.

For a time, Grubman appeared to have everyone fooled. As the stocks he championed moved steadily higher, his reputation among sophisticated investors running mutual funds and pension funds grew to immense proportions. These were the same people who voted in the *Institutional Investor* magazine's poll of the best Wall Street analysts, and they regarded Grubman as a saint. Stephanie Comfort, a former analyst at Morgan Stanley, found out just how loyal Grubman's followers were in 1997, when she began downgrading some telecom stocks Grubman favored. That same day she remembers an angry, expletive-laced phone call from one prominent money manager, Stewart Robinson. "You're wrong and Jack is going to be right," Robinson said before slamming the telephone down.

Grubman remained "right" for a few more years, as regulators, sophisticated investors, and many in the press turned a blind eye to his hyped research that found a silver lining in every problem faced by his favorite companies.

On the surface, Jack Grubman's Wall Street career looked like a true American success story. He was a poor kid who made it big, he bragged to friends, fighting as an amateur boxer while studying for a career somewhere far from his impoverished youth on the tough streets of South Philly, where he claimed to have hung out with made members of Philadelphia's criminal underworld in the working-class Italian neighborhood.

But the reality was quite different. Grubman grew up in Northeast Philadelphia, a white ethnic enclave comprised mostly of middle-class Jews who lived in neat row houses and saved for their kids' college educations. In fact, the real tough guy of the Grubman clan was Jack's father Izzy, a city worker and former boxer with a firm grip—strong enough to rip a telephone book in half with his bare hands. Jack's mom, Mildred, was a typical housewife who worked in a department store to help the family make ends meet.

Despite his boasts about his superior intellect, the young Jack Grubman was by most accounts, a good student, adroit with numbers, but with an exceptional gift for gab. During summers, Grubman sold umbrellas and worked as a busboy in Atlantic City. At Philadelphia's Northeast High School, far from the mean streets of South Philly, he served on the debate team and played in the high school band, according to his high school yearbook. There's no evidence that Grubman ever threw a punch in the ring, but that didn't stop him from telling anyone and everyone who would listen about his boxing exploits. "I always assumed he was a former boxer because he talked about it so much," says one friend.

After high school, instead of following his friends and applying to Temple University in downtown Philly, Grubman enrolled in Boston University, where he received a degree in mathematics. Grubman's next stop was Columbia University, where he received his master's in probability theory, a branch of mathematics that attempts to quantify whether a given event will actually occur. In 1977, after deciding to forgo his Ph.D., he took a job as an analyst with the nation's largest telecom company, AT&T, working in the company's "long lines" division located in Bedminster, New Jersey. By now, Grubman had a demonstrated talent in two distinct areas: bullshitting and numbers, and he seemed equally adept at both. At AT&T he was assigned to a team of math geeks who spent long hours cranking out economic models known as "demand analysis" to help AT&T project trends in long-distance usage.

But as Grubman would show, he was no geek. With his long hair combed straight back, Grubman seemed somewhat out of touch with AT&T's button-down corporate culture where top managers wore starched white shirts and dark ties. Several colleagues privately complained that his personal appearance always seemed to be marred by his ungroomed beard, which often attracted food particles. Still, he fancied himself a ladies' man, often showing up to work in double-breasted suits and colorful ties. "He would have a new date every time I saw him," said one former colleague.

By most accounts Grubman was a solid analyst who understood the telephone business and the regulatory environment, which was about to change dramatically. But he often complained about the long hours and lack of advancement at the company. Several former colleagues say he spent much of his time reading newspapers, talking about sports, and, most important, networking with other executives he believed would become major players in the telecom business, people like Dan Hesse, a future top executive for AT&T's wireless division, and Joseph Nacchio, a former top AT&T executive who went on to run Qwest Communications, and one of Grubman's closest future associates.

Grubman also displayed the one characteristic that would serve him well in his future career as an analyst: an ability to argue forcefully. At AT&T, much of this involved his background, but it also spilled over to his work product. While on the job, Grubman was loud, and his criticisms appeared "over-the-top" according to one coworker. "He was out of control," said another. When he criticized a piece of research, Grubman often made his case in an expletive-laced diatribe so that no one doubted where he stood on the issue. "He would talk about how this model was bullshit and that one was a piece of crap and go on and on like that," said someone who worked closely with Grubman.

Grubman's best friend during these days was another analyst named Jay Yass, who shared common interests and a common background. Like Grubman, Yass was a math whiz; Yass attended the Bronx High School of Science and earned a master's degree in math. Also like Grubman, Yass was a working-class guy trying to make it at one of the most white-bread companies in America.

Grubman and Yass bonded almost from the time they met, spending evenings drinking at local pubs and talking about everything from music to sports. During this period, Grubman was far from the cocksure executive that he was known as later in his career, and, according to some, he used Yass as a sounding board on everything from purchasing cars to major career decisions. "Jay, we're always going to be friends, right?" Grubman asked him one night after a particularly grueling day at work. "Of course," Yass said, "We're like brothers."

Grubman also followed Yass's instincts about a possible career change. Like Grubman, Yass believed AT&T management didn't appreciate the math geeks who worked long hours crunching numbers for the company's economic models, and in the early 1980s, he interviewed for a job as a Wall Street research analyst. Yass didn't take the job, but Grubman took the cue from his friend and began looking at a future in research as well. His timing was perfect. The Justice Department had just ordered the breakup of AT&T, spawning the seven regional Bell operating companies, a decision that would forever change the telecommunications industry. The Justice Department gave AT&T two years to spin off the Bells. As a result, Wall Street needed people to analyze the changing corporate environment, turning people like Grubman into hot commodities.

Wall Street would have to wait a little longer for Grubman. In 1982, he left the Siberia of the geeks and moved to the corporate-finance department of AT&T in New York, to help the company plan for the coming divestiture. The move gave Grubman even greater access to top officials at the company who did little to advance his career at AT&T, but who would prove useful in his next life as a securities analyst on Wall Street.

That new life began with a call from PaineWebber, a major brokerage firm that handled the accounts of thousands of small investors. Grubman reached out to Yass, who had since taken a new job at GTE. "What do you think, Jay, should I do it?" he asked. Yass advised Grubman that he didn't have much choice given some of the shifting political winds at the post-divestiture AT&T. "Too much is uncertain, and it sounds like a good move."

Grubman took the research job with PaineWebber in 1985, and wasted no time getting started on making a name for himself. He initially failed a required test for all analysts, the "Series 7," probably because he was too busy schmoozing to study. But Grubman's ability to network paid off as he quickly established himself as one of the nation's most quoted analysts. Grubman bragged that he charmed his way into a friendship with reporters, which led to numerous quotes early in his career. He soon built a reputation as one of the few analysts on the street who could accurately predict the earnings of phone companies before they were released to the public.

The prevailing wisdom held that Grubman maintained a network of former colleagues who provided him with tips about their company's financials. Indeed, there's no doubt that Grubman had one of the best Rolodexes in the business; the breakup of AT&T caused the company to shed thousands of executives who were now working at nearly every major telecom outfit, and Grubman wasn't bashful about leaning on his established relationships to gain an edge on his competitors. His old boss Marty Hyman, who left AT&T for a job at Sprint, recalls the first time he met with Grubman the analyst. "How's the quarter doing," Grubman asked, looking for some insight into the company's earnings. "Jack, even if I knew I couldn't tell you," Hyman said. Jack just smiled, but it didn't stop him from asking again and again.

Hyman claims he held his ground, but AT&T leaked like a sieve. By the mid to late 1980s, Grubman's ability to guestimate AT&T's earnings almost to the penny was legendary. The usual suspects were Grubman's friends, who were scattered through the vast corporate bureaucracy that existed even after the divestiture was complete. But some people believed Grubman had an even better source. Sometime in the late 1980s,

Grubman admitted to dating LuAnn Levick, a smart, elegant woman with straight brown hair, who worked in AT&T's public relations department preparing quarterly earnings statements. It's unclear when Jack and LuAnn first became an item, but when their relationship became public, speculation spread on Wall Street that LuAnn was the source of the leaks that made their way into Grubman's reports. Although there was no hard evidence, as LuAnn's relationship with Grubman became known among AT&T finance officials, she was relocated to another part of the company, an AT&T official confirms.

With or without his girlfriend, Grubman continued to predict AT&T earnings with remarkable accuracy and build his rep as the telecom go-to guy. He bragged that Peter Lynch, Fidelity Investments' legendary fund manager, began calling about buying opportunities, according to one person. Grubman reported back to friends that he loved his job, the respect Wall Street bestowed on experts like himself, and maybe most important, the vast sums of money he was earning. Securities analyst Susan Kalla, who worked as a consultant in the telecom industry in the 1980s, remembers what prompted her to search for a job on Wall Street at around the same time. "I remember hearing that Jack was making more than $1 million a year."

Grubman was living large and not afraid to flaunt his newfound wealth and power. Business meetings were often held at sporting events, mostly high-profile boxing matches at Madison Square Garden and Atlantic City, and baseball games. "For Jack, the personal and the professional always got muddled," said one former telecom exec who was the beneficiary of some of Grubman's largesse. The executive recalls one instance in particular. Grubman showed up at his office for a meeting, but before they could get started, Grubman shut the door and pulled out a bag of cocaine, which he separated into a series of thin lines on the executive's desk. The meeting began a few minutes later, but not before the two finished snorting. (Grubman's spokesman says Jack doesn't deny the incident.)

Grubman was now moving fast, and by 1990, all his hard work began paying off. He soon became ranked as one of the telecom industry's top analysts by *Institutional Investor* magazine, meaning he had gained a following among the sophisticated investors polled in the survey. More important, as investment banking had become the leading factor in how analysts did their jobs, Grubman excelled there as well. In 1991, he helped PaineWebber underwrite $32.5 million in stock for LDDS Communications, a small but growing telecommunications firm located in Jackson, Mississippi. The deal was a major coup for Grubman.

PaineWebber's investment banking business was the laughingstock of Wall Street, with most deals going to the big three: Goldman, Morgan, and Merrill. But Grubman turned on his considerable charm, flying down to Mississippi and wooing LDDS's iconoclastic CEO Bernie Ebbers over beers and greasy hamburgers at the Cherokee Inn, Ebbers's local bar, and the relationship was born. About a month later, Grubman justified Ebbers's loyalty by initiating coverage of LDDS with an "aggressive buy," calling the outfit "a well positioned, well run regional reseller of long distance services." It was the start of a beautiful, and lucrative, friendship.

Other successes would follow. Some months later in 1992, Grubman hit the Wall Street equivalent of a grand slam, securing PaineWebber a role in GTE's $6.2 billion merger with Contel in 1992, and a subsequent $1 billion stock offering. PaineWebber later got the lead role in a $963 million stock deal that GTE did in September 1999 over industry heavyweights Goldman Sachs and Merrill. The string of victories was big for PaineWebber, but even bigger for Grubman. For years, he had built a rep as a guy who knew the inside of every company in the industry. But now he offered something more valuable: access to top executives, who handed out lucrative investment banking deals. His potential seemed unlimited. If he could produce like this at PaineWebber, a mid-level player, imagine what he could do in the big leagues?

To go with his high-profile career, Grubman found the right wife. He married LuAnn Levick, the former AT&T public relations executive, in a small ceremony in New York City. Levick and Grubman appeared to be polar opposites. She was quiet and pensive; he loud and at times obnoxious. But Grubman was beaming as he introduced his beautiful new wife to family and friends. "She's a Midwestern WASP," Grubman would later say about his wife's cool demeanor. LuAnn appeared to find Grubman attractive for other reasons. "What I found most interesting when I met him was really his Jekyll-and-Hyde reputation," she told *The Wall Street Journal.*

But not everyone seemed to be sharing in the joy. Mildred Grubman found little in common with her daughter-in-law, and at one point turned to Yass and asked, "What do you think, Jay, is he making a mistake?" Yass said he didn't think so. "Jack is going places," Yass thought. "He's going to be a star."

Sometime in 1993, Salomon Brothers telecom banking chief Eduardo Mestre had similar thoughts. Mestre, a seasoned investment banking pro, knew firsthand how the business of winning investment banking deals was changing. The old relationship system, where corporations relied on one firm and one firm alone to handle all their underwriting needs, was finished. More and more, companies bid out work, holding "beauty contests" between big investment banks. One way to gain an edge was to hire a top-notch analyst, someone who would not just publish stock research, but act as cheerleader for the stocks he loved. And no one could cheer louder than Grubman.

Grubman had something else going for him: a burgeoning relationship with LDDS, since renamed WorldCom by its CEO Bernie Ebbers. By the early 1990s, Ebbers had built WorldCom into a regional telecom empire, absorbing a series of smaller companies, and, as a result, had become one of Wall Street's best corporate customers. But he was picky about his investment bankers; Ebbers directed much of the merger advisory business (millions of dollars a year for helping the firm with its acquisitions) to a small, Altanta-based brokerage firm, The Breckenridge Group. Officials at Salomon, sensing that the company wasn't finished growing, wanted a piece of WorldCom's underwriting bounty, and they reckoned Grubman could help.

If it seemed odd that as an analyst Grubman could be courted by one of Wall Street's top bankers, no one at Salomon seemed to care. Mestre simply dialed Grubman from his office and set up a breakfast at the Yale Club, an elegant setting in midtown Manhattan for graduates of the prestigious Ivy League school. Grubman was certainly receptive. Mestre was at the time one of the top bankers in the telecom arena, a man with an impeccable résumé, and someone who Grubman believed could help him get to the next level in his career. Equally important, Grubman was impressed by Mestre's pedigree. He was born in Cuba, but raised in Argentina, the son of a successful media entrepreneur. Tall and athletic,

Mestre was educated in the United States, received his bachelor's degree from Yale, and then graduated from Harvard Law. Though driven and disciplined (he worked out religiously), Mestre had little use for the trappings of the typical successful Wall Street hotshot, friends say. He bought his suits off the rack, lived in a comfortable apartment in Manhattan, and drove a seven-year-old Dodge van that he parked in the garage of the World Trade Center, which survived the 1993 bombing. That said, by the mid 1990s Mestre had made Salomon a top player in telecom banking thanks to his contacts at every major outfit.

The meeting was set for 8:00 A.M. Grubman arrived late, he would complain, because Mestre gave him the wrong address. Grubman later said he came well prepared, drawing up twenty-five key questions for Mestre to answer. But in the end, the most important question came from Mestre. "You're the most prominent analyst in telecom and we have a good franchise," he told Grubman. He asked him to come work at Salomon, adding that he'd make more money than he'd ever dreamed.

Grubman agreed, and in the coming weeks, he met with some of Salomon's top players, including CEO Robert Denham and research chief Jim Crandell. But Grubman wasn't so enamored with Mestre's sales pitch that it prevented him from dangling the offer in front of Paine-Webber, according to people at the company. The final decision was left up to PaineWebber's moneyman, Joe Grano. A former Green Beret who served in Vietnam, Grano had broad shoulders, a square jaw, and a bad temper. As a former stockbroker, Grano rose from humble beginnings to run the brokerage department at Merrill Lynch and then PaineWebber, which he helped build as a major player in the business of selling stocks to small investors. In 1994, PaineWebber CEO Don Marron anointed Grano his No. 2, putting him in charge of expanding the firm's ability to snare investment banking deals, the area where Grubman had begun to shine.

But Grano wasn't exactly a fan of Grubman's work habits. A few years earlier, he and Grubman had paid a call on AT&T, and Grano hated Grubman's know-it-all attitude with the potential client. Grano had other suspicions as well. While managers across Wall Street had begun making research a vital part of their firm's banking efforts, Grano had spent nearly his entire professional life serving the small investor as a broker or a manager of brokers. He was well aware that a good analyst could help a firm win banking assignments, and just how easy it was to screw small investors with conflicted research.

Seated in his office decorated with Army memorabilia, Grano recalls being apprised of the Salomon offer: a yearly salary of around $3 million and possibly more, depending on how much banking business he developed. Grano, who grew up in a tough Italian neighborhood of East Hartford, Connecticut, knew a shakedown when he saw one. "No fucking way," he snapped. "And tell Grubman not to let the door kick him in the ass on the way out."

Grano muttered a few more expletives before Grubman was told, in no uncertain terms, Grano's response. He was free to go.

Grubman joined his new firm in March 1994 with two missions: to remake the nation's telecom industry and, in doing so, become rich. The fastest way to achieve those twin goals was found down in Mississippi in the form of Bernie Ebbers.

A former high school basketball coach, milkman, and bouncer, Ebbers seems at first glance ill equipped to lead a major telecommunication company. His business career started when he invested in a local hotel and restaurant, which ultimately expanded into a chain. But after the breakup of AT&T, Ebbers and a few of his buddies saw the opportunity of a lifetime in selling low cost long distance service. They pooled their money and invested in a small telephone company, Long Distance Discount Services, or LDDS, in Jackson, Mississippi.

Ebbers may have come from humble beginnings, but he clearly knew how to make money. His original business plan for LDDS appeared as if it came right from a Wall Street arbitrage desk. The company would buy long-distance "time" and resell to local telephone outfits at a markup. Because LDDS didn't own the telephone lines, everything went to the bottom line. After experiencing some difficulty early on, LDDS became so successful that Ebbers decided to expand into other areas of the regional telecom business. Between 1988 and 1995, LDDS made eleven acquisitions, growing from a mom-and-pop operation to a company that had caught the eye of major Wall Street firms. Ebbers, however, remained loyal to the people who got him there. Breckenridge, a tiny Atlanta-based outfit that had banked LDDS when Wall Street wouldn't, served as an adviser on all eleven transactions.

Salomon now wanted a piece of the action. No more than five months after he joined Salomon, Grubman began working to set up a string of meetings with Ebbers. In one of the first, he arranged to have Ebbers fly into New York, where he met Mestre and the Salomon banking team. Grubman and Mestre turned on the charm, explaining how much a topflight firm like Salomon could help a growing company like WorldCom.

Ebbers apparently didn't budge. Sometime later, Grubman decided to fly down to WorldCom's headquarters in Mississippi and try his luck once again, meeting this time with CFO Scott Sullivan in addition to Ebbers.

Still, Breckenridge continued to handle the lion's share of the company's work, including three WorldCom acquisitions that closed in 1995. The company was by now a far cry from its days of LDDS, one that Grubman believed could make a serious run at AT&T as the nation's largest telecom outfit. Amid the negotiations, Grubman did what he does best: hype the stock. In April 1996, he issued a report recommending WorldCom for "aggressive growth managers." The other stock recommended in the report was MFS Communications, another Salomon banking client. MFS was important for another reason: Ebbers was eyeing the firm as a possible acquisition.

It was obvious that Ebbers took a certain degree of pride in sticking with the firm that brought him to the big time. But even Bernie's loyalty had a price. In early June 1996, Salomon bankers had just drawn up plans for Ebbers to acquire MFS, a proposal called "Project New Wave." A few days later, they did something else to get Ebbers's attention. On June 10, Salomon was the lead underwriter on an IPO for McLeod Communications, one of the upstart telecommunications firms like WorldCom that won Grubman's praise. But the deal served another purpose. Before the transaction was completed, Salomon allocated 200,000 shares of the IPO into something called "Account X," which turned out to be a new personal brokerage account for Bernie Ebbers. Even though the WorldCom CEO was not yet a retail brokerage customer at Salomon, the allocation was massive—four times larger than any other individual client at Salomon, and larger than the level of stock granted to several large "institutional investors," like mutual-fund giant Fidelity Investments.

For Ebbers it was free money. He bought the shares at the offering price, and was free to "flip" or sell the stock when the shares began to rise, as they almost always did for hot IPOs during the market bubble. Ebbers made an easy $2 million on the deal. Not bad for absolutely no work. But that was nothing compared to what he could now make in salary, largely thanks to Grubman's constant support. Ebbers's pay was now linked mainly to WorldCom options, thus the higher the stock price, the more money he was worth.

Not surprisingly, a couple of months later, Grubman and Salomon hit it big. Ebbers telephoned Grubman himself, informing him WorldCom was planning to use Salomon as an adviser for its planned acquisition of MFS Communications. Grubman quickly called Mestre with the good news. There would be additional meetings and conference calls, and Grubman would lead the way. When it came to convincing the World-Com board that the merger made sense, Grubman and Mestre gave a presentation. A banker at Salomon raised a seemingly obvious question with her supervisor: Why was an analyst so involved in a deal he's sure to rate in the weeks to come? The banker had been invited to a meeting with Grubman and Ebbers and noticed the two "bantering" not about the typical analyst concerns, like WorldCom's financial health, but about Salomon's role in the deal. After the banker left the meeting, she quickly notified Salomon's compliance department about what she believed was a serious breach of the firm's Chinese Wall.

Ironically, there was no breach. Grubman was now over the Chinese Wall, legally acting as a banker and restricted from writing research on the deal until his banking duties were complete. And when they were, Salomon collected $7.5 million in fees advising WorldCom and Ebbers on the MFS deal, one of the largest single paydays for the telecom department.

The deal underscored not just Grubman's conflicted business practices but also his vision of what it took to survive and thrive in the new wireless world of instant communications, cell phones, high-speed Internet traffic, and unbridled competition spurred by the 1996 Telecommunications Act. The law, passed in February 1996, essentially forced the Baby Bells to "unbundle" their services and open up the competitive landscape to the new entrants, companies like WorldCom, that Grubman believed were ready to make a serious move to gain market share on the more established player by expanding rapidly. With the MFS purchase, WorldCom in Grubman's view was ready to take over the world. MFS gave WorldCom miles upon miles of the fiber optic capacity it needed to compete with its bigger rivals. MFS also had a hidden weapon in its arsenal, an outfit known as UUNet, which provided access to the Internet for businesses. With Internet usage doubling every year, WorldCom had, in one acquisition, repositioned itself as a New Economy darling.

For Grubman, the broad industry trends seemed like a no-lose proposition. Consumers had an unending appetite for telecommunications services, meaning that the growth of the industry would all but pay for itself. Meanwhile, to expand phone lines and create new wireless, cellular, and high-speed cable business units, the telecommunications industry would turn to Wall Street in record numbers, requiring hundreds of billions of dollars in stock, bond, and bank financings—hundreds of millions of dollars in fees that would go to the brokerage industry's bottom lines. Grubman never seemed to consider the obvious counterargument to his theory, namely that all this competition would squeeze profit margins, making these newfangled technologies a commodity.

But why should he? A 1997 article in *The Wall Street Journal* laid out the success of Grubman's theory in stark terms: A $100 investment in WorldCom in 1989 would be worth $1,580 in January 1996. More startling was how WorldCom stacked up to its competitors. WorldCom's stock returns were "about 10 times the best returns generated by . . . the Big Three of long distance, AT&T Corp., MCI Communications Corp., and Sprint." The Ebbers-Grubman recipe for success was simple: Try to grow the business, hype the stock, and customers will come.

Now, all Grubman needed was to keep selling this "theory" to investors. Unlike his superstar counterparts, analysts Mary Meeker and Henry Blodget, Grubman avoided television, including CNBC, despite numerous requests over the years. But that didn't mean the king of telecom was without friends in the press, as evidenced by a string of positive newspaper articles that began appearing in major business publications underscoring Grubman's prominent role in the booming telecom business.

The most important of these articles appeared on the front page of *The Wall Street Journal* with the headline: "The Jack of All Trades; For Salomon, Grubman Is a Big Telecom Rainmaker." For Grubman, the article was the defining moment in his career. The *Journal* picked its profile candidates carefully, particularly those that appeared on the front page. The article demonstrated that Grubman was worthy of the same attention given to financial luminaries such as Warren Buffett, Henry Kravis, and Grubman's future boss, Sandy Weill. The reason was simple. More than just an analyst, the article said, Grubman had emerged as the single most important player in the rapidly changing telecom business. His reports moved markets. His advice was eagerly sought by some of the most powerful CEOs in the industry. What made Grubman the telecom superbeing was his ability to use his inside knowledge to help Salomon Brothers win some of the most important deals in the telecommunication business. Grubman wasn't just telling investors what to buy, he was telling the entire telecom industry how it should look.

Grubman, the story said, wasn't your typical Wall Street executive. He had grown up in South Philly, boxed and then attended college. But what separated "Grubman from the analyst pack is how skillfully he manages to walk the divide between banking and research, with his credibility intact."

After reading the piece, and noticing his "dot drawing," the paper's trademark profile sketch, prominently displayed on the *Journal*'s front page, Grubman was nearly orgasmic. The *Journal* failed to challenge his background (some of which turned out to be made up), and signaled to the world that his research was sound. As far as Grubman was concerned, he had officially arrived on Wall Street.

The story, it should be noted, wasn't entirely a puff piece. Grubman may have been a superstar, but the article raised the fundamental problem with the way he conducted business, namely that beneath his charm, Grubman was essentially promoting stocks of companies that paid his salary every time he completed an investment banking deal. Grubman's annual salary of $3.5 million in 1996, one of the highest on Wall Street, was paid in what people at the firm called "Grubman Units," based on how many deals he completed. Even more bizarre was the response of regulators to Grubman's dual role as analyst and dealmaker. They did nothing. SEC enforcement chief William McLucas appeared to care little about the broader question of whether investors were duped into buying stocks based on research that had been influenced by Grubman's conflicts. "There are no hard and fast federal laws that say you can do this and you can't do this," McLucas was quoted in the story. "It's really a case of navigating the problem case by case."

Whether he knew it or not, McLucas had just given Grubman the green light to take his way of doing business to the next level.

In the summer of 1997, British Telecom, the massive UK-based telecom outfit, launched takeover talks with MCI, then the nation's second-largest long-distance carrier. MCI had seen better days. Under its former chairman, the legendary Bill McGowan, MCI grew to compete with AT&T in the long-distance market, but since his death in 1992, MCI had floundered, spending billions of dollars on projects that did little to raise profits. BT, looking to expand across the Atlantic, reckoned that with a little work, the combination would create "a premier global company well positioned to take advantage of the rapidly evolving telecommunications market."

So did Grubman. In one news account, he described the deal's benefits and appeared certain that MCI would accept BT's bid. "There really is no chance of this being renegotiated," he said. Grubman loved the combination so much that he launched a major counterattack on one of the deal's main critics, Dan Reingold, the Merrill Lynch telecom analyst and Grubman's main competitor. Grubman began frantically calling top money managers, attacking Reingold's research as misguided. "He doesn't know what he's talking about," Grubman said.

But Reingold wasn't backing down. "This deal has got to be renegotiated at a lower price" or it would fall apart, Reingold declared in one report. His fear was based on growing evidence that MCI's earnings would continue to deteriorate, causing BT to rethink its bid. "Those who don't see" this possibility, he wrote in a report "must have taken those little pink pills that I refused to take in college." He didn't mention Grubman by name, but Grubman knew whom he was talking about.

It wasn't the first time the two squared off. Reingold and Grubman weren't just competitors, they were mortal enemies, trading jabs in research reports as they fought for the top spots in the *Institutional Investor* poll throughout the 1990s. The rivalry began in the mid 1980s when a young Jack Grubman, then at PaineWebber, blasted MCI in a research report. Reingold, who worked in MCI's investors relations department, countered, citing numerous errors in the research. "This is a disgrace to the profession," he told Grubman, who exploded in a string of curses.

When Reingold made the jump into the Wall Street research business in 1990, he found Grubman to be his toughest competitor, someone willing to push the limits. Reingold, it should be noted, wasn't exactly negative on the telecom business, nor was he above helping his firm win banking business. Like Grubman, he believed the telecommunications industry would grow for years to come, though he favored the "Baby Bells," while Grubman voiced his support for the "New Entrants." But where they differed was in their level of enthusiasm. Reingold considered himself an analyst first, and while he placed "buy" recommendations on WorldCom and other telecom outfits, he never tried to master the system of conflicts that brought Grubman so much success.

In fact, Reingold constantly complained that he couldn't compete against someone who was willing to do anything to win the next deal. "This guy is going to jail," he told several portfolio managers after hearing speculation that Grubman had begun leaking sensitive deal information to clients, giving them inside tips on acquisitions before they became public. For his part, Grubman didn't think Reingold had the balls to do what it took to win.

BT's planned acquisition of MCI was the latest round in the Grubman-Reingold slugfest. By midsummer, MCI's negotiations with British Telecom were clearly in trouble. Reingold drew first blood alerting investors of possible problems with the deal after MCI issued a warning in the summer of 1997 that it was suffering from larger than expected losses. Shares of MCI began to nose-dive, and BT was forced to renegotiate its bid lower. The deal was clearly in jeopardy, but Grubman continued to stand by his original prediction that it would be completed at its original price, and that Reingold didn't know what he was talking about.

Grubman, it was soon revealed, had good reason to keep pushing the merger. Salomon's "arbs," the name given to professional traders or "arbitrageurs" who buy stock in the target company and sell shares in the acquirer, had listened to Grubman and bet big that the deal would be completed, meaning that MCI's stock would rise sharply, since it was being acquired. But with the deal in trouble, just the opposite had occurred; shares of BT began to rise steadily and MCI's fell. Salomon's arb desk was bleeding tens of millions of dollars—some street estimates valued the losses at about $100 million—just from listening to Grubman.

Despite the mounting losses, Grubman wasn't ready to throw in the towel. Reingold was sitting at his desk when he got a frantic call from a money manager, one of his best clients. He had just gotten off the phone with Grubman, who claimed to have access to a "confidential appendix" to BT's merger agreement with MCI. Grubman, the money manager said, claimed the document laid out a provision in the BT-MCI merger agreement that prevented BT from renegotiating the deal. In essence, it would have to make the purchase at the original price tag of about $20 million. Reingold nearly hit the ceiling. It was hardly a secret that Salomon's arb desk was getting killed on the BT-MCI trade, and now Grubman was getting desperate. "Make him show you the document," Reingold shot back. The investor said he would. Reingold never heard back, but in the end he didn't have to. By late August, BT made its intentions clear to MCI: Accept a sharply lower price or we're done. For all intents and purposes, the deal had collapsed.

As an analyst, Grubman had failed miserably at what should have been his top priority, keeping investors in the loop about the flaws in MCI's business model, and BT's willingness to go the distance. But Grubman soon found a way to turn things around. Working with Mestre and another telecom banker, Tom King, he set up a series of meetings with WorldCom's CFO Scott Sullivan, who said he might be interested in buying MCI. His pitch was simple: Buy MCI. There were certainly good reasons why a WorldCom-MCI combo made sense. The deal would create the nation's second-largest long-distance company, nearly the size of AT&T. With MCI, Salomon argued, WorldCom would have all the pieces to become the preeminent telecommunications outfit. Sullivan liked what he heard.

As Grubman was working on the final details of the most important merger of his career, he received a phone call, but this time it wasn't from one of his top clients. Jamie Dimon, the No. 2 executive at Travelers Corporation, wanted to meet with him. Salomon Brothers was being acquired by the giant financial services company, run by Sandy Weill, one of Wall Street's most powerful players. Life for Jack Grubman was going to change dramatically.

The lunch meeting was held at Travelers' offices. Dimon, a Harvard MBA who had been with Weill for his entire career, was accompanied by Steve Black, his closest associate and the capital markets' chief of Travelers' brokerage business, Smith Barney. Dimon's motive was simply to keep Grubman happy. Salomon, he believed, was a troubled company, filled with gunslinger bond traders who made big bucks when times were good, but simultaneously took huge risks with the company's capital. Grubman, meanwhile, proved to be a steady earner. As the trio began their meeting, Grubman was preoccupied with the WorldCom MCI deal, something Dimon picked up on immediately. "You seem distracted, Jack," Dimon said. Grubman, surprised by Dimon's candor, said he was. "At some point you'll know why," Grubman answered.

The next day Travelers announced its $9 billion purchase of Salomon Brothers, merging it into its Smith Barney investment bank. Dimon's hunch about Salomon was fairly accurate, forcing him to slash staff, including some cowboy bond traders that had cost the bank big bucks on risky trades. Less than a week later, Dimon discovered something else, as WorldCom purchased MCI in a $37 billion deal. Thanks to Grubman's hard work, Salomon eventually would earn more than $50 million in fees, one of its biggest paydays ever, to complete the deal.

Top executives at Grubman's new firm were ecstatic, and so were investors, who viewed Grubman as omniscient. "This was a masterstroke," said William K. Newbury, an analyst at TIAA-CREF, a WorldCom investor, in an October 13, 1997, BusinessWeek article. No one, much less Grubman, seemed to care much about whether the deal made any financial sense. Ebbers had to come up with $7 billion in cash to buy out a stake BT already held in MCI. All told, MCI and WorldCom would accrue a combined $30 billion in debt, with the deal adding an estimated $500 million in additional interest expense. After the merger was complete, Grubman let the world know just how he felt. "Load up the truck and buy as much WorldCom as you can."

Amy Butte was breaking into the Wall Street research business in the mid 1990s, when she received some interesting advice. Butte was a junior analyst at Merrill Lynch & Company, and she had just finished working on her first big stock deal. A Harvard business school grad, Butte had considered some of the great investors of the era, people such as Peter Lynch and Warren Buffett, as her guideposts, people who studied balance sheets and invested for the long term. But after the deal, as she shared drinks with one top Wall Street executive, Butte was told to forget much of what she learned in college and pay attention to a new legend in the making.

"If you really want to amass power and influence, you want to be on both sides, working as an investment banker and analyst," Butte recalls the advice from Mark Loehr, head of investment banking at Wit Capital. "You want to be like Jack Grubman."

By now few doubted that Grubman had the Midas touch. His stock picks were setting records. Despite the pitfalls of the MCI deal, World-Com became one of the hottest stocks in the market. Inside Salomon, (renamed Salomon Smith Barney after the Travelers purchase) Grubman's Chinese Wall straddling was being taught to a younger generation of analysts as the model to follow during their careers on the street. Grubman's loyal assistant, Sherlyn McMahon, told a group of newly minted MBAs that being a "research analyst is an exciting and stimulating job, particularly in the telecom group," where Grubman is involved in "every M and A transaction" concerning the company's top telecom banking client, WorldCom. "We believe Jack has the longest standing and strongest relationship" with WorldCom on Wall Street and that shares of the company will keep trading higher.

So did many investors, who looked beyond Grubman's supervisors at Salomon and ignored his conflicted relationship with the company as long as shares kept rising. During the mid to late 1990s, some of the nation's most sophisticated money managers were convinced that Grubman was at the center of every deal, the ultimate source of information for the rapidly changing market. Grubman more than helped promote his reputation as the ultimate insider, by sprinkling tips among his best buy-side clients. To his critics and even some of the people on the receiving end of the tips, Grubman's actions seemed to border on illegality.

But Grubman seemed to walk the fine line between gossip and insider information on a regular basis. In the late 1990s, for instance, Grubman told one mutual fund manager that Sam Ginn, the CEO of a wireless company called Airtouch, was finally ready to sell the company after years of rejecting various offers. Salomon wasn't involved in the deal, the money manager recalls Grubman saying, but he insisted that his information was good. After buying a few thousand shares of Airtouch the next day, the money manager realized just how smart Grubman could be. Shares of Airtouch were rising steadily as rumors swirled about a possible takeover of the company. The portfolio manager made some calls to colleagues in the business. As it turned out, he wasn't the only one blessed with a Grubman tip. "This can't be insider information," he was told. "Jack is telling everybody."

Within a few days, the word leaked officially on CNBC that Airtouch was in play. A week and a half later, shares of Airtouch rose nearly $20 as a company named Vodafone won the bidding war.

As Grubman and the firm's highflying telecom group were busy on the WorldCom-MCI deal, Grubman found himself with a new boss. Sandy

Weill, the great Wall Street financier, was busy integrating Salomon Brothers into his growing financial empire with its massive Smith Barney brokerage unit that sold stocks to small investors. Grubman now became the official spokesman for millions of investors who bought stocks through Traveler's brokerage subsidiary, Smith Barney.

Grubman's WorldCom-MCI call brought him accolades outside Salomon as one of the nation's top deal makers, but within some parts of the firm, he was hardly a beloved figure. One of Weill's first moves was to kill the Salomon arb department as a result of the huge losses suffered on the BT-MCI debacle following Grubman's advice. Weill was no stranger to business risks during his long career on Wall Street, but he hated financial risk, and as far as Weill was concerned, stock traders like those at Sal-omon were some of the most dangerous people around. However, his view of Grubman was much different. The two were hardly friends; in fact, Grubman had only limited contact with the firm's boss of bosses, meeting or exchanging calls maybe once every other month depending on the topic. But Weill clearly understood Grubman's ability to add to the bottom line. Between 1998 and 2000, Grubman helped Salomon Smith Barney raise $53 billion in stocks and bonds for telecom outfits. That translated into hundreds of millions of dollars in fees, making Grubman possibly the best deal maker at the firm. WorldCom was by far Grubman's top client, contributing $100 million in fees since Ebbers ditched Breckenridge as his main adviser for acquisitions and other offerings.

But it wasn't just Salomon that came out smiling. Ebbers soon became a constant recipient of IPO shares into his brokerage account, often corresponding to Salomon's appointment as a lead manager or adviser on various financings. In 1997, Salomon earned $8 million in fees as lead manager for a large WorldCom bond deal, $37.5 million in fees as adviser on its takeover of MCI, and $1.5 million for an exchange offer of MFS notes. Ebbers's IPO shares from that year netted him a profit of close to $10 million.

By now Grubman was one of the hottest commodities on Wall Street, and in 1998, the top executives at Goldman Sachs, the prestigious investment bank, thought he would make a wonderful addition to their team. Top officials, including co-CEOs Jon Corzine and Hank Paulson, and investment bankers John Thornton and John Thain, all wooed Grubman with promises of untold riches once the firm went public. Grubman loved the attention, bragging that Corzine himself led the recruitment drive. Goldman's sales pitch, however, extended beyond money. In April 1998, Sandy Weill combined his Travelers brokerage and insurance empire with banking powerhouse Citicorp, creating the world's largest financial supermarket. On paper, the combination seemed like a no-brainer. The new company, called Citigroup, would benefit from the "synergies" between Travelers' investment bankers and its massive brokerage sales force that sold stocks to small investors, with Citicorp's commercial bankers to win deal after deal. But officials at Goldman emphasized that the Citigroup model would ultimately fail as commercial bankers and people like Grubman fought over control of key clients.

At Goldman, they said, Grubman would be in control. The negotiations continued for several weeks and Grubman appeared willing to accept when Goldman officials suddenly realized that they had forgotten something. Research chief Steve Einhorn, a partner at the firm, needed to meet with Grubman to complete the deal. If Grubman needed a sign of just how little regard Goldman had for research, this was it. Unlike with other analyst candidates, Einhorn didn't make the initial contact with Grubman, and top executives were already on board with Grubman's hiring even before Einhorn voiced an opinion.

The hastily scheduled meeting was held at 7 A.M., and Einhorn was visibly annoyed about being brought into the process at a relatively late stage. He coldly asked Grubman at one point, "Why do you want to join Goldman?" as if he were unaware Grubman had been recruited by the firm's top players. "You called me," Grubman shot back.

After the meeting was over, Einhorn was convinced Grubman wasn't right for the job. His main objection was that Grubman was an analyst in name only, and the firm was asking for trouble if they brought him aboard. But many more people inside the firm couldn't wait to get Grubman started. In the end, it didn't matter. Grubman had let senior executives at Salomon know about Goldman's interest, and they were ready to counter. Whether Grubman would have left for Goldman remains a matter of debate. Privately, Grubman said he would have jumped ship if Goldman was planning to remain a partnership (the firm was attempting to go public), which would have entitled him to the huge year-end bonuses Goldman paid these top executives. "At the end of the day, I would have been a managing director at another public company," he told friends. Meanwhile, more than a few officials at Citigroup believed that Grubman had no real intentions of leaving for a place like Goldman, with its stiff, white-shoe corporate culture and endless internal political battles.

But the prospect of losing the nation's top-ranked telecom analyst and deal maker was a risk that few officials were willing to take. Jamie Dimon, Salomon's most senior executive, had Steve Black draw up a new contract for Grubman that would be presented to Salomon's ruling body for approval. Nothing at Salomon Smith Barney was done without the support of the big guy, Sandy Weill, the notoriously tightfisted CEO, and Grubman's contract was no exception. But even a penny-pincher like Weill, who once ordered employees to remove plants from the office because of extensive watering costs, knew he couldn't resist Grubman's demands.

In the end, Weill approved a contract that may have been one of the most lucrative that any analyst, maybe any executive, had ever received. While the contract didn't pay Grubman specifically on the basis of how many deals he helped win, it provided the next best thing. The contract included terms and conditions that gave Grubman the ability to earn tens of millions of dollars a year depending on his performance "as measured by senior management." That meant the firm could pay him whatever it wanted as long as he kept making money.

Nowhere did the contract mention that Grubman had to publish research that actually helped *investors* make money. It was just the kind of incentive Grubman needed.

CHAPTER FIVE

Sucker Money

In July 1998, Sandy Weill and the corporate governance committee for the board of directors of his financial services empire, the Travelers Group, quietly made Wall Street history. Fearing that archrival Goldman would score a major coup in stealing their high-profile star, the company awarded Jack Grubman the mother of all contracts, promising a combination of stock, options, and cold cash worth an average of $20 million a year over the next five years. Grubman had certainly been well compensated before; in 1997 he earned around $8 million, according to company documents. But with the new pay deal, Grubman had achieved a special status on Wall Street. Not only was Grubman one of the highest-paid analysts in the history of research, but he now reigned as one of Wall Street's highest paid executives.

As it turned out, Citigroup had good reason to keep Grubman happy. It was well known that during the late 1990s, Grubman had become one of Salomon's top deal makers, helping to generate tens of millions of dollars in banking fees from corporations that were the beneficiaries of his positive research. But Grubman, like Mary Meeker and Henry Blodget, was valuable in another way. During the 1990s market boom, all three became high-priced salespeople for a "democratizing" stock market by helping to convince the broad middle class that Wall Street was not a crapshoot but a safe place to invest for the future. Average folk, people like the "Beardstown Ladies," who used to socialize at bingo parlors, began gambling on stocks with their savings. Construction workers, secretaries, bartenders, and schoolteachers, people who never even took an economics course, pulled their money out of the bank and began snapping up stocks, investing in mutual funds or turning to brokers to buy shares directly. Analysts encouraged investors to "buy on the dip," propping up the markets by pumping billions of dollars into scores of volatile high tech companies when they swooned.

The higher the markets rose, the more people worried they might be left out of the party. In 1980, American households held $875 billion worth of stock; at the height of the bull market in 2000, that number grew to $7.7 trillion. Despite some temporary setbacks like the 1987 stock market crash, Wall Street pointed to the market's wild growth as proof that long-term, "buy and hold" investing really worked. The Dow Jones Industrial Average, the key measurement of the nation's top companies, hovered near 11,000 by 1999, nearly twice its 1996 level and many multiples of its January 1990 level of 2,590. The growth of the NASDAQ stock market, the index that measured many of the money-losing New Economy Internet stocks championed by Blodget and Meeker, was even more astounding, surpassing the 5,000 level in 2000, compared to just 415 at the start of the past decade.

In some ways, investors had no choice but to believe what they were hearing from the Wall Street spin machine, which barely mentioned (other than in the fine print of their reports) that the analysts themselves had a vested interest in advocating the benefits of the markets. Many corporations had long ago ditched company pensions, forcing average Americans to save for retirement by investing in 401(k) programs that offered employees their choice of mutual funds, many of which were filled with risky high-tech stocks. Bonds had always been a safe and secure investment for people looking for higher returns than they could get from a savings account. But low interest rates made bonds, particularly low-risk U.S. Treasury securities and municipal bonds, simply too unattractive when compared to the huge returns offered by stocks.

As powerful as these broad trends were in luring the most unsophisticated people into stocks, the superstar analysts knew how to close the deal on the greatest pool of sucker money Wall Street had ever seen. Henry Blodget attracted a huge following among average Americans, directing them to a slew of high-tech Internet companies by preaching the benefits of the New Economy not only in his research reports, but also as a television news commentator on business channels like CNBC, and in his speeches to the firm's brokers, who dealt with three million small investors across the country.

By the height of the bubble, brokers were so hungry for anything

Blodget could give them, that Merrill had even made one of his speeches available to all fifteen thousand of its brokers by beaming the speech through the firm's in-house computer network. The speech was vintage Blodget. The Internet and the New Economy companies it had spawned, he said, had created a "profound economic trend that is hitting almost every sector" of the U.S. economy. "A lot of companies will fail," he warned, but the real risk, was staying out of the market as "pure play" Internet companies were stealing "market value away from some of the old-world industry leaders." It was a message that brokers seemed to love. After the speech was over Blodget was bombarded with questions from the audience about what stocks they should tell their clients to buy. Blodget reminded the brokers that they should consider their clients' risk tolerance before recommending these stocks. That said, nearly all the stocks listed by the Internet guru were Merrill Lynch banking clients.

Blodget's counterparts on Wall Street used similar methods to reach the masses. For years, telecom research king Jack Grubman, whose facial features never translated well on the big screen, refused to hype his stocks on television, but that didn't stop him from agreeing to massive cover stories in newspapers and magazines with reporters he felt would buy his spin. In fact, one of the most efficient ways that Grubman got his stock picks out to the general public was through something called Radio FCN, a daily radio show Salomon Smith Barney broadcast to its sales force around the country.

Salomon's management simply loved the show. Analysts like Grubman were asked softball questions by a moderator named Lee Degenstein, who used to be a broker himself. Afterward, brokers were encouraged to call up their clients with stock tips. One former broker named Phil Spartis recalled hearing Grubman pitch his stocks. Degenstein asked Grubman a question about WorldCom, both his favorite stock and his biggest banking client. Spartis says Grubman droned on for a full ten minutes about the company's amazing growth prospects (without disclosing his investment banking relationship with the company), before Degenstein stepped in and tried to change the subject, only to have Grubman persist in talking up the company. Spartis remembers turning off the show in disgust, but other listeners weren't as cynical. According to some Salomon Smith Barney brokers, the radio show was a highly effective tool used by management to alert brokers to the stocks that should be at the top of their sales pitch. WorldCom, thanks in part to

Grubman's many appearances on the show, was among the most widely held stocks among Salomon Smith Barney brokerage customers.

Mary Meeker's message was certainly more nuanced and less certain than either Blodget's enthusiasm or Grubman's over-the-top bullishness, but she too played a key role in enticing small investors to the market. For years Meeker claimed that her reports were intended for sophisticated investors, the traditional clients of the Morgan Stanley investment bank. But the reality was far different. Meeker's research was funneled through Morgan's own brokerage network and like Merrill, Morgan executives often piped her speeches and presentations about the markets to brokers so they could pass along her words of wisdom to small investors.

One such example occurred just days before the NASDAQ reached its March 10 peak, when the Queen of the Internet appeared in a well-timed "Live Web Chat" broadcast to brokers and other Morgan Stanley executives titled "The Internet: Where We've Been and Where We're Going." Meeker soberly pointed out that "it's critical actually for investors to realize that many of these companies are very high risk enterprises . . . people have to assume that their investment can go up or down 50 percent very easily in any given week or any given month."

But like Blodget, the Net Queen spoke about how the Internet was too big for investors to ignore. Put simply, the Internet was revolutionizing the world of business, "destabilizing" traditional businesses, and creating many, many new ones. "Web usage will be huge," she said, because "people do the same things on the Internet they do in real life," adding that "the number one channel on America Online is the—no surprise—the personal finance channel." It was also no surprise that AOL had been among Morgan Stanley's biggest investment banking customers, a fact Meeker failed to mention during her monologue.

There are many reasons why investors never picked up on the occasional warnings issued by the superstar analysts. Many investors, of course, just didn't want to hear that the good times weren't going to last forever. Others simply accepted risk as a fact of life and rolled the dice. But many more fell victim to the way such nuances were communicated through the vast networks of brokers that firms like Citigroup, Merrill Lynch, and Morgan Stanley employed to peddle stocks to small investors.

During the 1990s boom, stockbrokers became an important part of the Wall Street equation as firms sought to profit from the mad rush of small investors. The top Wall Street brokers pulled in yearly salaries well into the millions of dollars, and the most sophisticated knew all about research conflicts and various scams that put their most unsophisticated clients at a disadvantage. But many more weren't all that much different from the people they were selling to in terms of their knowledge of finance, the markets, and the problems that made the research they used to push stocks so dangerous.

Consider, for example, John Cunha. In 1998, Cunha was fired from his job as a broker trainee with PaineWebber's Iselin, New Jersey, branch after failing his Series 7 exam, a requirement to sell stocks on Wall Street. But that didn't stop him from following his dream, and trying to make a killing in the stock market. After leaving PaineWebber, he walked across the street, filled out an application, and signed up to work at Morgan Stanley as a stockbroker. He was hired virtually on the spot.

Part of the Wall Street con job during the 1990s market boom was to paint their brokerage sales forces as something more than mere order takers or salesmen looking for a fast buck. In politically correct Wall Street terms, brokers like Cunha became "financial advisers," whose main task was to help investors save for the future. But the reality was far different as Wall Street went on a massive hiring spree to find thousands of new brokers to meet the demand from a growing class of new individual investors, many with little if any real knowledge or experience in the markets. In addition to his experience working briefly for two Wall Street firms, Cunha had repaired broken skis at a resort in Colorado, and before that, worked his way through college by selling textbooks. At Morgan, he passed his Series 7 exam, but his primary source of knowledge about selling stocks wasn't gleaned from some finance textbook or employee sales manual. "I used to sell stocks by reading directly from Mary Meeker's research reports," he said in an interview.

With a starting salary of $30,000 plus commissions, Cunha got his job about a year after Morgan Stanley's 1997 merger with Dean Witter Reynolds, which combined Morgan Stanley's prowess in underwriting lucrative stock offerings, particularly in the booming technology sector, with Dean Witter's massive retail sales force, a brokerage network with eleven thousand "financial advisers" who sold stocks and mutual funds to investors across the country.

Cunha was one of about two dozen brokers in the Iselin, New Jersey, branch who were inexperienced but hungry to make a quick buck. As Cunha tells it, his supervisors weren't much better. The office was run by a crew of managers and experienced brokers, such as branch manager Brian Rogers, and his assistant branch manager, Kevin Johnson, a gray-haired Tom Selleck look-alike, whose job it was to look after some of the new recruits like Cunha, but who spent much of his day working on client accounts. The compliance officer, who was supposed to make sure all trading out of the branch met NASD standards, was a dour man by the name of Ed Tierney, who rarely spoke to brokers like Cunha. Despite his position as the office watchdog, Tierney also kept a sizable book of business. During the trading day, as brokers were handling tens of millions of dollars in trades affecting the life savings of scores of small investors, Tierney could be found in his office with his door shut, helping his own clients make money. (Morgan says Tierney's brokerage activities were consistent with its policies.)

At first, Cunha believed the job was a godsend. He grew up in a lower middle-class home, an adopted son of a housewife and an electrician in suburban New Jersey. At thirty-two years of age, and still living with his parents, he was eager to move out on his own, get married, and most important, get started on a career in the brokerage industry. At Morgan Stanley, brokers were required to complete a three-week training session in New York, at the firm's retail brokerage headquarters in the World Trade Center. Even for a novice like Cunha, the training seemed overly simplistic. Cunha recalls one session when the moderator read from the employee handbook, which implored brokers to act "in their customer's best interests."

Even these simple rules, Cunha soon discovered, were largely ignored the minute he showed up for work in late 1998. Whether he knew it or not, Cunha had just become a member of one of the most aggressive selling machines on Wall Street. Second only to Merrill Lynch in size, Morgan Stanley's brokerage network was considered among the most profitable retail systems on the street, thanks in large part to its no-holds-barred sales practices that earned the scorn of competitors, and occasionally stock regulators, but pumped huge profits into the firm's coffers.

According to former employees, the high-pressure tactics included sales contests, where brokers were offered free trips depending on production, and orders by management to "cold call" potential new clients by randomly dialing numbers from the telephone book with a simple pitch: "I'm calling today to find out what it takes to be your broker."

At a time when its competitors stopped pushing their own in-house proprietary mutual funds, Morgan found ways to ensure that the firm's mediocre fund family comprised 80 percent of all sales from its brokerage offices, including paying brokers extra to push the in-house products. After regulators raised questions, management simply redirected the payments to branch managers, who demanded that brokers continue to push the in-house funds. "I WANT A 100% PARTICIPATION," wrote John O'Neill in a May 1999 directive to brokers in the Greenwich, Connecticut, branch office, about a new fund being offered by the firm. "I WILL HELP YOU ACHIEVE YOUR GOALS IF YOU HELP ME ACHIEVE MINE."

For Cunha, the pressurized environment of a Morgan Stanley branch office was jarring. He spent his initial weeks working twelve-hour days seated in the office's "bull pen," a row of desks where young brokers worked, scouring the local community for potential clients and most of all, pushing Morgan's technology stocks by reading directly from Meeker's research. His standard line was, "She's the best and she loves the stock." For many investors, it was all they needed to hear, particularly as tech stocks continued to lurch ever higher. The heady days of the 1990s bull market created a fantasy world where even money-losing stocks seemed to never fall, and when they did, it was a chance to buy more because they would eventually move higher. Soon, average Americans who wouldn't purchase a dishwasher without first reading *Consumer Reports* began entrusting their entire life savings to brokers who were armed with little more than a few memorized lines from a Meeker research note.

This was not to say that their inexperience was immediately apparent. Cunha and many of the other newbies were moderately successful as the markets continued to roll through the end of 1999 and into 2000. He arrived at the office early, and stayed late. His training taught him to keep customers from selling stocks by reminding them about the benefits of "long-term" investing. Among the brokers, Cunha says, there was an old saying anytime the markets got wobbly, "Don't frown and double down." Their sales pitches were timed to meet certain events, such as speeches by Federal Reserve chairman Alan Greenspan, the release of favorable economic data, and last but not least, the release of research by Mary Meeker.

But as the markets began to crash in early 2000, particularly the tech-laden NASDAQ, erasing the wild gains of the past two years in a matter of months, investors began demanding real answers. The NASDAQ reached its peak on March 10, 2000, hitting a high of 5,132, before embarking on a slow, steady, and painful decline over the next two years. Cunha recalls investors flooding the office with so many calls that brokers couldn't handle the volume. They simply let the messages roll into voicemail. But ignoring the problem could only go so far, as the stocks continued their decline. During the crash of 1987, there were fewer inexperienced investors in the market, and back then, the crash hit blue-chip names that rebounded in the not so distant future. What made the current market decline so terrifying was that brokers had spent the past five years selling risky New Economy stocks. These companies weren't just experiencing temporary setbacks; many were being exposed as near frauds with little other than a dot.com next to their names.

As far as many brokers were concerned, Meeker didn't help matters either. She often rated Internet stocks not just on traditional balance-sheet measurements, but also on something called "usage metrics," like website page views and estimates on how many "eyeballs" viewed a particular website. Meeker believed such measurements were the best way to assess money losing but promising Internet companies because they measured possible future performance, although most small investors had no clue what they meant. Before Morgan Stanley teamed up with the Dean Witter brokerage firm, Meeker's customers were sophisticated institutional investors, mutual fund and pension fund managers who could pick apart her reports, understand the difference between a "strong buy" and her "outperform" ratings on stocks, and what she meant by all those eyeballs hitting a website.

But now Meeker's research was being distributed to brokers and small investors who had neither the background nor, in some cases, the intellect, to grasp these fine distinctions. During long cigarette breaks, Cunha and other brokers angrily complained that Meeker rarely updated her research on several stocks during 2000, the first year of the Internet crash and a time when investors needed her guidance the most. One such stock was AOL, which had merged with media giant TimeWarner in early 2000. What a scam, Cunha thought; the same firm that would spare no expense taking their best brokers on expensive trips to swanky resorts couldn't spring a few bucks to update its research.

Morgan executives blamed it on the firm's strict "quiet period" rule that lasted, they say, a full year after AOL's historic deal to purchase TimeWarner early in 2000. Morgan was an adviser for TimeWarner, and Meeker's role in the transaction turned out to be particularly important. She was one of the key players in pitching the deal to TimeWarner's board of directors, giving a rousing speech that heralded the vision of AOL's CEO, Steve Case, a man she compared to legendary Time Inc. founder Henry Luce.

While Meeker's reports may have been dated and conflicted, Cunha says he and other brokers treated them as if they were gold. In pitching shares of the postmerger AOL to investors, he says he and the others read straight from her old reports. "No one told us not to," Cunha says. "And management knew what we were doing." For a time it worked, but by the end of 2000 many of Cunha's clients were no longer trusting either him or Meeker. "You motherfucker, I just lost half my money on this stock!" an angry investor screamed one afternoon in late 2000. Cunha knew he had run out of excuses. "I'm sorry," he said, "I was relying on Mary Meeker's research."

Cunha's troubles were, in many ways, just beginning. He says he had followed assistant branch manager Kevin Johnson's advice and put clients into a small telecom company named Voicenet, supposedly a pioneer in the technology of voice recognition. Johnson said it was a no-lose situation—trading at around $8 a share, but worth "$100-plus," Cunha recalls Johnson saying. (Johnson did not return telephone calls for comment.) It was all Cunha needed to begin talking up the stock to his clients, including several family members. Because no major firm published research on the company, including Morgan Stanley, brokers couldn't "solicit" orders to investors. Cunha says that Johnson provided him with a simple way to get around the company's solicitation rule. "If you call someone with a stock tip, and they call you back later and buy the stock, mark it unsolicited."

By mid-2000, Cunha had placed about a half dozen people into Voicenet, echoing Johnson's sales pitch that the stock would reach above $100 a share. "You're getting in on the ground floor of a major technology," Cunha told one family member, who dumped nearly $100,000 into the stock. His dad, a retired technician at Verizon, bought about $25,000 worth. Johnson was ecstatic. "This is a no-lose stock," he assured Cunha. One of the biggest reasons to be optimistic, Cunha said, was that Johnson told him that Morgan was now seriously thinking of initiating research coverage on the stock.

With Morgan Stanley research behind it, Voicenet would be a sure winner. But it was in fact a loser. After the dotcom bubble burst, shares of Voicenet began to plummet and Morgan's research department never launched coverage. By the fall, Voicenet was trading in the single digits, around $3 a share down from $50 earlier in the year, wiping out Cunha's family's holdings. It wasn't just a case of the market crushing shares of the company. Johnson was telling people to be calm and stay in the stock, as he was selling shares for the company's CFO to meet "margin calls" on stocks he bought on credit, sales that further depressed prices of Voicenet. For a change, Cunha did a little research on his own. He checked into Voicenet's profile on Yahoo!, and learned that the company had its headquarters in Manhattan. But when he showed up, he discovered that Voicenet consisted of nothing more than a post office box.

Unfortunately for investors, the activities in the Morgan Stanley Iselin branch were hardly unusual. The white-shoe firm of Goldman Sachs was known for its high-powered investment bankers and swashbuckling stock and bond traders who took huge risks in the markets and often delivered big profits. The firm was widely regarded as the gold standard of Wall Street, operating on an ethical plane far above that of its competitors, but the truth was far different, particularly when investment banking business was on the line. By the height of the market bubble, Goldman was run by an intense investment banker named Henry Paulson, a teetotaling Christian Scientist and bird-watcher. When he wasn't studying wildlife, Paulson was busy fighting his way to the top, forcing out his co-CEO Jon Corzine, the man who led the effort to make the firm a public company. Under Paulson, Goldman was locked in a bitter battle with Morgan to become Wall Street's top investment bank. During the 1990s, Goldman underwrote some of the most questionable IPOs in the market, deals that were turned down by Morgan Stanley and Mary Meeker because the companies' business models looked even less sustainable than some of the shaky outfits Morgan was selling to investors. By the end of the decade, Goldman had effectively replaced Meeker and

Morgan Stanley as the market's leading investment bank for Internet companies.

But how Goldman did business is instructive. Goldman appeared to have perfected the practice of spinning, handing out hot IPOs to corporate executives who handed back lucrative underwriting assignments. Meg Whitman, the CEO of eBay, the high-flying Internet auction house Goldman brought public, quietly received shares in over one hundred IPOs between 1996 and 2002. Goldman says Whitman was a longtime brokerage customer, but the firm also earned $8 million in banking fees from eBay during that time. In the late 1990s, only days after Goldman had received a key piece of banking business from Tyco International, one former banker noticed that Tyco had miraculously been placed on the firm's "recommended list" of stocks that were being actively sold by the firm's sales force that deals with the super wealthy investors.

When the firm was shut out of high-profile banking deals, it managed to save face in other ways. Goldman was so embarrassed that it wasn't initially chosen to play a major role in the massive AOL-TimeWarner merger (AOL chose Salomon Smith Barney and TimeWarner hired Morgan) that the firm helped AOL engage in a bit of financial alchemy, according to one former Goldman executive with knowledge of the matter. After the deal was completed, Goldman CFO David Viniar, working with the firm's media banker, Tim Ingrassia, agreed to a plan hatched by AOL's moneyman Mike Kelly to temporarily park a piece of AOL's European joint venture on Goldman's own balance sheet. Under the accounting rules, the move allowed AOL to disguise losses in the joint venture in the months following the deal as the markets began to turn sour. Goldman, meanwhile, pocketed a sizable profit itself. The transaction was reversed about a year later and Goldman made several million dollars. Needless to say, the firm recommended AOL to its brokerage clients.

In fact, research and investment banking were so intertwined at Goldman that investment bankers had virtual veto power over what appeared in reports through a process in which they were asked to review reports published by the research team, particularly when the companies being researched are looking to issue stock, says one former Goldman executive. Sometimes this review consisted of nothing more than confirming data points and making sure that basic facts were accurate in reports. But if a company was in the market for a deal, the changes became more substantial, according to the former Goldman executive. "We basically edited out anything that could be construed as negative," that executive said. "Banking could prevent analysts from downgrading a stock," said a former Goldman analyst.

Salomon Smith Barney also emphasized the positive when it spoke to small investors about banking clients. One morning in late November 1999, Phil Spartis tuned into the company's internal "squawk box" to hear Jack Grubman announcing a major about-face on AT&T, placing his coveted "buy" rating on the stock.

Grubman's edict created tremendous buzz inside Salomon Smith Barney's massive retail sales force, which employed nearly twelve thousand brokers, the third largest on Wall Street behind Merrill and Morgan. Like its competitors, Salomon encouraged brokers to actively push those stocks that were being "recommended" by the research department. (Spartis isn't the only broker who said the rule existed; former brokers at Merrill Lynch and Morgan Stanley maintain they faced similar pressures from their managers.) After listening to Grubman, Spartis hit the phones. One of his first calls was to a client, Michael Grimley, himself a WorldCom executive. "Jack went to a buy on AT&T this morning," Spartis said, adding that it was "the first time in five years" Grubman had upgraded the stock. His price target: $75 a share, a large premium from its current price of around $50. But Grubman said shares could spike higher.

"There's an analyst meeting on December 6," Spartis added, "and he [Grubman] thinks they'll have to rent out Madison Square Garden" given all the excitement the new strategy will generate. Grubman, Spartis said, believes that if AT&T follows through on its plan, it could be a "$2,000 stock." The sales pitch worked. Grimley bought around three thousand shares, but as he would soon find out, Grubman's call didn't measure up. About a month later, he ordered Spartis to begin unloading his AT&T position as shares began to nosedive. In the end, Grimley racked up a $30,000 loss. Salomon, however, made a boatload from Grubman's call. A few months after the upgrade, the firm earned $60 million in fees as an underwriter on a large AT&T stock deal.

Spartis, who is now the target of a regulatory investigation over allegedly placing clients in inappropriate investments, was fired by Salomon Smith Barney in early 2002 and has filed a wrongful termination claim against the firm. But Spartis said he isn't to blame; he was only following company orders to sell stocks recommended by Grubman. "Jack was the leading telecom analyst in the country," Spartis said in an interview, "and we were trained to push his calls."

As important as the Wall Street brokers were in feeding the opinions of the superstar analysts to small investors, they were just a piece of a larger strategy designed to lure as much sucker money into the markets as possible. In the 1990s, as we have noted, the big Wall Street firms had broken out of their traditional lines of businesses, embracing the concept of the financial-services supermarket, in which one firm could offer everything from research and investment banking to stock trading and brokerage services for small investors.

The new financial model brought tremendous profits to Wall Street. Citigroup, the ultimate supermarket combining Travelers Group and its Salomon Smith Barney investment bank with Citicorp, the world's largest bank, became one of the market's most profitable companies. But these new mega financial corporations also carried tremendous risks for small investors. As the size of the typical Wall Street firm grew, so did the conflicts facing the average American who relied on research and their broker's advice to purchase stocks. Former Federal Reserve chairman Paul Volcker may have put it best when he called these monolithic entities "bundles of conflicts." The financial supermarkets' best customers were the large corporations that paid huge fees for investment banking and commercial banking expertise, as well as for the positive stock research that became a prerequisite for doing business during the bubble years. With Wall Street spending so much time serving the needs of corporate America, Volcker believed that small investors would never be given a fair shake.

He was right. By the mid 1990s, nearly every major Wall Street firm had embraced a business model that treated brokerage customers as second-class citizens. Merrill Lynch was founded on the principle of bringing "Wall Street to Main Street" through its massive brokerage sales force, but during the bubble years, the firm strayed far from its roots by expanding into investment banking, research, stock and bond trading, even commercial banking. Merrill had downplayed its roots so much that by the late 1990s, it no longer offered full-time brokers to the middle-class investor, mainly those with around $100,000 in assets. Those investors were forced to deal with a customer service center located in New

Jersey if they wanted advice. The firm's new attitude toward its traditional customer base may have been best summed up by Jeffrey Lippert, the branch manager of Merrill's massive Garden City, Long Island, brokerage office, who in an email to his staff said: "We don't have time to provide personal services to the poor."

Merrill's uptown rival Morgan Stanley made a similar transformation, though from a different vantage point. For most of its history the House of Morgan was the anti-Merrill of Wall Street. While Merrill was created to serve the masses, Morgan was born to serve the rich (the firm has its roots in the famous Morgan bank), and for most of its history, Morgan Stanley would reign as the nation's premier investment banking outfit for corporate America. It came as no surprise that when scores of technology companies needed an underwriter in the late 1980s and early 1990s, a Morgan banker named Frank Quattrone had already set up shop in Silicon Valley and was ready for the kill. But in 1997, as small investors started flooding the markets, Morgan Stanley made an abrupt detour and merged with Dean Witter Reynolds, a large brokerage firm. Almost overnight, a company that traced its roots to Wall Street nobility had joined forces with an outfit that once set up branch offices in the Sears Roebuck department stores.

A culture clash was predicted. John Mack, the Morgan Stanley chief, soon bolted from the company to become CEO of Credit Suisse First Boston after a public spat with Dean Witter's top executive, Phil Purcell, over control of the firm. But the widely expected catastrophe never came. For all the cultural differences between the two firms, Morgan and Dean Witter made a perfect match in a 1990s sort of way. For years, Dean Witter brokers had pushed stocks without a name-brand analyst, but now they had some of the best analysts on Wall Street including the venerable Mary Meeker, at their disposal to help complete the sale. Morgan, meanwhile, had been dealing with smart "institutional investors" like mutual funds and pension funds for most of its history. Now the firm had a massive brokerage network filled with "mom-and-pop" investors eager to get their hands on the next Microsoft or IBM brought public by Morgan's banking department.

Despite these mighty combinations of brains and brawn, one firm surpassed them all. By the late 1990s, after a long and contentious career, Sanford I. Weill had created the largest and most profitable financial services company in the world, Citigroup. As Merrill was growing organically, and Morgan was expanding through one grand acquisition, Weill had spent much of the 1990s building his empire piece by piece, with the capstone being the deal he struck with John Reed, the longtime CEO of Citicorp, in 1998 to create Citigroup. The merger was heralded as the deal of the century, and it would live up to its advance billing.

The glaring problem, of course, was that the firm would have been illegal as the still formidable law that prevented combinations of investment banking and commercial banking, known as the Glass-Steagall Act, remained in effect. Influenced, no doubt, by millions of dollars in campaign contributions to Wall Street–friendly politicians, Glass-Steagall had been whittled down during the 1990s, but not totally eliminated. That is, until Weill and Citigroup got into the act. With the help of friends in Washington, including his new No. 2 executive, former Goldman Sachs CEO and treasury secretary Robert Rubin, as well as Jesse Jackson, the civil rights leader turned Weill lobbyist, Weill rolled over what remained of the Glass-Steagall Act, prodding Congress to repeal the law, and ensuring Citigroup's survival.

Citigroup didn't exactly wait for Congress to give it the green light before making its mark on Wall Street. Not long after the merger, commercial bankers and investment bankers began sharing clients. Competitors complained that the firm linked its commercial lending business to bond underwriting; companies that hired Citigroup to sell a bond deal would be approved for commercial loans. One document labeled "AT&T Debt Financing/June 16 2000" listed for AT&T the amazing array of services the firm offered, from Jack Grubman's research, to Eduardo Mestre's investment-banking expertise, to Citicorp's ability to lend cash, and even the advice and counsel of the firm's ultimate rainmaker, Weill himself. Another Citigroup memo virtually bragged about the intricate and lucrative web of relationships that Citigroup offered another big customer, WorldCom. "Citigroup is one of the closest financial institutions to [WorldCom]," the memo says. "Citibank is one of Wcom's leading international banks, providing loans, trade, cash management and FX services to Wcom international subsidiaries . . . SSB is clearly the lead investment bank of Wcom."

Weill was meticulously making sure that his grand vision produced results, cranking out record profits all through the 1990s. But he was absolutely reckless in his disregard for how the structure of his new firm would affect small investors who needed unbiased information about stocks, as Citigroup produced some of the most overhyped research on Wall Street. Consider the example of George Zicarelli. A videotape editor at CBS, Zicarelli was the perfect brokerage customer for the times: desperate to make money in the markets, and completely ignorant of the behind the scenes wheeling and dealing that could skew the research he depended on to purchase stocks.

At fifty-five years of age, Zicarelli had made and lost huge sums of money thanks to his addictions to gambling, alcohol, and cocaine. Over the years he had sought treatments for cocaine and alcohol abuse. His penchant for gambling also led him to trade wine futures, turning a quick $450,000 profit in late 1999. But Zicarelli wanted more. A member of the New York Athletic Club in Manhattan, he often rubbed shoulders with Wall Street executives, like Alan Schwartz, a top banker at Bear Stearns. These were people who earned in one week what Zicarelli made in a single year. So when he approached his broker about investing in red-hot telecom stocks later that year, it didn't take much to get him to bet the farm on the high-flying telecom companies that analyst Jack Grubman said would spread enormous wealth for years to come.

In 1999, Zicarelli began buying shares of Global Crossing, a company run by a former Drexel Burnham Lambert investment banker who wanted to lay high-speed cable lines under the Atlantic Ocean to create a truly global telecom company. Global, as it was known on Wall Street, was one of Grubman's top picks, and after he was given some of Jack's research, Zicarelli was hooked. In a few months, Zicarelli had nearly 80 percent of his net worth in the stock.

But as telecom stocks peaked and ultimately blew apart in mid 2000, Zicarelli knew he had made a bad bet, and turned to his broker for help. The way Zicarelli remembers it, his broker's advice was simple: Grubman still loves the stock and the market is going to rebound. He didn't inform Zicarelli that Grubman had a great incentive to keep pushing shares of Global, based on Citigroup's lucrative investment-banking relationship with the company.

In the spring of 2001, another of Grubman's top picks, Winstar Communications, had just filed for bankruptcy. Zicarelli turned to his broker once again, this time asking if Global would suffer the same fate. "No way," he claims his broker told him, "Global Crossing is a different animal," again referring to Grubman's research on the company. But it wasn't. Zicarelli says he listened to his broker's advice and by the end of

2001, he was nearly broke, with his Global shares trading at just pennies on the dollar, as the company followed Winstar into bankruptcy court.

Debasis Kanjilal, a pediatrician from Queens, New York, found himself in a similar situation. One afternoon he was listening to CNBC when he heard an analyst named Henry Blodget speaking about Internet stocks. Blodget had been issuing a warning that many Internet stocks, "75 percent" of the Internet companies that had taken the markets by storm, wouldn't survive. But Blodget assured investors he had the inside track on the winners, and within a few months, Kanjilal, an immigrant from India, invested all of his children's college funds, about $500,000, in two of those, JDS Uniphase and an outfit named Infospace, a company that Blodget had called "the best technology platform for wireless Internet" in the market.

Kanjilal didn't bring Zicarelli's addictive personality to the table, but the two shared a lust for riches. Both JDS and Infospace had risen dramatically during the bubble years and Kanjilal believed they would just keep rolling. Of course, he also ignored one of the most basic premises of investing, "diversification," or spreading your money around different types of stocks and praying that not all of them decline at once. Kanjilal turned the concept on its head, betting all his shares on two bubble-induced stocks with nearly identical Internet-based business models.

Like most people swept up in the stock frenzy of the 1990s, Kanjilal can only be held partially responsible for the consequences of his investments. In 1998, he sought out and found a Merrill Lynch broker in Manhattan, who was supposed to take his account and help him understand the markets. Indeed, when Kanjilal threw his money at Infospace, this absurd gamble should have sent shock waves throughout Merrill's compliance office, which under NASD rules is supposed to monitor customer investments based on "suitability." Instead, Merrill handed over to Kanjilal some of Henry Blodget's research on the company, which he continued to plug in various reports and research notes through 1999 and 2000, even as the market for Internet stocks began to decline. By the summer of 2000, Infospace had lost nearly half its value since Kanjilal first bought shares at around $120. When Kanjilal demanded answers, he says his broker repeated his mantra—"Henry thinks it's a great stock."

A year later, Kanjilal lost nearly his entire investment amid a broad sell-off of Internet stocks. His wife was forced to find work and Kanjilal gave up his dream of being able to afford to send his children to Harvard.

Officials at Merrill would contend that Kanjilal knew the potential consequences and paid the price. They have a point; Kanjilal was hardly uned-
ucated, and even the most unsophisticated of the firm's clients should
know that research is nothing more than an opinion.

But that describes only part of the story. Unknown to Kanjilal was
Merrill's investment banking relationship with Infospace, and what
many people believed was Blodget's role in making sure that relationship
remained solid even as the markets were tanking.

CHAPTER SIX

Oh, Henry!

The 1990s were a glorious time to work on Wall Street. Between 1998 and 2000, the heart of the Internet boom, Wall Street reaped nearly $4 billion in fees for underwriting deals that involved the Internet and technology, producing one of the greatest periods of wealth creation in the nation's history. The federal government wiped out its much-maligned deficit and President Bill Clinton was heralded as an economic genius as unemployment sank to historic lows. State and local governments across the country were also flush with cash as the wealth effect from middle-class taxpayers flowed into municipal budgets across the land. A working-class stiff in Queens who scrimped and saved to put his kids through Catholic school now considered early retirement and a second home in Florida. In New York City, the epicenter of the market and the wealth it produced, a group of brokers with little more than a college degree and a gift for gab were earning so much money that they needed to offset their multimillion-dollar salaries and the capital gains on their investments by producing rap concerts and opening trendy restaurants frequented by Hollywood stars.

But the real stars of Wall Street were the analysts who seemed to have their finger on the market's every move. Mary Meeker, now a household name, bought a fancy apartment in Manhattan, a short cab ride from work, and a mansion in Silicon Valley, not far from her New Economy clients, as her salary ballooned to $23 million by the end of 2000. Blodget snared a townhouse in the fashionable West Village of New York City as his salary approached $10 million a year. Grubman became so rich that he purchased a townhouse in an elegant section of the Upper East Side of

Manhattan, near Central Park, presumably so he could work off the stress of his hectic deal making with early morning jogs.

But the end was near, not just for the bubble, but also for the celebrated careers of the superstar analysts who helped propel the boom. For them, judgment day occurred on March 10, 2000, when the symbol of the New Economy, the NASDAQ stock market index, rose above the 5,000 level, nearly double what it was a year before. From then on, it was all downhill. At first, the market's unraveling was barely noticed on Wall Street; many couldn't believe it was happening. Blodget, for one, had seen a similar swoon just a few months earlier, only to watch the markets recover the very next day. "All I could say is 'wow,' " Blodget told *The Wall Street Journal.*

Meeker continued to urge investor caution, much like she did for the past year, except, of course, for all those "ten baggers"—the catchy New Economy label she placed on her favorite stocks that she said would increase in value ten times. The market's unraveling, it seemed, barely registered on Grubman's radar. He continued to issue research, particularly on his favorite stock and banking client, WorldCom, which screamed "buy" even as the markets were telling people to sell like crazy. One small investor, who had turned an $80,000 investment into a $500,000 nest egg by listening to the superstar analysts, tried to comfort himself by repeating the brokerage industry's most popular sales pitches during the bubble: "Invest for the long haul" and "buy on the dip."

But with every downward tick of the NASDAQ after March 10 and into the summer and fall of 2000, the screws began to turn on investors and then the superstar analysts who helped create the mania in the first place. In just three months since the NASDAQ peak, the market had fallen more than 1,500 points to about 3,400, wiping out hundreds of billions in wealth. Wall Street felt the sting as well. Various lines of business that helped make the analysts rich began to sag. Initial Public Offerings, the deals most coveted by investors, analysts, and bankers, were among the hardest hit. During the market bubble, IPOs were the lifeblood of Wall Street—their fees were nearly twice as high as the average stock offering, and investors begged their brokers for a piece of the action.

But as the market began tank, so did the allure of IPOs. Companies began pulling offerings in the face of investors' skepticism. Those investors who rolled the dice and bought the shares that came public soon held near-worthless securities.

The crashing markets should have told the superstar analysts that their theories of never-ending growth were wrong, and that money-losing companies must someday make money if they want investors to own their stock. But in a mad dash to win what deals were available, many analysts cut corners even more than usual, becoming more outlandish in their predictions, and pushing even harder to use their research to win banking business. Such antics would have gone unnoticed during the bubble years, hidden by the rising tide of the markets. But with investor losses mounting, the immense shortcomings of Wall Street research could not be ignored. For years, people like Grubman, Meeker, and Blodget had given short shrift to their analytical work, spending the vast majority of their time seeking out investment banking work, and now it began to show. Meeker who prided herself on the fact that she had "one shitty year" early in her career, had her second in 2000. She was one of four Morgan Stanley analysts that maintained an "outperform" rating on thirteen stocks that fell a whopping 74 percent.

Grubman didn't fare much better. As the tech meltdown began infecting industries where business models were based on the growth of the Internet, Grubman's favorite telecom outfits were among the hardest hit. Companies like Global Crossing, Qwest Communications, and World-Com, which issued tens of billions of dollars in costly stock and debt to build and maintain their communications infrastructure, that Grubman advocated, soon faced the prospect of bankruptcy unless investor sentiment changed. Leo Hindery, the CEO of Global Crossing took a direct shot at Grubman's theory of never-ending growth, warning his boss, company chairman Gary Winnick in June 2000 that "like the resplendently colored salmon going up a river to spawn, at the end of our journey our niche is going to die rather than live and prosper." A few months later, Hindery was out of a job, but it wasn't long before his prediction proved remarkably accurate. As the market crashed, Grubman went from king to court jester among company brokers who were forced to push his lousy stock picks to investors. "There are no words to describe how deplorable and sickening his guidance has been," wrote one angry broker to Salomon Smith Barney management.

But it was Henry Blodget who seemed to hit bottom the hardest. In just six short years, he had transformed himself from failed journalist to corporate finance trainee, and now to the nation's top ranked Internet researcher at the nation's largest brokerage firm. Along the way, he unseated the skilled and respected Jonathan Cohen for a job at Merrill Lynch, and more recently, the popular and powerful Mary Meeker in the closely watched *Institutional Investor* beauty contest.

By late 2000, Blodget had been at Merrill less than two years, but he seemed to have aged a lifetime. His thick red hair had been thinning for some time, and colleagues noticed he was in a constant state of exhaustion from the long hours. Blodget had come to Wall Street as a committed Liberal, someone who believed that the markets could serve a larger purpose by helping the average investor participate in the great economic revival, centered on the growth of the Internet. But now he had been reduced to something of a robot who worked long days serving Merrill's various competing constituencies, including the firm's most demanding constituency, the investment banking department that looked at Blodget as its No. 1 weapon to win lucrative stock deals.

Physically exhausted, mentally drained, Blodget had just been castigated by an investment banker because of a scheduling conflict when he reached out to an unlikely source for advice. Scott Ryles, the head of Merrill's technology banking department, had developed a close relationship with Blodget over the past two years, taking credit for being one of the people who recommended that Merrill hire Blodget in late 1998.

But Ryles himself had been demanding more time from Merrill's boy wonder to help snare deals that were still going to Merrill's competitors, Goldman, Morgan Stanley, and Credit Suisse, so there was little he could do. "You need help with your calendar," Ryles recalls saying.

Blodget, it seemed, was all alone.

How much sympathy Blodget deserved is another matter. For the past five years he had willingly accepted the conflicts of his job, the dual nature of pitching banking business while providing research on the same companies. According to people at the firm, he barely gave a second thought to how mixing research with banking might help his company make a lot of money, but could also mislead small investors into thinking that his research was "objective." As long as the market behaved, who would notice?

But the market didn't behave as Blodget had predicted and his stock picks fell like dominoes, slowly but surely exposing his research calls as frauds. Instead of the star treatment, Blodget began receiving the cold shoulder. Angry emails from brokers started flowing into his computer as investors began to openly criticize his research methods.

Privately, Blodget hit the panic button. In personal emails to friends and colleagues, he openly questioned his own stock picks, often blaming the very process that mixed banking and research for his troubles. In an email to one of his supervisors, he even threatened that he would begin downgrading stocks, "just start calling the stocks . . . like we see them," no matter what the repercussions on the firm's sensitive investment banking relationships. In another, he complained about being sentenced to "banking hell." Blodget had spent so much time doing deals that he was falling behind in his research production. He was "getting scared about lack of product" or research he was able to publish given his heavy schedule, he wrote Virginia Syer, an analyst in his group. "We put out more last year during banking hell," he added. "I'm going to have to work like crazy for the next few months. Definitely have that burned-out feel. This just ain't a low-stress job." Syer told her boss to hang in there. "H you crank out product," she wrote. "Give yourself a break. Life is too short."

But nothing, it appeared, could stop his inner demons as criticism continued to mount. His boss, research chief Andrew Melnick, forwarded him the following email from a broker whose clients lost money following Blodget's advice. "Why in the hell are we paying these guys multimillion-dollar salaries for this kind of work?" the broker wrote. Blodget exploded. "The more I read of these," he told one colleague, "the less willing I am to cut companies any slack, regardless of the predictable temper-tantrums, threats and/or relationship damage that are likely to follow."

Blodget, however, lacked the courage to start calling them like he saw them. Three months into the bear market, Blodget appeared on Louis Rukeyser's widely watched television business show, *Wall $treet Week with Louis Rukeyser*. During the interview, he boldly predicted that his top stock picks would be the survivors as the market continued to nosedive. "I think over the long term we'll be vindicated," he said. "I think this [the Internet] is a tremendously powerful economic trend."

So powerful to Blodget that he continued to play by Merrill's conflicted rules, accompanying the firm's bankers on their various forays to underwrite shaky Internet stocks. While Blodget and his team didn't win every deal, those that became Merrill's clients enjoyed Blodget's almost unyielding support, even as the markets continued to tank. One example was Internet Capital Group or ICGE, a Web "incubator" that made investments in smaller Web companies, generating profits, it told investors, when those companies came public. Back in August 1999, Merrill and Blodget scored a major victory when they took ICGE public, and Blodget never stopped hyping the stock. Later that month, he placed a two-year price target of $125 and billed the outfit as a "must own" stock, a "blue chip" in the fast growing "business-to-business" Internet market, which Blodget believed held great promise for investors down the road.

It's hard to see why, other than the company's banking relationship with Merrill. In January 2000 when a reporter from the financial publication *Barron's* questioned Internet Capital's lofty valuation—it had risen 2,800 percent since its IPO—Blodget issued his own rebuttal that same day, pointing out the pitfalls of worrying about valuation as the momentum of the markets was surging. Several weeks later in April, ICGE was turning to Merrill to sell some convertible bonds, and Blodget plugged the company once again. Despite the market's current problems and its impact on net stocks, Blodget explained that ICGE had a good enough business model that it would "eventually bounce back" down the road.

That's what Blodget was saying publicly, but inside Merrill, ICGE was becoming a joke as shares fell from a high of $170 to around $10 by the end of 2000. Blodget and some members of his team even recognized the error of their research, albeit privately, as the company's stock was being pounded. In one email to his colleague Sofia Ghachem, Blodget wrote: "Sadly, I think brilliant might have applied to a short note entitled 'SELL NOW' back in March, but we must make the best of it. Never has there been a more humbling force than Mr./Mrs./Ms. Market." Edward McCabe, an analyst on Blodget's team, appeared to mock his boss's rating on the stock as shares fell. "Mr. Blodget," he wrote, "ICGE has also been weak lately. Do you have any comments as to why?" Blodget suggested that McCabe shouldn't be the one pointing fingers. "You LOVED ICGE at $200," Blodget wrote back, "and here you are silent as a fawking mouse at $35. Since you LOVED it at $200, why isn't it a screaming fawking buy?"

Blodget finally downgraded ICGE a few months later to an "intermediate-term accumulate." In November, ICGE announced a third-quarter loss of $236 million. Shares fell nearly $6 to $10.38 around this time, but eventually the outfit would trade like a penny stock, becoming one of the biggest blowups in the history of the Internet. But not before Merrill pulled in tens of millions of dollars in banking fees from the company, one of its most lucrative relationships with any Internet outfit during the bull market.

ICGE wasn't the first and it definitely wasn't the last stock the Blodget team had professed support for publicly, but bashed in private conversations. Around this time, Blodget and other Internet analysts began to cool on Aether Systems, a computer software and programming company that Merrill brought public, earning nearly $40 million in banking fees. In November 2000, one of Merrill's Internet analysts, Virginia Syer, circulated an email discussing a potential downgrade of Aether and two other Internet companies as the markets floundered. Syer forwarded her note to research management with the following caveat: "I may sound flip, but I am not being so—If banking is our top concern, I'd like us all to agree on it."

Syer certainly knew the drill and so did Blodget; analysts had already met with Merrill bankers to discuss a possible downgrade, according to a regulatory document. But Aether was considering a secondary offering, and Merrill was well positioned to win some banking business. Of the three companies, Aether was the only one saved from a downgrade.

Blodget seemed to cut another banking client, Infospace, a company that supplied handheld devices with information, similar breaks, only to question his own decisions in private emails. Through 1999 and most of 2000, when tech stocks were cratering across the landscape, Blodget gave Infospace his highest buy rating as shares reached $262 on March 2, 2000, just days before the Internet bubble burst. For Blodget, it seemed, Infospace could do no wrong. In one research report, Blodget said the company "has the best technology platform for the wireless Internet." Although the wireless Internet market was volatile and likely to evolve in "fits and starts," Infospace, he believed, was destined for success. "The company has signed 5 of the top 6 carriers in the US and is gaining momentum in Europe and Asia."

Blodget clearly identified Infospace as one of those technology companies that he believed would survive the growing storm. But much of Blodget's public optimism seemed to be based not on deep analysis but on conversations with company executives. In a March 2001 interview with The Wall Street Journal, Blodget conceded that he never independently verified Infospace's global expansion plans, which turned out to be wild exaggerations as the stock fell to single-digit levels over the next year.

There's also compelling evidence that he was fully aware of these exaggerations. In a series of private emails to colleagues just after the bubble burst, Blodget referred to Infospace as a piece of "junk," a "powder keg," and expressed his "enormous skepticism" about the company's fortunes, and even fretted when the shares were being placed on the firm's "recommended list" so they could be sold to small investors.

Again, Blodget's warning never appeared to make it out of Merrill's email system. In April 2000, Blodget began assisting Merrill's investment bankers in retaining investment banking business from Go2Net, another Internet company, which was soon to merge with Infospace. Under the terms of the deal, Go2Net executives wouldn't receive cash as part of the sale; they would receive shares of Infospace. The higher the stock price, the more they would get paid. For Merrill the stakes were huge as well. The market correction began squeezing the deal flow that kept Wall Street happy and profitable during the boom years. One memo said the firm would make at least $16 million if the merger went through, making positive research on Infospace even more important.

Blodget seemed to understand this equation well. As both companies set the merger process in motion, he issued a report on Infospace reiterating his buy rating, something known as a "booster shot." These reports served no other purpose than to stroke investor interest so shares would trade higher. David Aarvig, a broker in Merrill's retail system, immediately saw through the hype. Normally shares of a company will fall when it intends to use cash or its stock to make a major purchase, so Aarvig asked the obvious question: Why is Merrill telling its clients to buy? "We had the stock as one of our Favored 15 and yet we were advising [Go2Net] on the merger," he said in an email to Blodget. "Everyone should have known that [Infospace] would fall sharply upon announcing the proposed deal; so why was INSP left as such a highly rated company . . . My clients have lost a lot money in this highly recommended company."

It's unclear if Blodget responded, but the Infospace call continued to generate excitement inside Merrill's brokerage network, though not the kind Blodget or Merrill really wanted. As shares declined, one broker who had pitched the stock to his best customers emailed Blodget citing a

Wall Street Journal article that attacked Infospace's annual report as a "horror story" with its "high-school exam format."

The broker, Jeff Sexton, said "before joining Merrill Lynch, I was a securities lawyer . . . Shame on me for not doing the due diligence that I and other FCs [financial consultants] assume you and other analysts are doing . . ." Merrill ultimately downgraded Infospace on December 11, 2000, but only after the merger was finalized and the firm received its $16 million advisory fee. The downgrade pushed the stock off Merrill's recommended list as shares began to trade in the single digits. Blodget appeared relieved that the entire episode was over. "Oh my god," he wrote a fellow analyst in another email. "I can't believe it took until now."

It's impossible to gauge how much of the Infospace money flowed directly into Blodget's year-end bonus. But as a November 2000 memo suggests, Blodget certainly had something to gain from his conflicted relationship with investment banking. In this memo, Blodget described the "21 transactions" that Blodget and his team worked on during the course of the year, deals that generated $90 million in revenues for Merrill. Such memos were used by Merrill analysts to remind management about their contributions to the firm's bottom line during bonus time, and Blodget wanted his fair share. The report said two other "completed transactions" brought the team's revenue total to $114 million for the year. Blodget was sure to point out that there were thirty-two other transactions the team should receive credit on, "approximately half still pending, half withdrawn."

Blodget and his assistants were so cognizant of the relationship between their pay and banking that they continued to update their list until the very last possible day. "Did we get paid for GoTo yet?' Kirsten Campbell, an analyst in the Internet group, asked Blodget in an email about another banking client, GoTo.com (no relation to Go2Net). "If so, you should add to our IBK (investment banking) list."

As it turns out, GoTo.com, based in Silicon Valley, had become a key banking target for Merrill at the end of 2000. The company went public in June of that year, just weeks after the Internet bubble burst. Like many New Economy outfits, GoTo.com promised investors huge returns down the road. Though its business model of charging companies to be listed in its search engine with results appearing somewhat suspect, Merrill nevertheless viewed the company as a potential gold mine. Unlike other net outfits, GoTo.com wasn't "burning" or spending its cash at a rapid clip. Its strong financial condition meant that the market, which was now starting to squeeze weaker companies, would look favorably on a GoTo.com stock deal. Merrill wanted that deal, and Blodget's research became a key selling point.

It is easy to see why. The markets were falling, but at the end of 2000, Blodget had just beat out Meeker for the top honors in *Institutional Investor* magazine's annual rankings, which became one of the pitches Merrill bankers used in offering their services to GoTo.com. Blodget clearly understood what was at stake for Merrill, and he assigned coverage of the stock to Campbell, who began the process of initiating coverage on the company just as bankers started a full-court press to shape her research.

At first, Campbell was uncomfortable playing the conflicted role that Blodget seemed to embrace. Campbell believed the company deserved a lower rating than what bankers were demanding. When Blodget suggested that she reconsider, Campbell exploded. "I don't want to be a whore for f—ing mgt," she wrote in an email.

Blodget ultimately agreed to a compromise, issuing only a "long-term" buy on the stock, but urging investors to be more cautious over the next twelve months, with an intermediate-term "neutral" rating. In early January 2001, as shares of GoTo.com fell below $10, Blodget issued his report (his name was on the top of the report even though Campbell did most of the grunt work). GoTo was "growing quickly and probably has enough cash to make it to break even," possibly in the first quarter of the year, he wrote.

That's what he told investors. In private, he was much more cautious about the company's prospects. "What's so interesting about GoTo except banking fees????" John Faig, a fund manager asked Blodget in an email around the same time. Blodget's succinct response: "Nothin."

Over the next six months, small investors who bought shares through brokers could have used such candor, but Blodget had other matters to attend to. In the spring of 2001, nearly a full year after the Internet bubble burst, Blodget joined banker Thomas Mazzucco on a road show to promote shares of GoTo.com, and gain some credibility as underwriter on a future stock deal.

Edward McCabe issued a research report that upgraded GoTo.com for the first time since Merrill initiated coverage, after which shares of the company rose nearly 20 percent. Mazzucco now sought to capitalize on all the good will. His proposal was straightforward: Merrill should serve as the lead underwriter on a company stock deal that would generate some much-needed cash. Executives at GoTo got back to Mazzucco saying they liked his idea, but not enough to appoint Merrill as the top underwriter. Credit Suisse First Boston, led by tech superstar Frank Quattrone, would get the deal. Mazzucco, Merrill's lead banker, was furious. He drafted a letter to top officials at GoTo expressing his disappointment. "Not only did Henry Blodget show leadership by" issuing his rating on the stock when it was "near its low point, but he recently upgraded it and sponsored a set of investor and Merrill sales force meetings."

Blodget didn't seem too happy either. He received word of GoTo .com's decision at 5 A.M. while he was traveling on the West Coast. Within hours, Blodget did something he rarely did during the market bubble: he downgraded a stock. "I don't think we downgraded a stock on valuation since the mid-1990s," McCabe wrote Blodget in an email right before the firm published the downgrade.

"Beautiful fuk em," Blodget responded.

But life wasn't beautiful for Blodget. By the fall of 2001, the tech-laden NASDAQ had fallen below the 2000 level, a three-thousand-point drop in less than two years. Although Blodget had already downgraded some of his top picks, Merrill's vast brokerage network was in an uproar, demanding better research for their clients and using Blodget's stock selections on Infospace, Internet Capital Group, and Pets.com as exhibit A in their case that the company's guru was in fact a joke. Even Melnick, the research chief, got into the act. He reminded his analysts to "effectively differentiate our research through a combination of greater spadework on the fundamentals . . ." and specifically criticized the use of the rating "accumulate," which seemed to be Blodget's fallback position when he didn't want to disrupt a banking relationship. Such a half-hearted call "does not help your credibility or the long-term franchise," Melnick warned.

Melnick's words of wisdom couldn't stop Blodget's demise. Newspapers, which had made Blodget a star, now considered him the poster boy for the Internet bubble. His television face time (which made him the most recognizable analyst on Wall Street) trailed off dramatically. After making about eighty television appearances in 1999, he did just forty-six in 2000 and just a fraction of that level in 2001. Making matters worse, regulators, including a little-known attorney general in New York State, began sniffing around his soured recommendations, examining the GoTo.com situation as a "retaliatory downgrade," after a *Wall Street Journal* article disclosed the controversial stock call in July 2001. The problems piled up for Blodget even more as he faced an arbitration case from an investor, Debasis Kanjilal, the Queens pediatrician who said he lost his children's education fund listening to Blodget's stock calls.

At least publicly, Merrill continued to support Blodget. A spokesman for Merrill blamed Blodget's troubles on his staff. He said the team had been largely disbanded and several had "let Henry down" by producing subpar research. Blodget's name often appeared at the top of research reports even though the bulk of the work was completed by analysts who worked for him, the spokesman said. But with the vultures circling, Blodget was clearly looking for an escape route. In December 2001, he announced his resignation from Merrill, telling *The New York Times*, "It just seemed like a good time to pursue the next thing." Like Jonathan Cohen, whom Blodget replaced two years earlier, it was uncertain how much choice he had in his "resignation." Wall Street, after all, is an unforgiving place to those who miss the market.

Yet for all his troubles, Blodget accomplished much during his short stint on the street. Just a few years before, he couldn't land a job as a copy editor at *The Wall Street Journal*. Now he was a millionaire several times over with a townhouse in Manhattan's tony West Village neighborhood, a new wife, and a degree of fame that could catapult him, hopefully, to the next new thing. He left Merrill with $12 million in salary, bonuses, and severance, and an agreement that the firm would pay his legal bills if investors who felt they were burned by his stock calls kept suing. To keep busy, Blodget decided to go back to his first love, writing. He inked a lucrative book deal with publishing giant Random House to put the whole Internet craze, presumably his involvement as well, into perspective.

It was a wild ride, but Blodget couldn't leave Merrill without paying his respects to one of his biggest supporters. It wasn't so long ago, when Internet stocks were soaring, that Merrill CEO David Komansky had adopted Blodget as his official adviser on the Internet, inviting him to his office, overlooking downtown Manhattan and decorated with rare Japanese art, where they chatted about the risky markets Komansky and his wife loved to trade in. During those heady days, Komansky was firmly in control of the firm and Blodget had helped make Merrill a player in the race to underwrite Internet stocks.

But these days, Komansky was a shell of his former self. Slowing profits (not even Blodget's presence could help the firm's financial situation) finally caused Merrill's board to change course. Komansky was CEO in name, but the shots were now being called by company president and heir apparent, E. Stanley O'Neal, a no-nonsense, bottom-line-oriented manager who wanted to ditch unprofitable parts of the firm, Blodget included.

Now all Komansky could do was shake hands with his former boy wonder and say good-bye.

CHAPTER SEVEN

The Queen Falls

Savvy investors were said to predict the great crash of 1929 when their shoeshine boys began dishing out stock tips. For Meeker, the moment may have been a cab ride in New York City sometime in early 2000, when the driver turned to her and said, "Hey, you're that Internet lady." As the 1990s came to a close, Meeker was possibly the most important symbol of the new economy on Wall Street. She had just turned forty and was regaled as a cultural icon, helping millions of investors understand how the New Economy would change their lives. With every new deal, every successful Internet IPO, every research call, Meeker's star rose. *The New Yorker* called her the "Diva of .Com" in a flattering story about her successes as the Internet's top deal maker, her skittishness about Internet stocks. She was mobbed at conferences by people who wanted a taste of her wisdom, stopped on the street, and regularly hunted down at airports on the West Coast, after taking the red-eye from New York, where would-be Internet entrepreneurs handed her business plans and begged for a few minutes of her time. At the height of her popularity, Morgan was forced to hire three full-time assistants to go through the several hundred emails she received each day from brokerage clients, venture capitalists, and assorted nut jobs looking for information on one of the greatest fads in Wall Street history.

The Internet had turned the world upside down, but Meeker was on top. While other analysts begged to spend five minutes with the leaders of the New Economy, Meeker considered people like Amazon.com founder Jeff Bezos and Meg Whitman, the CEO of eBay, close friends, and lunched with Larry Page and Sergey Brin, founders of the search engine Google. Bizarre job offers (one television producer proposed the Mary

Meeker fly fishing show when he heard of her love for anglers) came flooding in, as did opportunities to run Internet companies. Frank Quattrone, her old comrade now at Credit Suisse First Boston, basically had a standing offer for Meeker to join his team. "We don't compete against Morgan Stanley—we compete against Mary Meeker," Quattrone remarked in a *Wall Street Journal* story that caused a near panic among top Morgan executives. The threat that Meeker would jump ship resulted in massive increases in her salary from $15 million in 1999 to $23 million in 2000, and for Morgan it was money well spent. Meeker was now snaring more Internet banking assignments than at any time in her career, and working harder. By the height of Internet mania in early 2000, even top clients had trouble tracking her down. She had more than two dozen people under her wing, and had expanded her universe to cover companies that had only marginal New Economy components (her name was placed on the research of Martha Stewart Living Omnimedia, which derived only 8 percent of its revenues from the Net).

But the market for Mary Meeker was ready to peak. She generated more than $200 million in banking revenue in 1999, a personal record that she was about to surpass in 2000 when her close friend, Joy Covey, the former CFO of Amazon.com, warned her that trouble was on the horizon. Both were attending the World Economic Forum in Davos, Switzerland, at a time when the economy, at least in the United States, was better than ever. Like Meeker, Covey had spent the past five years consumed by her high-pressure job and the "revolution" the Internet seemed to foment, putting off family and a normal life. During a late night telephone conversation, as the two were unwinding after a day full of panel discussions and meetings, Covey recalls telling Meeker that the mania that had propelled their careers couldn't last forever, and she advised Meeker to find a life outside work. "Maybe this is a good time to step back," she said. "There just may be more pain than pleasure."

"I'm not quitting," Meeker said. "I want to see this through."

In the coming months, Covey left Amazon, got married, and started a family. Meeker, on the other hand, kept pounding away. By early 2000, the number of Internet companies looking to come public was mindboggling, and bankers at Morgan wanted to underwrite every one of them. As her days seemed to get longer—she was already working in eighteen-hour shifts—her temper grew more intense, replacing the dry humor that had been a trademark as much as her black power suits.

"This sludge makes no sense," Meeker roared at an assistant who compiled some data for a pending research report. Her boss, Dennis Shea, had to remind her that "you don't have to yell to have impact."

Some people inside Morgan attributed her frequent outbursts to work overload, and they were at least partially right. But there was another equally compelling reason why Meeker seemed to be losing her grip. Despite her unabashed support for the companies she brought public, Meeker knew Covey was right: Internet mania couldn't last forever, and when it was over, someone was going to be held accountable for the damage to investors' life savings.

Meeker didn't want that someone to be her. In speeches, presentations, and in her research, she began to warn investors that the boom was likely to result in a massive bust. Meeker clearly wanted it both ways. She mixed her enthusiasm about some Internet stocks and her admiration of the New Economy's leading CEOs (Amazon's Jeff Bezos and AOL's Steve Case were "wicked smart dudes") with pessimism about others, leaving a trail of rejected stock deals in the process. In mid 1999, one warning she gave to Morgan's sales force was leaked to CNBC, where reporter David Faber remarked how Meeker was "saying not overly positive things" about Internet stocks to Morgan's sales force. Later that year, she reminded her supervisors in a memo that she was doing all she could to "maximize gain and minimize risk" of approving deals with companies that wouldn't survive the eventual shakeout. In early 2000, as the NASDAQ rushed toward the 5,000 level, Meeker put Morgan's investment bankers on notice: Begin toning down your "selling memos," the marketing pitches used to sell new Internet stocks to large investors. She no longer wanted the Morgan name to be associated with over-the-top projections for New Economy stocks that appeared everywhere else. When word of her edict made it to *The Wall Street Journal*, Meeker sarcastically noted, "You never want to catch a falling knife."

Meeker's warnings sounded good in theory, but the result was that they began costing Morgan serious money. A report that landed on the desk of investment banking chief Joe Perella put Meeker's problem in perspective. Morgan had fallen behind Goldman in a special category of Internet IPO's: those from New York City's Silicon Alley, where a slew of new Web outfits were coming public and boosting Goldman's earnings. By early 2000, bankers at Morgan estimated that Meeker rejected more than hundreds of millions in deal fees. When Shea made some inquiries about the matter he heard the same complaint again and again. Mary Meeker had become a cost center.

So much money, in fact, that many investment bankers inside Morgan wanted to dethrone their Queen. The pressure built slowly at first; but during the first months of 2000, as the NASDAQ reached new heights and companies were begging to come public in droves, a full scale assault was underway. One key moment occurred in early 2000 when Meeker voiced serious opposition—a diva fit as someone at the firm called it—to Morgan handling a potentially lucrative stock offering for Microstrategy, a company that manufactures electronic commerce software. "I'm not buying the company's story," Meeker snapped during a conversation with Morgan's global research chief Mayree Clark.

In Meeker's mind, that was the end of the discussion. Well, not quite. It wasn't long before Meeker was summoned to a meeting at the firm's thirty-fourth-floor conference room to defend her opposition. The gathering was a who's who of Morgan's banking and research team, including Clark, the research chief, and Chuck Phillips, the company's software analyst, who had direct responsibility for the deal if Morgan chose to participate. Ominously present were a host of investment bankers, including Perella and his No. 2, Terry Meguid. It seemed like a lifetime since Perella had mentored Meeker, convincing her to reject the job offer from Quattrone because Morgan was a "big organization," which would give her support when things got rough. Now that support seemed to be missing.

Clark opened the meeting by letting Meeker understand the stakes. Microstrategy was looking to sell upward of $400 million in stock, worth as much as $30 million in fees in what's known as a "secondary offering," or a stock deal following an IPO. The firm wanted Morgan, but would turn to Goldman if they didn't move fast. It was theirs to lose.

Meeker then laid out *her* case. She was unfamiliar with the company's top management (Meeker viewed strong management as a key to success), and the company's Internet business was the main factor driving its huge stock valuation, a major problem in an overheating market for New Economy stocks. The meeting lasted about an hour with little progress, that is until Clark accused the Queen of playing office politics; Meeker, she said, was opposing the deal because Phillips would get all the glory as its lead analyst. Meeker, who considered Phillips one of her closest friends at the company, exploded. "I wouldn't do anything to harm Chuck in any fucking way!" she said, before storming out of the room.

Clark soon found Meeker in her office crying. She apologized and asked her to come back and talk things through. Meeker said she would, but she wasn't backing down. In the end, Morgan didn't do the deal, and Goldman Sachs got the assignment.

But Meeker's hunch regarding Microstrategy turned out to be right. The deal Morgan's bankers had salivated over was pulled in early 2000 after Microstrategy announced a massive restatement of its earnings, which caused its stock to fall $140 in just one day and earned a front-page story in *The Wall Street Journal* about the company's shady accounting. When Meeker saw the article, she burst out laughing. "I told you so," she said to Shea.

Meeker won the battle over Microstrategy, but she was losing a bigger war with the firm's powerful investment banking department. By mid to late 2000, as the demise of the Internet stocks Meeker had predicted was in full bloom, Morgan bankers began a full-court press to squeeze out what remaining deal flow could be had from the technology companies that had been Wall Street's most lucrative business through the 1990s.

Meeker felt that squeeze immediately. Keep in mind that no firm on Wall Street had the research for banking trade-off down to a science more than Morgan Stanley. One reason Quattrone left Morgan was that he was blocked from having complete control over the firm's tech analysts, but that's about as far as the firm's separation between research and banking went. Meeker may have had the ultimate "sign-off" on the deals the firms brought public, but as long as anyone could remember, analysts and bankers worked arm-in-arm to find IPO and M&A targets, as well as secondary offerings, setting the stage for some of the most conflicted research Wall Street had ever offered small investors.

No investment banking practice seemed to cross the line for analysts at Morgan Stanley. During "road shows" analysts transformed themselves into traveling salesmen, dropping all pretense of the "objectivity" the public expected, to help their corporate clients sell deals to investors. Analysts were expected to be so involved in the deal process that they often helped their favorite companies craft business strategy, and the collusion of banking and research was so extensive that bankers played a key role evaluating analysts, providing comments about their deal-making skills that were used to gauge year-end bonuses.

For analysts, the message was clear: Piss off banking with objective research and get ready to take a pay cut. In determining how much banking-related compensation an analyst would receive, the firm kept track of every deal members of the research staff worked on, even assigning a rating to measure the level of analyst involvement. It should come as no surprise that Meeker often received the highest rating on her deals.

The conflicts didn't end there. The firm employed people known as "liaisons," who directed traffic between banking and research. One liaison reminded a banker pitching underwriting business to a company called Pilgrim's Pride that he shouldn't guarantee that the firm would issue positive research coverage on the company, "unless we get the books and at least $3-5mm [million] in fees with the money in the bank before we pick up coverage." Perella, the firm's banking chief, virtually promised a company called Loudcloud positive research if Morgan was chosen to underwrite its IPO. Morgan Stanley, he wrote in one email to company officials, had "developed a successful model which combines the best of technology and telecom research . . . to properly position Loudcloud in the capital markets." And it worked; Morgan won the mandate, and nearly $5 million in fees on the transaction.

Morgan's policy of giving its analysts final authority to kill a banking deal in their coverage universe was also a double-edged sword. Meeker's celebrity during the bubble gave her the muscle to ultimately pass on over $1 billion of Internet revenues from rejected deals and fend off complaints from bankers who lamented all the lost money. But as the markets kept rising through the first quarter of 2000, Meeker's strategy that the firm should be picky in choosing which firms to underwrite looked more and more suspect. "These deals are getting done by others," was the common complaint heard by both Shea and Meeker from bankers who watched Goldman and Quattrone mopping up the Meeker rejects.

Meeker tried to fight back, but the pressure was coming from everywhere. Goldman, she wrote to Shea in one memo, resembled a "kamikaze" pilot, while Quattrone acted like a "junkyard dog" whenever business was on the line. Meeker had never considered Henry Blodget to be much of a threat, but now he was getting into the act, making a serious run at Meeker's exalted status as the Internet's top power broker. Throughout 2000, Blodget seemed to be everywhere (she ran into him at an Amazon.com analyst meeting), stepping in to pick up the IPO of Pets.com after Meeker decided to pass. The company had no earnings, a weak business plan, and, Meeker believed, a dopey image generated by a sock puppet that appeared in its ads. But when Merrill brought the deal public, bankers at Morgan said it was another example of Meeker being too picky. Pets.com fell into bankruptcy as dotcom stock crashed in the coming months (Blodget had opened coverage with an "accumulate" rating), but not before Merrill took the lion's share of a $5 million IPO fee. At one point, Meeker asked Phillips, "What am I missing?"

Morgan's banking department had the answer, pressing Meeker during meetings and in private conversations with her supervisors that the "new paradigm" introduced by the Internet had radically changed traditional investing standards, meaning that companies like Pets.com, despite all their flaws, would find a market among consumers and survive as investments. The pressure grew to the point that Meeker soon developed a sense of "Stockholm Syndrome" Wall Street style: She began to identify with her captors, in this case, Morgan's investment banking department, helping the firm underwrite deals she would have rejected just a few months earlier. "It was so frustrating to have someone who could bring in just about any deal leaving so much on the table," said one high-ranking Morgan official. Even more frustrating for Meeker, who slowly but surely started to cave and approve some of the market's most risky deals. To this day, Meeker defends her decisions to bring public in 2000 such dotcom train wrecks as Women.com, HomeGrocer.com, and other Internet IPOs. "Given the same information we had, I would do the same things," she says defiantly. "The market was telling us we were wrong when we turned down Pets.com."

Maybe so, but there's no denying that Meeker lowered her own standards to meet the demands of her critics. Companies that would have been shown the door a year ago were now breaking through the Meeker vetting process. The same woman who "wouldn't cross the street if a banker asked her," now became more open to their suggestions. Her so-called rule of three (Meeker used to say she gave bankers three tries to convince her a deal was worthy before telling them to "fuck off") suddenly became the "rule of four," giving bankers an extra chance to change her mind. Meeker herself rationalized the change in her standards by pointing to the competition. She would recount how many companies she turned down that were then brought public by others and eagerly snapped up by the investors.

Bankers at the company, Perella included, were ecstatic that Morgan now had a fighting chance to unseat Goldman, which had climbed to the top of the "league tables," or the list of Wall Street's top underwriters of Internet stocks. But in making up for lost ground, Meeker's research began to suffer at a time when investors needed her most. Meeker was always super positive about companies she liked, but her February 2000 report on Amazon.com, "Correction: Inflection! Amazon.Calm," was more over-the-top than usual. On the eve of the dotcom crash, Amazon's finances were anything but calm; short sellers were circling, pointing out that not only didn't the online bookseller make money, but some deals it had cut with outside vendors seemed designed to inflate revenues and keep the company's stock valuation at its sky-high level. But Meeker wrote how shares of Amazon rose 13 percent in recent after-hours trading, not because the market was overheating, but because investors were reacting "positively" to the company's business model.

"Call us melodramatic? Go ahead," she wrote in the report. "But we continue to maintain that Amazon.com may be on its way to becoming one of the greatest companies of our day." But as *Barron's* would later point out, Meeker's analysis was breathtakingly bad. While Meeker said the vendor deals would generate $450 million in cash, Amazon actually received stock that was as risky as the market. She also failed to make clear that Morgan was preparing to underwrite a bond deal for the company around the time the report came out.

In early March 2000, just days before the NASDAQ pulled above the 5,000 level, Meeker reached another research low. More than a year before, she had passed on the IPO for Webvan, an online grocer that took its business to Goldman Sachs. Her major complaint was that she didn't think the company had a sustainable business model (the company was losing money and while it had big plans to branch out, its sales were concentrated in the San Francisco area). What a difference a year made as Meeker prepared to bring public a direct competitor, HomeGrocer.com, a company with an even riskier business model.

To this day, Meeker can't provide a good reason why consumers needed another Internet food-delivery service when the first one wasn't creating that much interest. But it didn't take Meeker long to hear from investors that the company was a loser. As she began calling her best "buyside" or large investor accounts to gauge their interest, Meeker recalls getting the cold shoulder. "People seemed to be tired," she said. As it turned out, tired would be an understatement. When the company went public, shares closed only $2 above the issue price, a key warning sign that the Internet boom was now coming to an end. But that didn't stop Meeker from placing an "outperform" rating on the stock. In fact, she didn't downgrade shares of HomeGrocer as they fell more than 80 percent. Meeker has rationalized her late downgrades, which certainly came well after Morgan received its sizable investment banking fees, as the mark of a "true believer."

Other similar disasters would follow, particularly as the NASDAQ started its steady decline through the rest of the year and into 2001. Companies like Drugstore.com, tickets.com, and lastminute.com helped Morgan earn millions of dollars in banking fees, but they also caused investors who relied on Meeker's positive research huge losses. It wasn't just the stock offerings of new Internet companies Meeker championed that cost investors so dearly. Throughout 2000, Morgan's brokers were continuing to push shares of AOL following its merger with TimeWarner, using old research issued by Meeker that didn't reflect the deteriorating market. As brokers clamored for a reassessment, Meeker was bragging that the fees she helped Morgan secure after the merger was one of the "most rewarding events of the year."

But with every decline of the market, Meeker would have less and less to be proud about. The press, which only a year prior regaled her as a queen, now turned negative. Instead of focusing on her years of warnings, newspaper stories began to link Meeker's hyped-up research on the falling dotcoms to her banking work. Inside Morgan, many brokers simply stopped reading her research as the decline evolved into a full-fledged crash. "We began ignoring it," said one longtime broker who felt burned by her research. Another broker said during cigarette breaks, "We would call her every name in the book." So did many investors. Throughout 2000, Meeker seemed to make her peace with the firm's powerful investment banking department, but her star power with the public was slowly evaporating. Gone were the TV offers, the love-ins with investors who hung on her every word. In early 2000, Morgan's public relations department began to limit her public appearances, fearing that their Net queen had become "overexposed." Now they had a new fear: that Mary Meeker would become the poster child for conflicted research.

Inside Morgan, Meeker's friends rose to her defense, reminding people of her famous pessimism during the boom times. "Mary had been warning everyone who would listen for years that the good times would come to an end," Shea told one executive at the firm. Ruth Porat, the investment banker on her team, told anyone who would listen about all the deals she passed on and all the fights Meeker encountered because of her standards. Meeker, meanwhile, came up with her own defense. Her reports, she said, were written for sophisticated institutional investors who understood the difference between a "buy" rating and an "outperform." Maybe so, but Morgan's 1997 merger with the Dean Witter brokerage firm guaranteed that her research would be handed over to some of the most unsophisticated investors in the market. When Morgan offered its own online trading platform two years later—a service pitched to small investors who wanted to buy stocks cheaply over their computer— Meeker's research was one of the key draws.

Which would have been fine except for the fact that no one at Morgan alerted investors that Meeker's own standards were crashing along with the markets. By the end of the 1990s, few people on Wall Street believed the so-called Chinese Wall was intact, but to many average investors, "research" published by a reputable firm like Morgan, with Meeker's gold-plated imprimatur, stood for something. But Morgan appeared more interested in making money than in alerting investors to the dangers they faced in relying on Meeker's reports. In 1999, Morgan Stanley served as lead manager on 9 percent of all Internet IPOs, 27 of 301 deals that came to market. In 2000, the year the tech market crashed and the quality of the companies seeking financing began slipping, Meeker helped increased Morgan's share of the IPO pie to 10 percent. Even by turning down most deals, Morgan earned hundreds of millions of dollars in fees from those companies.

Meeker herself appeared to understand the gravity of the situation in her 2000 "annual report," the document she handed Morgan's research management at the end of each year to summarize her work. In the report, she admitted to several "lowlights" during the course of the year, presumably the dotcoms she brought public that began to implode with the market crash. The year, she said, was one of "the most challenging periods of my career" thanks in large part to "internal IBD screams . . . gain, gain, gain IPO market share." Meeker passed on a comment made by a managing director in the banking department who said, "I couldn't believe how mean people in the firm are to you." With her battles with the bankers still stinging, Meeker wrote that she's "most proud of the deals we didn't do, the wealth destruction we didn't participate in and our performance vs. our competitors . . . These decisions were difficult, lonely and trying."

Lonely and trying, but many others were very, very lucrative. Meeker pointed out that during the great Internet crash of 2000, she and her team handled more IPOs than at any other time in her career, a "record year," she called it. The beauty of Meeker's job as defined by Morgan Stanley was that she could be a lousy analyst and still make a boatload of money. As her reputation came under fire, speculation swirled across Wall Street in late 2000 and into 2001 that Morgan had dramatically cut Meeker's salary from the $15 million she made in 1999, primarily because her research had been so bad. (Meeker deftly sidestepped the salary question in a March 2001 *Wall Street Journal* interview that made it sound like she took a pay cut.) But the reality was far different. Meeker's banking work resulted in an $8 million raise during a year when she ranked as one of Morgan's worst stock pickers.

Mary Meeker once said that "the biggest challenge to me was the backlash" from investment bankers angry when she didn't approve their offerings. But a bigger backlash loomed. The superstar analysts had rationalized the crash of Internet stocks as nothing but a pause in the euphoria, blaming general uncertainty surrounding the contested 2000 presidential election as the reason why investors chose to stay out of the market. But with each downward tick of the NASDAQ, with each dotcom failure, Meeker's reputation fell another notch. By the end of 2000, Meeker wasn't just an analyst who missed the market, she became a target of investor anger and media scrutiny over the massive losses people suffered following the advice of analysts. Feeling the heat, Meeker appeared on a CNBC show hoping she could explain away the Internet meltdown, and pointing to a better future down the road. That was until anchor Mark Haines pressed the obvious question: How could you have been so wrong about so many stocks? "If we sound a little too optimistic," Meeker said, according to a *BusinessWeek* story that described the interview, "it's really a function of the fact that this is the kind of environment that creates buying opportunities." Haines was unconvinced. "You're telling us to start from this point and put our money in the right places? But following your advice we put money in the wrong places."

Meeker summed up by saying that markets go up and markets go down, but the Internet was here to stay. When the interview was over, she was visibly shaken; Morgan Stanley complained to the CNBC producer that she had been set up, offering Meeker as red meat to their viewers who had been among the hardest hit when the Internet bubble burst.

Meeker would have to get used to the attention. In a blink of an eye, she became the target for all that she had once tried to avoid. Now all the rejected deals, the pressure from bankers, the early warning signs she issued that the markets were heading for a fall counted for nothing as investors and the press went on a witch hunt for culprits. For Meeker, it was the worst period in her career, far worse than her near blowup as a young analyst. Over the past ten years, she had given up much for the business she loved—friends, a family, and a normal life. She had embodied Wall Street's frenzied work ethic in boom times, and its outsized compensation system that rewarded success. At times, she took comfort in her belief that the Internet was not a flash in the pan, a fad like Beanie Babies or the Tulip mania. Companies like Amazon, Yahoo!, AOL, and countless others were here to stay, she believed, because the public had made the Internet a component of their lives. There was just one problem. The market was no longer buying her story.

Nearly a year after the crash, the NASDAQ was still heading south, falling more than 50 percent from the magical 5,000 level and going lower. The pressure on Meeker soon built to crisis proportions as the reporters drew the obvious inference from her dual role as banker and analyst: Mary Meeker sold out investors to make a quick buck. For Meeker it was a devastating charge, and one that her closest friends tried to dispel time and again, at times convincingly, with facts and figures about her warnings and the deals she turned down.

But Meeker's travails were just beginning. After years of ignoring analysts' conflicts, regulators were starting to wake up to the problem. A congressional subcommittee began holding hearings, making Meeker, along with her fellow superstar analysts Henry Blodget and Jack Grub-man, key targets in their probe (each analyst was asked to voluntarily tes-tify; each refused). In May 2001, as interest in conflicted research continued to build, Meeker suddenly found herself the center of the issue. Just as the *Barron's* article a few years earlier signaled her regal sta-tus, a *Fortune* cover story titled "Where Mary Meeker Went Wrong" showed just how quickly someone could go from famous to infamous. Meeker's fall was so pronounced that the dour-looking portrait on the cover of the widely read financial magazine actually made her gasp.

Fortune, like most financial publications, wasn't without blame for having hyped the market for Internet stocks, and inflating the reputa-tions of the superstar analysts. It famously placed Enron high on its list of the nation's most admired companies before a massive accounting scandal caused the Houston-based energy giant to file for bankruptcy. But in profiling Meeker, the magazine showed no mercy. "Of the 15 stocks Meeker currently covers, she has a strong buy or outperform on all but two," the magazine stated. "Among the stocks she has never down-graded are Priceline, Amazon, Yahoo and FreeMarkets—all of which have declined between 85% and 97% from their peak." Meeker was described as an analyst who started good but ended bad, someone who sold out for the greater good of her wallet.

Based on all the fawning press over the years, Meeker had a reputa-tion as being media savvy, but this time it didn't show. *Fortune* reported that "Meeker refuses to admit—or even see—how compromised she is." Underscoring the conflicts in her research that had hurt investors since the bubble popped, Meeker was quoted as saying that she felt a "stew-ardship" not toward small investors who lost money relying on her re-search, but to all those struggling companies she brought public that helped pad her enormous salary. Meeker said she was hesitant to down-grade these outfits because "if you take a company public and you are re-ally aggressive on the downside, it can be devastating."

When the magazine hit the newsstands, colleagues were aghast. "Mary clearly said things she wishes she could take back," was how one Morgan Stanley executive described the reaction internally. Meeker, meanwhile, was devastated, and briefly considered suing the magazine for libel after providing Morgan's legal staff with a list of what she said were mistakes in the article. But it wasn't the factual content that had her so upset, but rather it was the story's underlying theme that she sold out.

Did she lessen her standards during the height of the bubble? Of course, and Meeker would be the first to admit that pressure from bankers and the unyielding rise of the markets caused her to rethink her own rules for tech investing. But one thing Meeker always prided herself on was integrity. If she wanted to sell out, she reminded associates as the story made its way around Morgan's offices in midtown Manhattan, she would have been working for Frank Quattrone, making twice as much and bringing many more shaky companies public.

In the end, Meeker dropped the idea of a lawsuit, and instead, determined to set the record straight on her own. Friends in the industry started speaking out. Covey, while attending a conference sponsored by *Fortune*, openly defended her friend. "The media builds up people," Covey recalls saying, before reminding editors of the magazine of all those puff-piece stories they approved on the great New Economy riches available for investors. "And then the media looks to tear down people when it doesn't work out by publishing cover stories on Mary Meeker," she added. After her remarks, Covey said she was congratulated by more than a dozen people. Meeker spoke at Stanford Business School, the place that educated her old friend Frank Quattrone and countless other New Economy gurus, to give her side of the story. The event was part of Stanford's "View from the Top" lecture series and during her presentation, Meeker remarked that she was there to give "a view from near the bottom." "Did we do the best we possibly could?" she asked the crowd, "Yes. Did we do better than everyone else? Yes."

But it was unclear if anyone was listening. Like Blodget, Meeker was branded a con artist by the end of 2001. The same woman who never left the office and slept under her desk during the height of the boom now found it difficult to come to work. As the hate mail poured in, she had lost her support group as well, the bankers and analysts that faced the same pressure she faced during the height of the mania. Her friend and partner in bringing so many companies public, Andre de Baubigny, resigned from the firm, a casualty of overwork and the supercharged market. Porat, Meeker's soul mate during the Internet craze, took a banking assignment in London. Software analyst Chuck Phillips, one of her closest friends, remained at the company, but he was coming under similar pressure as Meeker, catching the eye of the SEC for owning stock in a company he covered. Even Shea, her constant defender, appeared to put Meeker on notice. "You are at a crucial juncture in your career," he wrote in Meeker's performance evaluation for 2001. "Do you want to be a research analyst?"

Porat, meanwhile, had other problems. She had been diagnosed with cancer in June 2001 and was undergoing chemotherapy when she was speaking to Meeker, who asked how she was feeling. Porat replied that she had seen better days, but things were going as well as could be expected. Then Porat inquired about Meeker's health. "Mary, how are you doing?" Meeker's reply was pure anguish: "They're attacking my integrity," she said, before adding, "How about trading places?"

Porat, for her part, survived her ordeal and resumed her career as one of Morgan's top investment bankers. It was unclear if Meeker would do the same.

CHAPTER EIGHT

Jack in a Box

During the stock market boom of the 1990s, there was a fair amount of competition among the superstar analysts and their various supporters in the Wall Street community. Although they were barely acquaintances (Meeker had met both Grubman and Blodget separately), each had taken a keen interest in the other's careers. In the beginning, most of it centered on who was getting the best press, and whose star was rising the highest. But by early 2001, as the decline in the stock market was in full swing, much of the competition turned to the negative, that is, who was getting hammered the worst by investors, clients, and the once adoring business media.

For months Blodget and Meeker took the brunt of the heat, as Internet shares began their correction in early 2000, exposing the weaknesses in their research, most notably the influence of investment banking on their stock ratings. But as the pain spread to the other half of the New Economy, the telecommunications sector, it was only a matter of time before Grubman found himself in the crosshairs. For Grubman, it was a rude awakening. During much of the 1990s, the swashbuckling analyst for the Salomon Smith Barney unit of Travelers Group, and ultimately the Citigroup megafirm, was a media darling. Celebrated by the press, he earned a reputation as a street fighter with an MIT diploma (though he never attended the prestigious college), the smartest, toughest man in the business, the "Jack of All Trades," as The Wall Street Journal described him near the height of his power.

But after nearly a year of continuous market losses, Grubman's stock-picking record and his reputation had taken a severe beating. No longer was he the popular guy among the throngs of investors who used his research to buy stocks of Global Crossing, Qwest, Winstar, and his favorite, WorldCom. Despite the horrendous losses each outfit suffered during their yearlong slide, Grubman remained largely optimistic about the prospects of these companies, causing a near revolt among stock brokers who not too long before had recommended that their clients follow his advice. Now the media were getting into the act as well. In December 2000, *The New York Times* began a series of stories on conflicted research of the superstar analysts, targeting Grubman as "one of the many analysts who got it so wrong," in a long, detailed account of the Chinese Wall straddling that made Grubman one of Wall Street's highest-paid analysts.

The article described Grubman, as well as Mary Meeker, as the walking embodiment of everything that was wrong with Wall Street research. It presented evidence of Grubman's hyped research and inflated ratings on companies that returned the favor by kicking back investment banking fees to Salomon. It also discussed Grubman's massive pay package, the direct result of his ability to win business from these same outfits. It certainly wasn't the first story that took issue with Grubman's brand of doing business, but timing was everything, and with the market pummeling his top picks on a daily basis, Grubman immediately felt the heat. Brokers and even some investors, already burned by Grubman's calls, seized on the story as further evidence of Grubman's failings as an analyst, calling for his immediate resignation, while others just wanted to wring his neck.

Grubman, according to friends and associates, was shaken by the sudden burst of notoriety. It was around this time that he received an email from a friend by the name of Carol Cutler. An analyst for the Government of Singapore Investment fund, Cutler had become one of Grubman's top clients, using his research to buy stocks and crediting Grubman by executing the trades through Salomon's stock-trading desk. In early January 2001, Cutler was traveling to a swanky resort in Scottsdale, Arizona, to attend Grubman's yearly telecommunications conference, which even amid the yearlong market decline, was still a must-attend event for the who's who of the telecom market.

Cutler was anxious to see Grubman for other reasons. Over the years, their relationship had evolved away from the business into something more intimate. Indeed, the two were now communicating almost daily, much of it by emails laced with sexually explicit references in which Cutler, stationed in Asia, often expressed her desire to consummate their relationship into something more formal when she returned home. As the conference got under way, Cutler now told Grubman she was hoping he would finally fulfill a promise to give her a Philadelphia Eagles football jersey so he could see her "wear it."

But Grubman wasn't in the mood. Still smarting over the *New York Times* profile, he had sent Cutler a short email saying that he had "just landed" in Scottsdale on Citigroup's corporate jet, without further explanation. "So hearing Mary Meeker got corp jet really got to you," she wrote back. "Must be nice, I could get use [*sic*] to that."

Nothing, it seemed, could change Grubman's sour mood. "Yeah," he responded, "she and I are now sharing news coverage too."

Sensing she hit a nerve, Cutler tried to set the record straight. "Listen there is a big diff. She didn't know what she was doing and is on the way out. U are, and always will be king. Actually, in not knowing what the fuck she was doing, she caused a great deal of our problems . . . NYTs doesn't know shit."

According to a copy of the emails, Grubman didn't answer, but Cutler wasn't through. "Actually I was impressed how smart Sandy is to treat you so properly," she wrote, referring to his boss, Citigroup CEO Sandy Weill, who apparently ignored the bad press and gave Grubman access to the company jet. "I was hoping I could fly with you. Coffee, tea or me . . ."

One thing was certain: The King of Telecom had seen better days. Grubman wasn't the only securities analyst who trumpeted the benefits of the vast expansion of telecommunications services during the height of the 1990s tech boom, from high-speed cable to various wireless products. But Grubman was the first to fully recognize how the combination of deregulation and the growth of the Internet created a special situation for Wall Street, where dozens of new companies would come to market in need of capital to finance their vast expansion.

And being first had certain advantages. Grubman's championing of the New Entrants, like WorldCom, Global Crossing, Qwest, and Winstar Communications, over incumbent companies like long-distance standard-bearer AT&T and the so-called Baby Bells, which once supplied all of the nation's local telephone service, put Salomon Smith Barney and its parent company, Citigroup, first in line to underwrite billions of dollars in stocks and bonds to build their massive networks. In the late 1990s, as telecommunications underwriting became one of the most profitable businesses on Wall Street, Grubman held the key to immense riches—as much as $1 billion in underwriting fees that these companies dangled before Wall Street investment banks.

Grubman certainly had many advantages over the competition in pursuit of these riches. By now the research-for-banking trade-off was ingrained in Wall Street's corporate culture, and Grubman knew how to work the system for maximum results. Grubman pushed companies to sell stocks and bonds and invest tens of billions in building or buying communication networks through Citigroup's investment bank—before they even had enough customers to meet their output. To blunt naysayers who believed the vast telecom expansion he advocated was a recipe for disaster, Grubman had an answer for that as well, contrasting World-Com, which had real earnings (at least on paper) and an "experienced" management team, with the scores of dotcoms that had come to market with no earnings and untested management.

And it worked. For much of the 1990s market boom, Grubman's research sold remarkably well to sophisticated investors, retail clients of Salomon's brokerage department, and most important for Grubman, his supervisors, who found all sorts of ways to keep Grubman happy. By 1999, he was earning an average of $20 million a year, had frequent use of the company jet, and near unlimited power to work on any deal that came his way. That same year, the company approved another interesting perk that underscored his power on Wall Street. Most brokerage firms have hard-and-fast rules preventing executives or their spouses from maintaining outside brokerage accounts. The fear is that company lawyers can't monitor whether analysts are trading stocks based on inside information they picked up while they were over the Chinese Wall, or working on sensitive investment banking deals.

But for the king of telecom anything was possible. The firm's legal team approved a request by Grubman to give his wife, LuAnn, the green light to maintain a brokerage account and trade stocks outside of Salomon Smith Barney. "Under normal circumstances we do not allow our employees' spouse to maintain accounts outside the firm," a

Salomon compliance official wrote Grubman in an August 16, 1999, memo. ". . . As per the attached letter, we have granted approval for you to maintain brokerage accounts away from Salomon Smith Barney . . . we have approved the accounts you requested based on your representations that you have no beneficial interest, control, influence over or investment therein." Grubman often boasted that he was so concerned about charges of profiteering that he avoided buying telecom stocks he was hyping. That didn't prevent his wife from owning some of his favorite stocks, such as WorldCom.

But as the 1990s came to a close and the markets began to shift from never-ending optimism to gloom and doom, Grubman's act started to wear thin. On May 15, 2000, *BusinessWeek* magazine featured Grubman in a cover story entitled "The Power Broker: From his Wall Street perch, Jack Grubman is reshaping telecom and stirring up controversy." The story wasn't unique in its subject matter; *BusinessWeek* scored a major scoop by exposing Grubman as a fabulist, a man who would make up almost any story, concoct almost any lie to get ahead. Grubman didn't grow up in South Philly as he told so many people for so long, the story said, nor did he graduate from MIT as his résumé stated. In fact, Grubman grew up in Northeast Philly, a middle-class section of the city, and earned his BA from the less prestigious Boston University. (Even Grubman's boasts about being an amateur boxer seemed to be contrived; his spokesman cannot provide the address of a single boxing club where Grubman would have trained.)

Just as the *Wall Street Journal* piece in 1997 established Grubman as a man on the rise, the *BusinessWeek* article marked the beginning of his downfall as it started circulating among Grubman's clients, the large mutual fund investors and the corporate executives who handed him banking deals. Grubman didn't help matters much either with a frank assessment of his own business practices. When the reporter, Peter Elstrom, asked Grubman if he was "objective" enough to publish sound research on companies like WorldCom, Global Crossing, and others that kicked back huge fees to Salomon, Grubman responded simply that, "What used to be a conflict is now a synergy." Objective research? Grubman said the "other word for it is uninformed."

It was one of those quotes that would forever haunt Grubman. When the article made its way around Citigroup, colleagues were outraged. In just a few words, Grubman had crystallized everything that was awry with Wall Street research. Some bankers demanded that Grubman keep a lower profile out of fear that someone at the Securities and Exchange Commission might one day begin to examine just what Grubman meant when he compared being objective to being uninformed. After the story, Mike Hayes, a broker from Salomon's Reno, Nevada, office, forwarded a complaint from an investor about Grubman's "maybe too close ties with companies he's supposed to be objectively analyzing," with the following comment: "It probably expresses what most [brokers] in the field are wondering about."

But it wasn't just the objectivity comment that had so many people inside Salomon looking for answers. The article essentially said Citigroup's main spokesman for the telecom revolution, the man who many believe was responsible for the tremendous growth of business based on a theory of never-ending demand, was a fabricator, someone who held so little regard for the truth that he distorted his family background and education. And if Grubman would blow smoke about such trivial details in his life, what were the chances that he was lying about the prospects of the companies that were paying SSB huge fees and making Grubman a millionaire many times over? Even John Otto, a banker who covered telecom and benefited from Grubman's activities, questioned Eduardo Mestre, the powerful head of Salomon's telecom department, about Grubman's résumé fabrications and whether any action should be taken. Mestre said he wasn't concerned. "That's Jack," he added.

Not everyone looked the other way. During the course of the great telecom boom, Robert Gensler, a mutual fund manager at T. Rowe Price Associates, had grown fond of Jack Grubman. Gensler credited Grubman with teaching him about telecom stocks at the time he broke into the business in the mid 1990s, when Grubman, already a brand name analyst, agreed to come down to T. Rowe Price's Baltimore offices to give Gensler a primer on the changing industry.

But when *BusinessWeek* crossed his desk, Gensler exploded, according to a person with knowledge of the conversation. "How could you have said that?" he asked Grubman. Grubman sheepishly described the résumé incident as an innocent mistake. He said he added the MIT stuff to an early job application and had never gotten around to taking it off his résumé as time went on. Gensler accepted the explanation, but from that point forward he thought twice before trusting Grubman's various claims.

As the Internet crash spread into the telecommunications stocks, the list of Grubman skeptics grew. At the heart of Grubman's theory was a never-ending demand for telecom services that would propel the stocks of his favored companies to greater and greater heights. But there was nothing like losing money to snap sophisticated investors out of their Grubman-induced stupor. As tech prices began to dive, the smart money began to focus not on the endless demand Grubman had been hyping, but on the impact increased competition was having on company balance sheets and whether companies like WorldCom could repay their massive levels of debt, much of it acquired with Grubman's assistance. Shares of WorldCom fell from around $70 during the height of the bubble, to below $20 in late 2001 and below $10 into 2002 before Grubman removed his long-held "buy" rating. For another Grubman darling, Global Crossing, the decline was equally disastrous. At its peak, the company traded at $64 a share, but Grubman didn't downgrade the stock until late 2001, when shares were trading at $1.07 and just months before the company filed for bankruptcy in January 2002. Grubman's reputation among sophisticated investors suffered another jolt when it seemed that his bullishness may have given cover to corporate insiders, like company chairman Gary Winnick, who sold $1.3 billion in stock before the bankruptcy filing in early 2002. During that time, Grubman served as an unofficial adviser to the company, helping Salomon become one of Global's top investment banks.

The backlash was particularly acute inside Salomon Smith Barney's massive brokerage sales force. Once voted the best analyst by Salomon's brokers, Grubman soon became a marked man among the very people who trusted his research to push investments on millions of small investors. What seemed to enrage brokers the most was his continued guidance to the sales force that the stocks of these shaky telecom companies, WorldCom and Global Crossing in particular, would soon recover, even as they headed for scandal and bankruptcy.

"I personally lost over $25,000 because I assumed he would not leave us hanging if this was going to zero," said one Salomon Smith Barney broker in an email to management about one of Grubman's post-bubble stock picks. "This bastard could have downgraded it @ 10.00 [$10 a share]. Oh well, it's just my daughter's college."

Grubman, the broker added, "could not spot a trend if it hit him in the face. I'm sorry I kept trusting him."

•   •   •

By most measures, Grubman could be called the primary villain of the great telecom debacle that caused investors so much pain. His hype surpassed anything Wall Street had ever seen from a research analyst, notable bulls like Blodget and Meeker included. When Grubman issued a stock rating, or felt he needed to reinforce it with some commentary, Grubman didn't just send out a research note, he "blasted" his opinion through voice mails that were sent to thousands of money managers at a moment's notice. When he needed to defend a company that was under attack from a rival analyst, he assumed the role of company flack, bashing his opponent like the prize fighter that he claimed to be. An analyst at PaineWebber got a full taste of Grubman's fury after suggesting that WorldCom might purchase a company called Nextel. "I was there. I was around the table," Grubman said at the time. "The idiot from PaineWebber wasn't there. I can tell you that WorldCom is not going to bid again for Nextel."

During the height of his power, Grubman developed his own enemies list, composed of people who either disagreed with him or couldn't stand his blowhard tactics. They included rival telecom analysts like Merrill Lynch's Dan Reingold, code-named "dimwit" and at times "dickless wonder" by Grubman and his acolytes, and others like Michael Armstrong, the CEO of WorldCom's main rival, AT&T Corporation, and a frequent target of Grubman's attacks. At one point, Armstrong was so incensed by Grubman's constant criticisms that he complained to his good friend, Citigroup CEO Sandy Weill (Weill was an AT&T board member and Armstrong a Citigroup board member) about what he viewed as Grubman's boorish behavior.

Weill let it be known that he wanted Grubman to act more professionally, but as long as he continued to produce results, Grubman had almost free rein to say and do what he pleased. And he did. Early one morning at an AT&T conference for Wall Street analysts, most of the attendees were sipping coffee, dressed in khakis and polo shirts. Grubman was spotted by one AT&T official walking around in the lobby in his underwear.

Grubman's various antics rippled through the Wall Street community. Other analysts were all but forced to copy his exuberance out of fear they wouldn't win business. Others, in order to cozy up to the WorldComs and the Global Crossings, began to mimic his mantra of endless growth of telecom services, making it seem as if the success of WorldCom and Global were all but assured. Analysts who couldn't bring themselves to stoop to Grubman's level felt abandoned by their own companies. Dan Reingold, Grubman's major competitor during the bubble years, came under intense pressure from the bankers at Merrill to match his opponent's deal making prowess. Reingold, however, had neither the connections nor the stomach to go toe-to-toe with the market's top deal makers. "I can't compete with this guy," he bitterly complained to a friend. It wasn't long before Reingold left Merrill for Credit Suisse First Boston.

But for all his faults, Grubman was hardly a lone wolf. In fact, his business practices, his many feuds, his over-the-top style were well known and often condoned at the highest levels of Salomon Brothers, and later Citigroup. The pervasive knowledge of Grubman's activities was demonstrated through dozens of emails, correspondences, and internal Citigroup documents, which show that his various supervisors not only ignored what he was doing, but became enablers of his practices. At times these same people forced Grubman to go further in misleading investors than even he would have gone on his own. And that pressure began at the very top of the Citigroup financial empire.

Sanford I. Weill is a man not known for subtleties. He would chew out a clerk just as fast as a million-dollar-a-year investment banker. Weill loved to drink gin, smoke cheap cigars, and eat rich food, which accounted for his hefty waistline. Everything about Weill is big, including his ambition. In the 1960s, he grew a mid-sized brokerage firm into one of Wall Street's largest, before selling his Shearson Loeb Rhodes brokerage empire to American Express Corporation in 1981. Years later, after being bounced from Amex, Weill embarked on one of the greatest comebacks in Wall Street history, taking a mid-sized insurance company and slowly building it into the nation's largest brokerage firm. The $83 billion merger of Weill's Travelers Group, with its Salomon Smith Barney brokerage, and the giant Citicorp banking empire run by John Reed, created the most powerful firm Wall Street had ever seen, Citigroup, and in Weill, Wall Street's most powerful man.

For years, Weill reveled in mostly positive press chronicling his remarkable comeback. But there was a dark side to Weill, which was less obvious to the outside world. He managed people through fear and intimidation, and his greatest business attribute seemed to be an ability to make ruthless cuts in personnel and employee perks after each and every acquisition. (He once ordered coffee machines to be removed from one outfit he had acquired, presumably to save on supplies and electricity.) As his appetite for power grew, Weill gave the ax to some of the most experienced Wall Street managers in the business, such as his longtime protégé, Jamie Dimon, whom he apparently believed was stealing too much of the limelight.

His bullying tactics were legendary. He once berated an investor-relations official so much he started to cry. In 1999, Weill was locked in a bitter battle to take sole control of Citigroup and remove Reed as co-CEO. People at the firm say Weill was looking to gain an edge over Reed any way he could. When Heidi Miller resigned as CFO of Citigroup in 2000 to take a job with Priceline.com, Weill exploded. "Is this because of John?" he said, referring to Reed. Miller said it wasn't, but Weill wouldn't accept her answer. "I'm going to put a stake through his heart," he snapped.

Weill eventually pushed Reed out of the firm, but when he heard that *The Wall Street Journal* had caught wind of what he said about Reed, and was preparing to use it in a story, he issued a denial to the newspaper. It wasn't long before Miller issued a denial as well. A coincidence? Maybe so. But Miller told colleagues that she felt pressured to support Weill's version of the events, which she later disavowed. (The "stake through his heart" quote ran in the *Journal*'s overseas edition but was pulled from the much larger U.S. edition.)

Like Miller, Jack Grubman was also on the receiving end of Weill's bullying, particularly as his research—or, to be more accurate, his research on one company—presented a not-so-insignificant obstacle in Weill's quest for power.

That company was AT&T.

Jack Grubman didn't always hate AT&T. He had worked for the company, as did his wife, and had been positive on the stock off and on through the 1980s and into the mid 1990s. Grubman's research got considerably more negative on the company in the wake of the Federal Telecommunications Act in 1996, which gave a big boost to the New Entrants like

WorldCom and other outfits that would emerge as Grubman's favorite stocks. But even as the competitive pressures on "Ma Bell" grew, Grubman's bearishness had its limits.

All that changed with the appointment of C. Michael Armstrong as AT&T's chief executive officer. Outgoing and smooth, Armstrong was a top salesman for IBM, and later the CEO of Hughes Electronics Corporation, where he received enormous praise for transforming the company from a stodgy defense contractor to a major commercial satellite operator. He was hired to work similar magic with AT&T, and from the minute he arrived at the company's headquarters in Basking Ridge, New Jersey, Armstrong vowed to shake things up.

It didn't take long for Grubman to turn negative on this strategy. Months after Armstrong's appointment, Grubman had a "hold" on the company's stock, signaling to the market that the nation's top telecom analyst had no faith in the new CEO's plan to grow revenues by slashing expenses and making a series of strategic acquisitions. Grubman said his bearishness on the stock was all business; the company simply wasn't prepared to compete with the likes of WorldCom. But inside the telecom industry, people knew it had a personal element as well. Put simply, Grubman despised Armstrong. At industry conferences, presentations, and chats with his top clients, Grubman didn't miss an opportunity to bash the AT&T CEO as an "empty suit," a "delusionist," or a "fucking fraud," a man who was taking a once great company and running it into the ground.

Despite its reputation as a place shrouded in numbers and complexity, Wall Street is really a business of relationships, where deals are made over cocktails at 21 or during fancy dinners at Campagnola, one of the city's best Italian restaurants. And Grubman's attack on AT&T ran head-first into one of the most symbiotic relationships on Wall Street.

Sandy Weill and Michael Armstrong had been close for years, with Armstrong serving as one of Weill's board members in his various companies on the way to building Citigroup. When Weill and Reed began selecting members for the new Citigroup board, Weill was sure to pick Armstrong as one of his guys. Armstrong, meanwhile, returned the favor in 1998 when he asked Weill to join the AT&T board, and the marriage was complete. With Weill and Armstrong joined at the hip, Salomon Smith Barney had become one of AT&T's top bankers, underwriting hundreds of millions in bond and stock deals during the late 1990s. The

Weill connection was certainly a wonderful asset for Salomon Smith Barney, and something the big bank loved to flaunt whenever business was on the line. One internal document, which was part of a banking pitch the firm made to AT&T for a large underwriting, listed members of the "Citigroup's AT&T Corp. Team," the people who presumably would ensure the sale was a success. At the top of the list was Weill. The memo even included Weill's email and direct telephone number just in case the big boss was needed.

But by the late 1990s, AT&T was clearly a troubled company, and Armstrong's comeback strategy, which included purchasing cable television giant TCI, was falling flat. In fact, AT&T's stock actually declined 2 percent during the first month after the merger, while WorldCom soared, thanks largely to Grubman's embrace of its merger with MCI. Grubman convinced investors that there was nothing Armstrong could do right, and nothing that WorldCom's CEO, Bernie Ebbers, could do wrong.

"Please pass my congratulations along to Jack for a great call on AT&T," wrote Paul Crovo, a money manager. "Jack deserves an 'A+' for objectivity and for ignoring all the corporate finance and banking interests at SSB who would love to be making money by schmoozing with [AT&T] and helping them do their deals. It's too bad that so many other sell side analysts have 'sold their soul to the devil' by recommending this stock just to get banking business in the door."

Grubman had a twinkle in his eye when the email popped on his computer, quickly forwarding the message to banking chief Eduardo Mestre with the following comment: "Eduardo, this is the other side—and the one with the II [*Institutional Investor* magazine] votes. Jack."

But there was something more important to Citigroup, and Weill in particular, than Grubman's II rankings. For Weill, one of the worst things about being on the AT&T board was the constant refrain from his fellow board members about Grubman's bearishness on the stock. Armstrong was reaching his limit with Grubman as well. He wanted Grubman to act more "professional" said one person with knowledge of the conversation. Armstrong had long complained to associates about the over-the-top statements in Grubman's reports, and the numerous personal attacks he made to industry professionals. But there was one thing about Grubman that really got under his skin. When Armstrong spoke during analyst meetings, Grubman could be heard noticeably clearing his throat and making obscene noises.

This behavior was so troublesome, he told Weill, that it was threatening "the relationship" between AT&T and Citigroup. Under normal circumstances this would mean that AT&T would no longer consider Citigroup and its Salomon Smith Barney banking unit one of its top underwriters, but for Weill the statement represented something more dangerous. By now, Weill had made his intentions for ousting Reed fairly clear to his top advisers, and the Citigroup board was evenly divided, Weill knew he couldn't afford even a single defection from his side. In other words, the AT&T-Armstrong "relationship" had to be preserved.

Weill approached the task at hand as delicately as he knew how. He ran into Grubman one night at Carnegie Hall. Weill, who was there with his wife Joan, introduced Grubman as "the reason I am persona non grata at AT&T." Later, Weill was even more direct. He told Grubman that he should rethink his rating. People close to Weill say he did little more than "nudge" Grubman to see some value in Armstrong's strategy. Weill, himself, would later say that he asked Grubman to do nothing more than take a "fresh look" at his negative outlook on AT&T. Whatever the exact words, Grubman got the message immediately: The guy who signed his paycheck wanted him to upgrade the stock.

Weill turned up the heat a few notches more after Armstrong complained that Grubman omitted AT&T from a list of the nation's top telecom companies during a speech at an industry conference. Grubman was ordered to write an apology letter to Armstrong, extolling his accomplishments and the company's position in the telecom business. "Despite our current investment stance on AT&T," Grubman wrote, "I view AT&T as one of the most significant companies in this industry . . . I am truly open-minded about changes in investment views."

The pressure on Grubman continued to build through 1998. When television commentator Louis Rukeyser slated Grubman to appear on his widely watched show, *Wall $treet Week with Louis Rukeyser*, Grubman was thrilled. Even as his stature grew, Grubman mostly avoided the glitzy CNBC with its growing audience of wannabe stock traders. But this show was a classic of its genre, watched by the top market professionals, while Rukeyser with his thick white hair and genteel manner was a throwback to another era. More than that, Grubman relished the opportunity to spew his worldview, which included promoting his favorite stocks and attacking those, like AT&T, that he had no use for.

But just minutes before he was about to appear, Grubman heard his cell phone ring. It was Mestre with the following message: "Don't bash Armstrong." Grubman shot back that he wasn't prepared to spend a lot of time on AT&T, but as the transcript of the show indicates, Grubman knew when to follow orders—somewhat. During the show, he spoke at length about the effect of deregulation on the consumer, what overseas telecom outfits he favored. "I would buy WorldCom all day long," Grubman remarked. Not even Rukeyser could pass up the opportunity to rib Grubman about his support for WorldCom, which had just paid him tens of millions of dollars in fees for the key role he played in the MCI merger. "They took your advice, and now you love them, huh?"

Then came the moment of truth. "A lot of people out there still own AT&T. How would you advise them?" Rukeyser asked. Grubman did his best to follow Mestre's advice. "I like Mike Armstrong a lot. I think in his tenure . . . he's done some remarkable things in just turning around the mentality of the company. The first thing he's doing is cost-cutting, which is long overdue." But even with two of Citigroup's top people on his back, Grubman couldn't pass up the opportunity to take at least one swipe at Armstrong. "To get me excited on AT&T," Grubman added, "he then needs to show a plan for top-line growth."

Armstrong was willing to meet Grubman more than halfway. In mid 1999, as Weill was plotting his final move against Reed, Armstrong had just approved giving Grubman special access to AT&T top brass (including himself) so he could fully understand the company's new growth strategy. It's not every day that analysts can conduct such a wide-ranging review of a large company's vital operations. Analysts usually get their information from the company's investor relations department, which will provide only the most flattering accounts of company events, and they often have to grovel to get a sit-down with the CEO. But Grubman was no ordinary analyst. He forged special ties with Bernie Ebbers of WorldCom and Gary Winnick of Global Crossing and with that access came enormous praise from Grubman about their companies' prospects. By developing his own relationship with Grubman, maybe Armstrong could get some of the same treatment.

Grubman's review lasted several months, and Weill received regular updates. Internally, people couldn't remember the last time Weill had cared so much about a stock rating from one of his analysts, but this was no ordinary stock rating and Grubman wasn't just another analyst. Despite his intense hatred for the telecom king, Armstrong spent two and a half hours discussing AT&T's new business model, which centered on the company's new cable strategy and its alleged plan to compete against WorldCom and the New Entrants. Grubman spent days at the company's Denver offices, where the cable operations were centered, and in AT&T's corporate headquarters in Basking Ridge, New Jersey. Much of the work seemed tedious; at one point, Grubman reported back to Weill that he spent a full day in AT&T's offices going through "dry, arcane costs and engineering analysis." Grubman was quickly concluding matters, he told Weill, looking to spend some more time in the firm's corporate headquarters in New Jersey to meet a few more people and "wrap things up."

AT&T officials felt fairly certain that they had finally turned Grubman into a supporter. In August, Weill accompanied Grubman to a meeting with Armstrong at AT&T's New Jersey headquarters. Armstrong got right to the point, chiding Grubman "for going out of your way to portray us as dopes." Grubman said he was ready to give AT&T a fair hearing, but inside Salomon, people were getting a different story. Sherlyn McMahon had been Grubman's assistant since he joined the firm in 1994. Her main job was to input data into Grubman's earnings model, which calculated the various financial ratios used to rationalize his ratings on companies like WorldCom. But for Grubman, McMahon was no mere assistant. McMahon was one of the few people who could decipher Grubman's handwritten notes, which she translated into research reports. She often had direct contact with various members of his inner circle, people like Ebbers and WorldCom's powerful CFO Scott Sullivan, and Grubman was confident enough about McMahon that he could even give her a peek at his close relationship with Carol Cutler, the buyside analyst at the Singapore pension fund that he communicated with either by phone or through email almost on a daily basis. Every now and then he would play for McMahon some of Cutler's sexually laced voice mails that explained, in vivid detail, the depth for her love for the telecom king, and how she planned to show it. McMahon just shook her head in disbelief.

Sex was one of the last things on Grubman's mind as he continued his analysis of AT&T. Grubman told McMahon he was holding fast to his current negative rating. His game plan, McMahon would later say, was to bury AT&T in paperwork, making his upgrade contingent on answering all sorts of questions and demands for confidential information. No company, he reckoned, would be willing to divulge so much information.

Then two things happened. First, word began to spread that AT&T was preparing a huge stock deal to finance a spin-off of its wireless telephone unit. The deal would be one of Wall Street's biggest ever, spreading tens of millions of dollars in fees to the firms at the top of the underwriting list. Like most large companies, AT&T liked to spread its money around, and would probably appoint three firms to "run the books," or manage the biggest chunk of the deal. Given the size and complexity of the transaction, the top underwriters could earn upward of $60 million in fees, the largest payday in Wall Street history.

Inside the firm, winning the deal became a top priority. Investment banker John Otto estimated that despite Weill's relationship with Armstrong, Salomon left tens of millions of dollars in fees on the table as AT&T began spreading its underwriting fees to other firms that had a more positive outlook on the company. When rumors of the deal began circulating through Salomon Smith Barney, Grubman sensed a new urgency among top officials at the firm: This was one deal they couldn't afford to lose.

Closer to home, Grubman faced another challenge. For more than a year, he and LuAnn had been asking colleagues about New York City preschools for the twins. Recently, they had settled on one of the best, the 92nd Street Y in Manhattan. Located on the tony Upper East Side, the 92nd Street Y is not just another elite preschool—it's more like an exclusive finishing school for toddlers. The barriers for entry are abnormally high. Children are given IQ tests and interviewed prior to admittance, as are the parents. In addition to paying the school's hefty tuition, which runs around $15,000 a year, parents are expected to make generous donations to the not-for-profit organization that runs the school.

As Grubman soon found out, money can only get you so far. Despite numerous meetings, and promises for support, his twins didn't even make the school's short list. While Grubman may have been the king of the telecom market, he had no clout with the people who ran a Manhattan preschool.

But he knew someone who did.

• • •

Jack Grubman and Sandy Weill weren't very close, but by the late fall of 1999, they were communicating daily, sometimes several times a day as the telecom king continued his "fresh look" into AT&T's stock rating. For Weill, Grubman's AT&T rating became an obsession, and Grubman clearly understood how his boss might be affected if Armstrong wasn't kept happy. It didn't take long for Grubman to come up with a solution that would make everybody happy, unveiled in a two-page memo he sent to Weill titled, "AT&T and the 92nd Street Y." In it. Grubman hit all the right notes. He reminded Weill of his meetings with Armstrong, the fresh look at the company's new strategy, and his "very productive" meetings with AT&T's top executives, including Armstrong, and how he planned to "keep (Weill) posted on the progress" of his work.

But Grubman wasn't finished. He said he needed to elaborate "on another matter," which he described as the "ridiculous but necessary process of preschool applications in Manhattan." Grubman went on to describe how Davis and Elizabeth Grubman, two-and-a-half-year-old twins, were planning to enter nursery school the following September, and they needed Weill's help. "Of the schools we've looked at, the 92nd Street Y is, without question, the one we'd love our children to attend." Grubman said the place was perfect, with the "right mix of educational and developmental programs and it has a healthy Jewish culture without being over the top on a religious scale." But there was just one problem, Grubman noted. "Given that it's statistically easier to get into the Harvard freshman class than it is to get into preschool at the 92nd Street Y"—(Grubman told Weill he verified that statement)—"it comes down to 'who you know' . . .

"Anyway, anything you could do Sandy would be greatly appreciated. As I mentioned, I will keep you posted on the progress with AT&T which I think is going well." Grubman even attached a list of Y board members for Weill to call. "If you feel comfortable and know some of these board members well enough, I would greatly appreciate it if you could ask them to use any influence they feel comfortable in using to help us as well."

Weill didn't wait long to fulfill his end of the bargain. Grubman said he had already reached out to 92nd Street Y board member Pat Cayne, the beautiful wife of Bear Stearns CEO Jimmy Cayne, so he should begin elsewhere. As it turned out, Grubman contacted Pat Cayne through a telecom executive, Verizon CFO Fred Salerno, who was a Bear Stearns board member. Cayne was initially open to Salerno's request, but when she asked her husband his opinion, he had only two words: "Fuck Grubman." Jimmy Cayne, one of the shrewdest CEOs on Wall Street, had seen too many deals go Grubman's way to aid the enemy. Pat Cayne simply told Salerno there was nothing she could do; the school's selection process was based on merit, not social connections.

Weill knew better, contacting Y board member and New York City socialite Joan Tisch, the wife of Loews Corporation chairman Preston Robert Tisch. Joan Tisch was receptive, agreeing to approach the leadership of the Y, including its executive director Sol Adler. Weill's proposal: a donation of $1 million if the Grubman kids were admitted. It wasn't long before the Citigroup CEO heard back that the school was receptive to his deal. Meanwhile, Grubman became more and more receptive to the AT&T business model, though he kept his upgrade plans quiet until around the third week in November. He had just returned from AT&T's Denver offices, the home of the firm's cable facilities, when he broke the news to McMahon. "I think I'm ready," he said. Given the mounting internal pressure, McMahon was hardly surprised. "Really," is all she said. Grubman then handed her about twenty pages of handwritten notes containing his analysis of AT&T's new cable strategy and, of course, his upgrade from a neutral to a "buy" rating.

On November 29, Grubman made his move, informing Salomon Smith Barney brokers in his early morning analyst call. Grubman put on quite a production. With the new cable strategy in place, there was no telling how far the stock could climb. If all goes according to plan, AT&T couldn't be stopped, he boasted. The market agreed. Shares of AT&T, the most actively traded stock that day on the NYSE, spiked about $2 after the upgrade. Later that evening, his good friend Carol Cutler called from Singapore. She was looking for Grubman, but got McMahon instead. Cutler was in tears. "I can't believe he caved," she said, quickly adding: "Why didn't he tell me first?" McMahon told her she would give Grubman her message.

Grubman, meanwhile, informed the SSB publications department that his thirty-six-page AT&T report "must be edited and mailed out to printers today so that it can be distributed in time to meet Sandy Weill's deadline."

As AT&T's board of directors was moving forward with the wireless stock deal Salomon hoped to underwrite, speculation on Wall Street spread that Grubman's upgrade was nothing more than a ploy to get a leg up on the competition. Among the first to pick up on this story were *Wall Street Journal* reporters Leslie Cauley and Randall Smith, who drew the connection between Grubman's reversal and the AT&T transaction in the paper's widely read "Heard on the Street" column. The story also raised the potentially thorny issue of Weill's possible involvement in "prodding" Grubman to upgrade the stock. It was common knowledge that bankers had applied pressure on analysts to skew their ratings, but now it looked like Grubman faced the ultimate squeeze play, taking heat from the powerful CEO. Giving legs to the story was Weill's odd, unconvincing denial. "I never told an analyst what to write," he said through a spokesman. Grubman and AT&T were more emphatic. "Anyone who knows me knows that I call them as I see them. No one tells me what to do." Armstrong declined to comment, but an AT&T spokeswoman said, "It is insulting to AT&T and to Grubman" to suggest that the rating was fraudulent.

A few weeks later Grubman was more candid when he told *New York* magazine, in a glowing profile titled "Cable Guy," that the *Journal* had simply made a fuss over nothing. "*The Wall Street Journal* tried to make a big deal out of the upgrade, but the reality of the world is that analysts are becoming increasingly important in the banking practice of firms, not just for underwriting but also for mergers and acquisitions. It just is what it is; it's part of the business."

That business was extremely lucrative for those who knew how to play the research-for-banking trade-off. A few weeks later, Salomon received the good news: It would be one of three banks on the upcoming wireless deal, a post that put the firm in line to earn $60 million in fees. Weill, meanwhile, successfully pushed out Reed as his co-CEO, with Armstrong staunchly in his corner. Despite his public support for AT&T and its "new" direction, Grubman still didn't miss an opportunity to privately bash the company and its CEO to his inner circle of money managers and telecom executives. When one of them started ribbing him about "selling out" his research to win a banking assignment, Grubman set the record straight. The upgrade, he said, had little to do with the wireless spin-off, he said. "I needed to get my kids into the 92nd Street Y."

• • •

With his children admitted to the exclusive preschool, Grubman must have felt he was millions of miles from his childhood home in Northeast Philly. His compensation for the 1999 calendar year reached $25 million, much of it the result of his role in making Salomon Smith Barney Wall Street's top telecom banking outfit. He had settled into a posh brownstone on the Upper East Side of Manhattan that he purchased with $6.2 million in cash. Grubman's telecom conference, at the exclusive La Quinta resort in Palm Springs, California, was among the most successful ever. Maybe the best quote summing up Grubman's sheer power came from Elliot Dorbian, a former Salomon broker and currently an independent investment adviser, who told *Money* magazine, "When Grubman said wonderful things about a company it was like a narcotic—everybody wanted it. He walked around like he was a god. And it was perceived in the industry that he was a god."

Whether it was God or Grubman, something supernatural seemed to be responsible for the market's continued strength. Through the first three months of 2000, telecom stocks soared to levels never seen before, buoyed by the overall strength of technology-laden NASDAQ stock market, the primary bellwether of the New Economy. Over the years, Grubman developed strong ties with print reporters, including those at *The Wall Street Journal,* where he provided much-needed scoops on the changing nature of the telecom business and events on Wall Street. But one morning, after *Wall Street Journal* reporter John Keller wrote a story that didn't quote the telecom king, Grubman exploded. According to Keller, Grubman said he was relaying a message on behalf of the Salomon telecom team: "The scoops will go to the people who play ball," he said, "Those who don't will be left in the cold."

As Grubman's power grew, so did the power of Salomon to snare just about any deal that came its way in the telecom world. When companies had second thoughts about hiring Salomon, bankers applied a little pressure in Grubman's name, pointing out that they couldn't "control what Jack does" in his research if the firm was passed over. Seeing what happened to AT&T, no company wanted to take that chance.

By March 2000, Grubman was possibly the most powerful analyst Wall Street had ever seen. Mary Meeker, the famed Internet queen, couldn't hold a candle to Grubman's absolute clout, both with investors who were buying his favorite stocks, and with the company executives who were selling shares to the public. Henry Blodget, the pretty boy of the Internet, had great name recognition with investors largely from his seemingly constant appearances on CNBC. But compared to Grubman, Blodget was a corporate pawn, whose main job was to help Merrill make up for lost ground in the great technology banking boom that showered so many profits on rivals Morgan Stanley and Goldman Sachs.

Grubman's biggest clients continued to spew tens of millions of dollars in banking fees, and Grubman continued to receive the lion's share of the credit even when presumably he had nothing to do with the business. This made Grubman's looming fall from grace especially historic. Almost overnight, as the technology stock crash of 2000 quickly spread into the market for telecom stocks, Grubman found himself treated no better than Henry Blodget, who had become the symbol for research hype once the market bubble burst. For Grubman, it began with the company's vast brokerage network. Grubman's most touted stock, WorldCom, was one of the most widely held stocks in Salomon Smith Barney's brokerage department, and the firm's brokerage sales force, which dealt with small investors, was first in line for the backlash once shares began to crater. Second in line was Jack Grubman himself, who continued to recommend the stock even as shares were getting killed. Grubman's once rock-star status among Salomon's sales force turned to mud as angry brokers began demanding answers for his enormous bullishness in the face of evidence to the contrary.

At first, Grubman had a fairly straightforward rationale for his continued support: He was a true believer. "My blind spot is that I tend to think long-term," Grubman once said. In other words, it was the market that was wrong, not his theory, and his stock picks would ultimately prevail. But evidence soon began to mount that Grubman's theory was wrong as well. Following Grubman's *BusinessWeek* profile, letters began to pour into Salomon Smith Barney questioning whether his conflicted role caused him to hype the companies that were now getting slaughtered in the market. At one point, John Hoffman, Salomon's global head of research, wrote in an email to a person on the company's research staff that he was "acutely aware" of Grubman's conflicted research and the problem it posed for investors.

"Obviously the degree of conflict between research and banking appears heightened when the stocks are not working, as is the case in telco right now," Hoffman said in an email. "I think that Jack is a very good analyst . . . he must be more discriminating on the stocks he recommends with the market working against him. I hope to be able to manage this process to prevent further damage to our client base."

Grubman soon looked to vindicate himself by issuing a massive new research report, a "major industry call" and a "reiteration of our investment position," to promote several of his favorite stocks, including Global Crossing, and Qwest. The plan was described in a series of confidential memos, the first one dated August 17, 2000, and sent to executives at some of his top stock picks. "Obviously, we believe that all of your companies can create a tremendous amount of shareholder value, but none of your companies are going to do that unless WE have the ammunition to respond to a drumbeat dramatically increasing in frequency from investors," he wrote. Grubman then asked for detailed financial information—"fiber miles . . . pricing and costs . . . recurring revenue" and other tidbits not normally found in public sources, so he could make his point that the industry was on the rebound.

At first, no one responded. Perhaps it was the level of detail demanded by Grubman that spooked the executives. So he sent out another letter, stating that "in order for us to react positively" to the investor angst, the information was critical. Silence once again. Grubman, unfamiliar with being ignored, was now getting desperate. "The longer, we in particular remain silent, the more worried investors will believe that you, at the companies, don't have a handle on this information," he wrote on September 19, 2000. "Investors are waiting to hear our viewpoint because they know we will move the market." What information, if any, he received from the executives in the hours after his last request is unknown. But the very next day, a glowing report extolling telecom stocks miraculously hit the street.

By the end of 2000, it was abundantly clear that there was very little Grubman could do to turn things around. Grubman's salary sank a few dollars to $23 million, but his theory had cost others much more. Following Grubman's worldview, the New Entrants expanded their cable lines and systems at a fevered pace, making Grubman and Salomon's bankers rich, but also sowing the seeds of their own demise as the supply they created far outstripped demand for these products from businesses and consumers. Since these companies did whatever was possible to expand, including raising enormous amounts of debt, the end results were even more disastrous as pricing pressure squeezed already weakening profit margins.

WorldCom and Global Crossing, Grubman's two top stocks, were hit particularly hard. Shares of WorldCom fell from its high of close to $70 in 1999 to around $25 in the beginning of 2001. Global suffered a similar fate. But it wasn't just Grubman's favorite stocks that were crashing. While AT&T received a temporary jolt from Grubman's upgrade in late 1999, by mid 2000, his flip-flop was exposed as one of the more disastrous stock picks of the year. Shares declined nearly 50 percent after the upgrade, and the market losses forced Grubman to do the unthinkable in his world: Downgrade a stock. In October 2000, Grubman slashed AT&T's rating two notches, from a "buy" to a "neutral." Since the time of his upgrade, Grubman said AT&T's core business of providing long-distance service to consumers declined faster than expected, and its new cable strategy never measured up to expectations. Grubman was sure to plug WorldCom at AT&T's expense, pointing out that AT&T can't match the "global scale and scope" of Bernie Ebbers's baby. Publicly, Grubman appeared chastened, telling *The Wall Street Journal* that "near-term stock picking has never been what I'm known for," but privately he was seething. Grubman told friends that his worst fears about the company and its CEO, Michael Armstrong, the "empty suit," had been confirmed. His anger seemed to boil over one Saturday afternoon in early January 2001 after a conversation with his email partner Carol Cutler, which would change both of their lives.

Known on Wall Street as a savvy stock picker, Cutler had been an early convert to Grubman's theory that deregulation combined with the power of the Internet would provide huge growth for telecom companies. Cutler had an eclectic career, starting off as an analyst at the Bank of New York before quitting to try to make a living as an artist. She joined the Government of Singapore Investment Fund, known on Wall Street as "GIC," in the late 1990s as an analyst, recommending stocks for the massive portfolio that invested the country's foreign reserve. More often than not, her stock selections mirrored Grubman's, though at times, Cutler's investment style went beyond Grubman's research. Friends and colleagues say that at various times in her career, she claimed to being somewhat clairvoyant in her investment decisions.

Whatever technique she was using, it worked for much of the 1990s, and given the size of the Singapore portfolio—the fund held a total of $100 billion during the bubble—Cutler became a key contact for Grubman, who was looking to influence sophisticated investors with his market calls and secure votes in the *Institutional Investor* survey. Grubman repaid Cutler's loyalty. She was often treated like telecom royalty by Grubman, seated at his table during his yearly conferences. One confidential Salomon Smith Barney document shows that the Singapore fund in 1999 received five hundred thousand shares of an IPO for a once hot telecom company, Williams Communications Group, a significantly higher number than that given to other well-known institutional investors.

Smart and good-looking, Cutler bore a slight resemblance to Susan Sarandon. Indeed, people often noticed Cutler and Grubman hanging out together during industry conferences. "She was always trying to get his attention," one analyst said. Cutler's feelings for Grubman were reflected even more strongly in emails where she would profess her love and devotion to the telecom king. Though Grubman had no intention of leaving LuAnn, he seemed to like the attention, and over time, he clearly regarded Cutler as a friend and a confidante, someone he could trust with his most intimate thoughts.

During 2000 and 2001, they were corresponding regularly, engaging in what can be best described as a truly New Economy version of the traditional office romance: email sex. For Grubman the exchanges provided an important release valve and an interesting diversion from the mounting pressure of his job. For Cutler, it was a chance to profess her love for the telecom king and possibly have a life outside of work. In one email, under the subject line "Hey Handsome," Cutler wrote that finally being in Grubman's "presence" was worth the wait of not seeing him for so long. "You really do it for me," she wrote. "In fact seeing you has shifted my whole mood—I was kinda dragging this week . . . I loved sitting there tonight watching you. And I guess someone else got a haircut too! It looks really good, really good. And you're wearing my favorite casual shoes—brown suede. Brown suede is so luscious and rich, it has such a yummy feel to it. Befitting for you to wear."

As the email conversations progressed, the subject matter got more outrageous, with both Cutler and Grubman growing comfortable with the increasingly salacious matter. "Are you trying to get me all juiced up that the great Grubman is the greatest thing in the world?" she complained in one email, though many others served as a gesture of support during a difficult time for Grubman. At one point, Cutler gave Grubman some interesting advice on how they could have livened up a particularly boring meeting they had with a high-profile money manager, Rob Gensler, who worked at T. Rowe Price Associates. Cutler suggested that Grubman "could have been fingering me under the table . . . And then . . . as I would of needed some fresh air to cool down, I would of taken a break and gone out into the hallway. You of course would have followed the pussy trail figuring there might be some good dog chow around. Then I would of pulled you into a corner, quickly unzip and unveiled the Big Dog. I would [have] kneeled in reverence and then I would of sucked your cock clean. You would [have said] that it was the best darn meeting you've EVER gone to."

Grubman's response: "Much better idea."

Cutler seemed to be Grubman's biggest fan even as the rest of his professional world was falling apart. At Citigroup, Grubman was the king of telecom as long as WorldCom and Global Crossing were cranking out deals, but with their finances falling into disarray, and their stocks tanking, both companies scaled back on their expansion plans, which meant far fewer big underwriting deals, and far less money flowing into Salomon's banking department. Bankers began lobbying Grubman to change his focus away from the New Entrants to the new sweet spot in the markets, the Baby Bells and the other telecom companies that Grubman had ignored. Grubman refused, but the pressure had been taking its toll, with Grubman telling people that he feared he would be fired. Cutler soon emailed Grubman something she thought might lift his spirits. It was a copy of one of a Joe DiMaggio baseball cards, only DiMaggio's name was replaced with "Slugger Jack" and the line: "The only major leaguer who batted 1000."

But by early 2001, Grubman would have been lucky to bat .250 as WorldCom, Global Crossing and the rest of the New Entrants continued to crash. Making matters worse for Grubman, his chief rival Dan Reingold began gaining ground on the telecom king among investors who began to turn away in favor of someone with a hotter hand at picking stocks. It was an amazing turn of events for Grubman. At around five foot six, Reingold may have been the shortest analyst on Wall Street, and for most of the 1990s, he came up short against Grubman, who snared the lion's share of the big banking deals and top honors from *Institutional Investor* magazine in its survey of Wall Street money managers. Reingold complained the deck was stacked against him; Grubman's deal making and propensity for giving tips about upcoming mergers and other transactions to large investors were nothing less than "criminal," he said on several occasions.

There was no love lost on Grubman's end either. Both Grubman and Cutler commonly referred to Reingold as "DW," shorthand for "dimwit" or "Dickless Wonder," depending on their mood.

But by early 2001, Reingold had turned the tables, scoring points because of his support for the Baby Bells and his more critical opinion of WorldCom. For Grubman, it was a fate worse than death, but something Cutler thought she could cure with salacious humor one afternoon, giving Grubman a chance to forget his crumbling stature on Wall Street.

"You won't believe this," she wrote in an email. "A source of mine, who insists on remaining unknown, says that DW has a big fantasy about you. He wants to give you a blowjob. Can you believe that! He's heard your reputation for being a Svengali so now he has this fantasy that if he drinks from the well than maybe he will finally understand telecom, what drives it and how it works. If you ask me sounds like a big excuse for wanting to do you."

Grubman didn't appear amused. "He's about the right height," was all he wrote.

But early one morning in January 2001, it was AT&T, not Reingold, that was on Grubman's mind. By now, Grubman's AT&T flip-flop had become a huge embarrassment. Members of the media, portfolio managers, and rival analysts labeled him a sellout as speculation swirled about Salomon's huge payday on the wireless deal and the company's shares kept falling lower. Grubman couldn't go public with the real reason behind his upgrade—the pressure from Weill—so he tried to change the subject by painting himself as a hero for doing what others were afraid to do, downgrade a stock even if it was after an upgrade that many people on the street believed was phony. "Let's call a spade a spade," he told *The Wall Street Journal*. "Nobody . . . puts negative ratings on stocks. Very few people have anything less than a positive rating." But few people were buying Grubman's excuse, and as his chorus of skeptics grew, Grubman desperately wanted to set the record straight, choosing the one person who, because she shared so much with him, he knew he could trust.

He got his chance at around 11:00 A.M. on January 13, 2001, when Cutler sent Grubman an email that began by discussing the marriage of his assistant, Sherlyn McMahon. Cutler then changed the subject. "You are a true friend and one needs to be a true friend before being a lover," she wrote. Grubman agreed. "Without question. The latter means nothing without the former. Now of course for cheap sex, I could always go to Gensler," Grubman said, once again referring to the T. Rowe Price telecom analyst Robert Gensler. Cutler brought up Reingold, or "DW," who she said would be "in the closet watching."

"Do you think DW could do himself, much less anyone else?" Grubman asked. "No," Cutler responded, "That's why he's called dickless," adding that Reingold is "delusional and desperate to learn anything. That's why he wants to be in the closet to watch the great one . . . maybe we should hook him up with fellow delusionist Armstrong [AT&T CEO C. Michael Armstrong]—now that's a perfect match made in hell."

Just hearing Armstrong's name put Grubman over the edge. "He's already been done by Armstrong just doesn't know it," Grubman said, referring to Reingold's positive recommendation of AT&T, before making the following statement: "You know everybody thinks I upgraded [AT&T] to get the lead for [the wireless deal]. Nope. I used Sandy to get my kids in 92nd ST Y preschool (which is harder than Harvard) and Sandy needed Armstrong's vote on our board to nuke Reed in showdown. Once coast clear for both of us (i.e. Sandy clear victor and kids confirmed) I went back to my normal negative self on T. Armstrong never knew that we both (Sandy and I) played him like a fiddle."

At first Cutler didn't seem to understand the significance of Grubman's statement. "Good for you!" she wrote back, adding: "Very good school for the kids." But it wasn't long before she realized that Grubman had just made an incredible disclosure. Everybody on Wall Street understood the conflict between investment banking and research. But when was the last time someone upgraded a stock to help a CEO win a high-profile board-room battle? And when was the last time the CEO repaid the favor by pulling strings so the analyst's children could attend an exclusive preschool?

Sensing she hit a nerve, Cutler responded quickly, writing that she knew "there was pressure" on him over AT&T. Grubman, meanwhile, continued to set the record straight. "The biggest thing that pissed me off is that T did exactly as I knew they would for precisely the reasons I thought . . . collapse because the core business would fall apart."

"At first I wondered if you didn't share the reason with me because you didn't know if you could trust me to keep a secret," Cutler shot back. "I hope you now realize you can trust me." Grubman simply answered that trust had nothing to do with it. "We just never discussed. I always viewed T as a business deal between me and Sandy."

Cutler soon changed the subject, letting Grubman know how much she wanted to see him so "we can go to our next level . . . for our eyes and ears only. Course there's nothing wrong with also throwing in a couple of lips, penis, pussy, etc., etc.."

Grubman and Cutler continued their exchanges during the course of the year, a form of mutual masturbation, as both their careers seemed to be plummeting along with the stocks they championed. "I love when you talk dirty to me," Grubman emailed Cutler at one point, and Cutler loved doing the talking. "Rolling my lips around your rod," she wrote in one particularly obscene email in the form of verse under the subject line LVLT: Visibility of Capacity Sales Key to Story, "would be like coming face to face with God; If only I could get you to stop being a clod; If only I could get you to give me a nod; Most would think it is very odd; that you have yet to get to my home—which is not made of sod now as I've got such a great bod, I really doubt you need much of a prod; So don't let work nor exhaustion make you nod get to my home ASAP so I can properly pay tribute to your rod."

Grubman's response was short and sweet. "Like I said, waxing poetically."

There was, however, nothing poetic about Grubman's stock picks. As 2001 progressed, the telecom meltdown was in full swing though Grubman continued to push his best stocks. At a retreat for Citigroup managers in early January, Mike Carpenter, the investment bank's chief executive, took issue with the obvious shortcomings of the firm's research: There were no sell ratings and only one "underperform" rating on the 1,179 companies covered by the firm's research arm, he pointed out. For Carpenter, it was a strange statement, since as head of the investment bank, he knew full well how Grubman used positive research to help win some of the biggest deals in the telecom market. Brokerage chief Jay Mandelbaum said "research was basically worthless" for the more than twelve thousand brokers who were being burned by the hyped stock picks of Grubman and other analysts. Mandelbaum's statement wasn't exactly news to global research chief John Hoffman, and U.S. stock research chief Kevin McCaffrey, who had been deluged with criticism about Grubman's research from company brokers. McCaffrey forwarded one particularly nasty message to Hoffman from a broker located in White Plains, New York, who complained, "As far as I'm concerned Jack Grubman no longer exists at our firm. If he talks in the box, [be] assured my box will be turned off," referring to the monitor on every broker's computer that displays analyst commentary. Hoffman responded to McCaffrey: "This will certainly shorten up the morning call."

Remarkably, Grubman remained as long-winded as ever, revving up his research hype machine to greater and greater heights as his critics grew. In 2001, one observer estimated that he cranked out forty research reports, compared to twenty-five in 2000 and nineteen in 1999. "Is there a bandwidth glut?" he wrote in early 2001, taking aim at the research of Susan Kalla, the analyst who published a lengthy report showing how the vast overbuilding and capacity among the telecom companies that followed Grubman's advice would squeeze profits and lead to lower stock prices. "As we have written many times: No."

Grubman would soon have another opponent, Manuel Asensio, a prominent short seller (an investor who profits when stocks fall in value) who, in early 2001, took aim at one of Grubman's top picks, Winstar Communications. Grubman, as it turned out, had a lot invested in Winstar, as did Salomon Smith Barney. The company was known in the telecom world as a Competitive Local Exchange Carrier, or CLEC, a fancy way of describing one of the handful of New Entrants favored by Grubman to take on the Baby Bells, which long dominated local telephone service. Grubman initiated coverage on Winstar in January 1998 with a "buy" rating and a $50 price target, given the company's embrace of New Economy technology that gave it many advantages over the competition.

Since then, Grubman had grown so close to Winstar's management (the firm had raked in $24 million in banking fees from Winstar since Grubman launched coverage) that he regularly consulted with top executives before issuing research reports, and accompanied them to social functions. "That same event is having Led Zeppelin this year," Grubman told Winstar CEO William Rouhana during a conference call with analysts. "I look forward to attending again, Jack," Rouhana replied. "And I suspect," Grubman continued, "as was the case last year, two of the four of us will be actually singing along."

Asensio certainly wasn't singing Winstar's praises. In January 2001, he was one of the first investors to announce that no matter how much money Salomon made from its relationship with Winstar, the company was in deep trouble. A wire-thin man, with short dark hair and a bad temper, Asensio approached his work much like Grubman, publicly confronting his targets as "frauds" and their supporters on Wall Street as "stock manipulators" who misled the public. The public dimension of Asensio's opinion—he made public all his research reports—often worked to his advantage as the negative spin he spread made its way into the market, sending shares even lower. Despite some high-profile mistakes, Asensio had put together an impressive record during the long bull market, successfully targeting a number of stocks that turned out to be worthless.

By early 2001, Asensio had added Winstar to his list. With $1.3 billion in bank debt, and another $1.6 billion in junk bonds, Asensio said the company was in such deep trouble that it "possesses no ability to . . . repay its debt." Taking a direct swipe at Grubman, he said Winstar was a figment of the Wall Street hype machine, and the analysts like Grubman who maintained their ratings in the face of his evidence were worse than frauds. Asensio told *Fortune* magazine they were "idiots."

Grubman was now ready for a fight. He issued a report, attacking Asensio as a "short seller" who simply didn't do his homework. During a conference call with the company, he referred to Asesnio and the company's detractors as "rumor mongers," who should be investigated by securities regulators. Grubman's bullying tactics may have worked with rival "sell side" analysts who worked at the big Wall Street firms, but Asensio reveled in the attention. He alerted every journalist he knew about Winstar's troubles, directing them to his popular website, Asensio.com, which provided regular updates of his battle with Grubman. At the same time, he wrote Salomon's management about what he believed were serious flaws in Grubman's research. "Please find attached report issued by your analyst Jack B. Grubman on Winstar Communications," he wrote to McCaffrey, Grubman's immediate boss. "It contains false statements and omits negative information." Accompanying the letter was a copy of Asensio's own research on Winstar, with a detailed examination of all those "false statements" issued by Grubman. Asensio then wrote Grubman himself, asking to be included in a "dinner meeting you are hosting for Winstar," where he could confront Winstar and Grubman directly.

Neither Winstar nor Grubman took the bait, and for a good reason. By mid March, shares of Winstar fell to the "penny stock" range, trading at around $2.50 as more and more investors woke up to the possibility that the company would not survive. Like a dog with a bone, Grubman continued to ignore the prevailing wisdom. In his annual "State of the Union" research report, Grubman came to Winstar's defense. During the bull market, his report was a yearly event anticipated by sophisticated mutual fund and pension fund managers looking for guidance. In the report, Grubman pointed out that "we believe in remaining visible, especially when stocks are down." He predicted "bankruptcies, scavenger hunts, no new entrants funded, and eventually consolidation," but that the demand for telecom service was "growing," and those investors who followed his research would eventually profit. Grubman made sure he addressed Winstar's critics specifically. "As far as Winstar's balance sheet, the noise surrounding its ability to make interest payments is just that." The company, he said, was a survivor and one of his best stock picks.

That's what Grubman was writing for the public; what he was saying in private was another matter. As of September 30, 2000, the company had a deficit of $2 billion, a loss of $227.4 million, and things only got worse in 2001. Later, in March 2001, Grubman was so concerned about the company's prospects that he tried to downgrade the stock, telling a Salomon broker in an email that he couldn't follow through because he got "shut down" by management. As it turns out, Grubman actually prepared a draft report downgrading Winstar from his long-held buy rating to "neutral," but Salomon's compliance department put a hold on the move, Grubman would later concede. At the time, Salomon bankers were pitching Winstar as an acquisition candidate to WorldCom. Investment banker Scott D. Miller told WorldCom CFO Scott Sullivan in one email that by paying $4.3 billion for Winstar, the company could boost its sagging stock price. If Grubman's "projections are right," Miller wrote, the deal "would enhance the WorldCom Group's revenue" growth rate by 1 percent, thus paying for itself. How seriously Sullivan took the offer isn't clear, but Salomon bankers appeared so obsessed with keeping Winstar afloat that they began working on another deal, something called "debtor-in-possession financing," that never saw the light of day.

Grubman finally downgraded Winstar in late March, but only after the company failed to make an interest payment on some debt, shortly before it fell into bankruptcy, as Asensio predicted. Grubman, himself, may have provided the best explanation for the Winstar mess. "Don't get me wrong I should be held accountable" for Winstar, he wrote in one email. "If anything the record shows we support our banking clients too well and for too long."

Grubman, however, remained resolute about two of his favorite stocks and biggest investment banking clients, WorldCom and Global Crossing. To reporters, he rationalized Winstar's lightning fast decline as an aberration, largely the result of a decision by Lucent to end a vendor agreement that supplied about $1 billion in annual revenues. Cutler agreed. She wrote to Grubman around this time that WorldCom and Global Crossing would soon benefit from something called "web hosting," a service that would create "big" revenues for the companies. "I like BIG things," she concluded. "Think BIG."

Grubman, however, couldn't help but feel puny as WorldCom and Global crashed. In another email, Cutler flagged a *Wall Street Journal* article suggesting that WorldCom might not survive unless it found another suitor, noting its failed attempt to merge with Sprint in June 2000 (the move was blocked by regulators). Grubman and his team, it seemed, were finally starting to have doubts about the companies he had championed for so long. At one point his assistant, Sherlyn McMahon, emailed WorldCom CFO Scott Sullivan a number of questions, including one that took issue with the company's own rosy analysis of its future. "Can you provide info on the change in working capital during 2000 showing up on cash flow statement at $4.8 billion and why it will be $2 billion in 2001?" McMahon wrote. "It seems high." McMahon, worried that she may have spooked an important banking client, made sure she ended the email on a happy note: "Love from 1 of your only 2 friends on the sell side. Sheri."

On May 16, 2001, Grubman reiterated his "hold" rating on Sprint in a voice-mail "blast" to his clients. For Grubman, it was a dangerous move. Around the same time, two of Salomon's top banking clients, Deutsche

Telekom and France Telecom, were selling their stakes in Sprint. Executives at both companies went into a frenzy, blaming Grubman for getting smaller returns as shares of Sprint fell, and threatening retaliation down the road if Grubman didn't "shut up and disappear" until the sale was over.

Grubman didn't and retaliation was swift. About a month later, Deutsche Telekom refused to appoint Salomon as a top underwriter on a lucrative bond issue, a key piece of business given the drought in underwriting caused by the telecom meltdown. The financial director of DT, Gerhard Mischke, delivered the news himself, telling a Salomon banking executive in Frankfurt, Germany, that he had no intention of appointing Salomon on the deal "after Grubman two times lowered his forecast."

Salomon's investment bankers went into overdrive. Frank Yeary, one of the firm's top telecom bankers, arranged what he "called a post mortem meeting" about the "Grubman issue of the last weeks." Another banker, Stephen Winningham, advised SSB chief Michael Carpenter that the clients believed analysts should be either "supportive or silent." Grubman told associates he was on thin ice at the company and that the bankers were trying to get him fired. At one point he warned U.S. stock research chief Kevin McCaffrey that if Yeary, his most vocal critic, tried any rough stuff at the meeting, "I will lace into him."

Grubman was accompanied by McCaffrey, and by most accounts, the meeting was cordial, though Mestre's presence was troubling. The vice chairman of telecom investment banking, Mestre was among the most powerful people at Citigroup. It was no coincidence that he was the one who had recruited Grubman five years earlier with promises of making him a star. Mestre lived up to his end of the bargain and now it was Grubman's turn, by adapting his "theory" to the market's new reality. Yeary tried a softer approach than Grubman originally expected, asking Grubman to be a team player and reshape his views for the "greater good" of Citigroup.

Grubman, according to people at the meeting, held his ground. But the message came through loud and clear: Mess with banking and you'll pay the price.

Now investors were paying the price as well. By the spring of 2001, all financial indicators for WorldCom pointed downward. Its stock had fallen more than 70 percent, rumors circulated that Bernie Ebbers might sell out, revenues were shrinking, and regulators began to investigate whether research conflicts were to blame for tens of billions of dollars in market losses suffered by small investors who bought stocks based on positive research. The press started to turn up the heat as well. *The Wall Street Journal* ran a series of articles exposing the conflicts in the research of famed Merrill Lynch analyst Henry Blodget, including one that showed how Blodget actually downgraded a company that rejected Merrill as an underwriter. *Fortune* magazine devoted an entire edition to research conflicts, featuring on its cover a sourpuss shot of Morgan Stanley's tech analyst Mary Meeker, under the headline "Can We Ever Trust Wall Street Again." Grubman made the cut as well, being featured in another story about his horrendous Winstar research. Inside Salomon, however, executives were just happy that their man wasn't displayed more prominently than Meeker. "Grubman took his licks," wrote Timothy Tucker, a manager in the firm's research department, to research chief John Hoffman. "But thank God he wasn't put on the cover . . . That photo of Mary Meeker looks every bit like a police mug shot. Not a look of contrition, more like resigned boredom with perhaps a trace of the 'banality of evil' type of look." Hoffman's response: "She's got her money. Now let the chips fall."

But Hoffman should have been looking closer to home, where it was still business as usual. The brokerage arm of Citigroup's massive banking empire continued to pump out some of the most absurd research on Wall Street. Like vultures circling a wounded animal, Salomon's bankers picked at WorldCom and the other new entrants for possible underwriting opportunities. Bullied into submission over the Deutsche Telekom incident, Grubman spun a string of setbacks into positive events for the company. "Given WCOM has global network of assets," combined with the implosion of other telecom outfits, the company is "stronger today than it was a year ago."

Even in its debilitated state, WorldCom still had much to offer Salomon and the Citigroup, at least according to one internal document that described the relationship in sharp detail. Shares of WorldCom were declining fast, down more than 70 percent over the past two years, as the firm continued to miss revenue forecasts. Financing a new major acquisition to replace the missing revenues would be difficult, if not impossible. But if WorldCom needed capital it could always tap into the bond market, buying time until the business improved. That appeared to be the plan in the spring of 2001 as the company eyed a massive bond deal, possibly as much as $12 billion in debt, and tens of millions of dollars in fees to Wall Street's deal-deprived bankers. Salomon clearly wanted in on the action. One document recommended the approval of a massive loan commitment to WorldCom, noting that Citigroup "is one of the closest financial institutions to WCOM," but also because of a promise of future business down the road. According to the loan-approval document, WorldCom's treasurer, "Susan Mayer has informed us that if Citigroup commits $800 (million) . . . SSB will be awarded a joint-book runner role in" the upcoming bond deal, that would help the company cover its negative cash flow for several years. The document pointed out that in recommending the loan, it was basing its calculations "on estimates by SSB analyst Jack Grubman," but also on the strength of WorldCom's management, including Ebbers, "one of the most celebrated entrepreneurs in the industry, who according to *Fortune* has created more shareholder value over the past eight years than any other telecom CEO," and his sidekick, CFO Scott Sullivan, who was well regarded by the financial community for his successful financial management of a rapidly growing company.

The entire Citigroup financial empire seemed to be available to WorldCom, but the loan document also pointed out that "due to recent deterioration of business fundamentals, long-distance companies such as WCOM . . . have suffered deterioration in their economic results and a significant reduction on the market capitalization."

Investors could have used a little of the same candor, but Grubman kept the hype machine on full throttle, urging investors to continue snapping up shares of the company's stock, and predicting a huge payday down the road. Salomon also supported WorldCom in other ways. Not only was Ebbers granted huge personal loans using his own depressed stock as collateral, he received shares of hot IPOs from Salomon's brokerage division that amounted to "free money" because Ebbers could immediately flip the stock at a profit. On the eve of the $12 billion bond deal, a Salomon banker, Scott Miller, emailed Citigroup CEO Sandy Weill with a request to place a "congratulatory call to Bernie Ebbers" after the bond deal was completed. Despite all that Salomon had done for WorldCom and Grubman's "ardent" advocacy of the company, Miller wrote Weill that Citigroup had some reason to be concerned about its lucrative relationship. JPMorgan Chase had managed to worm its way into the big bond deal, and Ebbers was impressed with a cocktail meeting reception attended by the bank's top officials, including Jimmy Lee, the high-profile chief of its lending division. Miller reminded the famously blunt Weill that Ebbers "doesn't mince words" and may bring up Weill's affiliation with AT&T. Weill, Miller advised, should be ready to fire back, pointing out that Citigroup hired WorldCom to provide a "very significant proportion of its (internal) communications business," not to mention the firm's support of "WorldCom's capital needs."

But these turned out to be mere side issues in a relationship that was mutually beneficial. Citigroup, and its telecom team led by Grubman, had been the most vocal supporter of the company, and to turn back now would have been unthinkable. Citigroup still served as a co-manager on the big bond deal along with JPMorgan Chase. Ebbers and Sullivan, despite their flirtation with JPMorgan and other banks, knew their way around Citigroup better than any other firm. Indeed, Grubman and Sullivan emailed each other almost daily, even planning to meet during vacation. But as the months passed, and the operating environment continued to deteriorate, it became harder and harder for even an experienced stock promoter like Grubman to remain on the positive side about his top stocks. In mid June, Sherlyn McMahon sounded the alarm bells once again, this time on Global Crossing. Still rated positively by Grubman, Global was sinking fast after Dan Reingold issued a note saying that the company provided information at an analyst dinner that was forecasting lower profits. Grubman considered attacking Reingold directly with his own note, saying no such guidance was given, but McMahon warned he was playing with fire.

"The big issue with clients is will numbers come down on GX [Global Crossing]," McMahon wrote in an email. "Given what I know about the industry, I think they will. I think all our companies are in jeopardy of having weak 2Qs which will last into" 2002. After hearing McMahon's explanation, Grubman replied: "Not sure what to do."

WorldCom wasn't faring any better. Shares were falling almost daily. Grubman and McMahon were bombarded with calls from buyside analysts asking for guidance, and questioning their continued optimism in the face of such obvious disaster. Then came Reingold. Grubman's old nemesis, now at Credit Suisse First Boston, issued another note suggesting that WorldCom put out misleading guidance that should have analysts worried. The note even took a shot at Grubman, stating that an unnamed "analyst" had based his research on "company expectations that are three quarters old." Cutler recommended that Grubman keep his cool ("no blast" voice mail refuting Reingold's claims) and let her do the talking for him the next time she met with CSFB officials. "I'm going to use the rope of all his written words . . . to wrap it around his little balls," she wrote in one email. "They will be blue balls when I'm done—that's if they are still attached." After Cutler complained to a CSFB salesman, Reingold was perplexed. "What did I ever do to this woman?" he said "I don't understand it."

The situation was even more perplexing for Grubman, who had always bragged that sophisticated investors held him in high regard while the retail brokers who sold stocks to average Joes wanted his scalp. But that began to change as well. "I realize you have a job to do," wrote Sean Connor, an executive for mutual fund company Van Kampen, "and I enjoy hearing your view, but I can't figure out why you are so promotional in your voice mails. The company just put up a shitty quarter, lowered guidance significantly, especially in the growth areas, and to me that is why the stock is down."

Inside the research department, Grubman's shortcomings as an analyst finally became too much to ignore. Over the years, the firm's research brass had ignored the conflicted nature of Grubman's work as he generated tens of millions in revenues for the "greater good" of Salomon and Citigroup. How could they not? Grubman not only helped pay their salaries, but he also came through for the firm's most powerful deal maker, Sandy Weill. But now they were paying the price. Congress began hearings on research analyst conflicts as the market's most hyped stocks continued to fall, and considered calling Meeker, Blodget, and Grubman as witnesses. Brokers, on the front line of customer complaints and potential lawsuits, became increasingly vocal. Timothy Tucker prepared a lengthy memo dissecting what was to date one of Grubman's worst research calls, his continued support of Metromedia Fiber Network, a telecom company Salomon brought public in 1997, earning $49 million in fees since that time. Grubman, needless to say, had a buy rating on the company, until it was trading as a penny stock and preparing for bankruptcy protection.

Tucker explained the facts surrounding Grubman's call, his continued hyping even when he should have been offering words of caution, and how he maintained target prices well above where the shares were trading in the market. As Tucker pointed out, one of his claims seemed particularly disturbing. Grubman said that Metromedia obtained a credit facility from Citicorp, Citigroup's banking affiliate, to help its funding needs. But the reality was quite different; Citicorp never finalized the agreement as Metromedia's financials deteriorated. Grubman, meanwhile, only cut his rating from a buy to a neutral when shares were trading below $1, and less than a month after that, one of his research notes suggested that Metromedia was still a buying opportunity. Metromedia eventually filed for bankruptcy protection.

"Explaining this isn't easy," Tucker wrote. "My candid opinion is that until quite recently Jack Grubman's team had not yet come to terms with the debacle in their sector. While share prices plummeted, they remained convinced of the longer-term potential of their group and were unwilling to cut ratings and adopt a more cautious stance. When you add the heavy layer of banking involvement into the mix this very problematic situation gets easier to understand."

Tucker offered a simple solution. Equity research pumped out thirteen thousand reports a year, many were scrutinized by the firm's legal department, but for the most part, the firm relied on people like Grubman "to do careful work" when he prepared his research. That, he said, had to change. "There was a failure of analysis, and it pains me to confess, a failure of management. This is the only real explanation I can offer."

It was, to say the least, an amazingly frank assessment of a disaster waiting to happen.

And that disaster was closer than anyone at Citigroup realized. By the fall of 2001, WorldCom was clearly a troubled company, hampered by a huge debt load, mounting problems with the costs of its massive telecom infrastructure, and pricing pressure. But Grubman was operating as if it were still 1999. Though he communicated with Ebbers approximately once a month, and Sullivan even more frequently, Grubman's public comments made him appear to be oblivious to just how much the company's finances had deteriorated. One explanation: Emails show that Grubman and his team were now running his research by top officials at WorldCom, including Ebbers. As she prepared to issue one research note, McMahon realized that she might have problems getting

Grubman's $60 price target approved by compliance because Citigroup had just imposed a new rule preventing price targets from being 75 percent above market price of the stock. Shares of WorldCom had sunk to about $13, well below the threshold. "I am going to try to slip this one by them," McMahon wrote WorldCom investor relations chief Scott Hamilton, as she sent him a research note she had just prepared. "But I may have to lower the price target." Hamilton responded with a simple, "Thanks," adding "Scott (Sullivan) is looking at" the note and that "Bernie is in a meeting for another 45 minutes or so" and will review it as well.

McMahon emailed back that "I'll sit on it until I hear from you," and then contacted the firm's compliance department about the price-target matter. Less than an hour later, Ebbers issued his go-ahead. Along with his "buy" rating, Grubman proclaimed the following: "WCOM is on the verge, within the next quarter or two, of returning to being a growth company."

By early fall 2001, Grubman was still hawking WorldCom, but Global Crossing was a different story. Grubman had maintained a buy rating on the stock even as it began to trade into single digits, for obvious reasons as far as his competitors were concerned. Grubman had personally advised its chairman and founder, Gary Winnick, the former Drexel Burnham Lambert investment banker, on the company's strategic direction, and helped Salomon win more than its fair share of the banking fees Global had spread around the street. Meanwhile, Grubman's reports on Global Crossing were as bullish as any he published on WorldCom.

But by late September, Grubman started laying the groundwork for his eventual downgrade. In an email to John Otto, the banker who covered the company, Grubman said he knew someone "who pegged every bankruptcy in this space." This person, whom Grubman didn't name, was "way ahead of the street or even the companies" and he "says GX is next."

Grubman added that given all the companies in his sector that had either filed or were heading for bankruptcy, "We cannot afford another [buy] rated stock going under. Can only take so many lawsuits and NASD investigations," referring to the fact that the NASD had begun to sniff around his controversial Winstar call. "So I think we have to pull the plug on this and frankly all other emerging names under $3 per share."

Otto responded by explaining how Global Crossing's management "has stabilized and is doing a solid job." He conceded that, "obviously, the problem is the balance sheet" and the "erosion of the equity value," but he added that he and other bankers were "working on" the company's problems. Grubman didn't seem impressed. "Fair enough," he added. "Look I staked a lot on these guys so trust me I hope you work magic." Grubman had enough invested in Global that he asked Otto for a favor: Confront Hoffman, the research chief, and get him to relax the price target rule so he could set it at $10 a share (it was trading far below that level). Later, Grubman sent the entire exchange to McMahon with the following note about Otto's optimism: "Hopefully, he is right."

But he wasn't. In November, as shares of Global fell even further to $1.07. Grubman cut his rating to a "neutral" from a "buy." Two months later, Global applied for bankruptcy court protection.

"Not a great call," Grubman conceded in an email to one broker, "but it's over."

WorldCom, meanwhile, was hanging on by its fingernails. A year earlier, the company was hoping for a positive reception from the market when it prepared to spin off MCI into a separate tracking stock for its consumer long-distance business. But the comeback was short-lived. On November 1, at the AXA Conference Center in Manhattan, Ebbers unveiled the track-stock plan to about 3,500 investors and analysts. While at the meeting, he also revealed something more important. Standing on a large stage with Grubman sitting in the front row, Ebbers explained how the company was lowering its earnings and revenue estimates for the fourth quarter of 2000 far below industry estimates. The culprit, according to Ebbers: competitive pressure in the telecom industry. It was a startling confession for a company that had been telling investors that prosperity was right around the corner. After the presentation was over, a crowd swarmed both men, demanding answers. Grubman seemed to know what was coming. He had a research note ready for release as soon as the meeting was over, easily beating the competition with the news. Before the meeting, he was taken "over the wall," and privately briefed on the company's deteriorating finances.

Grubman could have used his connections to give investors some insight about WorldCom's trouble into late 2001, but all he offered was spin and hype. Only now his hype seemed to fall flat as shares of the company continued to drop no matter what he said. As it turned out, private investors weren't the only ones to begin tuning Grubman out. Around this time, Grubman's wife, LuAnn, sold her stake in WorldCom, which had been getting killed in the crash. (Grubman says through a spokesman that she sold the stock following a companywide edict.)

It's one thing for multimillionaires like the Grubmans to take a beating on a stock, but when average people take losses the stakes are higher. Robert Goss, a WorldCom employee, was near suicidal when much of his savings, tied up in WorldCom stock, began to disappear before his eyes. "Oh, God, somebody just needs to take me out in the parking lot and shoot me," he told his broker, Amy Elias. "Maybe that would end my dilemma." Goss didn't do anything foolish, but a short time later, he said he was relying on a higher authority for help. "The wife and I are both praying," he told Elias. "She just called me a little while ago and . . . she says we gotta depend on God trying to help us out of here."

Elias said she was praying as well.

Grubman, meanwhile, was busy glossing over WorldCom's increasingly dire financial situation. On November 14, McMahon emailed Grubman that the company's latest "10-Q" or quarterly earnings statement was "pretty shitty." The next day Grubman decided to get some fresh information directly from Scott Sullivan, but the WorldCom CFO wasn't in the mood. Sullivan remarked that "Everything is for sale," and that the pessimism from Wall Street was hurting the company. "There is nothing to fear but defensiveness," he wrote Grubman. "Your notes, discussions only make it look like we are being defensive!"

The email seemed odd, as if Sullivan had something weighing on his mind. Grubman quickly forwarded Sullivan's email to McMahon. "FYI don't understand his last point," Grubman wrote.

"Yeah," McMahon said. "What notes and discussions?"

Grubman didn't push the matter and resumed hyping the stock. T. Rowe Price money manager Robert Gensler gave Grubman a recap of a meeting he had with Sullivan and Ebbers, who said the company's finances have improved. "Volumes have picked up" since the 9/11 terrorist attacks, and pricing of new contracts have been stable for months. Grubman was ecstatic. "All WCOM needs is a flat" quarter to be up year over year, he told Gensler. Later, he emailed Sullivan his upbeat assessment. "Sounds like q4 on track and in general landscape stabilizing." Sullivan did some sucking up of his own, telling him to "hang in there—your success attracts attention," referring to a rash of news stories that had bashed Grubman's stock hyping of companies like WorldCom that kicked back banking business.

Grubman, as usual, forwarded the emails to McMahon with the following remark: "Nice message."

It was one of the last nice things Grubman would hear from World-Com. Late in the year, *Institutional Investor* displaced him from the number one position in its ranking of telecom analysts, largely the result of his continued support of the floundering WorldCom, which was heading below $10 a share. Nothing, it seemed, could save WorldCom from the fate that struck Winstar, Metromedia, Global Crossing, and a host of other Grubman touts. In early February 2002, Grubman personally coached Ebbers on how to answer analysts' questions about his company's deteriorating finances. When Ebbers was finished, World-Com fell even further to $8 a share. In March, Grubman reiterated his "buy" recommendation on the stock, just as the SEC launched an investigation into possible accounting irregularities at the company. Grubman seemed to ignore both his own and McMahon's suspicions about the company's finances as shown in their email exchanges. WorldCom, he wrote, "is executing better than any time over the past 10 years," and the SEC inquiry "is mostly general in nature . . . very straightforward—almost boilerplate."

Ebbers, Grubman said, had recently provided ample evidence that the company was on the rebound in a speech the same day the SEC commenced its inquiry. The speech "reinforced that industry landscape is getting better." WorldCom, he reminded investors, "has the highest quality balance sheet in the telecom industry . . ." and the company believes its "growth will manifest from new products and expansion of its international business." How was Grubman able to make such a bold prediction? No one knows for sure. Later Grubman would concede that he never reviewed the company's contracts that backed up its stated level of capital spending overseas, though he managed to visit a few projects, including the installation of fiber optic lines in the Tokyo subway system.

In yet another sign of Grubman's diminishing power, shares of World-

Com barely budged with the report, while his critics inside his firm continued their assault. In the past, brokers couldn't wait to get their hands on Grubman's words of wisdom, now they couldn't wait to get their hands around his neck. One afternoon, brokerage chief Jay Mandelbaum received an angry email from one of his top brokers, a woman named Cheryl Schwarzwaelder, complaining about Grubman's research and looking for some help. "As far as Global Crossing, Jack had the stock at a buy rating from $60 all the way down to $1!!!" she wrote. "Now he is falling into the same footsteps with WorldCom . . . I can not have 2 bankruptcies with an analyst who keeps stocks at BUY ratings all the way to bankruptcy!!!"

It's difficult to know what pushed Grubman to finally downgrade WorldCom, but on April 22, 2002, he made his move. Emails show that Grubman had just read a news story that discussed lower bandwidth pricing for the foreseeable future, a condition that would continue to eat at WorldCom earnings. Whatever the reason, after he received approval from research management, Grubman announced that he had cut his long-held "buy" rating to a "neutral," citing growing concerns over the company's operations and the looming possibility of bankruptcy. For Grubman it was about as dour an assessment as he could give on his one-time favorite stock, though he still couldn't bring himself to use the word "sell."

"It would obviously be easier to not downgrade the stock, and therefore not suffer the inevitable and justified slings from various parties," he wrote sheepishly, adding, "clearly, we have been wrong on the stock."

While Grubman's hype ceased having much effect on the market, his downgrade sent the stock sharply lower to around $5 a share, prompting widespread fears that WorldCom was heading for bankruptcy. A few days later, the company hit a new low when Ebbers abruptly resigned, touching off another flurry of speculation about WorldCom's chances for survival.

It was an unceremonious end of a mutually beneficial relationship. In addition to all the IPO shares Salomon had granted Ebbers over the years, Ebbers also received hundreds of millions of dollars in loans, timed, as it turns out, by Salomon's appointment as underwriter on its massive bond deals in 2000 and 2001. Even more suspicious: The loans were secured by Ebbers's holdings in WorldCom stock, meaning

Grubman's hype was also protecting the firm's investment in Bernie Ebbers. A week after Ebbers resigned, Citigroup discovered what a bad investment Bernie Ebbers turned out to be. The company was forced to sell off the WorldCom stock Ebbers pledged as collateral, taking a $2 million loss.

But the losses for some investors weren't over. In late June, Grubman cut his rating once again from "neutral" to "underperform," raising more concerns over the company's financial condition. Shares of WorldCom were already trading at just $1.22, but at least Grubman saved himself from a Winstar-like embarrassment. Two days later, WorldCom put itself out of its misery and filed for bankruptcy protection, announcing a massive earnings restatement that led to the largest accounting fraud scandal in Wall Street history. Sullivan, one of the two architects of the company's tremendous rise and fall, was fired that morning.

The big question inside Citigroup: How did Grubman blow it? In his March report, Grubman called WorldCom "one of the most reviewed companies in the S&P 500," and presumably he was doing the reviewing. Now brokers at Salomon were outraged. Grubman, they believed, was either stupid or corrupt, and several led an effort to have Grubman replaced with Susan Kalla, now with a small brokerage firm, Friedman Billings & Ramsey, who was one of the first analysts to alert investors to the holes in his research. Similar outrage spread across Wall Street. Meeker was told by her supervisors to figure out if she wanted to stay in the business. In the wake of Henry Blodget's disastrous calls, Jerome Kenney, who oversaw research on Merrill's powerful executive committee, promised angry brokers a new day: Analysts would now be required to spend more time doing research and less meeting with banking clients.

But nowhere was the anger greater than at Salomon Smith Barney, where Grubman became public enemy No. 1 with the firm's sales force. One broker wrote in an email that Grubman should be "publicly flogged," while others just wanted him fired. Brokers realized a key fact that the company's management failed to recognize: Grubman represented short-term gain but long-term pain as investors turned away from the firm in droves. One Salomon broker was so upset by the impact of all the attention given to Grubman that he wrote an email to a *Wall Street Journal* reporter to complain. The paper, he wrote, was "biting the hand that feeds you," given the heavy amounts of advertising the paper gets from Wall Street.

When contacted by the reporter, the broker quickly apologized. He had been getting an earful from angry clients about Grubman's conflicted stock picks and sent the email in frustration. "If Jack Grubman was sitting here," he added. "I'd hit him with a baseball bat and piss on him."

CHAPTER NINE

Keystone Cops

When the dust finally settled, the damage done by the superstar analysts was nothing short of nuclear. The NASDAQ stock market that traded many of the dotcoms and tech stocks at the heart of the analysts' hyped ratings fell by 60 percent from its peak in March 2000 to March 2001. John Makin, an economist with the American Enterprise Institute, pointed out that these losses resulted in one of the largest destructions of "paper" wealth in the nation's history; the disappearing dotcoms eliminated nearly $2.5 trillion from the U.S. stock markets. As the tech fallout spread to the broader markets (bear in mind that WorldCom, Grubman's bankrupt New Economy baby, traded on the New York Stock Exchange, not the NASDAQ) the damage was even more severe—a total of $4.5 trillion wiped out during the first twelve months after the crash.

For Makin and other economists, what made the entire episode so disturbing was not merely its size and scope, but also the nature of the victims involved. The great stock market crash of 1929 wiped out huge amounts of wealth, but much of it came from rich speculators and investors who should have known better than to trust the markets to be infallible. But in the 1990s, however, a stunning demographic change swept the brokerage business. Lured by a combination of necessity—the need to save for retirement, greed, and, maybe most significant, the hype of the superstar analysts, millions of average, middle-class Americans with little if any knowledge of the way Wall Street worked began handing their life savings to brokers who knew the game all too well. For a time it worked; in just a couple of years, many in the middle class who followed Wall Street research became millionaires, at least as measured by the value of their portfolios. People didn't just sit on their "paper" wealth,

187

they spent much of it, buying homes, cars, and boats, expanding their lifestyle to match the market and the analysts' enthusiasm for future growth. When the market crashed, so did their lifestyles. The middle class went back to being middle class or even worse.

The experience of Ed Wolfe, a retired truck driver from a small town outside of Cleveland, Ohio, typified all the highs and lows that befell this new type of investor. In early 2000, after thirty-two years at the Rubbermaid factory in Wooster, Ohio, Wolfe amassed what seemed like to him a small fortune of $328,000 by stashing away a portion of his paycheck in a conservative bond fund offered through his company's 401(k) plan. Despite his sizable savings, Wolfe was for the most part financially illiterate; he rarely read the business pages of his local newspaper, and what little he knew about the stock market he got from television, having listened to the superstar analysts hype their favorite stocks. In other words, he was the perfect brokerage customer for a firm like Merrill looking to sell technology investments at the height of the bubble.

Merrill Lynch broker Joel Cessna clearly *looked* like he knew what he was doing when Wolfe showed up at his office in the local strip mall, seeking advice on how to put his nest egg to work and retire in style. Cessna had a computer on his desk with charts and graphs, Wolfe recalls. He wore starched shirts—"the kind that were done at the laundry, not home washed," with classy ties and a dark blue blazer. More important, Wolfe remembers that Cessna spoke confidently of how he would take care of his money and produce "a guaranteed 8 percent return." Wolfe was sold, but as he handed him a check for all his savings, just withdrawn from the local bank at the other end of the strip mall, Wolfe made one request. "No gambling," he recalls saying. Wolfe said he made it clear that he wanted his money in a safe place. Cessna, he said, agreed.

Whether he knew it or not, Wolfe had become a high roller. Thanks to a policy handed down from Merrill's headquarters in the World Financial Center in downtown Manhattan to boost the company's earnings, Merrill had embarked on a campaign to "cross sell" its various products to clients of its massive brokerage system. Instead of recommending mutual funds from companies like Vanguard or Fidelity, brokers across the Merrill empire were now put on notice to drum up corporate profits by pushing the company's own mutual funds, including several that were stuffed with Internet stocks championed by Henry Blodget. Wolfe, on Cessna's advice, invested in a number of tech stocks and three mutual funds packed with shares of bubble-induced Internet companies. One of those funds, the Merrill Lynch Internet Strategies Fund, had been part of the huge sales push at the firm, unveiled at a presentation in San Francisco where the guest speakers included Blodget as well as Michael Lewis, the author of *Liar's Poker*, a classic book about greed on Wall Street.

Wolfe, of course, had no way of knowing the pressure brokers like Cessna were under to sell these risky investments. Over the next year, he made several withdrawals from his account to cover living expenses, believing that Cessna had guaranteed an 8 percent return and that would make up the difference. Then he received an urgent call from Cessna. Wolfe had never bothered checking his brokerage statement over the past twelve months, but if he had, he would have learned that the NASDAQ crash had eaten a huge chunk out of his initial investment. That combined with his monthly withdrawals left Wolfe with a little more than $90,000 from his initial investment of $320,000. Cessna's advice: Stop draining money from the account or you'll be broke.

"When I heard that, I thought I was going to have a heart attack," Wolfe recalled.

Ed Wolfe's experience reveals much about Wall Street and its culture during the 1990s market boom. His lack of sophistication (and downright stupidity) should have been a signal that he needed high-level financial assistance; instead, it set him up for the kill. Wolfe asked very few questions, demanded little if any service, and relied totally on the advice of his "financial adviser" to pick his investments. In other words, he was easy prey for the big Wall Street firms that ignored their responsibility to the new class of investor who flooded the markets with little knowledge of the various ways Wall Street made money at their expense. An NASD arbitration panel apparently agreed, and in early 2003 ordered Merrill to repay Wolfe nearly $235,000 in compensatory damages and $75,000 in legal fees. After accumulating twenty-five similar customer complaints, Merrill decided to fire Cessna, according to a spokesman, because he "failed to follow management's instructions regarding recommending suitable investment strategies for clients." Cessna says his only problem was that he "should have turned Wolfe away because his objectives were too aggressive," as were his other customers who complained.

But Cessna was hardly the only broker to face difficulties during the bubble years. Throughout the 1990s, investor complaints soared as more and more average people found themselves holding risky technology stocks that had gone bankrupt or were now trading at a fraction of what they were bought for. People like Wolfe obviously came to the market with absurd expectations about how the stock market worked (he wanted an 8 percent return with no risk), but Wall Street compounded the problem in many ways. The compliance departments of the big Wall Street firms, which are supposed to keep tabs on improper activity, seemed to look the other way as fraud and abuse spread at epidemic proportions. In one extreme example, a broker working out of a Lehman Brothers branch in Cleveland stole tens of millions of dollars from clients while the executive in charge of compliance sat oblivious to the scam just a few desks away.

But the blame should be cast wider. All of this activity also occurred under the nose of Wall Street's chief regulator, the Securities and Exchange Commission, which seemed to be taking an extended coffee break during one of the greatest destructions of wealth in American history. To fully appreciate the level of ineptitude by the nation's top securities regulator—and its contribution to the mammoth losses suffered by investors once the market bubble burst—it's best to step back and examine not just what the SEC is supposed to do, but also the actions of the man who presided over the agency during a time of unmatched recklessness by the big Wall Street firms, its chairman, Arthur Levitt Jr.

The SEC likes to portray itself as Wall Street's top cop, an imposing federal agency with limitless power to track down criminals who use the financial markets as a haven for their scams, and no one embodied this image better than Arthur Levitt Jr. An appointee of President Bill Clinton, Levitt was one of the few chairmen of the agency who brought a practical Wall Street knowledge to a job that had been filled with politically connected bureaucrats. He had been a key player in Sandy Weill's creation of the Shearson brokerage empire in the 1970s and early 1980s, and was later named chairman of the American Stock Exchange. But where Levitt really excelled was in politics. The son of a New York State politician (his father was a longtime state comptroller, helping New York City survive near-bankruptcy during the fiscal crisis of the 1970s), Arthur Jr. had close ties to prominent members of the state Democratic Party who worked on Wall Street. During the 1992 presidential race,

Levitt helped rise $3.5 million for the Clinton campaign. When Clinton won, vowing to erase the "decade of greed," a liberal with Wall Street credentials like Levitt seemed perfect to lead the charge.

Levitt appeared to get off to a fast start. After taking office in 1993, he launched a series of measures to clean up the scandal-ridden municipal bond market by restricting how much money executives could donate to local officials in order to win lucrative bond deals, a practice known as "pay to play." Later, when he heard of abuses involving stockbrokers, Levitt dialed up one of his old friends from his Wall Street days, Merrill CEO Dan Tully, who helped him get every major firm on Wall Street to voluntarily agree to a set of rules to clean up some egregious practices by stockbrokers. On the rare occasion that people in the markets questioned the merits of one of his directives, Levitt quickly reminded them of his inside knowledge of how the Wall Street money-machine worked. "Listen, I used to work on Wall Street, I know how the game is played" was his common response.

Levitt certainly talked a good game. He created huge headlines through his criticism of various practices in the securities industry, using what's known as the office's "bully pulpit" to speak out on these issues and others. He tried to push through Congress measures designed to make auditors more independent and less likely to allow companies to fudge the numbers on accounting statements. For small investors, who had come to the markets in droves during the market boom, he forced corporations to give them the same information they handed Wall Street analysts, a rule known as "Fair Disclosure."

But by the end of the decade, it was quite clear that, for all his good intentions, Levitt had failed small investors. The SEC's own statistics paint an alarming picture about Levitt's record. Throughout much of his tenure, the number of enforcement cases launched by the commission remained relatively stable even as fraud exploded. At times, the SEC appeared even to be cutting back on its enforcement activity. Between 1994 and the SEC's 1996 fiscal year, new investigations declined 24 percent, while charges against alleged miscreants and their companies fell 12.7 percent. The commission tried to get back on track in 1997, but its record from the remainder of Levitt's service was uneven at best. In 1997, the commission launched a total of 489 enforcement actions and 525 in 1999. But in 2000, the year the bubble burst and the result of Wall Street's deceptive practices started showing up on investor account statements, the number of cases launched by the commission miraculously declined more than 4 percent to 503.

Levitt's various efforts to enact reform fell flat as well. His rule restricting campaign contributions in the municipal-bond market turned out to be so filled with loopholes that executives began funneling millions of dollars into "soft-money" accounts where there are no limits to the giving. Rule FD, or "Fair Disclosure," had become a laughingstock on Wall Street primarily because it had the practical effect of burdening small investors with data they had no expertise to understand. One afternoon in September 2000, a research analyst at SSB forwarded a post-FD earnings announcement from a company to Timothy Tucker, a manager in Salomon's research department. Tucker couldn't help but chuckle. "Such a high level of detail, clearly laid out. Now Joe Six-pack can really keep his [earnings] models up-to-date. Arthur Levitt must be thrilled!"

As for Levitt's set of rules for Wall Street brokers, many of the biggest firms, including Tully's own, openly violated its various clauses and often in plain view of SEC investigators, who were powerless to do anything because it was all voluntary. Levitt's political acumen may have been overestimated as well. He was a great fundraiser, but he had almost no stroke with his boss, Bill Clinton, or with some of Washington's top Democrats, who often joined with Republicans to thwart his "reform" efforts, including a proposal to create more independent accounting standards.

So what did Levitt accomplish? Not much, according to commission officials who worked for him. Levitt had juggled so many priorities at once that SEC commissioners could never focus on the most important. "We never knew what was on the agenda," said one former commissioner. Levitt, these people say, often crafted major policy decisions during one-on-one meetings with various industry executives, before they were even presented to his staff. SEC Commissioner Laura Unger was so miffed at Levitt's work habits that she asked for some advance notice of his initiatives. "Arthur, you can't announce these initiatives to the public before you tell us," she said. "We need to have a dialogue."

The SEC enforcement division—the unit primarily responsible for bringing charges against wrongdoers—can compel everyone from the lowliest broker to the most powerful Wall Street CEO to provide truthful testimony about alleged wrongdoing or face immediate sanctions up to and including being thrown out of the securities business. But during the 1990s bubble, Levitt wasted huge resources not clamping down on the big brokerage houses but targeting small firms, known as "bucket shops," that operated on the fringes of the business. Satirized in the movie *Boiler Room*, these outfits accounted for a small fraction of investor trading during the 1990s market boom, but under Levitt they received more than their fair share of attention. In the summer of 2000, as Wall Street peddled some of the most conflicted stock research in its history, the SEC and the Justice Department announced one of their biggest busts ever, charging nineteen people with ties to organized crime with stock manipulations that resulted in huge losses for small investors.

How much did their alleged rip-off actually cost the typical brokerage client? After all the hoopla was over, investigators fessed up that the price tag for the entire scam amounted to a paltry $50 million over the previous five years. That's $10 million less than the fees Salomon earned on one day's work underwriting the controversial AT&T stock issue after Jack Grubman's well-timed upgrade.

While the commission was spending its limited resources worrying about organized crime on Wall Street, the supposedly squeaky-clean mutual fund business, which attracted trillions of dollars in small investor savings during the bubble, became a cesspool of unscrupulous practices— everything from the charging of excessively high fees to secret deals where mutual fund companies paid extra fees to brokers to sell their funds over possibly better investments. Under Levitt, another scandal known as "spinning" was virtually ignored. SEC officials at the time said that the money involved wasn't large enough to constitute fraud, even though top corporate executives like Bernie Ebbers received tens of millions of dollars of hot IPOs in their personal brokerage accounts after handing firms like Salomon Smith Barney lucrative underwriting contracts.

Levitt's response to what may have been the biggest scandal of the 1990s bubble wouldn't be much different. By the time he took office in 1993, research conflicts had become a fact of life on Wall Street. Things got so bad that most analysts had given in to the pressure and embraced a system that encouraged them to hype research on companies that were issuing stocks and bonds. Those who didn't found themselves out of a job, like Marvin Roffman.

A gaming industry analyst for Janney Montgomery Scott, a Philadelphia-based brokerage firm, Roffman made huge news in 1990 when he was fired by his firm after making critical comments about the junk bonds issued by real estate mogul Donald Trump to finance one of his Atlantic City casinos. Roffman's prediction that the Trump Taj Mahal bonds would fall into default proved amazingly accurate, but his comments so angered Trump that he demanded a retraction from Roffman and the firm. Roffman refused, and a couple of days later, he was fired. As research chief James Meyer escorted him out of the building, Roffman recalls hearing the following words of advice: "Keep your mouth shut or you'll never work in this business again."

Meyer says he was merely reflecting reality, that whistleblowers have a tough time finding work on Wall Street. But Roffman was not about to keep quiet. He immediately filed an arbitration suit against Janney for wrongful dismissal and a lawsuit in federal court against Trump as newspapers across the country chronicled his case as an example of the pressures faced by analysts to hype stocks of big banking clients. The press made Roffman a hero for standing up for what he believed in, but some of his colleagues didn't see it that way. A headhunter told him that no firm would hire him because they were afraid he might "piss off" banking clients. Fellow analysts wouldn't return his calls as he looked for work.

But even more troubling for Roffman was the response of the SEC, where investigators were supposed to be policing this type of activity. They never contacted him about the matter.

More than a decade later, Roffman can rest easy. He won a large settlement from Janney for wrongful dismissal and an out-of-court settlement from Trump, and today, he runs a successful money-management firm with $215 million in assets. But one question still irks him. Where was the SEC? "I couldn't believe they never spoke to me about what happened," Roffman recently said, still incredulous. "Not once."

Many more stories like Roffman's would be chronicled in major newspapers as Levitt took office, and well into his tenure as SEC chairman. By the height of the 1990s stock market boom, Wall Street research had virtually no resemblance to the independent reports made famous by DLJ in the 1960s. Analysts weren't just under pressure from bankers to tone down their criticisms; now they faced edicts from upper management to hype their reports to win a piece of the $75 billion in underwriting fees offered by corporations during the bull market. The big brokerage firms defended these practices by claiming that the hype ratings, the dearth of "sell" recommendations, represented the honestly held opinions of the analysts who wrote the reports. Levitt must have believed these lame excuses himself, because during his tenure the SEC did not bring a single case against a major firm involving fraudulent research. In fact, it wasn't until mid 1999 that analysts' conflicts suddenly appeared on Levitt's radar screen. Why did he wait so long? In an interview, Levitt said he had been aware of the problems involving research for some time and even witnessed the conflicts firsthand during his days on the street, but he was busy with other issues that occupied his time, particularly his push to reform the accounting industry. "Had I not been involved in those issues, I would have done something more," he said.

Once he got started, Levitt certainly *talked* a good game. His first public comments on the issue can be traced to a speech in Boca Raton, Florida, at a conference sponsored by the Securities Industry Association, Wall Street's main lobby group. In it, Levitt said he was putting the brokerage industry on notice over its increasingly conflicted stock research that had resulted in a dearth of sell ratings at a point when the markets were overheating. "I don't have a specific proposal on this," Levitt later told the Dow Jones News Service. But he added that the commission was so concerned with the effect research conflicts were having on small investors that "we're going to examine this issue carefully."

How did this sweeping crackdown materialize? In September 2000, just months after the market bubble burst, the SEC took great pleasure not in charging Jack Grubman for issuing conflicted research on AT&T, but in pursuing sixteen-year-old Jonathan Lebed with securities fraud for touting in Internet chat rooms stocks that he owned and then selling them at a profit. In a settlement with the SEC, Lebed agreed to turn over $285,000 in profits and interest without admitting or denying wrongdoing, the first time a minor had been charged with securities fraud.

Both Levitt and his new enforcement director, Richard Walker, said the case underscored the SEC's get-tough attitude regarding fraudulent research. In a speech after the case was filed, Walker went even further, saying Lebed's fraud exceeded anything the SEC knew about standard practices on Wall Street. "Some of the press and others have gotten completely sidetracked and have attempted to defend Lebed's conduct by demonizing Wall Street and suggesting what Lebed did is really no different than what Wall Street analysts do every day," he said. "Of course, to the

extent an analyst intentionally manipulates a security, misleads investors
. . . makes unsubstantiated price predictions or other statements that
lack a reasonable basis . . . the analyst has a serious problem. But to suggest that these are 'standard brokerage house procedures' is sopho-
moric."

But it was Walker who seemed to be out of touch with reality. By now,
every major Wall Street firm had developed a system in which analysts
could hype stock ratings beyond all reason, hiding behind their sky-high
price targets on investment banking clients with the standard excuse that
a rating was just an opinion. Levitt's response was even more speeches.
During one, he pointed to a "web of dysfunctional relationships" involving research and investment banking that forced analysts to hype ratings
and put small investors in harm's way. In another speech, he used a little
humor to show how Wall Street research had stopped caring about investors' needs, pointing out that sell recommendations on Wall Street
were about as "common as a Barbra Streisand concert." He singled out
the television news media for failing to recognize such obvious conflicts
while they made people like Blodget TV stars. "How many times has an
analyst been asked to list his top five picks?" he asked. "And how often
has an analyst cautioned viewers, 'By the way, my employer recently underwrote three of these companies?' Not often."

Levitt certainly understood the scope of the problem. In another
speech he cited some disturbing statistics; the ratio of buy to sell recommendations during the bull market of the 1990s was running 8-to-1,
compared to a ratio of 1-to-1 during the bull market of the 1980s. He
asked at another speaking event for a show of hands of how many analysts were in the audience. Then he asked how many had actually placed
a "sell" rating on some stock. There wasn't one in the crowd.

But understanding the problem was one thing, addressing it was another. In mid 2000, Levitt's SEC remained noticeably silent even after his
old business partner, Citigroup CEO Sandy Weill, all but admitted to
having pressured Grubman to upgrade his rating on AT&T right before a
major stock deal. Instead of launching a major investigation into Weill
that would have put all of Wall Street on notice, he directed his staff to
reach out to both self-regulatory agencies, the New York Stock Exchange
and the National Association of Securities Dealers, and begin work on
drafting rules that would force analysts to disclose conflicts while they
appeared on television.

With the growth of television business news as a major source of information for small investors, Levitt believed the unedited hype of people like Blodget, particularly on CNBC, was a major problem. He wasn't far off. CNBC reporters David Faber and Joe Kernan had long questioned research conflicts, derisively referring to analysts as "penguins" for falling in line and hyping stocks when banking fees were on the line. But the station also fueled much of the hype that Wall Street used to mislead small investors, mainly by allowing analysts like Blodget to promote their stock picks without disclosing their role in securing investment banking deals.

Television producers immediately criticized the proposal. "You can't make a television appearance and then read four minutes of boilerplate," Bruno Cohen, CNBC's senior vice president, told *USA Today*. But Wall Street was breathing a collective sigh of relief. For all his rhetoric over the past two years, for all the evidence at his disposal about how small investors were being misled by hyped stock recommendations, Levitt's recommendations did very little to address the problem, which begins and ends with analysts hyping stock ratings to generate investment banking business.

Even more inexplicable was his trust that the Wall Street self-regulatory groups should take the lead in the reform effort. The NYSE and the NASD are basically private clubs run by the brokerage industry and their policies often reflect the wishes of the big Wall Street firms. Moreover, the NASD, the regulatory organization in charge of the NAS-DAQ stock market, had little incentive to enforce strict rules over analysts. The hyping of technology stocks that traded on the exchange, by analysts like Henry Blodget, gave the NASDAQ a huge competitive advantage over its main rival, the New York Stock Exchange, as millions of new investors began buying and selling stocks that traded on its system.

Despite all his years working in and around the brokerage business, Levitt, it appears, was blind to a basic fact of life on Wall Street: To accomplish anything, you must first instill fear in the hearts of the brokerage industry's top firms. Although Levitt seemed to say the right things about conflicted research and its effect on the small investor, he failed to instill the kind of fear into the Wall Street community that only a major investigation can accomplish. His inaction gave tacit approval to Jack Grubman's Chinese Wall maneuvers and Henry Blodget's hype. The election of a Republican president, George W. Bush, in late 2000, rendered Levitt even more irrelevant as Bush made it known that he would find someone else for the job in the coming months. Levitt spent the rest of his tenure as a lame duck, with no power and a dwindling audience for his speeches.

True to form, the self-regulatory organizations managed to drag their feet just long enough on Levitt's plan that he was virtually powerless to force them to act. When Levitt realized what had happened, he went ballistic. One of his first calls was to Frank Zarb, who had just stepped down as chairman of the NASD. Zarb, according to Levitt's recollection, said that his membership was uncomfortable with even the modest step of television disclosure of analysts' conflicts. (Zarb doesn't recall the conversation.)

The soon-to-be-ex-SEC chief then called Mary Schapiro, then president of the NASD's regulatory division.

"If you don't do something about this I will!" Levitt boomed. He screamed and cursed and was so angry that he briefly brought Schapiro to tears. Schapiro regained her composure and explained calmly that she was waiting for Levitt to get back to her on extending the measure to include financial advisers. But Levitt was unconvinced.

Later that day, Schapiro reported Levitt's outburst to the NASD board and her boss, NASD chairman Robert Glauber. "That's outrageous," Glauber said, offering to set the record straight with the SEC chief. But Schapiro told Glauber to let it die, adding, "I bet he didn't call Dick Grasso and scream at him," a reference to the street-smart chairman of the NYSE. She was right. Realizing that he had stepped over the line, Levitt called Schapiro to apologize. "You're such a good friend and I care for you so much I feel comfortable yelling at you," Levitt said, according to Schapiro's version of the conversation. Schapiro accepted his apology and said she was looking forward for some guidance on how to make the analyst disclosure rule better. Levitt said he would call her back in a few weeks with a more concrete plan. But there was little follow-through, as Levitt himself readily admits. "There's no question looking back that I should have done more."

With the SEC distracted, investors would have to wait for others to hold Wall Street accountable for misleading research. One person to step up was Eric Von der Porten, a forty-two-year-old former investment banker, who some years before had given up the fast track of the securities business to manage money in his hometown of San Carlos, California. Von der Porten worked out of a small office above a local restaurant, running what's known as a hedge fund, a pool of money he invested on behalf of a coterie of wealthy individuals. Hedge funds are different from mutual funds in that they are lightly regulated, meaning that investors like Von der Porten can take bigger risks, rolling the dice with trading techniques that allow them to profit when stocks fall in value, something known as "short selling."

As the dotcom bubble reached enormous heights through 1999, Von der Porten believed he had come across one of the biggest "shorts" in his career. Most of the top Internet companies didn't even have earnings, many were built on bizarre concepts. Despite these obstacles, they traded at levels that were clearly unsustainable by traditional financial measurements. One stock that was high on Von der Porten's list was Amazon.com, the online bookseller that Blodget had put on the map just months earlier with a $400 price target. Given the firm's messy balance sheet and lack of profitability, Von der Porten believed Amazon was ripe for a major correction from its current share price of more than $300 a share. Soon, he began "shorting" shares of Amazon at a rapid pace, betting the stock would nosedive once reality set into the market. There was just one problem: The stock wouldn't budge, at least not enough to make a difference. The reason, Von der Porten believed, could be traced to Wall Street, where analysts at nearly every major Wall Street firm were busy hyping shares of Amazon while the company geared up for a number of large stock and bond underwritings.

As Von der Porten began combing through research reports, he believed two top analysts had done more than just hype the stock; they also appeared to be glossing over major problems on Amazon's balance sheet. One was Jamie Kiggen, DLJ's top Internet analyst. The other was Blodget, who Von der Porten at one point telephoned for an explanation. Amazingly, Blodget took his call and admitted to making a mistake. "I wish I had more time to focus on one particular company like you do," he says Blodget told him during a short telephone call. "I'm always juggling ten different constituencies."

Von der Porten couldn't believe his ears. "When I got off the phone, I remember thinking this guy has got to be a fucking idiot for even talking to me," Van der Porten says.

It was also around this time that Von der Porten read a story about one of Levitt's speeches addressing research conflicts, and decided to give the SEC chairman some more ammunition in his fight. He began with offering Levitt some insight into Kiggen's research. "Mr. Kiggen's most recent reports on Amazon.com include statements I believe are, at best, grossly negligent," Von der Porten wrote Levitt on July 24, 2000, citing what he believed was Kiggen's reliance on "flawed data provided by Amazon.com."

"I have read the speech you delivered . . . and I wholeheartedly agree with your views regarding the conflicts facing Wall Street analysts," he wrote.

Von der Porten may have loved Levitt's speech, but the SEC chairman didn't seem to care much for his letter. After a few months with no reply, Von der Porten wrote to the enforcement division of the NASD, which is supposed to provide front-line regulation of technology stocks like Amazon and on the analysts who rate them. This time, he got an answer, but not the one he was looking for. "The evidence does not, at this time, warrant the institution of disciplinary action against Donaldson Lufkin & Jenrette and/or James Kiggen," NASD's investigator Ruth Brooks wrote Von der Porten on December 29, 2000.

Von der Porten was shocked, given the NASD's own rule stipulating that research reports must be reasonable and that analysts should have "a sound basis for evaluating the facts in regard to any particular security." But there was nothing, he believed, that was reasonable about Kiggen's research. So he went back to the SEC, which in addition to regulating Wall Street is also supposed to regulate the self-regulators like the NASD. "In my view this . . . indicates NASD Regulation has no intention of enforcing any rules of conduct with respect to securities analysts," he wrote senior SEC counsel Dean Conway in February 2001. "Instead of exercising their responsibilities, Mr. Kiggen and his supervisors apparently manipulated information and published reports that were extremely inaccurate and misleading."

The SEC apparently didn't see it that way, so Von der Porten turned his attention to a more high-profile target. By the end of 2000, Henry Blodget was Wall Street's top-ranked Internet analyst, but Von der Porten found he was making rookie mistakes. In one report, Blodget asserted that Amazon was going to produce "positive" cash flow at the end of the first quarter of 2001 by collecting cash from customers faster than they had to pay vendors. When Amazon missed that number by a long shot, Von der Porten placed another call to Blodget, who, as Von der Porten recalls, explained that his research was based on a "guess" and that he and his colleagues "will do more work" to get it right the next time.

Von der Porten couldn't wait to relay Blodget's comments to the SEC. "I am appalled that a prominent brokerage analyst would take such a strong position on a controversial—and critical—issue without having done the work to support his conclusions," he wrote in a February 21, 2001, letter. Within a few weeks, the NASD launched another inquiry, this time into both Merrill and Blodget. "Finally, I thought I had broken through to the bureaucracy," Von der Porten says.

But a few months later, Von der Porten discovered that regulators didn't have the stomach to deal with research conflicts at the big Wall Street firms. In his letter, Von der Porten provided investigators with a detailed account of Blodget's various mistakes and his hyped research on companies like Amazon that were frequent issuers of stocks and bonds. But on December 7, 2001, NASD senior supervisor Michael W. Hoffman wrote Von der Porten that the NASD had completed its review of Merrill and Blodget and "based on the assembled facts, the evidence does not, at this time, warrant the institution of disciplinary action."

With the NASD's letter in hand, Von der Porten went back to work managing money. For nearly two years, he had done what regulators with their vast resources and teams of investigators wouldn't do: Ask simple, obvious questions about what appeared to be flaws in the research published by some of the most reputable firms on Wall Street. Von der Porten stopped calling securities regulators with tips, but a year or so later, he was contacted by NASD officials who decided to take a second look at the issue. Von der Porten was invited to agency headquarters in Washington, D.C., ushered into a large conference room, and asked to provide his views on the problems with Wall Street research to about ten or so investigators suddenly eager to learn about the issue.

About halfway through the meeting, he abruptly stopped, and asked an obvious question: "What took you guys so long?" The answer, from one of the officials in the NASD's enforcement division, might actually be funny were it not for what it says about the quality of regulation during the 1990s stock-market bubble. "We didn't have someone on staff with the capability to analyze financial reports." Von der Porten just smiled.

• • •

While Levitt and his cohorts at the NASD and the NYSE may have been too incompetent or stymied by their connections to the brokerage industry to clean up Wall Street research, many of the other traditional political watchdogs were no better.

As the market soared during the 1990s, the brokerage industry cranked up its fundraising machine, targeting some of the market's most important lawmakers in charge of regulating the nation's securities industry. People like the liberal Democratic Senator Charles Schumer of New York, a key member of the Senate Banking Committee, and Michael Oxley, the conservative congressman from Ohio who headed the House Financial Services Committee, suddenly became strange bedfellows, receiving millions of dollars in campaign contributions from the street, and returning the favor by supporting the industry-friendly legislation. Schumer's record is particularly disturbing. He was one of the few Democrats to publicly oppose Levitt's effort to tighten standards on accounting, calling the proposal on auditor independence "a backwards way of doing things." One big incentive was money. Schumer received $4.3 million in campaign contributions between 1997 and 2000 from Wall Street firms and banks, and hundreds of thousands of dollars in contributions from accounting firms. Even Silicon Valley technology companies kicked into the Schumer war chest, a nod to both his pro-business voting record on various issues, and his relative silence on the growing evidence of abuse affecting small investors who continued to snap up risky high-tech stocks.

Levitt, meanwhile, left the SEC in early 2001 as the agency's longest-serving chairman, but he wasn't about go quietly. The stock market crash seemed to confirm all his warnings about Wall Street and its sleazy practices, which he blamed on Republicans who controlled Congress and bitterly opposed his reform agenda (ignoring, of course, the SEC's own inaction). In Philadelphia, during his last town hall meeting, Levitt asked people to say no to "trading systems or practices that favor brokers instead of their customers; to Internet frauds . . . and those who prey on the elderly by hawking high-risk securities; to analysts who never met a stock they didn't like; to regulators who take their eyes off the interests of investors, and politicians who care more about corporate interests than individual investors."

Levitt, himself, found a cushy job with the Carlyle Group, a white-shoe investment banking boutique where he could use his contacts on Wall Street and in Washington to make money, and sought to capitalize on his reputation as an investor advocate by writing a book about his years as SEC chairman. *Publishers Weekly* described the book, *Take On the Street*, as a "mini MBA course," a how-to guide for investors looking to make money and avoid Wall Street scams like conflicted research. But much like Levitt's tenure as SEC chairman, the book was long on the rhetoric and short on action. Levitt gave readers an overview of some of the scandals during the bubble years, from faulty accounting to conflicted research. There was just one problem: He failed to explain how all of these nasty things were able to flourish under his watch.

Left with Levitt's mess was Laura Unger, a former SEC commissioner, who was appointed interim chairman until the Bush White House could find a more seasoned person to fill the job. Well meaning and smart, Unger had labored under Levitt's leadership for several years, and took over at the worst possible time. The White House had imposed a "regulatory freeze," preventing the SEC from passing any new reforms at a time when the markets were reeling and investors were demanding answers. Not long afterward, Unger was given an order to trim the SEC's staff at a time when the commission should have been scouring the street for the people responsible for the massive losses investors suffered in the aftermath of the bubble. Unger tried to put the best spin on an impossible task, promising to continue Levitt's investor-focused agenda, but she encountered significant obstacles from nearly her first day, including inheriting a staff that didn't think she was qualified for the job.

It was in this vacuum of leadership that investors found another unusual ally.

Jake Zamansky had become an "investor advocate" not out of conviction, but out of necessity. A graduate of Temple University's law school, Zamansky wanted to make lots of money and live large by defending the owners of small "bucket shop" brokerage firms that operated on the fringes of Wall Street and were known for their unethical and often illegal sales practices. Zamansky loved his job so much that he left the white-shoe firm of Skadden, Arps, which frowned on his low-class client list, and teamed up with former NASD attorney Bill Singer to create one of the most successful bucket-shop practices in the country.

Zamansky's client list was a virtual who's who of the bucket-shop community, including its most notorious member, Stratton Oakmont Securities. For years, Zamansky had helped Stratton evade numerous regulatory probes and a flood of investor complaints that the firm was pumping out worthless stocks to unsuspecting investors. But his biggest victory for Stratton came in a libel suit Stratton filed against Prodigy Services, the operator of a popular financial bulletin board. Investors had posted scores of messages on the bulletin board referring to Stratton's brokerage activities as "criminal." As bad as Stratton was, prosecutors had yet to convict the firm of criminal securities fraud. That would come later. In the meantime, Zamansky claimed that Prodigy had slandered Stratton by refusing to remove the false and malicious messages. A judge ultimately forced Prodigy to remove the postings.

With his slick black hair and Armani suits, Zamansky resembled a cross between Senator Charles Schumer and actor Andy Garcia. Stratton's CEO called him "Jaws" for his ability to devour the competition and keep Stratton open through the early to mid 1990s despite the regulatory assault. But by early 2000, Zamansky's career had taken a sudden and nasty turn. The broad crackdown on the bucket shops had put many of his top clients, Stratton Oakmont included, out of business and their top executives in jail. Zamansky felt the pinch immediately. He began partying more, coming to the office late, and failing to bring in new clients. Singer warned Zamansky that he better generate business or start looking for another line of work. Zamansky asked for more time, but it wasn't long before Singer strolled into Zamansky's office flanked by three other partners and said, "We want you out." Zamansky begged for a second chance, but the best he could get was an agreement to use the office until he found a new job. That afternoon, Zamansky went home and drowned his sorrows in a bottle of vodka before falling asleep in front of the television, wishing it all was a dream.

Being fired from Singer was bad, but what was worse was the reception Zamansky received when he interviewed at other law firms: No one would touch him. It was one thing to hire a bucket-shop lawyer with clients, it was another thing to hire one who was fired for not bringing in enough new business. At one point, he thought about applying to the SEC, but what regulator would hire someone who represented some of the most sophisticated stock swindlers in history? These were the toughest times in Zamansky's career. With no work and few leads in sight, Zamansky decided to do something that would have made the boys at Stratton Oakmont cringe. He began to represent the little guy.

For years, Zamansky had weighed taking on cases from small investors, but Stratton proved too valuable a client to leave the dark side. Now he had no choice, and while his transition wasn't motivated by a higher calling other than the almighty dollar, Zamansky's timing was impeccable. The Internet bubble was running out of steam and customer complaints as measured by the number of arbitration cases filed were beginning to rise sharply, particularly after the NASDAQ crash in March 2000 exposed some of the high-pressure tactics used by brokers at big Wall Street firms to sell high-technology stocks.

Zamansky's game plan was to become the public face of the new investor anger toward the street. He hired a young attorney, Ted Glenn, to handle his arbitration cases and lawsuits, and began contacting newspaper reporters and television producers to promote his cases. By mid 2001, Zamansky had become a regular on CNBC, which had switched gears amid the market turmoil from promoting analysts who hyped the market to giving airtime to people like Zamansky, who hyped Wall Street's many sins. As Zamansky's name recognition grew, so did his roster of clients who said they were ripped off during the market bubble. By the end of 2000, Zamansky was back on his feet, paying his bills and enjoying his new life as one of Wall Street's leading ambulance chasers.

But Zamansky wanted more. His goal was to find the "right case and the perfect victim," a case so outrageous that it would underscore Wall Street's propensity to screw the most unsophisticated of the investing public, and take his public profile to a more respected level. Zamansky's search would take months. Many of the potential clients he came across had similar characteristics. While many were middle-income folks with little if any knowledge of investing, others openly embraced the mania that swept the markets, looking to make a quick buck by actively trading stocks as if they were professional money managers. They did have one thing in common. Almost all of the people he interviewed claimed to have been misled by unscrupulous brokers at major Wall Street firms who sold them stocks by plugging the knowledge and expertise of the superstar analysts.

It was around this time that Zamansky came across a document that described his defense of the Stratton Oakmont Securities back in the early 1990s. The crux of the government's case against Stratton was that its brokers were selling stocks they *knew* were fraudulent. Zamansky's defense was that brokers were selling these stocks based on the "opinions" of research analysts. "You can't go to jail over an opinion," Zamansky said at the time. He was, of course, proven wrong as the SEC closed down Stratton and prosecutors put many of its top officials in jail. But Zamansky's excuse was now being used by Wall Street in defense of its brokers for selling all those worthless tech stocks during the market bubble. It didn't work then, and, Zamansky believed, it wouldn't work now.

For the next month, Zamansky immersed himself in Wall Street research reports, spending weekends and long nights poring over the written words of top analysts, especially Grubman, Meeker, and Blodget. They had much in common; all were relentlessly bullish on the markets, turning even the most negative news into a positive for their favorite companies. For a time he considered suing all of them in a sweeping indictment of Wall Street research. But even a press hog like Zamansky knew better; for all the publicity such a suit would generate, eventually he would be overwhelmed by legal teams with limitless budgets. He decided to narrow his case to one analyst, though his selection process was far from scientific. Meeker, Zamansky reasoned, would make a horrible target because she was a woman and her reports contained too many caveats. Grubman, he thought, was too shrewd. "Why roll the dice on some smart Jew from Philly," he told Glenn (Zamansky, who is Jewish, also grew up in Philadelphia). But Blodget, with his Waspy looks and lightweight résumé, was different. "An empty suit with a British last name," Zamansky remarked. "He's the perfect target."

Now all he needed was the perfect victim. A telephone call in halting English solved the next part of the puzzle. Debasis Kanjilal, the forty-six-year-old pediatrician from Queens, told Zamansky he lost his children's college savings by listening to his Merrill Lynch broker who relied on Blodget's research. "My broker said Henry's the best," Kanjilal told Zamansky. That apparently was enough for Kanjilal to dump nearly $500,000 into shares of two technology stocks, including an Internet company called Infospace that had traded as high as $120 a share, but was now hovering at $3. Zamansky knew he had a winner when he visited Kanjilal at his modest apartment in Jackson Heights, the epicenter of New York's Indian community. Over a dinner of naan bread and chicken curry, Kanjilal told Zamansky how he came to the country in search of a better life for his family, two teenage children and his wife, and how it was being derailed through the greed of a Wall Street broker and the flimsy research of Henry Blodget. He spoke about how long it took to save all the money he had earned through his years as a doctor here and in India, where he volunteered his time to help the poor, even receiving a letter of commendation from Mother Teresa, which was hung proudly on his shelf.

Zamansky sat and listened as dollar signs danced in his head.

Zamansky ordered Glenn to start research on an arbitration claim against Michael Healy (Kanjilal's broker), Henry Blodget, and Merrill Lynch itself. Zamansky knew that to win he needed more than the obvious conflict of Blodget issuing positive research on a Merrill banking client. His order to Glenn was to find a smoking gun. Glenn said it wouldn't be easy. The big Wall Street firms, after all, had always been good at covering their tracks on such matters and Zamansky didn't have the resources to scour the globe for dirt on Blodget. Zamansky received some more bad news after turning to several attorneys for advice on how to proceed. They told him to drop it, Zamansky recalls. "I just don't see a case," said Jeffrey Liddle, the lawyer who won an $800,000 settlement for former Merrill analyst Suzanne Cook several years earlier by attacking the firm's research practices. Liddle thought Zamansky would find it difficult to prove that Blodget's ratings were anything but an "opinion," which is protected under the First Amendment. Another lawyer suggested that Zamansky check his malpractice insurance because Blodget would likely countersue for defamation after Zamansky failed to provide reasonable proof that the Internet guru had issued fraudulent ratings.

Zamansky spent the weekend at a friend's house in East Hampton weighing the possibilities. Without naming Blodget, he had a strong case of a broker stuffing "unsuitable" investments into Kanjilal's portfolio. He began to have second thoughts about a broad case that included Blodget, but his reticence didn't last long. For all the gains he had made over the past year, he was still working out of one of Singer's offices, still trying to take his law practice to the next level. With the public outraged over Wall Street's activities during the 1990s bubble growing by the day, Zamansky knew that if there was ever a time in history to take on the big firms, this was it.

If Zamansky had any further doubts, they disappeared after Glenn discovered several crucial pieces of evidence. At the same time that Blodget was pushing shares of Infospace, the market for Internet stocks was tanking, but the company had begun negotiations to purchase another Internet company named Go2Net.com. The deal was complex; instead of paying cash for the company, Infospace bought the other company with its own stock. But what made the whole thing so suspect, Glenn pointed out, was that Merrill was Go2Net's adviser on the deal. As a result, Merrill, and in his view Blodget, had a strong incentive to hype shares of Infospace. If Merrill let shares of Infospace crater, Go2Net would likely call the whole thing off as the price of the deal fell, reducing the profit from the transaction.

But Glenn said he wasn't through. He also found that Blodget's research appeared to be targeted to key points during Infospace's negotiations with Go2Net. In fact, Blodget had issued a positive "booster shot" report on Infospace only a day after Merrill was selected to represent Go2Net as its merger adviser. After seeing all the evidence, Zamansky was thrilled. "Let's see Blodget sue me for defamation now," he said.

On March 1, 2001, Zamansky filed an arbitration case on behalf of Kanjilal against Merrill, Blodget, and Michael Healy. He alerted *The Wall Street Journal*, which published a story on the case inside its Money & Investing section. Zamansky alleged that at the time Kanjilal's broker and Blodget were pushing Infospace stock, Merrill had been hired as a financial adviser to Go2Net.com, which was targeted as a possible Infospace acquisition. He said Blodget's recommendation "lacked a reasonable basis in fact and Blodget failed to disclose serious conflicts of interest with the company whose stock he was touting." Merrill issued a simple statement that Zamansky's case was "totally without merit," and vowed to fight it to the end. In an interview, Blodget was cool and collected. The fallen Internet guru who had seen his stock picks and reputation crash with the rest of the market, described the charges as "a lot of Monday morning quarterbacking," and compared Infospace to other viable companies that faced skeptics amid the crash. As for his research practices, Blodget denied there was any link between his research and Merrill's banking business. "The only way to succeed is to create the highest level of integrity and credibility," he said.

Inside Merrill, however, the case was stirring up a storm. Blodget said he didn't know about the Go2Net acquisition when he issued his July 11

Infospace report, but documents show that someone in his group may have. Sofia Ghachem, a member of Blodget's Internet research team, had been involved with helping Merrill's bankers get banking business from Infospace since at least May, when she took the company on a "non deal road show to introduce its new CEO," Arun Sarin. In an email, she called Infospace "very important to us from a banking perspective."

To believe Blodget didn't know about the Infospace's banking objectives would mean that the merger negotiations involving Merrill began immediately after the report was issued, and Ghachem wasn't involved any time before. Even Mary Meeker scoffed at Blodget's explanation when she read it in *The Wall Street Journal*. Morgan was Infospace's adviser on the Go2Net deal, and Meeker believed Merrill was playing dirty to get around "quiet period restrictions," having Blodget issue the report in his name, but using an analyst on his team to work directly with bankers. If Blodget was directly involved he could never have issued the booster shot report, she said. "I could have never gotten away with what they did," Meeker complained to someone on her staff, noting how Morgan's compliance department prevented a Morgan rating to be issued until after the merger was completed. (A Merrill spokesman denies Meeker's assertion, saying both Blodget and Ghachem were not involved in the merger negotiations until July 21, a few weeks after Blodget's report.)

Zamansky didn't buy Blodget's explanation either, particularly after he subpoenaed and received a document from Infospace showing that Merrill stood to make about $17 million if the deal was completed, and that Blodget's research was a key selling point in Merrill's deal pitch to Go2Net. Armed with this information, Zamansky reached out to Merrill to start settlement talks. Merrill refused. The firm's huge PR department, one of the biggest on Wall Street, quietly began to bash Zamansky's reputation with other lawyers as someone who operated on the fringes of the legal community. Merrill's legal strategy was simple: Bury Zamansky in motions and paperwork and attack his credibility. Zamansky, the company believed, didn't have the stomach or the resources to go head-to-head with the massive Merrill legal and public relations team. "Jake, you're not getting a dime from us," one of Merrill's outside lawyers said. "This is just another arbitration."

But Merrill misjudged both the public's discontent with Wall Street research and the feistiness of its adversary. In the weeks ahead, Zamansky peddled his lawsuit to television news shows and newspapers across

the country. Just as Blodget became a household name hyping stocks during the bubble, Zamansky soon became one of the key spokesmen for the
bubble's victims. The story picked up additional steam as Congress
began demanding answers from the brokerage industry. Representative
Richard Baker, a Republican from Louisiana, decided to hold hearings on
analysts' conflicts. Baker suspected he had hit a nerve when, after announcing his plans to hold hearings on research, he received angry calls
from Wall Street analysts, saying the entire controversy was "old news"
and not worth his time. As Baker delved into the issue, looking at press
accounts of analysts' conflicts, his interest grew, and Zamansky did his
best to make sure Baker stayed with the program. A lifelong Republican,
Zamansky used his contacts in Washington to get a sit-down with
Baker's staff and explain how Wall Street used conflicted research to win
banking business and mislead small investors. Zamansky was amazed by
how little these young men and women knew about Wall Street and the
issue that Baker was making a national priority. Even more bizarre was
their almost knee-jerk response that the Wall Street firms were good and
all trial lawyers were evil bloodsuckers looking to increase their billable
hours. "All some of these kids wanted was a cushy job working on Wall
Street," Zamansky would later remark.

With Baker ramping up his investigation, Merrill was now in a state of
turmoil. In June 2001, Blodget brought on more controversy after he
downgraded shares of GoTo.com, another Internet company (not connected to Go2Net) to a "neutral" from "accumulate." What made the
move so unusual was not just that Blodget had downgraded the stock,
but that it came after Merrill lost an underwriting assignment to CSFB. It
was one thing to hype the stock of a banking client, a practice virtually ignored by regulators. But it was quite another to issue a retaliatory downgrade that could have a material impact on a company's financial
condition if enough investors sold shares.

When Merrill's PR department received a call from *The Wall Street
Journal* about the downgrade, the firm launched an all-out effort to kill
the story. Blodget declined to comment, but his boss, Merrill research
chief Andrew Melnick, flanked by several company attorneys, agreed to a
face-to-face meeting with the *Journal* to make their case. The meeting
lasted about two hours as Melnick and a lawyer who worked in the research department provided their version of Blodget's work on
GoTo.com. Melnick underscored the fact that at Merrill analysts aren't

paid on a deal-by-deal basis (what Melnick didn't say was that under the system he created, analysts were asked to submit proof of all their banking work when the company doled out year-end bonuses) and that Blodget wasn't involved in banking GoTo.com. Still, there was one question for which Merrill had no good answer: When was the last time Blodget actually issued a "sell" rating on a stock? In fact he hadn't, not once since he joined Merrill.

The *Wall Street Journal* story was published on June 13, just as the Baker subcommittee was taking testimony from various industry officials, including those at the Securities Industry Association, Wall Street's top lobbying group. Zamansky recalls sitting in the audience during the hearings, listening to one congressman taking testimony from SIA chief Marc Lackritz. The congressman read aloud the "lead" or introductory paragraph of the *Journal*'s story questioning whether Blodget's downgrade of the stock was just a "coincidence." As Zamansky remembers it, Lackritz "didn't know what to say."

Neither did Merrill as Zamansky took to the airwaves, pumping the story to greater heights. "We can't keep up with the Zamansky PR machine," one flack at Merrill complained. At Merrill, the man on the spot was George Schieren, the firm's veteran attorney, who had had a long and distinguished career fighting and settling various legal cases filed against the firm. With the media firestorm over Blodget's research growing by the day, Schieren knew this case was one that needed to be settled.

In mid June, Zamansky was sitting in his office planning for a television appearance when the call came in. "Jake, we ought to sit down and talk," said Gerald Rath, Merrill's outside counsel.

Within a couple weeks, Merrill made its offer: a $400,000 payment (Zamansky kept one-third) and a confidentiality agreement, meaning Zamansky couldn't comment on the specifics of the settlement. Zamansky agreed to the settlement and the secrecy. "Don't worry, you can trust me," he added.

But details quickly leaked, first to *The Wall Street Journal* and then throughout the Wall Street media establishment. Far from putting the controversy to rest, the settlement gave the story legs. Legal experts soon portrayed the settlement as an admission of guilt that would ignite a flood of lawsuits from aggrieved investors who claimed they were misled by faulty research. Only a few months before, Zamansky could barely pay his rent. Now he was a media star as the case got worldwide attention.

His family in Israel read about his exploits in the *Jerusalem Post* and his girlfriend gushed as she watched Zamansky attack sleazy research on *Good Morning America*.

Conflicted research had become the hottest financial news story of the year. The superstar analysts themselves told associates they were being scapegoated for the Internet bubble. Threatening letters and emails began to pour into Wall Street from Middle America. One analyst even went so far as to hire a bodyguard after several threats. Like any good politician looking to increase his profile, Baker seized on the public's anger by holding more hearings, and ignoring the requests of the securities industry to put the matter to rest. The big Wall Street firms were in an uproar. Over the long bull market, firms such as Merrill Lynch had funneled millions of dollars in contributions to the full committee's chairman, Mike Oxley, to protect themselves against the type of negative publicity he was dishing out. But Baker saw little downside in letting Wall Street twist just a little while longer, despite Oxley's ties to the brokerage industry. At one point, Baker even toyed with compelling Grubman, Blodget, and Meeker to explain their actions, but he ultimately backed down, and instead issued an invitation for them to defend their research. All three declined.

Baker turned up the heat in other ways. When the SIA issued a set of best practices, Baker was quick to dismiss the actions as too little too late, and raised the possibility of legislation to enact reforms. The SIA responded with a message to Baker's chief spokesman Michael DiResto. One morning while DiResto was in his office in Baton Rouge, his phone rang. It was a lobbyist from the SIA, who wasted little time issuing a warning: "This is going to hurt Baker's fundraising." DiResto asked if "this was a threat." The lobbyist said it wasn't, just the reality of being a congressman who relies on Wall Street for money. But when DiResto passed on the message, Baker wasn't swayed. "I'm not that much of a fundraiser, anyway," he said with a laugh.

The SEC, sensitive to all the publicity generated by the issue, finally pursued its own inquiry, ratcheting up the pressure on Wall Street even more. Except for Levitt's ineffectual speaking tour, the SEC had taken no action in the area of research conflicts, and the agency's lack of attention was now being blamed for the huge losses suffered by investors. Unger, still the acting chair, directed her staff to launch a probe of analyst activities. The investigation was headed by Lori Richards, a long-time SEC official, who focused on eight firms and whether analysts hyped stocks in their reports that they also owned.

The investigation's focus demonstrated just how little the commission's staff really understood about the way Wall Street research worked during the bubble years. Of course, many analysts owned stocks, and the incentive to hype their own holdings was huge. But the benefits seemed to pale in comparison to the huge bonuses analysts pulled down during the bubble years by using their research to help their firms win banking assignments.

Even so, Unger boasted that Richards had discovered solid evidence of widespread improprieties. Speaking before Congress, Unger said many top Wall Street firms paid "their analysts largely based upon the profitability of the investment banking unit," while bankers had direct "input into analysts' bonuses." Whatever Chinese Wall separating banking and research previously existed had been obliterated during the market boom, Unger explained. Six of the eight firms under examination provided companies with prior notice when making a rating change.

But the most damaging revelation, at least as far as the SEC was concerned, involved analysts' personal involvement with companies they had rated. During the bubble, analysts had the opportunity to invest in start-up companies before they went public, and "always issued positive research on the company," she said. Several analysts sold stocks in their own portfolio that they rated a "buy" to the public. Unger cited one particularly egregious act in which one analyst, according to Richards's examination, had "shorted" a stock (hoping it would go down in value) while urging investors through his research to buy shares. It was an explosive charge. For years analysts had been suspected of boosting shares of companies that they owned in their personal portfolio. Now an analyst thought so little of his own research that he actually bet against himself.

Unger stopped short of saying the SEC was ready to file charges anytime soon. "It's something we're taking a close look at," is all she would say, adding that the self-regulatory agencies should enact tougher guidelines and promising a more detailed investigation by her staff in the coming weeks. One could only hope.

CHAPTER TEN

The Accidental Attorney General

Little did Unger know that the SEC's long-held reputation as Wall Street's top cop was about to be put to the ultimate test by an unlikely source. In 1998, Eliot Spitzer, a thirty-nine-year-old Democrat, was elected New York State attorney general by a razor-thin margin over the Republican incumbent Dennis Vacco in a state where Democrats outnumber Republicans two to one. Spitzer, it should be noted, said all the right things. He ran as a New Democrat, on a platform that supported the stuff that made Bill Clinton unbeatable as president: gun control, environmental issues, and the death penalty.

But Spitzer's campaign reeked like an old Democratic precinct house. During the race, he was embroiled in a nasty fundraising scandal after he failed to disclose that his father, a Manhattan real estate developer, had loaned him millions of dollars to finance his campaign. The move had so angered the *New York Times* editorial staff that it grudgingly endorsed Spitzer only after attacking his "dishonesty" and "evasions," calling him the best choice of "two flawed candidates."

But the ultimate indignity for Spitzer came a bit later, when political wonks around the state began referring to him as the "accidental attorney general." Vacco, as it turns out, only lost the election because he refused to accept the nomination of the state's tiny "Right-to-Life" party, which would have given him the margin of victory.

Initially, Spitzer did little to change the general perception he didn't deserve the job. Many in the state's Democratic Party establishment regarded him as a political opportunist, a "limousine Liberal," who bought the election by doing anything he could to get ahead. Minority politicians in the state openly criticized Spitzer for not appointing enough African

Americans or Latinos to prominent positions. Spitzer, the conventional wisdom went, was a young man going nowhere fast.

But Spitzer's detractors had severely underestimated his political skill and ambition to advance his career. As a prosecutor for the Manhattan district attorney's office in the early 1990s, Spitzer had displayed a knack for finding cases that would generate career-advancing publicity. His successful prosecution of the Gambino crime family landed him numerous newspaper citations. When he took over at the AG's office, he began looking for similar headline-grabbing material, but to do so, he needed to infuse the AG's office with new blood. He immediately began beefing up the office's legal staff by hiring seasoned investigators from the Justice Department, like Dieter Snell, who served as a prosecutor during the World Trade Center bombing, and others from his old stomping grounds in the Manhattan district attorney's office.

Most important, Spitzer dusted off a valuable weapon in addressing white-collar crime, an obscure but powerful state law known as the Martin Act, which gave his office tremendous leverage in pursuing corporate criminals. Unlike federal laws, under which investigators must allege "intent" to file criminal charges, the Martin Act requires nothing more than an appearance of criminal intentions, such as an undisclosed conflict of interest. Spitzer found that just the threat of a Martin Act prosecution was enough to get his targets to the table and begin settlement discussions. Just weeks after taking office, Spitzer announced a crackdown on cable television companies that he said would increase competition and lower rates for consumers. Later he headed a task force to reform the prizefighting business, and created a new unit to crack down on violence at abortion clinics. As more and more investors began using computers to make stock trades, Spitzer made his first foray onto the turf of the Securities and Exchange Commission and opened up an investigation into possible fraud in the booming online investing industry. He even took a shot at Wall Street bucket-shop brokerage firms, then being prosecuted and regulated by the U.S. attorney's office and the SEC, by indicting fraudulent stockbrokers.

Spitzer seemed to be making all the right moves. At one point he tapped into a family friend, famed political consultant Dick Morris (Morris's dad and Spitzer's are friends), for some advice. Spitzer says that during their lunch meetings, he and Morris spoke mostly about local and national politics. Perhaps, but when Spitzer turned his attention to Wall

Street corruption that many believed was the root cause of the stock market bubble that hurt so many average people, his political timing couldn't have been better.

For the past ten years, publications like *The Wall Street Journal* and *The New York Times* and *Fortune* magazine regularly featured average people who benefited from the long bull market: barbers, mechanics, and housewives who became millionaires overnight by investing in technology stocks and mutual funds pumped during the bubble. Now that the party was over, Spitzer became intrigued by the victims of Wall Street's unabashed bullishness. The cases were there, he told his staff. It was just the matter of finding the right ones.

In late 2000, Eric Dinallo, who ran Spitzer's investor-protection office, thought he found exactly what Spitzer was looking for. Dinallo was a native New Yorker with short black hair, an athletic build, and an unquenchable appetite for old comic books, particularly anything involving Spider Man. He graduated from New York University law school, spent time in private practice, before taking a job with the office of Manhattan District Attorney Robert Morgenthau, where he got his first taste of prosecuting white-collar crime. His biggest case was a 174-count indictment against A.R. Baron, a small brokerage firm accused of defrauding investors out of tens of millions of dollars. The case received nationwide publicity because it nearly ensnared one of Wall Street's biggest players, Bear Stearns, which "cleared" or processed many of the suspect trades.

Bear ultimately escaped criminal prosecution, but Dinallo earned points as a tireless worker who wasn't afraid to go up against major Wall Street players. He had another thing going for him when he applied for the job as the AG's new investor-protection czar: His knowledge of the Martin Act.

Before Dinallo interviewed with Spitzer, he spent a week reading up on the Martin Act, tracing its roots to a former state legislator, Francis J. Martin, who in the 1920s sponsored the law as an effective anticorruption tool to crack down on corporate fraud. Dinallo reminded Spitzer that until the mid to late 1970s, the Martin Act had made the state AG one of the most powerful corporate crime fighters in America, but as Dinallo explained, in recent years the office had all but forgotten that the law existed, and its reputation had suffered. Spitzer must have liked what he heard. A few days later, Dinallo was offered the job, and it wasn't long before he became one of Spitzer's favorites. Around the office, Spitzer referred to Dinallo as "The Hammer" for ramping up the investor-protection department's productivity, including thirty-three criminal convictions for securities fraud during his first two years in the job. The cases were good, Dinallo knew, but none of them were particularly memorable. That would change after a conversation with his father, Greg Dinallo, a screenwriter and an active investor. The elder Dinallo had been getting calls from his broker about stocks, but only those that the firm's in-house analysts had recommended. He couldn't understand why their sales pitches had been so limited.

Dinallo did some digging, and came across several newspaper stories that described the practice of Wall Street firms hyping stocks of companies that are also investment banking clients. In a memo to Spitzer, Dinallo asked to be given the green light to launch a formal investigation. "A recent *New York Times* article reported that many analysts at investment banking firms have a conflict of interest that prevents them from making sell recommendations or otherwise negatively evaluating companies they follow." He told Spitzer that his investigators "intend to look into this alleged practice, which if it is not being disclosed, could be a significant fraudulent practice."

Spitzer understood the issue well. No stranger to Wall Street, he often bragged that "30 to 40 percent" of the people he went to law school with either worked at a hedge fund, an investment house, or as a lawyer on Wall Street. In early 2001, Spitzer began quizzing some of his friends about Dinallo's research idea. The responses were strikingly similar: Everybody on Wall Street knew that research was utterly conflicted and corrupt. The problem was that most investors didn't have the foggiest idea what was going on behind their backs. He gave Dinallo the green light to proceed.

Dinallo's initial focus was on two firms—Merrill and his old friends at Bear Stearns. Dinallo had friends that worked in both law departments, so he believed these were the best places to start the probe. Another investigator in Spitzer's office said the firms were chosen for a different reason. Bear Stearns, rightly or wrongly, had a reputation among regulators as a firm that regularly bent the rules to win business, while Merrill was considered among the most reputable firms on Wall Street. What better way to dramatize analysts' conflicts than by contrasting the best with the worst?

Initially, Dinallo issued subpoenas to Merrill and Bear Stearns that focused on their use of positive research to win Initial Public Offerings from high-tech companies. But this approach hit an immediate snag. Neither Merrill nor Bear Stearns were big underwriters of Internet IPOs, although thanks to Blodget's positive research, Merrill handled many other types of technology financings, including mergers and secondary offerings.

Then, on a sweltering day in mid June, Dinallo caught a break. He was riding on the uptown No. 6 subway and reading *The Wall Street Journal* when he came across the story discussing Blodget's downgrade of an Internet company called GoTo.com (unrelated to Go2Net). Despite Merrill's reputation for fair dealing, the story alleged that Blodget had issued a retaliatory downgrade, slashing its rating of the company only after Merrill was rejected as an underwriter on an upcoming stock deal. The story also said that the research conflicts with Blodget ran deeper than one stock. It pointed to the lawsuit filed by lawyer Jacob Zamansky on behalf of a Merrill brokerage customer Debasis Kanjilal, who alleged that he was misled by Blodget into buying shares of Infospace. Blodget, the lawsuit stated, had hyped the stock to help Merrill serve as an adviser on Infospace's acquisition of another company, Go2Net, and earn a $17 million banking fee.

Dinallo wasted little time jumping on the story. The following day, he ordered his top deputies to subpoena Merrill for documents concerning the GoTo.com and Infospace ratings, including email conversations between Blodget and his colleagues. Merrill had closely guarded documents like emails between employees as confidential communications, and had recently blocked Zamansky's request for the emails. But the firm had no such leverage when faced with a subpoena from a major criminal prosecutor, and within a few days boxes of emails showed up at Dinallo's office in downtown Manhattan.

As the case became a top priority, Dinallo put together a team of seasoned prosecutors, including Gary Connor, a longtime investigator in the AG's office, Patricia Cheng, as well as Bruce Topman and Roger Waldman, another investigator in his office. One of his first moves was to contact Zamansky. That chore fell to Connor, who asked for a briefing on his now famous lawsuit. Zamansky loved the attention, but he told Connor that a confidentiality agreement prevented him from discussing the matter unless the AG's office made a special request. "Send me a subpoena and I'll tell you everything I know."

Connor agreed, and a few days later, he called on Zamansky, this time with a subpoena for information about his case in hand. Zamansky, as Connor soon discovered, had clearly done his homework. Over the past six months, he had interviewed dozens of bankers, investors, and analysts, including Tom Brown, the former DLJ researcher who claimed that he was fired from the company after criticizing a banking client. He even met with Jonathan Cohen, the bearish former Internet analyst who was replaced by Blodget after the famous $400 Amazon call. In laying out his case against Merrill and Blodget, Zamansky explained the relationship between investment banking and research, how a positive recommendation from one of the superstar analysts was like money in the bank when underwriting business was on the line.

Zamansky also tried to show how the fraud wasn't confined to Merrill or Blodget. He crunched some interesting numbers: Out of eight thousand stock recommendations, he said, less than four-tenths of 1 percent or twenty-nine ratings were sells. What was even more staggering was that the firms had maintained this level of hype even in the face of sliding markets and continued investor losses. At one point, Zamansky pulled out one of the few documents he was able to secure from Merrill as part of his lawsuit. Merrill had stonewalled his request for Blodget's emails, but one memo, he believed, laid out the dimensions of the fraud. It showed Merrill's financial gain in the Infospace/Go2Net merger. Merrill would receive $17 million, "payable in cash" after the deal closed, according to the document.

"Without Blodget's buy recommendation on the stock, Merrill leaves $17 million on the table," Zamansky recalls saying. "There's no way they allow him to do anything but issue a 'buy.' "

Zamansky says he remembers Connor's reaction: "That's amazing," Connor said. Zamansky, not known for understatement, agreed. "It's the greatest fraud ever."

With his stock research being called into question on a daily basis, Blodget had certainly seen better days. But things for the former King of the Internet were about to go from bad to worse. In July 2001, Spitzer had approved Dinallo's request to launch a wide-ranging investigation into research conflicts at Merrill Lynch, focusing on two of Blodget's most recent and controversial calls: Infospace and GoTo.com. Blodget, for the first time in his career, was subpoenaed to testify in a case where he was the target of the probe.

For Merrill the stakes were huge. Federal regulators like SEC or the self-regulatory organizations like the NASD can file only civil charges against firms or individuals. Spitzer had the power to indict both Blodget and, more troubling, the firm itself, and Merrill's lawyers knew no major securities company had ever survived a criminal prosecution.

When Blodget arrived at Spitzer's office at 120 Broadway in Manhattan to give his deposition, he must have felt as though he were in another world. With its drab industrial décor, Spitzer's offices were nothing like the posh surroundings Blodget had grown accustomed to a few blocks west in Merrill's World Financial Center headquarters. The furniture was vintage 1970s, produced by New York State prisoners. The walls were decorated with cheesy posters. Over a small kitchenette outside Dinallo's office hung an ominous sign: "Do not use toaster oven when the shredder is on."

Dinallo assigned Bruce Topman to lead the Blodget questioning on GoTo.com. A small, aggressive man with thinning hair and a black belt in karate, Topman had spent twenty-five years in private practice, much of it as a litigator specializing in corporate law for the firm of Webster & Sheffield. There he met Roger Waldman, also a partner at the firm. The two became friends, and when Waldman, who was active in the state Democratic Party, took a senior-level post with the new Democratic attorney general, Topman decided to take a job as well. "What did I have to lose," he would later remark. "My kids were grown, I didn't need the money, and I could at least have some fun."

Topman and Waldman made a great team. While Waldman's style was understated and polite, Topman often assumed the role of office attack dog, and Blodget looked like fresh meat. Topman was most interested in Blodget's explanation for the series of emails in which he denigrated stocks that had higher public ratings. A particularly enticing email was the one in which Blodget appeared to have a simple three-word answer for executives at GoTo.com when Merrill was rejected as an underwriter: "Beautiful, fuk em." A few moments later, Blodget downgraded the stock. In Topman's mind, those three words were the best evidence yet that Merrill and Blodget had used negative research to retaliate against the company for choosing another underwriter.

On Wall Street, Blodget had been widely regarded as a lightweight, someone whose knowledge of finance was as deep as the shaky companies he hyped. But as Topman would discover, that wasn't the person who showed up for the deposition. Blodget came to Spitzer's office knowledgeable about the business, and more important, well prepared to sidestep key questions about his conduct, claiming he couldn't recall events that had occurred just weeks before the deposition took place. On the subject of investment banking, Blodget was his cagey best. Investment banking had been just one factor in determining his pay, he said, explaining that when he did work with bankers, he was little more than an adviser on the company's strategy and finances. The way Blodget described it, Merrill had tough rules separating research and investment banking, and for the most part, he knew little about the firm's overall investment banking activities.

When Blodget was asked about his downgrade of GoTo.com, he described the call as "one of his best," an example of unbiased research on a company that could be back in the market at any time. As for the controversy surrounding the downgrade, he pointed the finger at the *Wall Street Journal* story and a competitor, CSFB's aggressive technology banking team, which served as the deal's lead underwriter. CSFB was embroiled in its own messy scandal involving charges that lead tech banker Frank Quattrone had demanded that some investors pay huge commissions in exchange for hot IPOs (Quattrone was not charged but CSFB was forced to pay $100 million to settle the case), so in Blodget's mind, they were the likely source of the leak.

Topman couldn't have cared less about press leaks. At one point, he asked Blodget if he recalled a press release that GoTo.com issued announcing the underwriters for the deal where Merrill was excluded. "I don't remember," Blodget responded. Topman was incredulous. "We're talking less than two months ago here, you don't remember whether you ever saw the press release?" Blodget said that while he didn't recall ever seeing the press release, one of his junior analysts could have told him about the decision. When asked if he had any "conversations" with executives at GoTo.com about the deal between May 18 and the time of his downgrade in June, Blodget said, "Not that I recall." Topman asked him, "How come you don't remember?" But Blodget corrected him. "I didn't say I didn't remember, what I said was I don't recall any conversations." He then explained there could have been other forms of communication with company officials that had nothing to do with the deal.

If the deposition had been a boxing match, Blodget would have been way ahead on points. But Topman had much more in his arsenal than was immediately apparent. As part of his document request, Topman had discovered that Blodget was invited to a dinner in mid May with bankers and GoTo.com executives who earlier in the day met with officials at Merrill's headquarters. Though Blodget didn't attend the dinner, he did help the bankers introduce GoTo.com's executives to the firm's institutional sales force, where he discussed his upbeat assessment of the stock. When confronted about the meetings, Blodget described them as nothing unusual. Yet Blodget's little seminar helped the firm achieve the desired results. Even in a bear market for Internet stocks, GoTo.com jumped about $3 after the Merrill meetings.

Blodget's close involvement with bankers suggested that he was more in the loop than he was letting on about the banking aspects of his work. Topman then seized on another important hole in his story. Blodget testified that he had no idea that Merrill had been booted from the GoTo.com deal when he downgraded the company's stock. But the date of his rating change was suspicious. On May 25 one of the analysts in his group, Edward McCabe, wrote a draft downgrade of GoTo.com shares and emailed the report to Blodget. That was the same day Merrill's bankers received word they weren't in the deal.

"The reason you did it was because you had learned that Merrill Lynch might not become the book manager?" Topman asked. "Absolutely not," Blodget shot back.

That's when Topman produced another email from Andrew Siegel, one of the bankers responsible for GoTo, to Tom Mazzucco, another banker on the GoTo team. In it, Siegel told Mazzucco he was "very dismayed" to learn Merrill didn't get the deal, given Blodget's "leadership" in launching coverage on the stock, and more recently promoting the company to "Merrill's sales force . . . which dramatically moved the stock price." Topman asked if that refreshed his memory of being told of the lost business before the downgrade. Again, Blodget held his ground—he had no recollection of GoTo.com's decision to exclude Merrill. Topman asked Blodget to "note the date and time of that" email. Blodget did, and Topman handed the analyst another email, sent from Edward McCabe the same day, but several hours later, at 5:01 P.M.

"H, I don't think I downgraded the stock on valuation since the mid 1990's."

Again, Blodget said he didn't recall the email, which was only two months old. That's when Topman handed him his reply email sent two minutes later: "Beautiful, fuk em'."

"Mr. Blodget, was your response to the downgrade by Mr. McCabe 'beautiful, fuk em'?" Topman asked.

For the first time during the many hours of depositions he had given, Blodget appeared flummoxed. "Just a second, could you repeat the question?" he asked. Topman did, asking him if his response to McCabe was as it appears in the email. Blodget responded, amazingly, that he didn't make that statement. Topman was astounded. "Did you write the response that we have on this exhibit," Topman asked. "Who are you fucking?"

Blodget's answer: It was all a joke. Since "the response was spelled F-U-K, E-M," not the proper spelling for either fuck or them, it was clear he was "being tongue in cheek . . ." In any event, the target of the fucking wasn't GoTo.com over its decision not to include Merrill in the stock underwriting, Blodget pointed out, but all those people who "complained that we are doing what some institutional investors think [Wall Street analysts are] not supposed to do, which is downgrade stocks based on valuation." But Topman wasn't buying it. "Mr. Blodget, isn't it a fact that the only reason you were doing GoTo and rating it was for banking fees and no other reasons." This time Blodget was emphatic. "No" is all he said.

Topman decided to turn up the pressure a few more notches. He handed Blodget another email exchange, this one from John Faig, a money manager for American Express, who asked Blodget in a January 11 email, around the same time Blodget was ready to promote shares of the company, an obvious question for sophisticated investors. "What's so interesting about GOTO except banking fees????"

Blodget's one-word response spoke volumes: "Nothin."

To Topman, the combination of the two emails was devastating. Unlike small investors who bought shares through their broker and had no contact with analysts, Faig's position made him very important to people like Blodget. He traded millions of dollars of tech stocks on a daily basis, and part of Blodget's annual bonus was tied to how many trades these investors placed through Merrill. Sensing his client was getting into deep trouble, Sandy Winer, Blodget's lawyer, offered an explanation: "Could you ask him if he was serious or not?" Topman said the statement spoke for itself. "I don't see how there could be an explanation.

"Is Mr. Faig a client?" Topman continued. Blodget said he was. Faig was a client he had known for two years. They "had a relationship," Blodget added, and Faig had a "good sense of humor," adding "I think I have a reasonable sense of humor" as well. The email was a "kind of funny note from a client that I sent a funny note back."

Topman wasn't laughing. Just before the end of his testimony, Blodget requested some time to address his accusers. "I sense a significant amount of skepticism in terms of what I was testifying or some of the theories I was espousing or what have you," he said, before speaking about his "credibility" and "integrity" in the marketplace. "What people most respect is people who are right," he added, and in retrospect GoTo.com had performed much as Blodget had said it would, falling along with the rest of the market. "Retaliating against a company for not choosing Merrill Lynch as an underwriter would be absolutely moronic from a reputation point of view, from a message point of view, from a point of view where this GoTo is a viable company that they will probably do banking business with in the future."

Later, Blodget seemed to be convinced he had dodged a bullet. The entire affair, he believed, was a witch-hunt and he made a convenient target, though he conceded in an earlier email to a former analyst in his group, Kirsten Campbell, that "some of the communication with the [GoTo.com] people and bankers prior to the initiation may have been a technical violation of the firm's written policies and procedures." Blodget, however, was far from admitting guilt. The Merrill lawyers told him that whatever he and his staff did on the GoTo.com deal "is no big deal." As for the case that started it all—the lawsuit brought by Zamansky on behalf of Debasis Kanjilal, and the controversy surrounding Merrill's $400,000 settlement—Blodget said the matter "was totally misrepresented by the press."

"I was dismissed from the case [i.e., exonerated]," Blodget added. "The decision to settle was still mystifying to me given that we hadn't done anything wrong, but it is what it is." Campbell, whose duties included research on GoTo.com, was preparing to speak to Spitzer's deputies as well. "There's nothing to be concerned about," Blodget wrote, offering to talk with Campbell "prior to the meeting" if she needed any advice. If not, "have fun with the lawyers, and don't worry about it. (I was scared to death in the beginning, but have since learned that these things happen all the time.) Look forward to having lunch at some point. H."

But his comments to Campbell were well off the mark. It wouldn't be long before Blodget was out of a job, and his book deal to describe the Internet bubble was stymied by a confidentiality agreement he had signed in exchange for his multimillion-dollar severance. Even without hearing Campbell's testimony, Topman heard enough from Blodget to convince him that he had a strong case against Merrill, Blodget, and possibly his entire Internet research team for misleading investors with fraudulent research.

Except for Blodget, Zamansky, and the lawyers at Merrill, the full extent of the Spitzer investigation remained a secret throughout the summer even as the SEC continued with its own inquiry into research conflicts. SEC examinations chief Lori Richards briefed Unger about her most explosive finding: An unnamed analyst at a well-known firm had "shorted" a stock that he recommended as a "buy" to public investors. The charge, if accurate, would mean that a major Wall Street brokerage firm published stock research that its analyst *knew* to be false, a clear violation of civil and possibly criminal securities laws. Unger couldn't wait to share the news with the Baker committee, and when she did, the financial press put out an all-points bulletin to find the miscreant. Bombarded with calls from reporters, the SEC's new enforcement chief Stephen Cutler took a deep breath and demanded a full investigation. There was just one problem, as Cutler and the enforcement staff would soon discover: Richards had made a mistake. When SEC enforcement officials started piecing the puzzle together they found that Morgan Stanley analyst Chuck Phillips, the unnamed researcher in Unger's testimony, had invested in a start-up Internet company, and engaged in a technique designed to reduce taxable gains on any stock he received once the company become public, something called "shorting against the box."

When Unger heard the developments, and more important, that she had given what amounted to false testimony, she had just two words: "Oh shit." Unger was preparing to relinquish the SEC's top spot to Harvey Pitt, President Bush's recent nominee for the job, and return to her post as a commissioner, possibly heading up an SEC task force to deal with research conflicts. If she was forced to publicly announce a mistake of this magnitude, it could deal a damaging blow to the initiative, embarrassing the commission at a difficult time. But if she said nothing, Unger would have effectively lied to Congress. In the end, Unger chose a middle ground: She personally informed Baker about the screwup and asked if they could just let the matter slide. Baker agreed. Now all she needed was to get Pitt to agree as well.

A heavyset man with a thick black beard, Harvey Pitt looked more like a college professor than possibly the most powerful lawyer on Wall Street. But by the end of the 1990s, Pitt had compiled a twenty-five-year record of helping some of Wall Street's top firms and executives deal with everything from criminal prosecutions to lobbying members of Congress. His knowledge of the nation's securities laws was so encyclopedic, his ability to get things done so immense, that both politicians and his clients described him in godlike terms. "He is well described as the Zeus in his field," Senator Schumer said during Pitt's confirmation hearing. "Like Churchill, he is a man for his times." Pitt was confirmed unanimously.

Pitt began his legal career at the SEC, rising to the post of general counsel and earning a reputation as an expert in securities law. After he moved to private practice in the early 1980s, Pitt became a star of the white-collar securities bar when he helped disgraced stock trader Ivan Boesky cut a plea deal that brought down former junk-bond king Michael Milken. Many more high-profile cases would follow. In the late 1990s, when the accounting industry needed a voice in Washington to help quash Levitt's reform efforts, Pitt lobbied both sides of the political aisle so effectively that Democratic Senator Chuck Schumer became a key critic of the plan. Back in New York, Merrill Lynch needed someone to counter SEC charges for its role in the Orange County, California, bankruptcy and Pitt was able to deliver once again, this time convincing the SEC's enforcement division that Merrill should not be charged with securities fraud and instead pay only a small fine. And it wasn't just Wall Street insiders who sought Pitt's counsel. He was usually the first call for seasoned Wall Street reporters looking for tips about the most explosive cases in the securities industry. If Pitt wasn't handling the case himself, it was usually a good bet he knew the person who was.

For all his power and status, Pitt wasn't the first name to surface for SEC chief after Bush's election. But when rumors swirled about his appointment, it was hard to find someone in Washington and on Wall Street who thought he wasn't the right man for the job—including Pitt himself. For years, Pitt had made no secret about his ambition to run the place where he began his career, nor his distaste for Arthur Levitt's leadership there. During the 1990s, he and Levitt had butted heads over nearly every policy to come out of the commission, from Levitt's push to reform the accounting industry to his creation of Rule FD or "fair disclosure" that was designed to force corporations to give small investors the same information they dole out to sophisticated Wall Street types. Pitt, like most of Wall Street, believed that the practical effect of the rule would be that corporations would simply release less information. But where they differed the most was in style. Pitt believed Levitt's endless public appearances criticizing Wall Street were counterproductive, building up walls between the firms and the chief regulator, who needed all the help he could get.

From the moment he started at the SEC, Pitt left no doubt that he wanted to remove any and all vestiges of Levitt's leadership. During his first meeting with commissioners and top staffers, he read a long memo criticizing the agency's approach to Wall Street crime. He wanted to turn down the rhetoric that had been a staple of the Levitt regime, and create working relationships with the big brokerage firms, such that they would report abuse to the commission before things got out of hand. The firms themselves should not always be held accountable for the actions of a wayward executive as they were for years under his predecessor; shareholders should not be footing the bill by paying fines when the culpability stemmed from a single person.

Much of Pitt's remarks were expected, given his well-known distaste for Levitt. But where he shocked many of the people present was in his assessment of the commission's enforcement record. "You people are going easy" in many of your cases, he said. For all Levitt's tough talk, Pitt believed the SEC accomplished very little during those years.

Pitt believed research conflicts was one of those places where Levitt talked a good game but did very little to reform the sleazy practices. Like most Wall Street insiders, Pitt knew full well that research reports were more reflective of a firm's investment banking needs than the analysts' opinions about a particular stock. While he often remarked that he had "never met an investor who bought a stock based on an analyst's report,"

Pitt was astounded by some of the most recent disclosures about Wall Street's use of research to win banking business, and as public anger mounted, he was fully prepared to make some meaningful changes. On September 10, 2001, he asked Unger to meet him for dinner at the tony Georgetown Club in Washington, D.C., to discuss research and other matters. Flanked by his chief counsel, David Becker, and another commissioner, Ike Hunt, Pitt laid out his plan to deal with the issue. There would be no task force to address the issue as Unger had hoped. Pitt and his staff would be dealing with the heads of the firms privately, the first step toward having the self-regulators at the NASD and NYSE craft new rules to address some of the problems that made research so dangerous for small investors.

Unger couldn't believe her ears. "You're making a big mistake," Unger recalls saying. The self-regulatory organizations will just drop the ball like they did with Levitt, she said. For all its shortcomings, the SEC is the only agency capable of doing this right, and given the findings of Richards's examination, the time was right to move. Pitt said he agreed about the need to do something, but on his own terms. SEC's recent examination of the issue, he believed, was slipshod (he had been briefed about the Lori Richards screwup involving Morgan Stanley analyst Chuck Phillips). Pitt knew Unger was disappointed, but pressed his own plan to convene a "summit" with leaders of the top Wall Street firms and the heads of the NYSE and NASD. The meeting would be on his "turf," he said, where he could make specific demands on the industry, getting the CEOs of the big firms to guarantee research reforms. Such an approach, he said, would make it difficult for Wall Street to pull on him what they pulled on Levitt.

This time, Unger exploded. "Harvey, you're essentially handing the baton to the securities industry. It's a bad idea to put it into their hands. It's like the foxes watching the henhouse." But Pitt wouldn't hear of it. He said he was confident of his ability to handle any issue, and make sure Wall Street got the message and cleaned up research once and for all. He told Unger one more thing: Find a way to correct your testimony before Congress.

But Pitt's research plan would be postponed as Wall Street and the nation faced an even bigger crisis. A few hours after Pitt's meeting with Unger, terrorists targeted Washington and New York in a devastating attack designed to cripple the country's political and economic infrastructure. A jumbo jet crashed into the Pentagon. Another, presumably heading for the White House, crashed after a group of heroic passengers forced the jet to crash on an open field in Pennsylvania. In New York, two jets crashed into the World Trade Center, the city's largest buildings, known as the twin towers, causing the structures to collapse and killing nearly three thousand people.

It was the largest single loss of life due to an attack on American soil in the country's history, even larger than the Japanese attack on Pearl Harbor, and nowhere was the damage more devastating than on Wall Street. Brokerage firms located in the Trade Center were forced to relocate immediately, creating a mad dash for office space in midtown Manhattan and across the river in Jersey City. Without power and telephone service, Merrill Lynch and Lehman Brothers, both headquartered in the adjacent World Financial Center, began sending their workers across the river in New Jersey and looking for space uptown.

After the attacks, the New York Stock Exchange, the nation's largest stock market, was still standing, but barely. Despite having a backup generator that kept the floor of the exchange operational, NYSE chairman Dick Grasso had one major problem: Wall Street's voice and data infrastructure had been so badly damaged that only a few firms could send orders through the Big Board. But that didn't stop the opening of the exchange from becoming a major political issue. Grasso's sources in Washington began telling him that the White House believed that the country would be sending a powerful message if the exchange opened immediately after the attacks, possibly even the next day. New York State banking commissioner Elizabeth McCaul said she was "calling on behalf" of Governor George Pataki when she told Grasso to open the exchange even if it were for only "fifteen minutes." Grasso nearly exploded. "I can open for one minute and you'd get the same result," he said, explaining that with so few firms ready to trade, the market would be almost nonexistent. McCaul seemed unconvinced, so Grasso said if she really wanted the exchange to open for fifteen minutes, she should get the governor to make that request directly. After the call, Grasso turned to Pitt for help. "Harvey, you know there's nothing stopping me from opening," Grasso said. "But there will be no customers." Pitt told him to take the time necessary to get the job done right, adding, "I'll take the heat."

•   •   •

For Wall Street, the 9/11 tragedy switched the media's focus away from the various scandals and investor losses that had permeated business news coverage for most of the year and on to the rebuilding of American finance. The press, which had been on a tear for nearly two years about how shady research misled the small investor, now began focusing on stories about the broader implications of 9/11, namely the impact of the attacks on the national economy and the human tragedy stemming from the attacks. Zamansky began frantically calling friends in the press to try to revive the research issue, but the media's appetite for scandal had suddenly evaporated.

Almost everyone who worked in the financial business knew someone who perished in the attacks, and some of the best reporting focused on how 9/11 affected individuals in the brokerage industry, both the victims and the survivors. Wall Street can be an unforgiving place, but 9/11 seemed to soften some of the street's rough edges. Sandy Weill, having successfully "nuked" John Reed as his co-CEO of Citigroup, offered Lehman CEO Dick Fuld, who was still looking for office space, several floors in his midtown Manhattan building. Earlier in the year, Morgan Stanley CEO Phil Purcell and the firm's president John Mack had become bitter enemies after Mack said Purcell had broken a "handshake" agreement to hand him the top job at Morgan. Mack resigned to become the CEO of CSFB, and vowed to "kick the shit" out of his old partner when competing for business. But during the first post 9/11 meeting of the top brokerage executives, Mack quickly sought out Purcell for a status report on his old firm, which had offices in the World Trade Center. The two shook hands and agreed to put aside old grudges to get Wall Street up and running.

With Pitt watching his back in Washington, Grasso reopened the stock exchange a week after the attacks, working night and day to make sure trading went as smoothly as possible, and in doing so, he became a national star. Though the markets fell more than 600 points during its first post 9/11 trading session, Grasso came to symbolize the resilience of America's financial system in the face of terrorism as trading slowly returned to normal. Grasso always had a flair for publicity; he held boxing matches at the exchange, pitting top-notch prizefighters like Roy Jones Jr. against Wall Street executives, including himself. Because of the precarious nature of the markets, Grasso understood that he had to do more than fix the NYSE's communications grid to rebuild Wall Street. So he turned the opening bell on September 17 into a grand celebration of patriotism. Burly cops and firemen, not Wall Street CEOs, were on the NYSE podium as trading commenced that day. During the course of the day, Grasso roamed the trading floor like a general inspecting his troops, shaking hands with traders, getting constant updates on how well the specialists were handling customer orders. When the day was over, the markets were down, but Grasso was clearly up. On Lou Dobbs's CNN television show, shot on the floor of the stock exchange, Schumer referred to Grasso as "a giant of a man" for his post 9/11 work. But at five foot seven, Grasso couldn't be seen on the television screen. He was blocked from view by the six foot three governor of New York State, George Pataki.

Few people would disagree with Grasso's status. In the weeks ahead, he unveiled a large flag over the front of the exchange, as he put it, his "Fuck You to Bin Laden," and urged Wall Street's biggest players to refrain from selling stocks, but when they did, there was an unwritten rule to trade listed stocks only through NYSE. Most people agreed, but not everyone. At one point, Goldman Sachs was ready to move a large block of stock for a client on the NYSE's main competitor, the NASDAQ. When Henry Paulson called Grasso with a heads-up, Grasso was shocked Paulson would go to his main competitor, since the NYSE now symbolized the country's economic resilience. "How dare you?" Grasso said. "Where is your patriotic duty?" Paulson said he would compromise and trade the shares in the overseas markets.

The era of good feeling lasted through the end of the year. The Baker committee postponed its hearings indefinitely to give Wall Street an opportunity to rebuild. Pitt canceled his research powwow with the Wall Street heavyweights and Spitzer put his own inquiry on hold, while Blodget seemed to take a hint from his detractors inside the firm and resigned from Merrill without a hint of the danger he was facing. After a dismal year of press, Merrill seemed to be on a mini roll, earning kudos for being the first major firm to return to its downtown Manhattan headquarters in early October. CEO Dave Komansky and president Stan O'Neal got all the credit from various local politicians, including Schumer, Wall Street's favorite Democratic senator, and one of the largest recipients of campaign money from the brokerage industry. But it was the rank-and-file

Merrill employee who felt the pain of working in a virtual war zone. Paul Critchlow, Merrill's top spokesman, says that during one of his first days on the job, he was gazing out a window, looking at what was left of the Trade Center, when he saw a worker pulling a body from the wreckage. Critchlow, who saw combat action in Vietnam, nearly broke down and cried.

Investors weren't that happy either. Despite Wall Street's rare show of civility, the markets themselves continued to behave badly, shaving countless millions from the holdings of those investors who continued to hope for a rebound. President Bush presented a plan of tax cuts he believed would reinvigorate the economy barely standing from the one-two punch of the bursting of the Internet bubble and the terrorist attacks. But Bush couldn't catch a break. A little more than a month after the attacks, came the mother of all corporate scandals: Enron. The Houston energy giant always enjoyed a special status on Wall Street with major firms like Citigroup, JPMorgan Chase, and Merrill earning huge fees for underwriting stock and bonds for the company, as well as helping Enron's CFO Andrew Fastow arrange a series of thinly disclosed limited partnerships that were designed to move the company's risky operations off its balance sheet and out of investors' sight.

When the entire charade began to blow up in late 2001—the company restated five years' worth of earnings, leading to a massive bankruptcy filing—Wall Street ran for cover as billions of investors' wealth vanished almost overnight. Despite the obvious financial treachery, all fifteen of the analysts who tracked the stock had rated Enron as a "buy" when the firm filed for bankruptcy in early 2002. Caught red-handed, the big Wall Street firms claimed they, too, were victims of Enron's deceit. But not even the street's biggest defenders, like Harvey Pitt, believed the story. The SEC launched a massive investigation into the firm's accounting, including its relationship with its auditor, Arthur Andersen.

Levitt was once again basking in the glow of his self-righteousness, taking credit for his stance on the shady dealings of corporate accounting that seemed to be at the heart of the Enron fiasco. But Levitt appeared to ignore the role of conflicted stock research in hiding the company's off-balance-sheet chicanery and his own failure to address the issue. Investment banking conflicts may not have been the only reason Enron's problems were so well hidden from the investing public, but it certainly looms large in explaining how the company got away with so much for so long. Many of the off-balance-sheet maneuvers that caused the company's demise were disclosed in various documents that objective analysts usually love to read to gain greater insight into a company's finances. And many did, though none of them appeared to have survived at a major Wall Street firm that counted Enron as among its biggest clients for underwriting business. One analyst, John Olson, a veteran energy researcher for Merrill Lynch during much of the bubble, said he was fired by Merrill research chief Andrew Melnick for his well-known bearishness on the company after Enron CEO Ken Lay complained to Merrill's bankers. On several occasions, Melnick had reminded Olson that he was alienating an important constituency at the firm, investment banking, which was giving him "negative reviews" during bonus season. Melnick says he fired Olson because he had also lost the confidence of Merrill's sales force. Still, after Olson left the firm, his replacement upgraded the stock, calling the company the "General Electric of the New Economy." Merrill's relationship with Enron appeared as solid as any on Wall Street after it was hired by Fastow to arrange one off-balance-sheet maneuver and receive about $4 million in fees.

The Enron debacle underscored the total breakdown of watchdog function by major institutions that investors had relied on for protection. And it wasn't just the Wall Street researchers who let investors down. In 2000, the SEC under Levitt decided to forgo a three-year review of Enron's books, which could have revealed the company's shady finances before it was too late. Even as Levitt was on the receiving end of countless accolades over his position on corporate accounting, he feared that his Enron misstep would cost him big time. At one point, he told Pitt that if the new SEC chief released that information it would "skewer me," Pitt recalls Levitt saying. Pitt said he wouldn't. "Arthur, on policy issues where you and I don't agree, you're fair game," Pitt said. "But on administration issues, we won't let you take the hit. It hurts the agency." (Levitt for his part, doesn't recall the conversation, but denies he would ever use the word "skewer.")

Pitt may have been a stand-up guy, but the Enron scandal refocused the financial press on the need for reform on Wall Street, and Pitt would soon be caught in the crossfire. Critics like Jake Zamansky began to target the SEC chairman as a patsy for his former clients, the big Wall Street investment houses. "He's siding with the securities industry," Zamansky said at one point. Levitt's achievements may have been few, but he talked a good game, giving the impression that he was fighting for small investors. Pitt, meanwhile, didn't say much publicly and he gave the impression that he was doing nothing.

It was an impression that people inside the SEC, including attorneys in the agency's enforcement office couldn't understand. It's not that they particularly liked Pitt. Most people inside the SEC considered him egotistical and unwilling to listen to others. But Pitt's directives to his staff show he was hardly in bed with his old clients. "If you had a case, Harvey wanted you to nail the people involved," said one SEC official. In November 2001, Pitt even lived up to his promise to deal with research conflicts "on his own turf" by calling a meeting of Wall Street top officials and using his own money to rent out a large conference room at the Wall Street Regent hotel. Pitt said all the right things. He ordered executives to once and for all clean up their acts. "You guys basically put out sales literature," he said, "and if you were smart enough to label it sales literature you wouldn't have this problem." Pitt said he wanted research to be revamped through new NASD and NYSE rules, which would include more disclosure in reports on banking clients, as well as the stock-picking records of the analysts. He also wanted a certification in which every analyst would be required to sign a document stating that the rating was his honestly held belief, not something swayed by banking conflicts.

There was just one problem: The entire meeting was held in private. In sharp contrast to his predecessor, Pitt thought that was the best way to get Wall Street to do what's right. It was a miscalculation that would haunt him for years to come.

CHAPTER ELEVEN

And the Walls Come Tumbling Down

By the end of 2001, Eliot Spitzer had resumed his own investigation into Wall Street research, but unlike his counterpart in Washington, Spitzer had no intention of keeping his efforts a secret. After giving Merrill some time to recover from the terrorist attacks, his prosecutors continued to depose various company officials on their way toward building a case against Merrill, Blodget, and possibly others at the firm.

As Spitzer resumed his probe, Merrill had made some major changes in its research department. Blodget was gone, as was research chief Andrew Melnick, who firm officials say left amid a cost-cutting drive. Those changes did little to convince Spitzer that the firm had changed its ways as Ray Abbott, a Merrill lawyer who helped oversee analysts at the firm, started his testimony. Right off the bat, Abbott made some startling concessions. He admitted that under Merrill's current guidelines analysts could "send the written (research) report to the company" before its publication. The reports, he said, couldn't contain the stock rating. Later, Abbott conceded that the firm had at least two different kinds of ratings that signaled investors should sell a stock, one simply labeled "sell," and another labeled "reduce."

Blodget, as it turned out, never once issued a "sell" or "reduce" rating during his three years with the firm, nor did many of his colleagues, as Merrill officials sheepishly conceded during the testimony. Indeed, it was only after Merrill's research came under greater scrutiny that the "reduce" rating was eliminated and Melnick issued a firmwide edict discouraging researchers from relying on the firm's "neutral" rating if they really thought a stock was likely to fall in value, he said.

Abbott's testimony on GoTo.com confirmed something else. Merrill tried to paint Blodget's GoTo.com downgrade as a routine part of his job as an objective analyst. But Abbott said people inside the department were bracing for trouble nearly from the moment it became official. Abbott said he knew that Merrill was rejected by GoTo.com as an underwriter, so when he heard Blodget was going to downgrade the stock, he wanted a second opinion from research chief Andrew Melnick. According to Abbott, Melnick told him, "I am not going to stop Henry from downgrading his opinion if that's what he wants to do." But Abbott apparently wasn't satisfied that the matter would just blow over. At one point, he asked the firm's PR department to alert him to press calls questioning the timing of the move, and that he even took part in an unsuccessful effort to convince *The Wall Street Journal* to kill a story on the GoTo.com that sparked the Spitzer investigation. Why was Merrill so concerned? Abbott admitted that a downgrade on a company that had just denied the firm banking business was highly unusual. "No, I don't recall that . . . scenario having happened before," he said during his testimony. The big question for Spitzer's investigators was what else was slipping through those very big cracks in Merrill's Chinese Wall?

Another witness, Kirsten Campbell, provided some answers. Under Blodget, Campbell's research duties were diverse. She covered the ill-timed Pets.com, the now defunct online pet-food company that Merrill brought public near the height of the bubble, as well as eBay, the online auction house that managed to survive and thrive despite the Internet depression. She picked up coverage of GoTo in late 2000, just as Merrill's banking department began pitching underwriting business to the company.

Campbell was no longer with the firm, having left some nine months earlier as Merrill was forced to downsize its workforce following the Internet crash. But Campbell, as her emails showed, was well versed in the company's research practices. Even though Blodget's name often appeared at the top of most reports, signaling he was the "lead analyst," analysts in his group appeared to do most of the heavy lifting, Campbell suggested. Blodget had assigned specific companies in the Internet universe to people like Campbell, who during her testimony described her job as "just to do the research and dig everything I can and present him with it.' When asked if Blodget knew "anything about these companies that he wanted to initiate on before he discussed it with you," Campbell said, "It's hard to say what he knew or didn't know."

For a time, Spitzer's investigators believed Campbell could easily be turned into a cooperating witness. In her emails, Campbell spoke openly to Blodget about research conflicts and how they hurt small investors who relied on Blodget's research. In one, she told Blodget she didn't want to be a "f-king whore for management" of a company that might be a possible investment banking client.

But as Campbell's testimony shows, she had no intention of joining the Spitzer team, and came prepared to fight for her old boss. At one point she simply refused to answer a question, remaining silent and peering at Topman. "I'm not going to have a staring contest with you, Ms. Campbell," Topman snapped. Later she labeled Topman's line of questioning as "absurd," to which he responded, "I don't think ad hominem attacks help us here, Miss Campbell."

Like Blodget, Campbell appeared to be well prepared to evade most questions, though she later made some interesting disclosures about her relationship with Blodget that may have had something to do with her attitude. She and Blodget seemed to be in fairly regular contact; they met before her testimony and briefly discussed the GoTo.com situation. Campbell testified that Blodget told her that "he's frustrated" over all the negative publicity surrounding the GoTo.com rating, which was an example of calling a "stock better than any other." Blodget, as it turned out, was paying her to do research for his book on the market bubble.

But Topman wanted more. At one point he confronted her with an email where Campbell wrote that she didn't want to be a "f-ing whore for management" when she began the rating process on GoTo.com. The same email contained a chilling critique of Merrill's research practices: "The whole idea that we are independent from banking is a joke."

"And F-ING stands for, excuse me, fucking?" Topman asked. Campbell was stunned. "I don't like to write like that," she stated. Topman broke in once again. "Can you explain what you meant by the sentence 'I don't want to be a whore for f'ing management'?"

Campbell could do nothing but state the obvious. "I wanted them to stop trying to force their opinions on us," she said, adding that she wrote "that this whole idea that we are independent from banking is a big lie" as a way of getting bankers to "back off" and let her do her job.

As good as things were for Spitzer's investigators, they would soon get even better after the deposition from Robert Dobler, another lawyer who provided oversight of analysts at Merrill. Dobler conceded that one analyst had actually confided in him that research management prevented her from changing "an opinion on a stock" from a positive to a more negative one. He later checked out the scenario with research chief Andrew Melnick, who said it wasn't true, but for Dinallo, it was a telling detail about how Merrill's research department worked.

By now, Dinallo's team had uncovered scores of documents showing how Blodget used spicy language in his emails to describe his disdain for companies he was hyping to the public. Dobler was asked about one particularly vivid description, in which Blodget called Infospace a "powder keg" despite labeling the stock a "buy" in his public reports.

"In your opinion should the investing public be made aware that a research analyst believes a particular stock is a powder keg?" asked Gary Connor, the assistant attorney general who stepped in for Topman.

Dobler knew there was only one answer: "Yes."

In mid March, Dinallo presented his case to Spitzer. Based on the emails, Merrill had clearly issued research that was fraudulent on GoTo.com and Infospace, Dinallo said. Over the past six months, he had kept a chalkboard in his office, on which he had listed some of the most sensational of Blodget's Internet rants, and what Dinallo believed they meant when translated into standard English. "POS," Blodget's abbreviation for a "piece of shit" stock, had actually turned out to be an "accumulate" in his reports to the public. To keep it simple, Dinallo simply wrote "POS= Accumulate."

But the testimony from analysts like Kirsten Campbell and others seemed to confirm a fraud that expanded beyond just two stocks. Stock analysts at Merrill faced tremendous pressure to skew their ratings to help the firm win deals, he said. The depositions from Dobler suggested that managers in the research department knew the problem existed for some time, but did little to address it.

Dinallo believed he should be looking at emails that involved every stock Blodget had rated during his short but tumultuous career at Merrill Lynch. Spitzer needed no convincing. "Get me the damn emails, all of them," he said.

The following day Dinallo's next subpoena covered tens of thousands of additional emails on companies people inside the AG's office never heard of, but were all too familiar to the scores of Merrill clients who were now sitting on almost worthless investments. In the weeks ahead, Dinallo's hunch turned out to be right as his crew began combing through stacks of emails that covered companies like Aether Systems, Excite@Home, Lifeminders.com, and 24/7 Media.

Some of Blodget's negative comments on these stocks were downright amusing. He called 24/7 Media a "piece of shit" and Excite@Home a "piece of crap," even though these stocks received positive public assessment. Dinallo and Topman could be heard laughing at the other end of the building when they saw a little cheat sheet Blodget had passed around so people could understand the abbreviations he often used when emailing colleagues.

Maybe the most damning new email was discovered by Elizabeth Block, who headed a unit that investigated fraud involving the theater business, but now was helping with the case. In it, Blodget had laid out the dilemma he was facing. If he downgraded some stocks, bankers would be at his throat. If he didn't, he wasn't fulfilling his obligations to small investors. Confused and angry, Blodget lashed out at his boss for not providing guidance about what to do.

"If there is no new email forthcoming on how (ratings) should be applied to sensitive banking clients we are going to start calling these stocks (stocks, not companies) . . . like we see them no matter what the ancillary business consequences are."

Block rushed into Dinallo's office, handed him the sheet of paper and waited for a response. Dinallo had just two words: "Holy shit." When Topman reviewed the email, he was a little more expansive. "This is an amazing fucking document."

A few moments later, Dinallo burst into Spitzer's office and whipped out the sheet of paper. Dinallo told his boss that he had found what he considered the best evidence in the case, maybe the best piece of evidence he ever uncovered as a prosecutor. Spitzer was impressed, and ready to make his case.

But Merrill was ready to fight. David Komansky, the firm's CEO, was in the process of handing the firm to his second-in-command, Stan O'Neal, who represented a distinct change from the typical Merrill CEO. The grandson of a slave, O'Neal grew up poor and as a teenager worked on a GM assembly line, before earning a Harvard MBA and fighting his way through the Merrill management ranks. In the summer of 2001, just as the stories about Henry Blodget's research broke, O'Neal was named president and heir apparent to Komansky, who announced he was planning to step down in the coming years.

O'Neal certainly wanted to shake things up at "Mother Merrill." During his years with the firm, he watched Merrill grow fat and underproductive. His solution was a massive overhaul of the firm, put in motion right after 9/11, discarding business units he believed weren't carrying their own weight, as well as remaking the firm's management structure. Inside Merrill, people said it was no coincidence that Blodget left the firm just as O'Neal took power.

By the spring of 2002, O'Neal began to focus on the firm's legal department, which he felt had also fallen behind during the Komansky years. And with good reason. Once known as the best on Wall Street, Merrill's legal staff had transformed itself into a cash cow for regulators and securities lawyers looking for quick settlements. O'Neal fumed when he learned that firm lawyers never consulted management before handing Jake Zamansky the $400,000 check for his suit against Blodget. As the Spitzer investigation heated up, his orders were simple: No more quick settlements.

Robert Morvillo was the perfect man to carry out O'Neal's new mandate. Morvillo was considered one of Wall Street's best white-collar defense attorneys, and Merrill had used him more than almost any other outside attorney to handle its various legal entanglements over the past twenty years. Most recently, he had been sitting in on many of the Spitzer depositions, and he didn't like what he saw. A short, round man with thin oily hair and a thick Long Island accent, Morvillo was a former assistant U.S. attorney who had gained his reputation as a premier Wall Street lawyer thanks in large part to his no-nonsense, sometimes bullying tactics that seemed to produce results when negotiating settlement deals with government investigators.

Morvillo wasted little time making his presence known as the depositions continued seemingly with no end in sight at Spitzer's drab offices in lower Manhattan. Topman was his most frequent target, particularly as he began taking testimony from another high-level Merrill research executive, Deepak Raj. At one point, after Topman complained that Merrill had not turned over some documents he requested, Morvillo accused him of using it as an excuse to intimidate one of the firm's research officials who was giving testimony. "What relevance is it that we have all this hyperbole," Morvillo boomed. "It's just meaningless and allows Mr. Topman to pop off with some purpose to intimidate the witness. It's kind of outrageous that he's making these statements in this context today, and actually quite foolish."

Topman shot back, "Wait a minute, you call it hyperbole, but the failure to produce important central documents with no explanation I do not consider hyperbole." But Morvillo wasn't through. "Nonsense," he snapped. "You've been attempting to intimidate witnesses since the first day I stepped in this room and for you to fulminate today after we produced seventy-five thousand documents is nonsense."

Topman added that Morvillo's "ad hominem attack is completely unnecessary," and continued with the deposition, but the battle between Morvillo and Spitzer's lieutenants and Spitzer himself continued as the two sides began settlement negotiations in late March. In a series of angry, expletive-laced discussions with Morvillo, Spitzer laid out what he needed to reach a settlement, namely, a large fine, a separation of research and investment banking, meaning that analysts could no longer help snare investment banking business, and the release of evidence, mainly the explosive Blodget emails. Spitzer labeled many of the details negotiable, such as the amount of fine involved. (Privately, Spitzer told his deputies that he was willing to settle for a fine of less than $10 million.) But one thing wasn't negotiable. Spitzer wanted all of the emails released.

Morvillo's response was unequivocal. No way.

For weeks the two sides were deadlocked. Merrill argued that Blodget's emails were being misconstrued and "taken out of context." Spitzer threatened to indict the firm if a deal wasn't reached, people at Merrill complained. Dinallo turned to one of Merrill's in-house lawyers on the case, Andrew Kandel, who headed the investor-protection unit under Vacco, and was well versed in the power the Martin Act gave to the New York attorney general. Dinallo believed Merrill might be more willing to settle if they knew more about the seriousness of the case and that Spitzer was reaching his limit. Spitzer gave Dinallo the approval to warn Kandel that the investigation was "broader than just a couple of emails."

Kandel said he understood, but appeared powerless to do anything. Morvillo was in charge.

Spitzer's limit was reached at the end of the first week in April 2002, when he met with Merrill's lawyers. Merrill's response hadn't softened. Paying a large fine was one thing, but Morvillo said Merrill would never agree to a settlement if the emails were released. Spitzer and Morvillo continued to negotiate, though at times the discussions turned heated with both men screaming and cursing. People at Merrill were astonished by Spitzer's dark side; he looked like a prep-school yuppie, but fought like he was from a tougher neighborhood in the Bronx than the tony Riverdale section where he grew up. At one point, Ed Yodowitz, another Merrill lawyer and a friend of Spitzer's, attempted to add a degree of sanity to the discussions, asking Spitzer if he could grant him the favor of a heads-up telephone call if Spitzer was ready to file a case. Spitzer said he would.

But Spitzer's mood would soon change after speaking with Morvillo once again, who tried to give the young attorney general some stern advice on how to deal with big Wall Street firms. "Eliot, if I were you, I'd be careful. Merrill has lots of powerful friends," he said. This time, Morvillo went too far. "Bob, you'll never win playing that game with me." (Morvillo in an interview said he had many heated conversations with Spitzer using those words, but he doesn't recall when they occurred.)

Morvillo had badly miscalculated. As a practical matter, Spitzer had little to lose in filing a case against Merrill, given the market slump that many Americans blamed on unscrupulous practices in the brokerage industry. More than that, he also had the law on his side. Part of the power of the Martin Act is that it gives a savvy prosecutor the ability to file a case, without stating whether it's criminal or civil in nature, and continue to negotiate a more favorable settlement as the target worries about being indicted. That's exactly what Spitzer did. After his conversation with Morvillo, Spitzer quickly ordered Dinallo to work the weekend to prepare a "354 case" against Merrill, which under the Martin Act gave the attorney general power to charge Merrill and Blodget with criminal securities fraud at some later date if settlement talks continued to stall. Despite his promise to Ed Yodowitz to provide Merrill with a "heads up" if he was to file a case, Spitzer believed that the element of surprise would be crucial in a coming public relations battle over the substance of the case.

Dinallo, meanwhile, had more immediate worries. His wife had gone into labor with their second child. At one point, while he and wife were at the doctor's office (she was practicing her breathing technique), Dinallo's cell phone rang. It was Spitzer. He wanted Dinallo to work the weekend and be prepared to file a Martin Act proceeding against Merrill and Blodget before a state Supreme Court judge by Monday morning. The call had barely ended before his wife went into labor and gave birth to a beautiful baby girl. That weekend, as Dinallo put the final touches on the case, some of his colleagues ribbed him about his dedication to his job, and suggested he should name his newborn "Merrill." Dinallo just laughed.

Not everybody found Dinallo's work so amusing. Despite all the histrionics between Spitzer and Morvillo, the Blodget investigation had barely registered on the screen of the Securities and Exchange Commission. That is, until a frantic telephone call from Merrill to SEC headquarters just days before Dinallo started writing up his court order. Merrill's legal team informed the commission that their negotiations with Spitzer had been so rocky that Spitzer had even threatened the firm with the Wall Street equivalent of nuclear war, warning that he might indict the company if an agreement wasn't reached.

For the SEC the situation was dicey. Given chairman Harvey Pitt's prior relationship as one of the firm's top lawyers, any direct involvement by him would be a clear conflict of interest. But if the SEC did nothing, the consequences were conceivably worse. No Wall Street firm had ever survived a criminal indictment, and Spitzer was threatening to take down the firm that dealt with more small investors than any other on Wall Street.

Stephen Cutler, the head of the SEC's enforcement division, was in charge of finding out what Spitzer was up to. A forty-one-year-old Yale law school graduate, Cutler had been with the SEC for only three years, having spent most of his career in private practice. Since taking the job as chief of the enforcement division, winning over his staff hadn't been easy. Many of his most experienced investigators had resented Cutler for his lack of enforcement experience, though he had recently won their respect for his successful case against Credit Suisse First Boston, forcing the firm to pay a $100 million fine for allegedly charging higher commissions to some large investors in exchange for access to hot IPOs brought public by its star banker, Frank Quattrone. (Quattrone wasn't charged.)

Now Cutler was facing possibly the biggest crisis in his short tenure. The SEC had done little to address research conflicts in the aftermath of the stock market bubble, and Pitt's analyst reform had clearly fallen through the cracks, giving Spitzer a huge advantage in claiming the issue as all his own. Cutler knew he needed to act fast. After hearing from Merrill, Cutler asked his staff what they knew about the Spitzer case. The investigation didn't seem to register with anyone just yet. But Bill Baker, a fifteen-year enforcement division veteran and one of the SEC's best investigators, said he knew how to find out. He had worked with Eric Dinallo on a bucket-shop case a few years back and he seemed to be a straight shooter. Baker volunteered to give Dinallo a call and see what he knew.

Baker began the conversation with a simple question. "Are you guys ready to file anything about analysts' conflicts at Merrill?" he asked. But Dinallo's answer was more complex. "Why do you want to know?"

"Because it's Merrill," Baker shot back. Baker didn't need to tell Dinallo that taking on such a high-profile target was of major concern to the SEC. He then explained that the SEC had been looking at the issue for some time, and offered to lend its support to the investigation. "We can do a joint investigation," Baker said. Dinallo said he would talk to Spitzer and let him know if anything would change.

But of course, things were changing rapidly. By the time the Baker telephone call was over, Spitzer's negotiations with Merrill had nearly broken down, and Dinallo was busy drawing up his complaint. Spitzer, meanwhile, scrambled to find some political support to help with the Merrill counteroffensive once the case became public. One of his first calls was to Senator Schumer. As a ranking member of the Senate banking committee, Schumer could be a great ally for Spitzer. He had closer ties to the securities industry than any Democrat in Washington, thanks to his support of Wall Street–friendly legislation, such as ending Glass-Steagall and killing Levitt's accounting reform measures. He also received tens of thousands of dollars in campaign contributions from the top firms and had regular meetings with Wall Street's biggest CEOs.

Schumer was also a press hound, and Spitzer believed he just might want to lend his support to the case, given the growing investor anger at Wall Street in the aftermath of the bubble. Spitzer gave Schumer a description of his evidence in the Merrill case. "You should care about this, it's a big issue," Spitzer told Schumer. "You're on the banking committee and these guys are screwing investors." But Schumer wanted no part of Spitzer's crusade. "These are New York companies, and I don't want to be involved," he said before adding not to do it. (Schumer says through a spokesman that he told Spitzer that "New York politicians should only publicly attack New York companies when necessary.")

Spitzer had no intention on turning back now, especially after his next conversation. By the spring of 2002, former New York City mayor Rudolph Giuliani was still basking in his status as a national hero, primarily for his work getting the city up and running following the 9/11 terrorist attacks. After leaving office earlier in the year, Giuliani set up his own corporate consulting firm, aptly named Giuliani Partners, composed mostly of his old cronies from City Hall. As the negotiations with Spitzer bogged down, Merrill turned to Rudy for help.

Like Spitzer, Giuliani launched his own political career cracking down on Wall Street fraud, with splashy cases that included handcuffing alleged miscreants in front of their colleagues. It didn't matter that some of his targets were not convicted, Giuliani used his rep as a corporate crime fighter to win two terms as New York City mayor, where he enhanced his image with a successful crackdown on street crime.

But Merrill badly overestimated Rudy's power, at least with Spitzer. As it turned out, Giuliani had crossed swords with Spitzer more than a few times in recent years. Giuliani was still smarting over the time Spitzer called him a "dictator" after a series of police brutality cases surfaced during his years as mayor. Aides to Spitzer say the attorney general felt dissed because Mayor Rudy at least once failed to return Spitzer's telephone call.

Looking to avoid confrontation, Giuliani simply asked Spitzer to reconsider any action against Merrill, a company vital to the New York economy. Spitzer told Giuliani he was missing the point. His investigation uncovered some disturbing behavior, possibly fraudulent activities that cost many small investors a great deal of money. At times the conversation got heated; Giuliani explained that Merrill deserved a second chance given its record of returning to downtown Manhattan after 9/11 and not fleeing across the river to New Jersey. Spitzer said he was simply helping aggrieved investors.

On a final note, after both men had regained their composure, Giuliani asked Spitzer for a favor. "Eliot, could you just take some time to consider the case I laid out?"

Spitzer said he would. A few minutes later, Dinallo was in court filing the case.

Dinallo had already left a voice-mail message with Bill Baker at the SEC alerting him to the filing, a move that angered Cutler as he caught wind of some of the most sensational emails in the case. Top officials at Merrill, meanwhile, were in a state of panic as the headlines began to appear on the Dow Jones News Service that the New York attorney general was ready to file a case against Merrill, Blodget, and several members of his research staff for issuing biased research. "We don't know what's happening," complained James Wiggins, a senior PR official, when asked for a comment.

That was an understatement. As Merrill's vast PR machine scrambled to come up with a game plan, Spitzer was preparing to make his findings public, including confidential emails and documents that would describe the fraud in all its gory details. At a press conference in the attorney general's office, just blocks from Merrill's headquarters, Spitzer put on quite a show. "Today, I'm announcing the preliminary results of a ten-month investigation of one of the nation's most prominent Wall Street firms, Merrill Lynch," he stated. Using the emails as props, he walked reporters through his nearly yearlong inquiry into Merrill's research practices. For the past two years, Blodget had been pummeled as someone too enamored with the Internet to see its imminent downfall. But if Spitzer was to be believed, Blodget not only saw the decline coming, he also hid it from small investors as Merrill continued to squeeze banking fees from the companies he was hyping in his research.

Standing before reporters, it was clear that Spitzer was no longer the "accidental attorney general" as he calmly but forcefully explained Merrill's various transgressions, brought to life through Blodget's emails. He pointed out how Blodget labeled a company called Lifeminders a "POS" (his shorthand for "piece of shit") just a month before he recommended the stock as an "attractive investment" to small investors. In another email, Blodget referred to Infospace as a "powder keg" even as he was urging small investors to buy the company's stock. As for GoTo.com, Blodget issued positive research to the public in early 2001, but told one important money manager that there was "nothin" interesting about the stock except banking fees. Only when those fees were lost to a competitor did Blodget downgrade the stock a few months later.

Spitzer had a lot of material to work with in making his case that Merrill's research wasn't just conflicted but fraudulent as well. Elizabeth Block's crucial finding that Blodget was threatening to start "calling the stocks . . . as we see them," obliterated Wall Street's old excuse that all those positive stock ratings on banking clients were honestly held opinions of the analysts. Kirsten Campbell's email that "John and Mary Smith are losing their retirement" because analysts want to cozy up to company officials underscored that the real victims of the conflicted research were average Americans. Spitzer described his findings as "a shocking betrayal of trust by one of Wall Street's most trusted names."

When the press conference was over, Spitzer's staff took to the phones telling reporters that Merrill's troubles were far from over, while Dinallo headed to state Supreme Court to obtain a judge's order that would force Merrill to enact several modest "structural" reforms in its research process. Part of Merrill's miscalculation was that it didn't take Eliot Spitzer seriously as a political force, and now it was paying the price as he made the rounds with television and newspaper reporters blasting the Blodget emails across America.

In various interviews, Spitzer began upping the ante. He continued to hint that filing criminal charges against both Blodget and Merrill was an option if a settlement couldn't be reached. Not only would Merrill have to pay a fine, but also the firm would have to adopt a strict separation of investment banking and research functions, and at one point he argued that Merrill should "spin off" its research unit into a completely separate entity. Merrill countered that in doing so, Spitzer would be putting Merrill's research department out of business, because banking revenues are needed to pay for analysts' salaries and support.

Spitzer would later soften his stance, demanding additional safeguards, but he wasn't softening his rhetoric. Under the Martin Act, top officials at Merrill could be compelled to appear at public hearings. Spitzer's staff said a short list had been put together composed of some of the firm's top research executives, including Rosemary Berkery, Merrill's new general counsel and a key member of Stan O'Neal's management team. Berkery was significant because she had been part of the Merrill negotiating team, but for a stretch in the late 1990s, she and Melnick also shared the job as director of the firm's research department.

Merrill's response to Spitzer's attack appeared to make a bad situation even worse. The Blodget emails, the firm's massive PR department said, were taken "out of context," a ludicrous excuse given the fact that Spitzer released a huge, three-hundred-page book that contained even more emails than were in the filing. But Merrill stuck to its script for weeks, issuing a statement that Spitzer's case had "no basis" in fact even as reporters openly derided the strategy. "A fair review of the facts will show that Merrill Lynch has conducted its research with independence and integrity," the firm said.

Merrill's problems, however, seemed to grow by the minute. By seeking a court order, Spitzer had sparked a little-known clause in the Investment Company Act, the law that regulates the massive mutual fund business. Under the act, any firm that finds itself under a court order must close its mutual fund business. Such a move would place in jeopardy the investments held by many of Merrill's brokerage clients, the people Spitzer was trying to protect.

When Spitzer heard this he called Cutler, the SEC enforcement director, for some legal advice. As an expert in securities law, Cutler knew the Investment Company Act possibly better than almost anyone in the legal community, but for now, he had something else on his mind. "Bill Baker says Dinallo gave him misdirection" on the suit, Cutler snapped, referring to the Dinallo-Baker exchange prior to the case being filed. Spitzer promptly apologized for any mix-up and said he would try to be more cooperative in the future. Cutler didn't necessarily buy Spitzer's story, but he went on to explain that Merrill's legal department wasn't bluffing. The fund business was in jeopardy if a court order was filed.

On Spitzer's orders, Dinallo returned to court accompanied by Dieter Snell, one of Spitzer's top prosecutors, with an amended complaint against the big brokerage firm. As Dinallo and Snell stood before the bench waiting for Judge Martin Schoenfeld to arrive, they made eye contact with their old friend Bob Morvillo, who growled, "This is irresponsible." Snell, a seasoned criminal prosecutor, just rolled his eyes. "I don't think so, Bob," is all he said.

Schoenfeld agreed to amend the order, allowing Merrill's mutual fund business to continue in operation, but ordered that the firm begin implementing other reforms sought by Spitzer, such as forcing Merrill to disclose in its research whether the firm has or intends to have a banking relationship with the company being recommended. Spitzer also wanted Merrill to post on its website how many "buy" and "sell" recommendations it had issued in any particular sector of coverage. By the end of the day, top Merrill executives had been put through the wringer. Henry Hu, a professor of finance at the University of Texas, likened the Blodget emails to the "Atomic Bomb" for their clear explanation of how pressures to satisfy banking clients were the driving force behind the positive recommendations that seemed so out of touch with reality during the market bubble. Attorneys vowed lawsuits against the firm to recoup millions, perhaps billions, of dollars in losses that investors suffered by listening to Blodget's false research. Brokers at the firm were in an uproar, complaining that they would lose clients unless investors could trust analysts to write objective research.

On Wall Street, the reaction wasn't much better. Shares of Merrill closed only 45 cents lower after Spitzer announced his case, but the worst was yet to come; over the next week, Merrill lost $5 billion in market value. By the end of the month, Merrill's stock declined $11 billion as traders began to factor in the possibility of criminal charges, which no firm had ever survived.

Even Pitt, the SEC chief who in his past life was an outside lawyer for Merrill, was shocked by Spitzer's findings, telling Merrill's CEO Dave Komansky that the emails "showed contempt for your customers." Komansky had a similar reaction. Hearing about Blodget call one stock a piece of shit, "made me sick to my stomach," Komansky said. Bill Baker was still furious with Spitzer and Dinallo for blindsiding the SEC, but even he conceded to an associate that the case was a "doozy." When he heard Merrill's position that Blodget's emails were being misconstrued, Baker could barely control his laughter, according to one person with knowledge of the matter. "What was Blodget talking about when he called that company a piece of shit?" he said at the time.

The biggest joke, however, was on Blodget, himself. Almost overnight, the popular image of Blodget had been transformed from a misguided but true believer in the New Economy, to that of an angry, personally conflicted man, someone who seemed to betray his own principles for the almighty dollar. Blodget not only was threatened with criminal charges, it was unlikely that he would ever find employment on Wall Street again.

As the pressure built, Blodget complained to friends that his "reputa-

tion is being trashed" by a renegade politician, and considered going public with his side of the story, namely that he didn't invent the conflicted
research system that he had come to symbolize. But as the press calls
came flooding in, Blodget suddenly realized there was nothing he could
say. When he left Merrill in December 2001, he basically signed away his
side of the story in a confidentiality agreement that covered any issue involving his years at Merrill.

But there was one call he couldn't completely ignore. A little more
than three years ago, Scott Ryles, the former head of Merrill's tech-
banking department, had been instrumental in helping Blodget get the
job that catapulted him to stardom and now brought him so much pain.
Ryles had left the big brokerage firm in late 1999 to start his own investment bank specializing in tech issues, and it pained him to see another
loyal employee being held out to dry by the firm that was once known as
"Mother Merrill." At one point Ryles offered Blodget his assistance. "I
could be a character witness, I could testify," Ryles recalls telling Blodget
during the call. But Blodget seemed too beaten to fight back. "They're
not debating the facts."

Whatever they were debating, the evidence uncovered by Spitzer had far-
reaching implications. Caught off guard by Spitzer's findings, the SEC
scrambled to come up with its own case. Cutler sat down with Pitt to plot
strategy. Under Pitt's leadership the SEC had launched more investigations than at any time in its history—he ordered his staff attorney to file
charges against WorldCom just a day after the company said it needed to
restate $4 billion in earnings, the quickest turnaround for any major in-
vestigation. But the myriad of scandals that found their origins under former chairman Arthur Levitt Jr.—Enron, Arthur Andersen, WorldCom,
and now research conflicts—had badly damaged the reputation of the
SEC and by extension Pitt, who failed to understand that his low public
profile created the appearance that he was covering up for his former
clients. Maybe most damaging, Spitzer had exposed holes in the SEC's
enforcement apparatus. One criticism that followed Cutler in the days
after Spitzer went public was how Wall Street's top cop managed to miss
the damaging Blodget emails when the SEC conducted its own probe a
year earlier. "Who would have thought that these guys would be so stupid to put this stuff into email," he responded. But Cutler knew better.

During the investigation, SEC inspections chief Lori Richards didn't bother to subpoena emails.

Now Cutler offered Pitt what he thought was an easy solution: Join Spitzer's probe. "Embrace him," Cutler said. "Make him a hero."

But Pitt wasn't interested. Pitt believed that Spitzer had come up with significant evidence of fraud at Merrill, but he also believed Spitzer's motives were suspect. At bottom, he viewed Spitzer as a political opportunist looking for headlines and a ticket to the governor's mansion in New York State. Embracing Spitzer, Pitt believed, would hurt the SEC's position as the national regulator of the securities markets. For the first time in modern history, a lone state official would be setting national standards involving Wall Street.

But Cutler remained unconvinced about Pitt's strategy. Spitzer was tougher and smarter than most people thought, and, most important, he had developed some damaging evidence against Merrill. If the commission didn't react quickly, he believed, Spitzer could make a lot of people in Washington look weak in the face of burgeoning corporate fraud. At the very least, the SEC should launch its own probe. "Harvey, you've got to turn me loose," Cutler said.

Again, Pitt told Cutler he would have to wait. It was yet another bad call from one of the smartest men in the financial business. As the SEC was standing still, Spitzer's office went on the offensive once again, attacking Pitt as a lackey for the securities business by blocking his enforcement director from joining forces with the AG's investigators. For about two weeks, Pitt remained underground, weighing his options as calls for his resignation started to grow. Then something changed. Schumer, who enthusiastically supported Pitt during his Senate confirmation, entered the picture offering to broker a peace treaty between Spitzer and the SEC. "We can have a meeting in my office," Schumer told Spitzer, who agreed to attend the meeting.

But as quickly as Schumer entered the scene, he would exit. A few days later, Schumer said he had a scheduling conflict, and the meeting was rescheduled to Pitt's office at SEC headquarters. The Schumer flip-flop foreshadowed even more problems to come, as Spitzer and Dinallo arrived at SEC headquarters in Washington, D.C. With his thick black beard and massive waistline, Pitt was an imposing figure. Today he was seated behind a large oak desk, flanked by SEC general counsel David Becker, Mary Schapiro, the second highest ranking official at the NASD, and NYSE regulatory chief Edward Kwalwasser. Cutler, the enforcement chief, was noticeably absent.

One of Merrill's chief complaints about the Spitzer probe was being singled out for industrywide practices, and Spitzer seemed to understand the firm's dilemma. Spitzer told the group he wanted to extend the "structural reforms" to the rest of the brokerage industry. Mary Schapiro, now the NASD's vice chairwoman, quickly objected, noting that the agency was already considering tough rules for analysts. Spitzer seemed bewildered. "Who calls the shots?" he fired back. "Aren't you guys the regulators?" Schaprio just rolled her eyes.

Pitt, for his part, mostly sat and listened as the regulators continued to exchange blows. Toward the end of the meeting, he told Spitzer that he had officially recused himself from any enforcement action involving Merrill because the firm had been a client. But his past associations with Wall Street wouldn't prevent him from playing an active role in reforming Wall Street research. And while Spitzer could help in crafting the new measures, any reform of Wall Street research must come out of his office. In other words, stay out of our business. Spitzer simply responded that his office would support anything that protected small investors.

Pitt didn't know Spitzer well, but the overriding impression he had after spending a few hours with him was that Cutler was right—the SEC needed to get back in the game or Spitzer would continue to upstage the agency any way he could. Almost immediately, he gave Cutler authority to launch his own competing inquiry into research conflicts on Wall Street. The SEC mailed formal notices to the biggest Wall Street firms to provide the agency with documents and other information concerning their research process. It would be one of the largest probes of Wall Street the SEC had conducted in years, and its first serious attempt at uncovering research fraud. The firms under scrutiny were diverse: Morgan, Merrill, and Salomon Smith Barney dealt with small investors through their huge brokerage departments. Goldman and CSFB specialized in selling stocks to sophisticated institutional investors. Cutler realized he had failed to include one of those West Coast "boutiques" that specialized in the dotcom underwriting during the bubble. Someone on his staff threw out the name Thomas Weisel Partners, the San Francisco–based investment house created by veteran tech banker Thomas Weisel. "Add them to the list," Cutler said.

Pitt was ready to go on the offensive as well. In one speech before business journalists, he took a swipe at Spitzer and the Martin Act, remarking that the SEC has federal laws and powers that go beyond anything that can be found on the state level. He also approved the new set of research rules that he had been working on since late 2001. For Pitt, the best part of the rules were that they went beyond anything Levitt had attempted to push through the system. In addition to television disclosure of investment banking ties, analysts could no longer promise positive research in exchange for banking business, and bankers could no longer have any role in supervising researchers.

Publicly, Spitzer applauded such measures as good news for small investors. Privately, he called on his staff to regain the momentum and expand their investigation beyond Merrill to include other firms and analysts that were at the heart of the bubble: Morgan Stanley and its high-profile Internet analyst Mary Meeker, and, of course, Citigroup's Salomon Smith Barney unit and Jack Grubman. Spitzer turned to his friends in state government for support, bringing together a coalition of state finance officials that would also investigate Wall Street for research abuses. The hyperaggressive Massachusetts Secretary of State, William Galvin, launched an investigation into CSFB, focusing on the practices of Frank Quattrone. Goldman came under scrutiny from the State of Utah, while Spitzer focused on Morgan and Citigroup. "That's great," one Morgan executive said ironically. "We get the Green Berets and Goldman gets the guys from Utah."

Wall Street was now bracing for a long war. It was one thing to have to answer to national regulators like the SEC and the NASD, where investigators have been dealing with lawyers from the securities firms for years. But now each firm faced the possibility of answering to fifty state regulators, all of them ambitious politicians who looked to copy Spitzer's strategy with Merrill and use Wall Street as a stepping-stone to higher office.

Merrill had clearly been fighting the longest. As the settlement discussions entered their second month, the firm's top officials appeared to switch strategies from merely responding to Spitzer's attacks to one in which the firm went on the offensive, trying to win over favorable members of the press, planting op-ed pieces in friendly newspapers, and playing good cop/bad cop with Spitzer. In late April 2002, CEO David Komansky, who had exerted little influence during the negotiations, suddenly appeared and issued a statement conceding that Blodget's emails "fall far short of our professional standards, and some are inconsistent with our policies." Komansky also said the firm was ready to make "meaningful and significant actions to restore investor confidence."

One morning Spitzer received a little gift from Merrill. It was a video-tape of the firm's return to its World Financial Center headquarters following the 9/11 terrorist attack, with clips of New York City Mayor Mike Bloomberg and Senator Schumer applauding the move. After viewing the film, Spitzer wasn't impressed. He immediately dialed one of Merrill's top lawyers to let him know he understood the firm's message, but wasn't impressed. "I love the fact that you guys returned to lower Manhattan," Spitzer told one Merrill lawyer, "but it's irrelevant."

For a time, Merrill's strategy seemed to produce some results. Merrill's stock price began to stabilize after its sharp decline and after a favorable *Wall Street Journal* op-ed that suggested the Merrill emails were "taken out of context." Some conservative commentators, like Steve Forbes, also began parroting the Merrill talking points. But Merrill's good fortune didn't have much practical impact as Spitzer stepped up his public criticism of the firm, prompting more stories about the Blodget emails and further declines in the firm's stock price. At one point an internal Merrill poll showed that nearly 70 percent of all brokerage clients had an unfavorable opinion of the company.

And things were about to get even worse. Spitzer's office had now become a clearinghouse for documents about research conflicts from class action and private attorneys, meaning that the investigation could soon be expanded to involve not just the firm's Internet group, but other areas of research. For the past five years, attorney Jeffrey Liddle had been sitting on piles of documents and transcripts from the arbitration case filed by former Merrill energy analyst Suzanne Cook, who had claimed Merrill's research chief Andrew Melnick had developed a system that dated back to the late 1980s whereby analysts were paid based on their banking work. Merrill had forked over $800,000 to settle the case and keep it confidential.

Liddle contacted Roger Waldman in Spitzer's office, offering all the documents for the price of a subpoena, which would allow him to avoid the confidentiality agreement. Liddle explained that the information would show that the AG's case "goes beyond Blodget" to include the firm's former research chief Andrew Melnick, who had since left Merrill and taken a job as co-head of research at Goldman Sachs. Waldman sounded intrigued. "That sounds great," he said, adding that Spitzer would undoubtedly be interested.

But how much help Spitzer needed from Liddle was unclear. Melnick, as it turns out, was far less conflicted than he first appeared. Though he created the system that required Merrill analysts to list their banking work for their year-end bonus, Spitzer found in his emails that he also called on analysts not to skew their ratings to win deals. In one, he told an analyst: "WE ARE NOT IN THE BUSINESS OF WRITING PRESS RELEASES." Even so, by the first week in May, shares of Merrill had fallen nearly 25 percent since Spitzer began the probe, amid constant speculation about the firm's future. Some of the rating agencies chimed in with warnings as well, issuing reports about how the markets might react if a big Wall Street firm was indicted, and what investors might do to protect their holdings.

Though Spitzer conceded to his staff that an indictment of Merrill was unlikely, publicly he continued to press all the right buttons, refusing in interviews with reporters to rule out criminal charges of either the firm or individuals. Merrill's problems seemed to grow by the hour. Initially, Spitzer had considered settling for a small fine, as little as $10 million, if he could reach a settlement agreement with Merrill that included the release of the emails.

But now that the emails were a matter of public record, Spitzer's staff began pushing the chief to think big, demanding a fine from Merrill in the $100 million range. And it wasn't just his staff that put that number in Spitzer's head. Despite all the press he was receiving, Spitzer was astounded that the business paper of record, The Wall Street Journal, had yet to put his story on page one. He was even more surprised since the Journal story in June 2001 basically touched off the inquiry. One night, he ran into Paul Steiger, the Journal's managing editor, and decided to pop the question. Steiger's response stuck in Spitzer's mind: "$50 million gets you C-1," Steiger said, referring to the front page of the newspaper's Money & Investing section. "Get me $100 million and I'll give you page one." (Steiger says the conversation was intended as a joke.)

With Steiger's words ringing in his ears, Spitzer made $100 million the magical number. Merrill, of course, had other ideas. When The Wall

Street Journal asked if the firm was willing to meet Spitzer's demand, spokesman James Wiggins responded that "a payment of $100 million is not acceptable to Merrill Lynch." But before the paper went to press, press officials at the firm asked the *Journal* reporter to leave Wiggins's quote out of his story. They wouldn't give a reason, but later it became clear that a new consensus had started building inside Merrill that given the nature of Blodget's emails, a payment of $100 million would be getting off easy.

By the spring of 2002, New York Stock Exchange Chairman Richard Grasso had more than a few worries on his hands as well. A short, intense man, with a shaved head, Grasso was a New York success story. He grew up in working-class Jackson Heights, Queens. When he was young, his father ran out on the family, leaving childrearing to his mom and two aunts. A graduate of the New York City public school system, Grasso served in the army, briefly attended Pace University and failed the eye exam to become a New York City cop. That's when he took a job as an $81-a-week clerk with the New York Stock Exchange, where he stayed for the next thrity-five years.

These days, Grasso was earning significantly more than entry-level pay. Around the time Spitzer was ready to file charges against Merrill, the New York Stock Exchange board approved Grasso's salary and bonus at more than $30 million, and for the big Wall Street firms, it was money well spent. During the dotcom craze, no one protected Wall Street's interests better than Grasso. While pundits predicted the demise of the NYSE's specialist system—where professional brokers match buyers and sellers of stock—Grasso preached the benefits of humans over computers like a Baptist minister spreading the word of God. Some people didn't think he would succeed; indeed, several of his own members tried to push regulators to replace the specialists with a NASDAQ-computer model. But Grasso would defy the skeptics, not only beating back the computer advocates, but also by increasing the NYSE's valuable "listings," adding a slew of new corporations to trade on the Big Board even after the bull market had run its course in 2000.

Grasso's greatest moment, however, would not be as a businessman, but as a leader. In the aftermath of the 9/11 terrorist attacks, Grasso became a national hero by meeting a presidential directive to send a valuable message to the terrorists and open the stock exchange in a timely fashion. For Grasso, his 9/11 experience wasn't business, it was personal. He grew up with scores of New York's cops and firemen, and was friends with several who died in the attacks. Now he wanted the stock exchange to be not just a place to sell stocks, but also a symbol of America's resilience in the face of terrorism. With an aggressive PR campaign, the strategy worked, enhancing the NYSE's image beyond Wall Street, and making Grasso a star. His name soon circulated as a possible treasury secretary or future SEC chief, and he was a frequent guest on mainstream television shows when they needed a talking head to describe the economy. Fearing that Grasso might take another job, the NYSE board paid him like a Wall Street CEO, increasing his salary to more than $30 million for 2001. Wall Street CEOs, however, generally don't get standing ovations when they walk into restaurants, as Sal Lombardi, the maître d' of Campagnola, discovered one night as he ushered Grasso to his favorite table and saw the crowd cheer.

But in the spring of 2002, Grasso faced yet another crisis. The two-year decline of the stock market was not filled with the human tragedy of 9/11, but it was threatening Wall Street, Grasso believed, in a significant way. What made Grasso so uneasy about the markets was that the economy, by many measures, appeared to be recovering. The Bush tax cuts were kicking in and people were spending money. But they weren't buying stocks and Grasso believed the corporate scandals were to blame. "People don't trust us anymore," he said at the time.

His worst fears were confirmed one afternoon in mid May as the Merrill research scandal entered its second month. Seated in his office, filled with photos with firemen and police officers, the "the real heroes of 9/11," as he used to say, Grasso picked up a copy of *BusinessWeek* magazine. "How Corrupt Is Wall Street?" the headline screamed. The magazine featured a series of stories on the scandals that had been rocking the financial world, from Enron to the failure of corporate boards to provide oversight. But its lead story featured Spitzer and the research scandal that "has plunged Wall Street into a crisis." *BusinessWeek* predicted that the scandal was likely to expand beyond Merrill Lynch to other firms as Spitzer looked for "smoking guns" across Wall Street.

Grasso was no fan of the liberal media, but he read every word of the story. "This has got legs," he told one colleague. It was time for Grasso to earn his paycheck.

As he dialed Spitzer's office in lower Manhattan, Grasso was prepared to turn on the charm. On a personal level, the two couldn't be any more different. Grasso, the outer borough working-class kid, was a Republican with close ties to former NYC mayor and Spitzer critic, Rudy Giuliani. His circle of friends included the biggest group of Spitzer haters on the planet: the CEOs of Wall Street. While Grasso made his fortune after working thirty-five years at the Exchange, Spitzer grew up rich in the ritzy Riverdale section of the Bronx. Spitzer even bragged about his inheritance; he called it "fuck you" money when people questioned his decisions as being politically motivated.

But the two weren't as far apart as it appeared. Despite Spitzer's life of privilege—prep school at the Horace Mann academy, undergraduate at Princeton, and Harvard law—his father, Bernard, was a self-made man, raised on the Lower East Side of New York, who instilled working-class values in his son. In college, young Eliot spent summers working in construction and even operating a jackhammer, and often spoke about how public service was his way of giving back.

Grasso, meanwhile, had already managed to find some common ground with Spitzer when the two attended some charity events for victims of 9/11. His good friend, Merrill CEO David Komansky, felt nothing but disdain whenever Spitzer's name came up, but Grasso remarked that he found Spitzer engaging and smart, someone he might be able to do business with in the future. He wasn't disappointed as he offered to mediate a sit-down between the two sides, "where everyone can sit and talk without lawyers in the room." He reminded Spitzer that no firm had survived a criminal indictment, and that Merrill was a major engine of New York's economy. Spitzer said he was well aware of the firm's contribution to the state's bottom line, but asked Grasso to keep in mind something else. "People are flipping hamburgers because of some of this stuff," Grasso recalls Spitzer saying.

Grasso indicated that he understood the scope of the problem, but was ready to offer himself—something he knew Spitzer couldn't resist. Grasso knew he could be a valuable ally in Spitzer's effort to gain national recognition by reforming Wall Street research practices. It's unclear what Spitzer said in response, but the argument made sense. Before hanging up, Spitzer suggested that Mr. Grasso call him in the coming days, and that the two should stay in contact as the talks continued.

Grasso's intervention appeared to work. Though there would be many more hours of tense negotiations, on May 22, nearly two months after Spitzer released the now infamous Henry Blodget emails and two weeks after Grasso's phone call to the AG, both sides announced that they had reached a deal. Spitzer held fast to his demand that Merrill pay his $100 million fine, and the next morning, *The Wall Street Journal* published its first page one story on the topic, headlined: "Merrill Will Pay $100 Million Fine to Settle New York's Analyst Probe."

With his $100 million in hand, Spitzer now said the deal was more than just money. The sides had crafted new reforms that would protect small investors for years to come, replacing parts of the Chinese Wall that had been obliterated over time. Though many of these reforms had already been put in place by Harvey Pitt and the self-regulators, Spitzer described the deal as "historic" and "significant." Under the settlement, bankers could no longer determine analysts' compensation, and a new "monitor" must also be appointed to keep tabs on how the firm would comply with various structural reforms in the agreement. Komansky, for his part, issued another "statement of contrition," this time for failing to address conflicts of interest.

As for the size of the fine, Spitzer said it would "send a message . . . that this type of behavior is unacceptable." Still, none of the money went to investors who were victimized by Blodget's research, and as Gretchen Morgenson of *The New York Times* would point out, the $100 million fine paled in comparison to the millions of dollars the firm earned from Blodget's conflicted research. She made one other salient point: $100 million is less than one-third of what Merrill had spent for office supplies and postage the previous year.

Spitzer even agreed to back off of his most far-reaching proposal—making research a separate unit in the firm that cannot be financed through investment banking revenues. A close look at the terms of the accord shows that analysts still had all the incentive in the world to hype their research on potential banking clients, and it didn't take long for other firms to try and head off a probe by agreeing to similar conditions.

Just minutes after the settlement was announced, Jack Grubman's boss, Citigroup CEO Sandy Weill, agreed to adopt all of the Merrill reforms without even a negotiation.

Class action attorneys and lawyers had a vested interest in Spitzer turning the screw as tightly as possible; the more severe the charges, the more money the firm would have to fork over in claims to investors who say they were misled by Blodget's research. But given the mountains of evidence in the Blodget case, they couldn't believe that Spitzer had settled for so little. Liddle was sitting at his desk preparing to hand over to Spitzer the documents from the Cook arbitration, when one of his top associates, David Greenberger, ran into his office. "Jeff, it's all over CNBC, Spitzer cut a deal with Merrill." Liddle couldn't believe what he was hearing. "But Waldman said he wanted the documents," he snapped as he turned on the television to hear the details: No admission of guilt, no separation of investment banking and research, and maybe most important, no indictment of Blodget or his supervisors at the firm.

Liddle just exploded. "You got to be kidding me," he screamed. "This is bullshit."

Liddle was right. The Merrill settlement did far less to break the corrupting influence of investment banking than Spitzer wanted to admit. Spitzer had never offered a clear rationale for not charging Blodget or the other analysts despite the mountain of evidence demonstrating their involvement in the fraud, and the $100 million fine was hardly a deterrent for a firm with a market value in the tens of billions of dollars. But for all its problems, the Merrill settlement had clearly put Spitzer on the map as Wall Street's most aggressive regulator, prompting much-needed soul searching about how the SEC and the NASD largely ignored the biggest scandal to hit Wall Street in years. For Harvey Pitt, the SEC chairman, his worst fears were now being realized: A lowly state official had embarrassed the federal regulatory establishment so much that national standards for Wall Street were now being set in Albany, New York.

While his reforms may not have gone far enough, they were better than nothing, which is exactly what investors had before he launched his probe. Newspapers, magazine and television shows featured him in glowing profiles about Wall Street's new "Enforcer." He was running for reelection in 2002 largely unopposed, facing a candidate that had so little clout that not even Republicans knew her name (Dora Irizarry was a former state judge). More important, his release of the Merrill emails put every Wall Street firm on notice that the New York attorney general was a force to be reckoned with.

Just a few short years ago, analysts were the most coveted employees on Wall Street; now they were pariahs, hated by investors, brokers, and their firm's legal departments for causing so much trouble. Many began leaving the business or finding other jobs. CSFB telecom analyst Dan Reingold, who for years battled Grubman for the attention of investors and journalists, basically stopped making outgoing calls to fund managers as his top stock picks, the Baby Bells, declined with the rest of the market. Reingold says he stopped because he too was about to quit Wall Street, but those who wanted to stay didn't act much differently. Mary Meeker went so far underground that she scaled back publishing research during the first half of 2002, and remained noticeably out of the press for the rest of the year, unless, of course, she was being cited for alleged conflicted research.

Grubman toned down his act as well. In the spring of 2002, he published a report titled, "For Whom the Bell Does Not Toll," which accurately warned that the Baby Bell operating companies would continue to face tough times ahead. But without his blast voice mails and constant ranting on conference calls, no one seemed to notice that Grubman was the author even as shares declined significantly.

The superstar analysts, however, couldn't erase years of hype from the market's memory. Even before the Merrill settlement, Spitzer had his sights squarely focused on Meeker and Grubman. And their firms Morgan Stanley and Citigroup. Michael Schlein, Citigroup's politically connected flack, clearly understood what was at stake. Schlein had been chief of staff for Arthur Levitt at the SEC before taking a job with Citigroup, where executives were impressed with his connections inside the New York State and national Democratic Party apparatus. In fact, Spitzer and his wife, Silda Wall, had attended Schlein's wedding reception a few months earlier, where they were seated near Citigroup founder Sandy Weill and Charles Prince, his former general counsel and still his trusted adviser.

But the ink on the Merrill settlement was barely dry when Schlein tracked down Silda Wall at the New York State Democratic Party convention in New York City, handing her what he described as an important document: a new plan by Citigroup to reform analyst practices. Wall quickly passed off the document to a member of Spitzer's staff.

In the proposal, the firm agreed to adopt all of the reforms that the attorney general had imposed on Merrill, and nothing more. There would be no discipline of Grubman. (Schlein continued to tell reporters that Citigroup believed Grubman did nothing wrong.) Spitzer publicly characterized the move as a good first step to dealing with the problem of research conflicts, but privately he let his staff know that Citigroup would have to do much more.

"I have just two words for those guys," Spitzer later remarked to an aide. "Jack Grubman."

Like Schlein, Donald Kempf, the general counsel of Morgan Stanley, had been closely monitoring the Merrill dealings with Spitzer. Plainspoken and aggressive, Kempf had an uncanny resemblance to Senator John Mc-Cain and he certainly brought a military-like precision to the job. As a young man, he spent three years in the Marines, attended Villanova University, where he was a mediocre student, but managed to get into Harvard Law after acing his LSATs and later convincing a former Marine on the admissions committee that a leatherneck would make a great diversity candidate for a school populated by geeks.

Kempf spent most of his thirty-five-year career at the law firm of Kirkland & Ellis and was considered one of the nation's top trial corporate attorneys, defending companies like General Motors and Dow Chemical. His Marine Corps training came in handy in the courtroom. Kempf developed a reputation as a lawyer not afraid to fight for a client and take a case to a jury if he thought he could win.

When he came to Morgan in 1999, the firm was embroiled in a nasty scandal involving a former employee, Christian Curry, who had posed nude for a gay men's magazine. When he was fired, Curry claimed he was the victim of sex discrimination (he also said he wasn't gay). Morgan said Curry had cheated on his expenses. The situation turned ugly for Morgan after it was disclosed that officials there made a $10,000 payment to an informant who said he had information about Curry. The conventional wisdom on Wall Street would have been to write a check to Curry and end the matter once and for all. But Kempf took another route. Over a series of dinners at his favorite Manhattan restaurant, Kempf convinced

Curry's lawyer, defense attorney Benedict Morelli, that he didn't have much of a case. In the end the two sides did indeed settle, without Curry getting a dime. Morgan, however, agreed to make a $1 million payment to the Urban League.

Kempf also showed Wall Street that he was willing to play by a slightly different set of rules, fighting rather than settling cases against brokers and other executives, and earning the enmity of investigators at the SEC and the NASD. Private attorneys accustomed to Merrill's practice of cutting deals despised Kempf's style so much that they nicknamed their nemesis "Mein Kempf." But Kempf seemed to enjoy the notoriety. "My competitors on the street keep saying how they have such a good relationship with everybody," he once told a colleague. "I would have a good relationship with these people too if I shelled out $10 million every time something happened."

In Spitzer, Kempf was facing his biggest challenge yet. Like many of the superstar analysts, Meeker had been a key component in Morgan's investment banking machine, and Kempf knew there were sizable risks in any aggressive defense strategy against Spitzer. As a former prosecutor, Spitzer wasn't part of the Wall Street–SEC club that Kempf disdained and would be less likely to cut the firm a break if he had the goods. Maybe more daunting, Kempf believed, Spitzer had the Martin Act, which basically gave him the power to indict over the Wall Street equivalent of a parking ticket.

So on Kempf's orders, his staff had scoured Meeker's research reports, spoken to her colleagues, and reviewed thousands of documents, including her emails. Kempf did a little research of his own, immersing himself in Meeker's research reports, and spending some time with Dennis Shea, her immediate supervisor, grilling him about the fine points of how research is practiced at Morgan Stanley. He assembled dozens of newspaper articles in which Meeker had clearly warned of the coming Internet collapse.

Under the intense grilling from Kempf and the others, Meeker initially believed the lawyers didn't buy her story about being a true believer. When it was over, they all agreed that Meeker may have had a couple bad years as analyst, but the evidence showed she published research that she believed in. Even better, there were no emails of the Henry Blodget variety. Meeker had worried that she had "written something stupid," but for someone who helped popularize the use of Web-based technology, Meeker seemed to prefer to communicate the old-fashioned way, over the telephone.

One of the lawyers on his staff, Alex Dimitrief, put it bluntly. "Don, we have a good story to tell." Kempf said he had come to the same conclusion. "Okay," he said, "I'm willing to fight this one out."

In early June, Kempf arrived at Spitzer's office for a morning meeting with Dinallo about the investigation. Dinallo and his staff were ready to play hardball. They had been reading over Meeker's research with its over-the-top predictions for companies like Women.com and other Internet failures that Morgan brought public during the bubble years as the premier firm in the sector. But what made Meeker such a big target was her role inside Morgan Stanley as the firm's chief Internet banker. Blodget was a tool of investment banking, Mary Meeker was the franchise.

Kempf began the conversation with a compliment. "Ya know, I really enjoyed reading the Merrill case," he told Dinallo, who was the primary author. "It read like a dime-store novel." Kempf said he had tried "all types of complicated cases in areas that I know very little about," during his long career, and what made him successful was his ability to "tell stories." Kempf added. "That was one hell of a story you told about Blodget, and I got my own dime-store novel to tell."

Dinallo thanked Kempf for the compliment, but explained it would take much more to make Spitzer to go away. Dinallo's opening offer: A $150 million fine, a possible fraud charge for the firm, and "structural" changes to the research and banking relationship. Meeker, he said, may have to face charges as well.

But Kempf came armed. "We're not Merrill Lynch," he told Dinallo. "And Mary isn't Henry Blodget." Kempf said Morgan was ready to fight tooth and nail with Spitzer to protect Meeker. "By the time Merrill began fighting back they were already dead," he said. Morgan would make the public know that unlike Blodget, Meeker hadn't issued any inflammatory emails. "We checked and she's clean," Kempf said. More important, Meeker's standards were superior to any Internet analyst on the street, he observed, sharing with Dinallo a little known fact about Meeker's research. Morgan had only underwritten 8 percent of all tech IPOs because Meeker had helped the firm turn down $1 billion in fees on deals that got done elsewhere, including the prestigious Goldman Sachs investment bank.

Kempf also warned Dinallo that he had had his public relations staff draft a number of op-ed pieces and advertisements that would underscore the statistical evidence supporting Meeker's innocence. His personal favorite, he told Dinallo, was an open letter by Morgan CEO Phil Purcell that compared Mary Meeker's record as a stock picker to baseball great Ty Cobb's record as a hitter. According to Kempf's analysis, Meeker's stocks underperformed the market only once, in 2000, the year the Internet blew up (he left out Meeker's first year with the firm when she nearly lost her job). Ty Cobb batted .240 in 1904.

"Even Ty Cobb had one bad year," the advertisement read.

"I'm not telling you not to charge us, but if you do you better get it right. We're ready to fight." Dinallo calmly told Kempf that he would talk to Spitzer. Deep down, Dinallo wondered if this was a battle he could win.

With Kempf's legal assessment in hand, Morgan's CEO Phil Purcell couldn't wait to let the world know Meeker would survive. Since Spitzer's assault, Morgan's stock had been getting crushed, falling nearly 25 percent on the assumption that Meeker would go down like Blodget. But in a speech to brokers, Purcell confidently predicted that both Meeker and the firm would be cleared. Emboldened by the lack of evidence against Meeker, Purcell attempted to push through Congress a bill that would bar state officials, like Spitzer, from the regulation of Wall Street.

When Spitzer heard about Purcell's move, he went ballistic, publicly attacking what Purcell did as "a perversion of American law. The only good this does is that it helps Phil Purcell and Morgan Stanley because he wants to be excused from the scrutiny that he's subject to—and it won't work." If Morgan was hoping for a quick settlement, it ended with that gesture. Despite Kempf's threat to fight tooth and nail to save the Internet Queen, Spitzer soon ordered Dinallo to make their simultaneous investigations of Grubman as well as Meeker his top priority.

Dinallo put two of his best on the cases. Roger Waldman was assigned to investigate Mary Meeker and Morgan Stanley, while Bruce Topman was appointed to lead the Citigroup inquiry that focused on Jack Grubman.

Spitzer seemed to get bolder in his rhetoric as well. No longer was he looking simply to clean up research. He was now talking about a broader goal of reforming the vast conflicts on Wall Street, where they dealt with the massive financial conglomerates that were spawned by the end of Glass-Steagall. These huge companies, Spitzer explained, controlled market access for millions of small investors, but they mainly served the interests of the rich and the powerful. How could anyone expect Jack Grubman or Mary Meeker to publish honest research if their firms were chasing huge fees from corporate America for everything from bank lending to investment banking?

While it would be impossible to bring back Glass-Steagall, Spitzer said he wanted the next best thing—a broad new regulatory apparatus that recognized that small investors were placed in harm's way.

Watching Spitzer get all the glory, from admiring newspaper articles to puff-piece television profiles, was a gut-wrenching experience for NASD chief Robert Glauber. Since a 1996 settlement with the Securities and Exchange Commission over its failure to police trading practices, the NASD had been in the process of beefing up its regulation of Wall Street abuse. Glauber, a former undersecretary of Treasury for George Bush Sr. and a Harvard Business School professor, was brought in to help complete the task. But Glauber's record in addressing analyst fraud had been a weak one. Nearly all the technology and Internet stocks promoted by Henry Blodget had traded on the NASDAQ, yet the agency hadn't brought a single case against a major analyst for issuing conflicted research. Making matters worse, the NASD had blown a big chance to be the first regulator to bring an action against Blodget as far back as 1999, when fund manager Eric Von der Porten had alerted the agency to the problem.

Now, with Spitzer in the news daily challenging the NASD's ability to regulate the securities business, Glauber let his staff know that he wanted results immediately. As it turned out, his timing was perfect. By the summer of 2002, the agency had made progress investigating Jack Grubman's disastrous Winstar call. Though it lacked the pizzazz of Blodget's emails (in fact investigators had not yet found many emails involving Grubman, only thirty to thirty-five emails), investigators believed the case hit all the right notes. Grubman had been the most popular analyst during the 1990s bubble, but his Winstar call was an ob-

vious disaster. At the very least, NASD officials believed, Grubman violated agency rules, which state that analysts must have a "sound basis"
for their recommendations. (Grubman had a $50 price target on Winstar
when it was trading as a virtual penny stock.) During his testimony,
Grubman also conceded that he had attempted to downgrade Winstar,
but was prevented from doing so by Salomon's compliance department.
As it turned out, the firm was arranging for some last-minute financing
for the cash-strapped outfit.

The NASD's enforcement chief, Barry Goldsmith, said his division
was ready to roll with a case against Grubman, the first time Wall Street's
most prominent analyst was charged by a regulatory agency. But he
pointed out something else to his immediate supervisor, Mary Schapiro.
During breaks in testimony, Grubman often bantered with NASD investigators about his interest in jogging and sports, before leaving the room
to frantically send out a series of messages on his BlackBerry. Given the
dearth of emails, Goldsmith suggested that the agency dig deeper.

"You never know what you will find," Goldsmith said. Schapiro
agreed.

News that the NASD intended to charge Grubman with fraud over his
Winstar rating caught Spitzer's staff flat-footed. Dinallo had already told
his boss that the evidence he uncovered against Grubman, thus far, was
sketchy at best. The few emails that he had found showed that Grubman
had also butted heads with bankers who sought to have him conform his
recommendations to the market realities in the post bubble world—
namely to begin recommending companies that were not in financial
distress and could issue stock. Others showed that when Grubman did
fold, he did so because of immense pressure from Salomon's power
banking arm.

But the NASD's case changed the equation. The Winstar investigation revealed that Grubman had cut a valuable investment banking client
huge breaks in his research, and now Spitzer scrambled to get back into
the news. As the scandals continued to spread, he joined the growing
chorus of detractors that called for Harvey Pitt's resignation. A day before his congressional testimony about the corporate scandals, Spitzer
asked Pitt if he would support his effort to strike down Purcell's attempts
to remove state officials from securities regulation. Pitt said he believed

the states deserve a place at the table, but he would have to support any bill that underscored the SEC's role as the nation's top securities regulator. "Not good enough," Spitzer insisted. A few hours later, Spitzer spoke out about the lack of leadership at the SEC, pointing to the commission's missed opportunities to address market abuses, including the research conflicts his office had uncovered.

After Spitzer's testimony, Dinallo told his boss that maybe he should temper his statements and not condemn the entire agency. "Steve Cutler is a pretty good guy and he's going to be pissed," Dinallo said. Sure enough, Cutler placed a call to Spitzer, asking if he would "lay off" the commission at a sensitive time. Spitzer said he would, but Cutler still wasn't happy. Later he scoffed at Spitzer's promise, telling one person that Spitzer had "set up" Pitt on the issue. There would be more setups to come.

CHAPTER TWELVE

Jack on the Stand

At forty-nine years of age, with nearly twenty years of Wall Street experience under his belt, Jack Grubman should have been basking in the sweet spot of a long and prosperous career on Wall Street. But by the summer of 2002, Grubman had become Public Enemy No. 1 in the burgeoning research scandal. Journalists demanded answers for his soured stock picks, investors blamed him for their shrinking retirement accounts, while brokers at Salomon Smith Barney who had been burned by his research calls launched an all-out effort to get him fired. Grubman, the self-described prizefighter from the streets of Philly, had to avoid certain parts of his own firm if he wanted to survive.

It wasn't long before Jake Zamansky, the man who helped propel research conflicts into a major scandal in 2001 with a case against Blodget, added to Grubman's misery. Zamansky filed an arbitration claim against Grubman on behalf of investor George Zicarelli, the CBS cameraman who claimed to have lost his life savings following Grubman's advice. "Grubman and Smith Barney must be held accountable for misleading investors with thoroughly conflicted stock research," Zamansky told Reuters. "This was brought to show it goes way beyond Blodget."

Zamansky seemed to relish a fight with Grubman, calling him "Wall Street's most conflicted analyst" and sought $10 million for his client. Citigroup's lawyers scoffed at the case as nothing more than a nuisance suit, but for Grubman the attacks hit home. As it turned out, Zamansky and Grubman actually grew up together in Northeast Philly, smoking pot and chasing girls during their high school days.

Grubman immediately made the connection with his old buddy, but Zamansky was clueless. "I went to school with Grubman?" he said after being informed by a reporter. Zamansky quickly asked his mother, still living in the old neighborhood, if she remembered a friend named Jack Grubman. "Of course I remember Jack," said Zamansky's seventy-five-year-old mother, who pulled out Jake's high school yearbook. Sure enough, there was a photo of a young Jack Grubman smiling, with his thick hair covering his eyes. Next to his photo, Grubman wrote a short note to his friend. "Jake, we had fun in English all year and I'll miss you in Boston. Best of luck, Jack."

Perhaps most surprising to Zamansky was the list of Grubman's high school interests, which included "debating society" and the "marching band." Boxing? The legendary Wall Street fighter never mentioned it. "I guess he lied about that as well," Zamansky later remarked, bragging that he couldn't wait to squeeze another big settlement out of a guy who "forgot where he came from."

Grubman probably wished he were back home in Northeast Philly, because in New York, virtually all his top picks were in bankruptcy or heading that way. On June 25, his favorite stock, WorldCom, announced it had misstated earnings by nearly $4 billion, undetected by Grubman despite his close ties to company officials. The announcement marked the largest accounting scandal in the nation's history, even greater than Enron's massive account fraud. Grubman managed to slip in a downgrade of the company just a day before WorldCom made the announcement, cutting his "neutral" rating to "underperform."

But that did little to stem the controversy surrounding his research. Newspaper reporters left messages day and night at his various residences, the town house on the Upper East Side of Manhattan and his home in the Hamptons. One television reporter, Mike Huckman of CNBC, camped out in front of Grubman's ritzy town house with a television crew hoping for an impromptu interview. "I have nothing to say," Grubman said as walked down the street, his arms flailing. "This is a huge invasion of privacy. Nobody saw this coming."

"Do you regret staying so bullish" on WorldCom? Huckman asked.

"Why are you harassing me?" Grubman shot back, turning the corner and rushing off.

Grubman's life had now become a tabloid story. In the coming weeks, his name would make it into the celebrity gossip pages as the long-lost cousin of controversial New York socialite and hit-and-run driver Lizzie Grubman (he denied they were related). The New York Observer wrote that just a few days after Huckman's interview, he had transferred the deed to his town house, purchased for $6.2 million in 1999, to his wife, LuAnn.

Spitzer raised the stakes even higher, demanding information regarding AT&T, a clear sign that he was zeroing in on one of Grubman's most controversial research calls and the $60 million in banking fees Salomon made on the AT&T wireless deal after Grubman went positive on the stock in 1999. Spitzer's office didn't have to dig much to make the connection. Jeff Liddle put aside his grudge with Spitzer over the Merrill settlement and during a meeting with Spitzer mentioned the November 1999 *Wall Street Journal* article that discussed Grubman's upgrade of the stock and, specifically, how it was timed to help win the wireless underwriting, with the pressure applied by Weill, who was an AT&T board member.

By now, Spitzer had made "structural reforms" the main point of his investigation, but Liddle told him Wall Street didn't need any more rules. "If you piled up all the regulations preventing research conflicts it would reach the ceiling," Liddle said. "But people like Sandy Weill won't listen to you unless you indict someone." Liddle recalls that Spitzer said it was too early to talk about indictments, but he wasn't ruling anything out.

Spitzer had good reason to keep his options open. The House Financial Service Committee decided to hold hearings on the burgeoning World-Com accounting scandal with its focus not just on Ebbers's and Sullivan's alleged deceit, but on Grubman's as well. With the Republicans in the majority, the committee was run by Mike Oxley, a congressman from a rural district in Ohio, who was among the largest recipients of Wall Street campaign cash, and as a result, one of the brokerage industry's biggest supporters in Washington. Oxley, it should be noted, was careful not to overplay his Wall Street allegiance as the stock market bubble burst and investors were demanding answers for the rash of corporate scandals that swept through the markets. He allowed the congressional hearings by a member of his committee, fellow Republican Representative Richard Baker, to go on for several months without much interference either pro or con, people on Baker's staff say. But after 9/11, the Baker hearings mysteriously disappeared from the congressional calendar. Baker later attributed the move to new priorities after the terrorist attacks, but political insiders say Oxley had finally intervened following complaints from the brokerage industry.

With Spitzer's investigation gaining momentum and WorldCom's bankruptcy looking more and more like fraud, Oxley needed to show that Republicans weren't tone deaf to one of the biggest scandals that involved the brokerage business. Even Wall Street's biggest defenders in Washington had to admit that the facts didn't look good for Merrill, Morgan, and now Citigroup, given Jack Grubman's unabashed support for WorldCom almost to the day the company filed for bankruptcy, and the firm's long relationship as WorldCom's top underwriter of stocks and bonds.

In the hearings, scheduled for early July 2002, Oxley and the ranking Democrat on the committee, John LaFalce, vowed to put politics aside and hold the bad guys accountable. Staffers for the various congressmen on the committee soon began a series of round-the-clock meetings to accomplish the hearings' real objective, namely, to make their guy the star of the show. On the front line of that battle was Mike Paese, a senior counsel for the committee's Democratic leadership, who specialized in financial issues. Paese had the right mix of Wall Street and Washington to make him perfect for the task ahead. He had been with the committee for nearly two years, but before that had worked five years as a securities lawyer on Wall Street. During that time, he got to know many of the street's top players, from super-lawyers Martin Lipton and Harvey Pitt to the senior executives at many of the leading Wall Street firms. Equally important, Paese also became familiar with many of Wall Street's dirty little secrets, including conflicted research, which everybody knew existed, but only Eliot Spitzer had the guts to address.

As he prepared for the hearings, Paese received an interesting tip about one of those secrets. It came from a Washington lawyer/lobbyist named John Cuneo. The tip, Paese recalls, went something like this: Cuneo said a lawsuit had been filed against Salomon Smith Barney alleging that hyped research wasn't the only way the firm won investment banking business from WorldCom. Salomon had also enticed top executives to hand the firm lucrative underwriting deals by allotting shares of hot IPOs to the executives' personal brokerage accounts, a practice known as spinning.

"Ask Jack Grubman," Cuneo advised, "if he ever helped direct shares of IPOs to WorldCom in exchange for business." Paese said he would.

The lawsuit, as Paese would soon discover, was filed by a former Salomon Smith Barney broker named David Chacon, who claimed he witnessed first hand how WorldCom's CEO Bernard Ebbers was the beneficiary of spinning, and how Grubman played a role in the scam. Several years ago, *The Wall Street Journal* had published a series of stories on the topic, but the SEC dropped the case, complaining that the amount of money involved was too small to have mattered. But if Chacon was to be believed, the deception was huge. Salomon Smith Barney had tremendously enriched Ebbers by spinning millions of dollars in IPO shares into his brokerage account, in exchange for sending tens of millions of dollars more in banking business Citigroup's way.

If this stuff was going on at Salomon, Paese believed other big firms must be involved as well. So he began taking steps to expand the hearings to other firms. There was just one problem. Oxley's hearings focused on WorldCom and Salomon Smith Barney, the Wall Street firm with the closest ties to the Democratic Party. Thanks to Sandy Weill's association with people like Jesse Jackson and his hiring of former Clinton Treasury Secretary Robert Rubin, Citigroup was labeled a "Democratic firm" by Republicans in Congress. Grubman didn't help matters when he made a $100,000 contribution to the Democratic Senatorial Committee right around the time the WorldCom scandal was announced.

Despite Paese's best efforts, Oxley wasn't budging. "What about Morgan Stanley and Merrill Lynch?" Paese asked Andrew Cochran, one of Oxley's key advisers. "Why are we only picking on Democrats?" But with the Republicans in the majority, Paese was powerless to do much more than complain. "We feel very strongly it's got to be Citigroup, and Citigroup alone," is all Cochran said.

The ranking Democrat, John LaFalce, had long advocated broad-based hearings on Wall Street's role in the scandals, and now he was prepared to make the most of his opportunity. In fact, LaFalce had planned to cover so much ground that Paese believed the Grubman-spinning question would get lost in the mix. As a result, he and another staffer, Todd Harper, handed the question to another Democrat on the committee, Pennsylvania Congressman Paul Kanjorski, who couldn't wait to turn the screws.

The hearings, set for July 8, certainly featured an all-star cast of characters. Ebbers, Sullivan, and Grubman, three of the most prominent executives during the bubble, would testify before the full committee. The smart money had Ebbers and Sullivan invoking their Fifth Amendment right against self-incrimination, while Grubman was the wild card. By now Grubman was doing everything he could to distance himself from WorldCom and its fallen leaders. At one point before the proceedings began, Ebbers attempted to physically embrace Grubman, who abruptly pulled away. The man he once considered a friend was a friend no more.

As was expected, Ebbers and Sullivan took the Fifth. Grubman, however, chose to speak. By now he was a shell of the man who once commanded the attention of the markets and the media as the street fighter with an MIT degree. As Grubman raised his right hand to take the oath of truthfulness, he appeared frail, with dark rings under his eyes as if he hadn't slept the night before.

The committee appeared to have little sympathy for the fallen superstar. Almost immediately, he was asked about the WorldCom bankruptcy and accounting fraud. Grubman said he had no advance knowledge of the matter. "I regret I was wrong in keeping my rating on WorldCom highly for too long," he simply stated. When he was asked about his massive salary and whether it was linked to snaring banking business, Grubman said there was no "direct" link, but he did confess the size of his massive pay package. Over the past four years, Grubman said, he averaged around $20 million a year. Banking, he finally admitted, played a role along with other factors in calculating his year-end bonus.

Kanjorski came next. "I have information that Salomon Smith Barney was offering special IPO (allocations) to executives of WorldCom on a specialized basis."

Grubman didn't duck the question, although he should have. "I am trying to think if I can answer that specifically yes or no," he said in a nasal voice. "I just don't recall because that's not something I would be involved with. So I can't recall. I'm not saying no, I'm not saying yes, I just can't recall." For Grubman it was the worst of all possible answers. Reporters took special note of Grubman's nondenial, and continued to dig for anything that would link him to the IPO allocations. Paese, sitting in the audience, knew his guy had just stolen the show. "I can't believe he just said that," he muttered to an aide. Zamansky, watching the spectacle in his office, began to mimic Grubman's answer with a hearty laugh. "What a fool," he told an associate. Jane Sherburne, Citigroup's Washington attorney, was shocked by Grubman's weaselly response. "It was not the answer we were hoping for," she later told Paese.

The Grubman testimony was among the most closely watched events on Wall Street that year. The *Wall Street Journal*'s newsroom, now located in a SoHo loft after 9/11 destroyed its World Financial Center headquarters, virtually shut down as reporters and editors gathered around several newsroom television sets to catch a glimpse of the show. Uptown at Morgan Stanley, Mary Meeker also watched in amazement as the Grubman spectacle unfolded. At first she thought how horrible he looked on TV. "He looks like a chipmunk," Meeker thought as she watched the proceedings with Morgan's PR director Ray O'Rourke.

Soon, it dawned on Meeker: This could be me! Meeker was visibly shaken as she tried to remember if she sent out any emails that could be construed the wrong way, and if she would have to testify next.

Following the hearings, Robert Rubin, the former treasury secretary brought to Citigroup as Weill's top rainmaker, unbelievably claimed that the Grubman testimony "hasn't been much discussed" among top Citigroup officials, in an interview with CNBC's Maria Bartiromo. But he did add that Grubman's theory of never-ending growth in the telecom business "had some flaws in it." Bartiromo never pressed him on what those flaws could be, but inside Citigroup, people understood Grubman's shortcomings all too well. A few days after the testimony, Sherburne conceded to Paese that it would be "better if he was gone," and the Grubman deathwatch began. It's unclear if CEO Sandy Weill watched Grubman's testimony, but several people close to him say he was outraged by Grubman's poor performance. Two years earlier, Weill was quoted extolling Grubman as one of the best analysts in the business. Now he could barely contain his anger. "Based on what I've heard, I think Jack Grubman believed in what he said, but it turns out that, at the end of the period some of his thoughts about where the industry would go and how it would be put together didn't work out," Weill said in a rare interview with *The Wall Street Journal* shortly after the hearings. Weill was then asked if Grubman had a future at the firm. His answer left little doubt. "Jack is a smart person but he was definitely wrong. In retrospect, you might say he stayed too long in those positions, but I think he believed what he was saying."

Soon Grubman suffered the ultimate indignity for any major Wall Street figure. His "dot drawing" that appeared almost daily in *The Wall Street Journal* was changed from one with a big smile and a full head of hair to a more somber portrait, with his eyes sunken and hair thinning. It seemed as if Grubman just couldn't catch a break. He continued to show up to work, listening in on analysts' conference calls with company executives and attempting to write research, but the controversy made it nearly impossible to perform. Like many New Yorkers, he escaped the stress of living in the New York City pressure cooker by jogging in Central Park, but now for Grubman, during the very hot summer of 2002, there was no escape. One morning in early August, Grubman headed for the park when a man in a T-shirt and shorts stuck out his hand.

"Hi, Eliot Spitzer," he said.

Grubman, who had yet to be deposed by Spitzer's office, was shocked by the appearance of his chief tormenter. "People would be mad if they knew you and I were talking," Spitzer said, with a laugh.

But Grubman wasn't laughing. "Yeah," Grubman agreed. "It's going to be nice when this is all over."

"That's right," Spitzer said. "But we have a lot of issues to resolve."

Grubman was well aware of the issues on the table. "Yeah, but conflicts are inherent on Wall Street," he said. "I don't know how you're going to resolve them without some kind of general reform."

To Grubman's surprise, Spitzer agreed. "Yeah, you're right."

When Grubman got back to the office, he retold the story to a colleague. "I can't believe this is the guy who wants my head on a silver platter," he said. Spitzer, meanwhile, called Grubman's lawyers to let them know he wasn't conducting an informal deposition.

That would come later. By the late summer, Citigroup had replaced Merrill Lynch as the face of conflicted research as investigators started to focus on his controversial upgrade of AT&T in November 1999. AT&T certainly wasn't Grubman's worst research call; following his bullishness on WorldCom from its high of around $70 a share would have cost investors much more money. But as Spitzer's team looked at their evidence, Grubman's AT&T flip-flop crystallized much of what was wrong with Wall Street research during the market bubble. Grubman had been negative on the stock for years, and only turned positive, it appeared, when the company was dangling tens of millions in banking fees as it prepared to spin off its wireless telephone unit in a massive stock deal. Grubman downgraded the stock a few months after Salomon was paid its $60 million underwriting fee for the wireless deal. The only losers appeared to be investors.

But what made the AT&T case so mouthwatering for Spitzer was that it had star quality. Grubman's boss, Sandy Weill, was an AT&T board member and reportedly pressured Grubman to upgrade the stock. Adding to the intrigue was speculation that AT&T's CEO Michael Armstrong, a Citigroup board member, was pressuring Weill to keep his analyst in line around the time of the deal.

The unfolding scandal had grave implications for the Citigroup CEO. Before the Grubman morass, Weill had been considered the greatest Wall Street CEO of his generation, and Citigroup with its combination of investment banking, commercial banking, insurance, and brokers an unmatched power on Wall Street. In early July, *CEO* magazine named Weill CEO of the year; some people on Wall Street considered him CEO of the decade for what he accomplished during the bubble.

But now regulators were combing through Weill's creation for its excess. Enron, WorldCom, and Grubman's research were only the most prominent of the multitude of scandals rocking Citigroup midway through 2002. Weill took this criticism particularly hard. Friends say he began drinking more, and then noticed that he had lost a lot of weight. The reason for the rapid weight loss, Citigroup officials said, was his new workout regimen. (*The New York Times* called Weill and his No. 2, Charles Prince, "occasional jogging partners.") Not everyone bought the story of Weill's conversion from heavy drinker to fitness nut. "The only diet Sandy went on is the Spitzer diet," NYSE chairman Dick Grasso told one associate. "He's shitting his brains out."

And losing money. Aside from the potential legal problems facing Weill, the Spitzer investigation hit Weill where it hurt him the most: in his wallet. Weill is known to obsessively watch the company's stock price because much of his massive wealth (estimated at around $2 billion) was tied up in Citigroup stock. As shares began to fall sharply, Spitzer began to ramp up his inquiry and Weill's personal holdings began to shrink considerably. For top officials at Citigroup, drastic action was necessary, and all fingers pointed at Jack Grubman.

For months, Citigroup officials including the bank's chief spokesman, Michael Schlein, had said that the firm believed Grubman (a) did nothing wrong and (b) could stay at the firm as long as he wanted. But in mid August 2002, the company's position took a dramatic turn. Grubman received a call from Michael Carpenter, the head of Weill's Salomon Smith

Barney investment bank. "I think it makes sense that you leave the firm, but I'm willing to listen." Grubman replied that he was ready to go as well, though only under certain conditions.

First he wanted his salary through 2003, as well as all stock and options granted to him under his famous five-year contract that helped him earn more money than almost any analyst in history. Grubman appeared to have given the size and scope of his package a lot of thought. He also wanted complete "forgiveness" of the $15 million "loan" that Citigroup gave him as part of its counteroffer when Goldman sought his services back in 1998. (Under the terms of his contract, Grubman was forced to repay the loan if he left the firm because of a regulatory action.)

Grubman certainly wasn't going down cheaply. He wanted an office in midtown Manhattan, and to be paid for his time talking to lawyers about Citigroup research even after he left the firm. Most significant, he wanted Citigroup to pay his legal bills, which would amount to millions of dollars. The entire package surpassed $30 million, a huge sum of money for someone accused of so much treachery. But Carpenter agreed. In exchange, Grubman would have to sign a confidentiality agreement, and cooperate with Citigroup in its defense.

On August 15, 2002, Jack Grubman, once the nation's most important stock analyst, announced he was leaving Citigroup. In his resignation letter, Grubman lashed out at the "current climate of criticism" that "made it impossible to perform my work to the standards I believe the clients of Salomon Smith Barney deserved." Anyone waiting for an apology would be disappointed. After all, Grubman pointed out, he was far from the only conflicted analyst on Wall Street. "I did my work as an analyst within a widely understood framework consistent with industry practice that is now being second-guessed."

It was the most believable statement Grubman had made in some time.

NYSE chairman Dick Grasso didn't spend much time second-guessing Grubman, but the "peace dividend" he had hoped for when he approached Spitzer in May over the Merrill investigation never came. Investors, skeptical about Wall Street's promises that it had reformed, stayed out of the markets as stocks continued to slide with every story detailing various investigations involving research conflicts. Grasso's "member firms," the financial companies that served on the NYSE board, were leading the losers in the market. Shares of Citigroup, Morgan Stanley, and even Merrill continued to slide as the investigations continued unabated.

The problem for Wall Street wasn't just Eliot Spitzer. Class action lawyers, like Mel Weiss, the most famous and successful of the breed, and private attorneys like Zamansky and Liddle eyed the research scandals as their biggest paydays in years, particularly now that they had a number of competing regulators digging up dirt that could be used as evidence in lawsuits. Liddle, for his part, was now representing Chacon in a wrongful termination suit against Citigroup. A new consensus emerged among Wall Street insiders about the financial impact of the investigations: The fines by Spitzer and the SEC would pale in comparison to the potentially huge legal liability that could accrue once the investigations were over and investors attempted to recoup their losses. "Mel and the boys are going to have a field day," Grasso remarked at one point.

And there was no end in sight. Only a few days after Pitt announced a plan to force Wall Street firms to agree to a more formal separation of research and investment banking, Spitzer one-upped the SEC chairman. He ordered Dinallo to work all weekend and quickly turn a batch of Citigroup emails into a major case against five of the nation's top telecom executives, including Bernie Ebbers, for "spinning." The case, the first of its kind, alleged that Ebbers and the others personally benefited from their cozy relationship with Grubman and Citigroup by receiving shares of hot IPOs in exchange for banking business. Spitzer demanded that the executives return to him a whopping $1.5 billion in improper gains.

But even more important than the amount of money Spitzer was demanding, he had embarrassed the SEC once again by not giving Cutler a courtesy call that he was treading on his turf. Cutler immediately called Spitzer and complained that Spitzer had front-run several civil and possible criminal cases already in the works, making it much more difficult for prosecutors to finish the job. Spitzer didn't say much, but when Cutler got off the phone, he was livid, telling colleagues that Spitzer was nothing more than a political opportunist, using Citigroup's recent document production of emails as a way to score cheap political points with a dubious case. (There were no smoking guns showing a direct quid pro quo between the IPO allocations to the executives and Citigroup's winning of banking business from their companies.) Cutler was so outraged that he told a colleague that Spitzer had even screwed Ebbers by filing the action even before he started settlement discussions with the former World-Com CEO.

Grasso, whose reputation had been built restoring public confidence in the markets after 9/11, was now watching all his good work evaporate as the investigations rolled forward and the markets slumped. After his initial meeting with Spitzer, Grasso had touched base with Dinallo and said he was all for the AG's office "giving the death penalty" to the bad guys. But now, his main concern was that "the competition for headlines" among the regulators had added an unnecessary level of doubt in the markets already ravaged by the dotcom bust and 9/11.

"I've never seen anything like this before," Grasso told one friend. Grasso believed that having so many competing probes blasting out headlines every day was the major problem facing the markets. What was needed, he said, was a little "détente" among the warring regulators, and he had no problem getting the process started.

His first call was to Pitt. Grasso and Pitt had been close friends since at least the mid 1990s, when Grasso hired Pitt to represent the NYSE, which had become the focus of an SEC investigation into the trading practice of its floor brokers. (The case was settled for a small fine and no charge of securities fraud.) During 9/11 and its aftermath, they were nearly inseparable, talking every day as Grasso tried to get the NYSE operational and Pitt gave him the political cover to take as much time as necessary.

Given their relationship, Grasso believed he could speak to Pitt like a friend. "Harvey, public confidence is getting murdered. We've got to stop this nonsense," Grasso said, proposing a dinner where all the parties could sit down, agree to work together, and settle their differences like "gentlemen."

Pitt was initially skeptical. He viewed Spitzer as a political opportunist, someone more concerned with headlines than meaningful reforms. But Grasso was insistent. "Harvey, I know you don't like Spitzer, but we have to bring this to an end," he said. He reminded Pitt that Spitzer could be reasonable, pointing to the final terms of the Merrill settlement, which were far weaker than what he initially demanded. Then he reminded Pitt of something else. No firm had ever survived a criminal indictment, and Spitzer's targets were major players. If Morgan or Citigroup went down, the economy could be destroyed. Pitt agreed to meet, and promised to bring the NASD aboard as well.

With Pitt locked in, Grasso turned his attention to Spitzer. Grasso knew Spitzer wasn't as much of a wild card as people on Wall Street believed, and a joint investigation with the SEC was clearly in his interest, as Spitzer planned to run for higher office. Ultimately, he would be viewed as the man who cleaned up Wall Street research once a global settlement was reached. Grasso's instincts were right. After a brief conversation, Spitzer agreed to come on board.

The meeting would take place at Grasso's private club, Tiro A Segno, the oldest Italian-American club in Manhattan. Located on a quiet street in the West Village, the club traditionally catered to Italian immigrants who loved to hunt. One of the perks of membership is a still-operational firing range located beneath an elegant dining room; guns are provided by the staff. More recently, Tiro's had become a popular business meeting place for New York's Italian-American elite, business leaders like investor Bill Fugazy, Charlie Gargano, New York State Governor George Pataki's economic development czar, and, of course, Richard Grasso.

Grasso reserved a private room with a long dinner table replete with bread and bottles of wine. Spitzer arrived with Dinallo. Pitt was accompanied by Cutler. Robert Glauber and Mary Schapiro represented the NASD. Given all the conflicting agendas, Grasso immediately sensed the tension in the room. As the parties sat down, Grasso tried to break the ice by comparing the meeting to a scene in his favorite movie, *The Godfather*, where the leaders of the five families agree to stop a nasty gang war that was hurting business. Doing his best imitation of Don Corleone, Grasso even thanked everyone for attending the summit, "even those who traveled as far as Staten Island."

Grasso knew he didn't do the scene justice, but at least Pitt and Spitzer were laughing, and the meeting began. Over courses of pasta and veal, Grasso explained why he decided to reach out to all the parties. Despite an improving economy, the markets were still in a funk; the Dow had declined nearly 10 percent in September alone, and brokers reported a sharp decline in small investors' interest in stocks. "We have to close the chapter on this difficult period," he said. Wall Street must pay, he said, but it also must be left to survive.

Surprisingly, he found Spitzer and Pitt in total agreement on the main issue: The need to separate research and investment banking in some meaningful way. "We can work together on this," said Pitt, and Spitzer said he was ready to join forces as well. One potential roadblock: Without all fifty state securities officials joining the party, there could be no global settlement. Spitzer said he thought he could bring in the states, particularly if reform was part of the agenda. And that agenda would be a "global settlement," a deal in which every Wall Street firm would have to pay a fine and adopt a series of reforms that protected small investors from banking conflicts. Cooperation would be key, Grasso said. The wine must have helped, because for the first time in months, all the nation's securities regulators agreed on something.

The joint investigation was announced the following afternoon. Almost immediately, Pitt seemed to fade from the scene, which was good news to Cutler, who now had near total autonomy to work with Spitzer to get the deal done. Dinallo, meanwhile, caught some flack from a group of state securities regulators who were unaware of the meeting until they read about it in the press. "How was the tiramisu?" Matt Nestor, one of the top investigators for the state of Massachusetts, asked sarcastically. Dinallo just laughed and promised to do a better job communicating in the future.

Grasso thought it would be a good idea for the group to meet regularly, and he asked everyone to attend a second dinner meeting two weeks later at the Georgetown Club in Washington, D.C. There, regulators for the first time began to create the broad outlines of a possible "global settlement," and the most dramatic overhaul of Wall Street research since the end of the fixed-commission structure in 1975.

The outlines of the deal were straightforward. Any settlement must include a large fine, as well as structural reforms that separated investment banking from research. Spitzer threw into the mix a new element, namely forcing Wall Street firms to provide small investors access to "independent research" produced by small investment houses that don't underwrite stocks.

But getting the diverse group personalities to agree on specifics at times proved more complicated. NASD chief Robert Glauber and Spitzer had little use for each other; Spitzer considered Glauber a dilettante. Glauber regarded Spitzer as a publicity hound. At one meeting their mutual distaste boiled over after Spitzer made a remark about Glauber's unusual attire. He had come dressed in a tuxedo and was forced to explain that he was scheduled to attend the opera that night.

The situation soon turned ugly when they began arguing over how regulators should deal with the issue of "spinning," which had made already rich executives even richer. Spitzer wanted it ended. The way to do it was to prevent corporate executives from receiving shares of IPOs once and for all, he said. But Glauber had other ideas. "We shouldn't make it a status crime to be a CEO," Glauber said. Spitzer could barely control himself. "I'm not here to protect CEOs!" he shot back.

Cutler stepped in and asked to table the matter. Later, as new information was released about the millions of dollars in free money Ebbers made from his Citigroup broker through IPO allocations, Glauber agreed to include the spinning ban in the global settlement, and Spitzer, according to his spokesman Darren Dopp, suggested that the two even attend the opera with their wives. Glauber said he was up for it.

Despite these flare-ups, the new era of détente was now producing results. Cutler and Spitzer consulted almost daily, and seemed to become close friends, though privately both Cutler and Spitzer distrusted the other's motives. Cutler had been burned too many times by Spitzer not to watch his back when dealing with the attorney general. Spitzer privately worried that the SEC was being cooperative in order to give Pitt political cover until the congressional elections were over in November. (Both the House and Senate were up for grabs and Republicans couldn't afford to look like they were soft on Wall Street crime.) "I want to make sure you're in this for the long haul," Spitzer told Cutler at one point. Cutler said Pitt was behind the effort 100 percent. "This is no election year gimmick." More important for Spitzer, Cutler agreed that they should go wherever the evidence led them.

That message obviously filtered back to Citigroup. Feeling the heat, Weill replaced Salomon Smith Barney chief Michael Carpenter with Citigroup's former general counsel and current chief operating officer Charles Prince. The move underscored the deepening crisis. By appointing a lawyer to run a business unit, Weill signaled that Citigroup's legal problems were significant. Though Citigroup continued its "we've done nothing wrong" public posture as Prince took the new job and began meeting with regulators, there was a distinct tone of resignation in his voice. Prince emphasized the firm's commitment to settle the investigations as soon as possible. Citigroup, he said, would do almost anything to clean up this mess, including paying a large fine and agreeing to additional structural reforms.

Prince also suggested that the investigators should conclude their case as soon as possible. Prince didn't say that the case could not extend from the company to its CEO. But he didn't have to. Already, several regulators said Citigroup's lawyers had dropped plenty of hints to lead them to conclude that Citigroup's cooperation in the global settlement would end the minute their leader was charged.

CHAPTER THIRTEEN

Upgrades and Preschools

While the regulatory cooperation was good news for the market—stock prices recovered slightly after the deal was announced—it was bad news for Citigroup and Sandy Weill as investigators ramped up their probe. At one point, both Spitzer and Cutler complained to Citigroup's lawyers that their email production was too slow—they both wanted more of Grubman's emails before even thinking about a settlement. Don't just send us boxes of emails, Cutler said. Sort them and "show us the best ones."

As it turned out, Barry Goldsmith's hunch that there were additional Grubman emails was right. The NASD forced Citigroup to hire an expert to do a much more rigorous search through the firm's computer network, and they discovered a gold mine of additional documents, as Beth Golden, one of Spitzer's deputies, would find out.

Golden, a University of Chicago law school graduate and former federal prosecutor in her home state of Minnesota, spent several years investigating white-collar crime and even served as an associate independent counsel on the Whitewater investigation. But her past dealings couldn't prepare her for the strange new direction the Grubman case was about to take. As Golden remembers it, there was something odd about the demeanor of Citigroup's outside attorney, Robert McCaw, a straight-laced partner at the firm Wilmer Cutler Pickering, when he arrived at the AG's office in downtown Manhattan. "He seemed embarrassed about something," Golden recalled.

Golden was accompanied by Dieter Snell, one of Spitzer's top prosecutors, while McCaw brought another partner from his law firm, Lewis Liman, the son of the legendary Arthur Liman who developed a friendship with Spitzer after doing some pro bono work for the AG's office. Seated across from Golden, McCaw nervously pulled out a dozen or so sheets of paper containing emails from a binder and slid them across the table.

Golden studied the documents and soon discovered why McCaw looked so odd. The emails contained the private, intimate conversations between Grubman and his email confidante, Carol Cutler (no relation to Stephen Cutler). For Golden, Cutler's name definitely rang a bell. She had already seen several emails between her and Grubman that seemed a little odd. (In one email that investigators examined, Cutler told Grubman "I like big things—Think BIG.")

But that was mild compared to what McCaw had just produced. The most sensational emails occurred over the two-day period in early January 2001, the beginning of what was to be one of Grubman's most trying periods as a stock analyst. On Saturday morning, January 13, Cutler began the exchange with a comment about former President Ronald Reagan's ninetieth birthday. "I wish I could have had the opportunity to meet with him," Cutler told Grubman, since like Reagan, she had come from the Midwest. The conversation soon turned away from Reagan to office politics, including crude comments about the two people Grubman seemed to despise most in the world, Dan Reingold and AT&T's CEO Michael Armstrong.

Golden was surprised by the vulgarity of the dialogue, the references to various sexual organs, and Cutler's suggestion that she and Grubman "hook up" Reingold with his "fellow delusionist Armstrong." But for Golden, that was all window dressing compared to Grubman's explanation for his controversial upgrade of AT&T in 1999. It was not to win a slot on the massive wireless spin-off. Rather, he needed Weill's help to get his kids into the 92nd Street Y preschool. Weill needed the upgrade to persuade Armstrong, a Citigroup board member, to help him "nuke" John Reed.

To Golden, Grubman's explanation seemed plausible, though no less problematic for the people involved. The conventional wisdom on Wall Street was that the two CEOs were so close that Armstrong had never wavered in his support for Weill. But when Spitzer's people took testimony from Armstrong they found that this relationship was not as solid as first thought. The reason was, of course, Jack Grubman. Armstrong confirmed to investigators that he told Weill on at least one occasion that

Grubman's continued personal attacks on his leadership of AT&T were "damaging the relationship" and must end immediately, several regulators said.

"This stuff is amazing," Golden said, as she and Snell studied the documents. Citigroup's lawyers understood the importance of the documents as well, and immediately began discrediting Cutler as a "nutcase" and "clearly demented," based on some of the more sexually explicit content in her emails. At one point, McCaw handed Golden a long, single-spaced love letter of sorts that Cutler wrote Grubman in early 2002, where she attempted to convince the former star analyst to leave his wife and have her children. "There is a potential to have three children in total," she wrote. "This is crazy," McCaw said. "She's obviously delusional."

But what Golden found interesting about the document was that it seemed to support Grubman's rationale for upgrading AT&T. In the letter, Cutler explained to Grubman that she remembered the internal pressure he was under, given the demise of his stock picks. "I felt like there were some serious attempts at real back stabbing at SSB . . . But you will not take the fall. Your life and livelihood are not meant to be sacrificed," she wrote. Citigroup, Cutler added, didn't need any more bad publicity, given its role in the Enron scandal. "That's why I left you that crazy cryptic VM about the sands of time," She wrote. "I meant Sandy and how he won his battle against John Reed, using Armstrong's vote and how he got Armstrong's vote. I mentioned it to you for I hoped you would use that info if you needed.

"If you learn to use me more directly in the future I will help you more directly. I'm a clever fox Jackie, and I'm your clever fox . . . IF you choose it to be so." But there was just one catch, according to Cutler. She wrote, "This relationship . . . has to get off email." Apparently, Cutler wanted to be something more than a plaything for Grubman and "Emails contain great risks . . . I don't know who might read your emails . . . I didn't want them to discover personal ones."

When she got through the letter, Golden thanked McCaw for his time, and immediately rushed into Spitzer's office with the goods. "Who puts this stuff in email," someone blurted out. Dinallo remarked that there was an "unusual degree of kinkiness" in Cutler's stuff. Golden pointed out the obvious: Cutler may be a flake, but the incriminating passage came directly from Grubman.

Spitzer's investigation had taken a new and more compelling turn.

288 • CHARLES GASPARINO

Barring a memo or an email, it would have been next to impossible to establish securities fraud by asserting that Grubman's upgrade was directly
intended to win a spot on the AT&T wireless deal. The Grubman/Cutler
email solved that problem. Even more, the emails showed that research
conflicts went beyond the analysts and the bankers who were directly involved. They also involved Wall Street's top executives, and in this case,
the executive at the very top of the Wall Street power structure.

With the emails in hand, Spitzer ordered his troops to verify Grubman's
and Weill's connections with the 92nd Street Y, and find Carol Cutler.
Deputy attorney general Michele Hirshman found that Weill had indeed
pushed to get Grubman's kids into the school by relying on his vast network of Manhattan social friends to seal the deal. Weill turned to Y board
member, Joan Tisch, the wife of Loews Corporation chairman Preston
Robert Tisch, to pave the way with the preschool's executive director, a
man named Sol Adler, who was supposedly impressed with such high-
level contacts. Hirshman discovered that Adler was impressed by something else: money. In negotiating the Grubman twins' admission, Weill
agreed to donate $1 million of Citigroup money to the preschool.

Bruce Topman then came across a memo from Grubman to Weill
titled "AT&T and the 92nd Street Y." Grubman wrote the memo three
weeks before his now infamous upgrade of AT&T. In it, Grubman directly
linked the upgrade with the preschool admission. The memo showed
that Grubman had given Weill an unusually complete update on his
meetings with AT&T officials and his research, especially significant
since CEOs rarely get so involved in analyst stock calls—unless, of
course, something very important is on the line. Then, about halfway
through, Grubman switched gears and asked Weill to help with the preschool application. "Anyway, anything you could do Sandy would be
greatly appreciated," Grubman wrote. The best thing about the document? Carol Cutler was never mentioned.

In the fall of 2002, Carol Cutler was out of work, but she was paying close
attention to the press surrounding Grubman, the man she still loved. She
had already tried to reach out to Grubman, who made it clear that whatever relationship they had was over. But it wasn't. While Cutler's name

hadn't surfaced publicly, she had become a legend in the regulatory community, as her salacious emails and Grubman's responses became required reading for the growing list of prosecutors, regulatory officials, and congressional staffers investigating the Grubman research scandal.

"Did you see what they wrote?" a senior SEC official said, comparing their raunchy rants to Wall Street's version of Penthouse Letters, after reading Grubman's boast to Cutler that his first sexual experience took place with the "sister of my best friend when I was 12 and she was 16," and that he preferred Italian girls because "Jewish girls always wanted to 'save' themselves for their wedding nite. But they gave head at a drop o [sic] a hat." One regulator could barely contain her anger, not because of the obscene nature of the emails but because Cutler was such a "lousy writer" after she came across an email in which Cutler promised to apply so many "licks and flicks" to Grubman's private parts that he would "succum to what I'm doing now (and will only keep you guessing as to exactly what) until you can no longer stand it any more . . . and you just explode. WorldCom, the 'shot' that was heard around the world."

With speculation swirling about Spitzer's interest in the AT&T rating, Cutler was hardly surprised when she was contacted to provide testimony about Grubman. She hired an attorney, explaining her relationship with Grubman, and the emails that she knew would come back to haunt both of them. She also made it clear that despite their salacious content, they never had real sex. She refused, she said, because Grubman would never commit.

Cutler arrived at Spitzer's offices dressed conservatively. Her long red hair was tied neatly into a bun. Dinallo was surprised by her demure appearance, remarking to at least one person in the AG's office that she looked nothing like she wrote. Dieter Snell called her "ethereal," saying she came across smart in a "metaphysical way," as Cutler calmly described her background, the vast changes in the telecom market, Grubman's theory about the markets, and her relationship with the telecom king.

Dinallo decided not to give her advance warning that they had the emails, using details, times, dates, and places found in the documents to test her credibility. Everything checked out as she answered every question directly. A common technique among well-coached witnesses is to avoid answering thorny questions with the phrase "I don't recall." It's usually a clue among prosecutors that a witness is hiding something. But

Cutler seemed to recall nearly all the significant details about her relationship with Grubman, including the pressure he faced to upgrade AT&T.

About midway through the testimony, Dinallo slid across the table the now infamous email trail involving AT&T. At first, Cutler didn't flinch. She told investigators that she remembered the day of the exchange quite vividly. Grubman had been under pressure for months to upgrade AT&T for a variety of reasons, including Weill's connection with Armstrong. He was a good father, so it seemed logical to her if he had to sell out, it wouldn't be just business-related, that he should get something in return that helped his kids get into a premier preschool.

But Cutler would lose her composure a few moments later when she was provided a copy of the love letter containing her most private thoughts about marriage and children with Grubman. "I can't believe you have this," she said, wiping tears from her eyes. At one point, Golden asked about the letter, and its description of her relationship with Grubman.

Once again, Cutler answered the question directly. "Some people do it and some people write about it." Cutler made it clear that she was in love with Grubman, but because he would never commit, emails became the next best thing.

When the meeting was over, Dinallo believed Cutler would come across as a "credible" witness and the way things were going, Spitzer seemed to be heading for a major showdown with the world's biggest financial firm. In late October, he had Golden call up McCaw and Liman to explain that the investigation had reached a new and critical stage. Golden was on the telephone just a few moments before Spitzer broke into the conversation with a warning. "There may be divergence," between the interests of Citigroup and Weill himself, he said. He advised that Sandy Weill should begin thinking about a defense strategy separate from that of the firm and get his own lawyers.

Spitzer's heads up was a typical prosecutorial procedure to alert potential defendants about the possibility of legal action. But for Citigroup, it was a crushing blow. It was one thing for Spitzer to target Grubman, but Weill was a different story. Despite his age (Weill was sixty-nine years old at the time), Weill was perhaps the most powerful man in corporate America and he had no intentions of stepping down from his lofty post anytime soon. Under Weill's tough as nails management style, Citigroup's earnings soared and its stock had outperformed all its peers, but his leadership had serious flaws. Citigroup's compliance system was simply unprepared to deal with the volume of business the company had begun to generate. The result was a corporate culture that failed to recognize when analysts like Grubman or top executives, like Weill himself, stepped over the line.

Weill clearly knew he was in trouble when he turned to Martin Lipton for help. The general partner of Wachtell Lipton Rosen & Katz, Lipton had run one of Wall Street's most successful law firms that handled everything from merger advice to antitrust. But lately, his firm had developed a booming business defending corporate executives accused of white-collar crime. His team of Larry Pedowitz and John Savarese were handling (along with Merrill's outside lawyer Bob Morvillo) the Martha Stewart insider trading case. Weill was now added to their growing roster of high-profile clients.

In crafting a strategy for Weill, the Pedowitz/Savarese team followed the same script used by many of the superstar analysts to defend their hyped ratings during the bubble. Weill, they argued, was a "true believer" in AT&T, and only asked Grubman to reconsider his bearishness as any true believer would. (Weill's specific defense on Grubman's AT&T upgrade was that he "never told any analyst what he or she had to write.") As for helping the Grubman twins with their preschool education, they pointed out that Weill was a generous person who gave millions of dollars to charities, and who was doing nothing more than helping out a valuable employee.

Inside Spitzer's office, investigators weren't impressed with these arguments or the demeanor of Savarese or Pedowitz, who treated some of Spitzer's staff as if they were recent law school grads. Weill's behavior suggested that his motive for urging the AT&T upgrade went beyond his love of the company. According to phone logs and other records, he and Grubman seemed to be communicating on a daily, even an hourly basis, around the time of the upgrade. Since when did the CEO of Wall Street's biggest firm take such a personal interest in a stock rating? Dinallo told people in the office that they had such a great case that Citigroup would pay a fine of at least $500 million to settle the matter, one of the largest fines in Wall Street history.

It wasn't long before these sentiments began to leak to the press. In late October, *The Wall Street Journal* reported that Spitzer had uncovered new evidence prompting his warning to Weill, as well as the hiring of Savarese and Pedowitz. The *Journal* also reported Spitzer's intention to take testimony from Weill about the AT&T upgrade.

The story was accurate, though it failed to address one major question: What was this new evidence? No one close to the investigation would comment. "I go down to the bottom of the ocean with that one," said one official from Spitzer's office. Cutler, her emails, and the 92nd St. Y angle remained safely hidden, at least for now.

Even without the most incriminating evidence in the public domain, Citigroup exploded when the story hit the newsstands. The next morning in a "Sandy Weill Memo to Employees," the firm accused the *Journal* of exaggerating Weill's predicament. "Today's *Wall Street Journal* carries a story that contains outrageous speculation and inferences," Weill wrote. Weill said he had "volunteered to testify" to Spitzer and others as "part of our ongoing cooperation with the various regulatory inquiries." On the issue of divergence, Weill quoted Marty Lipton: "The notion that there could be any charge against Sandy Weill is inconceivable."

It was a classic nondenial denial, but most of the media bought the spin. CNBC ran segments all afternoon taking shots at the *Journal*'s story. Rival reporters were gloating, pointing out to Spitzer's staff that the *Journal* had finally "gone too far" in its coverage of the Citigroup research scandal. Ted David, a CNBC anchor, lashed out at the *Journal* asking in an interview if Weill could get his reputation back. *Kudlow & Cramer*, a raucous new CNBC talk show featuring conservative television commentator Larry Kudlow and financial columnist Jim Cramer (a friend of Spitzer's from Harvard Law who once managed the AG's money in his hedge fund) devoted a portion of the program to the controversy. Cramer said it's Citigroup versus *The Wall Street Journal*, and went on to attack the story.

Even Spitzer's office seemed to join the *Journal* bashing. Several investigators complained that the story made it more difficult for them to complete their probe. One of the NYAG's key investigators on the Citigroup probe was quoted in a wire story stating that Weill was not the "target" of the probe. She later explained that the reporter left out the word "yet" in her comment.

• • •

By the end of the day Citigroup seemed to have dodged a bullet by dispelling the notion that the research probe had clearly reached the very top of Wall Street's biggest firm. But the reality was far different. Spitzer's deputies informed Grubman's lawyer that they wanted the former analyst to answer questions about the Cutler emails and Weill's involvement in the AT&T upgrade. The pressure was now becoming intense for Grubman. "I want closure," Grubman complained to one person. He also wanted a second chance at a career, but with each passing story, Grubman's return to Wall Street became less and less likely. Grubman, however, could be thankful for one thing: All the publicity surrounding Weill had taken the heat off him. "If Spitzer wants to get me on AT&T he has to get Sandy," he said at the time.

Indeed, there was some talk that Grubman might be willing to give up his old boss in exchange for a deal. Whether intentionally or not, Grubman's lawyer Lee Richards, appeared to give some credibility to the rumor when he offered what some people in the Spitzer camp thought was an olive branch: cooperation to show how research conflicts were a firmwide issue. But when Grubman showed up at Spitzer's offices for his testimony, he was anything but cooperative. Spitzer's deputies found him brash, almost arrogant, certainly not a man looking for redemption. Under intense grilling from Golden and later Topman, Grubman provided few clues for the AT&T case, and not many about firm-wide conflicts either.

Grubman had spent months locked in his lawyer's office reviewing nearly every one of his research reports, committing to memory their key points much like an actor memorizing his lines in a script. And it showed. Throughout his interview, he kept referring to his philosophy about the telecom market, his long held belief that the New Entrants like World-Com would be the ultimate winners. Grubman said AT&T's new cable strategy made him a true believer that the company embraced the New Economy and could now compete with WorldCom and the other companies he believed would rule the telecom business. When it was clear that AT&T didn't follow through with its cable plans, Grubman said he had no choice but to downgrade the stock.

When they asked him about Weill's pressure on him to upgrade

AT&T, Grubman didn't stray from the Citigroup position. Weill may have asked him to take a "fresh look" at AT&T, but he never told him what to write. As for his excuse for the Cutler emails, Grubman said he fabricated the Weill–AT&T–92nd Street Y story to "impress" a friend.

Golden, who spent hours reading dozens of email exchanges between Cutler and Grubman, was incredulous. After all, most of the online chats were initiated by Cutler who seemed genuinely in love with Grubman, not the other way around.

"Why would you need to impress someone you already won over?" she asked. Grubman stiffened up, but he stuck to his story.

Later, Spitzer received a progress report on the testimony. "We found him almost impenetrable," one investigator said. "Thirty million dollars buys a lot of loyalty," Spitzer commented wryly.

Then it was Weill's turn. Spitzer agreed to hold the meeting at Marty Lipton's office in midtown Manhattan. Spitzer sent his A Team: Hirshman, Topman, Golden and Dinallo. There were representatives of the SEC and NASD present as well. Citigroup's lawyers were present along with Weill's new legal team.

But for all the advance billing, the Weill "interview" turned out to be a nonevent. Like Grubman, Weill wasn't asked to provide a formal deposition under oath. The reasoning behind this move was odd. (Spitzer's investigators have never provided a good explanation.) Mary Meeker, Henry Blodget, and their various supervisors faced intense grilling under oath. Shea, who supervised Meeker, still talks about how terrified he was during his deposition when Waldman threatened him with perjury if he wasn't truthful. The technique worked, as Shea dug deeper into his memory to recall key facts.

Weill took full advantage of the leniency. People in the meeting say he had little recollection of a series of telephone calls with Grubman that took place around the time of the AT&T upgrade. He did make one key concession. He admitted that he asked Grubman to take a "fresh look" at his AT&T rating, sometime in late 1998 or early 1999, but reiterated that he never told Grubman what to write. As for his help in getting the Grubman twins in the 92nd Street Y, Weill said it was something he would do for any valuable employee. As for many of the other facts and details that involved Grubman and his research, including a string of phone calls between the two around the time of the AT&T upgrade, Weill simply stated he couldn't recall. After all, he said, the two weren't that close.

• • •

As the investigation continued, Citigroup became desperate to keep the details of the case a secret. But it was only a matter of time before word leaked out. Scores of regulators had seen the Cutler emails and the various documents at the heart of the explosive case. Even worse, the emails had been given to various congressional committees, which had launched their own investigations into the matter.

On November 13, *The Wall Street Journal* drew first blood. The newspaper had spoken to people who had seen the Grubman-Cutler email exchange with its comments about the upgrade of AT&T and Weill's efforts to repay his famous stock analyst by getting his children into an exclusive preschool. With a page one story under the headline "Grubman Boast: AT&T Rating Had Altogether Different Goal," the newspaper was first to report that winning the underwriting for the wireless deal was not the only reason for the upgrade; that Grubman was looking to help Weill "nuke" John Reed.

The story, however, left out the second part of the deal. As it turns out, Deputy Managing Editor Dan Hertzberg called the 92nd Street Y connection a stretch and it was removed from the story. *Journal* editors say they were not persuaded that Weill's help was anything more than a commonplace favor, and thus wasn't newsworthy, despite Grubman's boast that it was connected to the AT&T upgrade. Even without the preschool angle, the story was explosive. The media firestorm began early in the morning, when CNBC broadcast the *Journal* story. Grubman, who had declined to comment to the *Journal*, now issued a statement similar to what he had maintained with Spitzer's people, that he basically made up the whole scenario to impress a "friend." The emails to Cutler, he added, had "zero basis" in reality (apparently not much different than much of his research). Weill tried to seize on Grubman's denial as proof the whole thing was a joke and repeated his contention that he "always believed that Mr. Grubman would conduct his own research and reach independent conclusions that were entirely his own."

But Citigroup and Weill were in a state of panic. The day the story broke, Weill disclosed for the first time publicly what he had told to investigators, that he had asked Grubman to take a "fresh look" at his AT&T rating. This only added fuel to the developing media firestorm that pounded away at Grubman, Weill, and Citigroup. CNBC reporter David

Faber tried to advance the story by telling viewers that his sources had told him the word "nuke" didn't appear in the emails. That was, of course, wrong. Reporters for *The New York Times* scrambled to play catch-up, placing a call to Spitzer, who adamantly denied he or anyone in his office was the source of the leak to the *Journal*. That was right. The contents of the emails were well known to dozens of regulators, congressional staffers, and lawyers in Washington and New York.

After the conversation, though, the *Times* now had what the *Journal* refused to publish: the 92nd Street Y connection. For the *Times*, the news call was a no-brainer: Run a story focusing on the problems rich people have getting their kids into a hoity-toity preschool and call it a "New York Story." At the *Journal*, resistance to the 92nd Street Y connection by Hertzberg vanished when the reporter on the story learned that not only did the *Times* have knowledge of the email and its reference to the 92nd Street Y, but also that Weill had agreed to pay the preschool $1 million in Citigroup money to help get the kids into the school.

The 92nd Street Y connection took the scandal surrounding conflicted research to a level Wall Street never could have imagined. The *Journal* summed it up perfectly: "Kid Pro Quo," and advanced the story by citing another part of the email where Grubman said the admission policy is harder than Harvard's. The *Journal* then became the first news outlet to obtain the actual copies of the emails, and maybe more important, the Grubman memo to Weill titled "AT&T and the 92nd Street Y." Editors at the paper had an almost morbid fascination with Cutler and her crude rants, as they passed around not only the more salacious elements of her emails, but also her now semipublic love letter to Grubman. This time, editors decided to include key emails in the paper's story, minus Cutler's sexual fantasies, while noting that the emails "included sexual banter."

Grubman's only fantasy these days was staying out of the press. By now, he had dropped out of sight, spending as much time as possible at his home in the Hamptons. But with the controversy growing by the day, Grubman became a marked man wherever he went. Several Wall Street brokers spotted him at a Rolling Stones concert in Madison Square Garden as soon as the lights went on. "Hey there's Jack Grubman," one said, making eye contact with the former analyst, who just looked away. One morning Grubman was sitting on a bench in East Hampton, reading a newspaper and drinking coffee. Trying to conceal his appearance, Grubman wore a baseball cap, and a jacket with its collar turned up. But he wasn't fooling anyone. At one point, he made eye contact with a woman who apparently was keeping close tabs on the preschool saga. "Busted" she muttered as their eyes met. Grubman just looked away.

Weill tried to hang low as well, turning down speaking engagements and staying out of the limelight unless of course, he was issuing a statement about his involvement in Grubman's research. For years, the rank-and-file Citigroup employee viewed Weill as a savior mainly for his record in boosting the firm's stock price. Now they believed he operated in a world of double standards. Veteran telecom investment banker John Otto recalled to a colleague that despite Weill's alleged generosity he hadn't even responded to Otto's request for a small donation to the Boy's Club of Greenwich, Connecticut, where they both live. But then again, Otto couldn't upgrade AT&T.

The company's high-powered board of directors, composed of people like former president Gerald Ford and TimeWarner chief Richard Parsons, came under scrutiny as well. Under law, corporate boards have a "fiduciary responsibility" to monitor executive behavior. But these people acted as if they reported to Weill, not the other way around, and now they were paying the price as Spitzer's deputies arranged interviews to determine their knowledge of the AT&T upgrade fiasco. For some it was a humbling experience, particularly when they learned that Weill had used Citigroup money to coax the 92nd Street Y into admitting the Grubman twins. It's unclear what they planned to do about it, but Spitzer's investigators gave them a hint about what they should do by raising another question on everyone's mind: Does the company have a succession plan? In other words, who's going to take Weill's place when he resigns?

Back at Spitzer's headquarters, Roger Waldman was grappling with a different problem. For more than six months, he had been taking testimony, reviewing documents, listening to lawyers, and trying to figure out whether Mary Meeker deserved to be charged under the Martin Act for her research during the market bubble.

Waldman is a thin, pensive man, who speaks in quiet tones, masking a reputedly nasty streak that several Morgan officials noticed when giving their testimony. Since the investigation widened during the summer,

Waldman believed he had uncovered serious flaws in the firm's research process. For all intents and purposes, analysts at Morgan served as investment bankers, the best example being the firm's top analyst, Mary Meeker. Meeker's self-evaluations showed that she spent much of her time meeting with investment banking clients and completing deals. Given her banking duties, writing research reports seemed to be an afterthought for Meeker, and Waldman believed it showed in the quality of the final product. Waldman had reviewed most of Meeker's research reports and found them to be superficial and filled with hyperbole. Maybe even worse, Meeker's supervisors never objected to her over-the-top style.

Waldman nevertheless still had strong reservations as to whether he could mount a successful case against Meeker. Kempf kept his promise to put up an aggressive fight. Meeker and the other witnesses came well prepared for their testimony, and Kempf provided mountains of evidence, from Meeker's public statements, to newspaper stories and even analyst presentations that documented her various warnings that the bubble was ready to burst. Aiding Spitzer in his case against Citigroup was Grubman's unabashed support of companies like AT&T and WorldCom even in the face of deteriorating markets. Meeker was harder to pin down. As the Internet mania reached fevered heights, she began to use more amorphous concepts to rate stocks. Waldman noticed a plethora of "outperform" ratings. Taken literally, Waldman wasn't sure if he could prove that Meeker was actually hyping a stock, or merely suggesting that shares might outperform an underperforming market when the bubble burst.

The biggest obstacle, however, was Meeker's emails, or at least those that Morgan said they could provide. Throughout the investigation, Meeker openly worried that she might have said something foolish out of anger that would come back to haunt her. But regulators immediately complained that those emails Morgan had produced were amazingly bland, as if Morgan had deleted those with the most explosive content. Morgan denied the charge, suggesting at various times that she either preferred to communicate the old-fashioned way, using the telephone, or that the 9/11 terrorist attacks had destroyed key documents.

It's unclear if Waldman bought either explanation, but there was one way to find out if Morgan was telling the truth—do what the NASD did with Citigroup and make Morgan conduct a more intensive examination of its computer records. Spitzer, of course, had the final word on what action would be taken.

But for Spitzer, time was running out on what he considered a more important issue. Even as the Citigroup investigation became a national story, and the Grubman emails tabloid fodder, Spitzer's overarching goal was to create national standards for research, a so-called "global settlement." Since Grasso's Italian restaurant meeting, the various regulatory bodies had been working fairly well together despite an occasional dustup between Spitzer and Glauber. They even came up with the broad outlines of a deal. Each firm would have to pay a fine depending on the level of conflicts, agree to structural reforms in its research, and provide investors with some form of independent research.

But getting the top firms on the street to agree on the details remained elusive through the fall and into the winter of 2002. One problem may have been the resignation of Harvey Pitt as SEC chairman. On November 5, just after the midterm elections were announced in which Republicans picked up seats both in the House and Senate, Pitt announced he was stepping down as SEC chairman. Pitt's departure was certainly tragic. No other SEC chairman took the job with so much experience and promise, and based on the numbers, Pitt clearly delivered. He launched high-profile investigations into every major scandal, including World-Com, in which the SEC filed fraud charges against the firm just twenty-four hours after the company announced its earnings restatement. Under his watch, enforcement actions brought against alleged miscreants hit near record levels after falling during Levitt's last year in office.

Pitt may have been a better SEC chairman than his predecessor, but he could have used some of Levitt's political moxie. The specific reason for his departure had been a controversy over his appointment to an accounting oversight board, though the political types in the White House had increasingly grown worried about his many public gaffes, from a speech in which he seemed to suggest the SEC would take a "kindler gentler" approach to regulation (Pitt says he was taken out of context by his critics) to his proposal to get a pay raise by elevating the SEC chairman to a cabinet position.

Nevertheless, when Pitt left town Wall Street lost a valuable ally, and the big firms grew increasingly hostile about the terms of the deal. Dinallo at one point told one aide in Spitzer's office that he could see Citigroup paying $500 million to settle its case, but Citigroup pushed back, insisting that the firm's conduct was not five times worse than Merrill's, which coughed up $100 million. Kempf, the Morgan Stanley general counsel, considered dropping out of the global settlement by settling with Spitzer and fighting the SEC in federal court. His rationale was that he couldn't beat Spitzer, who had the "Martin Act" on his side, but the SEC would have a higher barrier to prove securities fraud under federal law. At one point Kempf even arranged an impromptu call by his boss, CEO Phil Purcell, to Spitzer on Thanksgiving Day to press his case. Spitzer said he couldn't agree to anything that would undercut the global settlement and the SEC. "I made a deal with these guys," he said.

Kempf was disappointed, but not as much as the top executives at Goldman Sachs when they heard about Meeker's lack of incriminating emails, and that their biggest competitor over the past decade was unlikely to face charges. While Goldman didn't have a name-brand analyst, the firm's cut-throat business practices had made it just as successful as Morgan at snaring technology banking deals during the bubble. The last thing Goldman needed was to be singled out for its research conflicts, while Morgan received a pass. CEO Hank Paulson soon tried to convince Dick Grasso to make sure the language in Goldman's final settlement agreement omitted the word "fraudulent" to describe its research practices. But Grasso was no fan of Paulson, whom he regraded as a "snake" for his effort to infuse more computerized trading at the exchange at the expense of Grasso's cherished specialist-trading system. "Hank, you better talk to Eliot," Grasso said. Later Grasso would remark that Paulson "couldn't have cared less how much he paid in a fine, just what the document said."

It's unclear if Paulson ever spoke to Spitzer, but one thing was certain: Complaints like his had taken their toll. By mid November, it was clear that regulators wouldn't get the settlement finished until the new year, and given all the moving parts, it was unclear if it would ever get done. The meetings with Wall Street and regulators often turned ugly. Kempf was openly ridiculed for bragging that Morgan's research practices were aboveboard, and at one point got into a heated argument with SEC enforcement chief Steve Cutler, who told Kempf that he had a bad reputation at the commission for being "unpleasant." Kempf responded that "the feeling is mutual." Ted Levine, the general counsel of UBS AG, lashed out at Spitzer about leaks to the press, particularly *The Wall Street Journal*. Spitzer countered that he wasn't the only one talking to reporters. Even so, the exchange was reported in the press the next day, making the negotiations even more difficult to bring to conclusion.

Several firms tried to take advantage of the confusion. Led by the Bear Stearns CEO, James "Jimmy" Cayne, several firms—including UBS, Lehman Brothers, and Bear—threatened to drop out of the settlement and fight the charges unless Spitzer and the SEC gave them a pass. The threat was real and Spitzer knew it. Compared to Morgan, Merrill and Citigroup, these firms had been bit players in the tech-banking boom, and their research conflicts were nowhere near the level of the bigger outfits.

But their best weapon was political: How could Spitzer advance his career by claiming credit for a "global settlement" when several of Wall Street's biggest firms were opting out of the deal?

Once again, Grasso came to the rescue. In addition to being the head of the world's largest stock market, Grasso was also an expert salesman, and now he had to sell his members on a deal that would cost them big bucks. His strategy was to pick off the dissenters one at a time. His first call was to Cayne, the wily chairman of Bear Stearns. Cayne ran one of the most profitable firms on Wall Street for longer than anyone in the business, except possibly Sandy Weill. His secret: Cayne was a championship bridge player who brought a card shark's mentality to the boardroom, and at least for now, Cayne knew he held a winning hand. "I shouldn't have to pay a dime," he said. "This is extortion."

Without saying good-bye, Cayne slammed down the phone. Grasso's next call was to Richard Fuld, the CEO of Lehman Brothers. Lehman had just gone through one of the most embarrassing periods in recent years when it was revealed that one of its top brokers, Frank Gruttadauria, had stolen tens of millions from his clients by creating phony account statements without a peep from the firm's compliance department. Grasso knew the last thing Lehman needed was more bad publicity.

Grasso turned on the charm, explaining how research was a black stain on the industry, and how vital it was for the industry to put the year of scandals to rest, and his plan worked to perfection. Fuld said he was on board, and would make a call to his counterpart at UBS, CEO John Costas, to make the case to him as well. Grasso had already laid the groundwork at UBS, telling his friend Joe Grano, who ran the brokerage department, that if the firm didn't agree to the settlement, it would be rolling the dice; Spitzer, Grasso said, was ready to perform a "proctologist exam" on the firm's research practices. It didn't take long for Costas to conclude that UBS was in the deal as well.

That left Cayne. Hearing that he had Lehman and UBS in the deal, a jubilant Grasso placed a mid-morning call to the card shark at his new offices on 47th Street in midtown Manhattan. Grasso told him he was the only holdout of the major firms, and he would be doing everyone a favor if he just joined the crowd. "Okay, I'm ready," Cayne said. But he still wanted to know how much he was going to have to pay. Grasso told Cayne his share had just increased by $10 million, to $80 million from $70 million. Cayne couldn't believe what he was hearing. "You can't fight these fucking people alone," Cayne said.

When Grasso announced he had put down the uprising, Spitzer was ready to cash in. With lightning speed, he contacted Cutler and suggested that the regulators start working on plans to announce an "agreement in principle," leaving the specifics for later. The decision for Spitzer was easy; he needed to declare some kind of victory before the end of the year or the public might lose interest. He ordered Dinallo to issue a directive to the big Wall Street investment houses at the center of the scandal to be ready to meet. Spitzer, Dinallo told them, wants this thing over, immediately.

On December 19, at 9 A.M. sharp, the general counsels of the top securities firms packed themselves into a small conference room on the twenty-fifth floor of Spitzer's office, sitting around a conference table. Kempf, Morgan Stanley's general counsel, brought along Morgan's CEO Phil Purcell. Much to Purcell's surprise, he was the only CEO present.

It wasn't long before Purcell wished he wasn't in the room. At one point, Spitzer looked Purcell straight in the eye, and said he had enough of the bickering, fighting, and mostly, the delays. "It's now or never," he threatened, according to several people present. "There's going be a deal or we're going to start bringing cases. I'm tired of all your fighting and acting like children in a sandbox."

Each firm, Spitzer explained, would be required to sign a small sheet of paper that said they would be part of a tentative agreement and fax it to his office. The details would be figured out in the new year. The total price tag was set at $1.4 billion, though the amount each firm paid would depend on their level of conflicts. Citigroup and Merrill, which had recently been forced into the global settlement despite its earlier deal, would be charged with "securities fraud" for their research practices. Merrill would have to cough up $25 million more to fund independent research, Citi's price tag would be close to $400 million. As Kempf studied the documents, he realized that he didn't get as much differentiation as he was looking for, but at least Morgan Stanley's fines were among the lowest of any firm charged in the case.

Spitzer said he wanted the faxes returned to him by midnight and reminded the group that those firms who didn't were taking a considerable risk—the so-called proctologist exam Grano warned Costas about. A few hours later, Spitzer got what he was looking for as the faxes started rolling in. By the end of the day, all but one firm, Thomas Weisel Partners, had agreed to the broad outlines of the settlement. Weisel settled the case in August 2004, agreeing to pay $12.5 million.

Despite Spitzer's tough talk, the settlement was something both sides could live with. Spitzer had backed off his earlier idea of spinning research into a separate part of a company that survived without investment banking revenues supporting the salaries of analysts. Instead, firms would be forced to strengthen their Chinese Walls and other synthetic barriers that may or may not protect investors during the next bubble. Meanwhile, much of the $1.4 billion in fines and penalties, as *The Wall Street Journal* pointed out, would be tax deductible, meaning that for the firms that had already reaped hundreds of millions in fees for investment banking business through fraudulent research, the price tag might barely reach $1 billion. As for the much touted "structural" reforms, it wouldn't take the big investment houses long to find the loopholes. Analysts could no longer attend "road show" deal pitches with bankers, but nothing stopped firms from linking research coverage to the companies that provided them with investment banking business.

There were other shortcomings. Neither Spitzer nor Cutler had demanded a fuller investigation of Mary Meeker's emails, like the one performed by the NASD, which could have proven once and for all Meeker's true believer status. Goldman CEO Hank Paulson apparently successfully removed the word "fraud" from any part of the agreement, even though banking and research at Goldman had worked so closely during the bubble that bankers had edited some reports before they were distributed to the public. The deal gave Morgan CEO Phil Purcell enough leeway to call Mary Meeker a "pioneer on the Internet" and that she "protected investors much more than anybody knows from the press" despite her role in propping up all those dotcoms that went bust, not to mention her support of AOL after Morgan served as an adviser on one of the most ill-advised mergers of all time.

Maybe the biggest disappointment involved Citigroup. Under the deal, Grubman would be banned from the securities industry and pay a $15 million fine. But the world's largest financial firm, whose research and banking departments had helped support some of the greatest frauds in history, walked away relatively unscathed. Spitzer was even leaning toward not charging its now-disgraced CEO Sandy Weill, who not only led the firm during a period of unbridled scandal, but played a direct role himself in one of the sleaziest episodes in Wall Street history, namely Grubman's AT&T upgrade. Cutler, the SEC enforcement chief, remained uncharacteristically mum on the issue, pointedly reminding Spitzer "to come to his own conclusions," according to one person with knowledge of Cutler's thinking. In reality, Cutler was scared that he was going to be "set up" by Spitzer if the press turned negative on whatever decision he made.

Spitzer said he made his final decision as he does most of his difficult ones—after a jog through Central Park, people in his office say. While running his usual three-mile course, Spitzer recalled thinking, "This would be a great case to try." The prospect of Sandy Weill on the stand would be the media event of a lifetime, and clearly feasible under the Martin Act, where the bar for securities fraud was much lower. But Spitzer also knew it would be a bruising battle, and Weill, who had close ties in the state and national Democratic Party, wouldn't go down without a fight. Spitzer was already getting an earful from people with close ties to the 92nd Street Y, many of them politically connected Democrats, for his investigation that shed light on the preschool's slippery admissions process.

The case was also far from the lay-up portrayed by the press. Spitzer believed that in order to be successful prosecuting Weill he would have to prove not just that Weill pressured Grubman to upgrade the stock, but that the Citigroup boss allowed a fraudulent rating to be published by his firm that he, himself, knew was fraudulent. And there was one additional problem—there could be no global settlement without Citigroup, the globe's largest financial firm playing a role. Citigroup had little incentive to join the pact if Spitzer was ready to charge its top executive.

Just as Spitzer was ready to drop the case against Weill, he faced an unlikely opponent in Barry Goldsmith, NASD's director of enforcement. Goldsmith was seriously considering filing a charge of some kind against Weill for his involvement in the AT&T rating. With the research settlement hanging in the balance, Spitzer placed a call to Mary Schapiro, the NASD's second-in-command. "Mary, it's now or never," Spitzer said in a telephone conversation. The pact, he said, "is too important" to the future of the securities business to jeopardize it with a charge against Weill. Schapiro said she'd get back to him. A few hours later, she did, explaining that Goldsmith had decided not to take action against Weill over the AT&T matter.

Across Wall Street the word went out that Spitzer "blinked," cutting a deal with Weill rather than holding Wall Street's top executive accountable. At one point, the attorney for Carol Cutler confronted Dinallo directly. "I can't believe you guys let him walk." Dinallo replied: "It ain't over till it's over," implying that Weill would face some sanction that wasn't going to be announced just yet. Despite these complaints, nothing could stop Spitzer from spinning the "global settlement" into a colossal victory. He won bragging rights to one of the largest settlements in Wall Street history and a host of changes to the way the brokerage industry provided research to small investors on behalf of corporations that were also investment banking clients.

The grand announcement was made as soon as Spitzer could schedule a press conference, nearly a day after he received all the faxes back from the Wall Street firms. Immediately, location became an issue. Glauber believed a "neutral" site should be chosen, meaning that the regulators would agree to hold the unveiling anywhere but at the offices of his archrival, the NYSE. But Spitzer had other ideas. Given Grasso's contributions, it seemed only fitting to hold the affair at the NYSE. It was a bitter pill for Glauber and his staff to swallow, given Goldsmith's contribution to discovering the most compelling evidence in the case, the Grubman-Cutler emails. As one high-ranking NASD official put it, "In the end, we were the reason why there's a research settlement."

Spitzer, of course, didn't see it that way. The press conference would be held at the NYSE's swanky sixth-floor boardroom, a place that could accommodate the massive coverage regulators were seeking. It was standing room only as reporters huddled close to the podium while the regulators took center stage to unveil the "historic agreement to reform investment practices." Dressed in his customary dark suit, Grasso declared that "Restoring investor confidence is paramount," adding that the deal closed "one of the darkest chapters in the history of modern finance."

Stephen Cutler explained what he described as the vast structural changes that the research settlement would enact. "I believe this settlement will result in significant reforms that will serve investors for many years to come." A few moments later, Robert Glauber, the opera-loving chairman of the NASD, gave his two cents. The settlement, he said, is a "vital step in restoring investor confidence," though he failed to mention how the agency ignored the issue for so long, including Eric Von der Porten's prescient warnings back in 1999.

But those details would be left for later as Spitzer and Grasso took center stage. Though the research settlement left much to be desired, their *political* triumph was indisputable. In only a few short years, Eliot Spitzer had made a remarkable political comeback, rising from the public perception of a rich kid who lied about his campaign finances to a valuable public servant looking to protect the interests of small investors. The deal, meanwhile, allowed Grasso to burnish his already sizable reputation as Wall Street's most important power broker. Though he never graduated from college, Grasso was smart enough to understand that Eliot Spitzer meant business.

Indeed, both men could have gloated over their hard earned victories, but they thanked the people on the ground who made it all happen, investigators like Dinallo, Topman, Waldman, and Beth Golden, the people at the NYSE and the SEC who put up with the political gamesmanship to craft historic change.

"When we began this investigation over a year and a half ago, we were concerned about protecting the retail investor," Spitzer said. "It was Joe Smith in Utica, New York, or Jane Smith in Topeka, Kansas, who might not understand the ways of Wall Street." The problem with Wall Street research, Spitzer added, was "captured by a quotation from somebody whom I won't name but an undoubtedly very smart analytical mind who was quoted as saying 'what used to be viewed as a conflict is now viewed as a synergy.' " Spitzer didn't get the quote exactly right, but he didn't have to; everyone knew whom he was talking about and the message he was delivering.

But before he was finished Spitzer was sure to pay homage to the man who did the most to make it all happen: Dick Grasso. "Let me turn to Dick and say . . . Dick you are not only a consummate diplomat, you are also a great chooser of restaurants," a reference to the dinner at Tiro's that made the global settlement possible. "I hope the investment banks don't take this the wrong way, but I may need to find another excuse for us to have dinner together, Dick, and that doesn't mean we're serving subpoenas today." Grasso just smiled. The poor kid from Queens and the rich kid from Riverdale came out on top.

Epilogue

Two days before Christmas 2002, Sandy Weill addressed Citigroup's massive workforce from an undisclosed location in France. According to the *New York Post*, Weill couldn't have been in better spirits. Both he and the firm he created had survived one of the most difficult periods in their existence, a point he was sure to make as he thanked Salomon's chief executive Charles Prince, who led the negotiations with regulators that turned out so favorably for Citigroup.

"Chuck . . . if it weren't for your tenacity we wouldn't be here right now," Weill said.

Weill certainly had good reason to be happy. As regulators finalized the global settlement in late 2002 and 2003, it became increasingly clear that Citigroup dodged a major bullet. Its $400 million payment as part of the deal translated into little more than a rounding error given the company's huge earnings. By not charging the Citigroup chief, Spitzer appeared to give Weill the green light to continue as Citigroup's CEO, presumably until the day he dies, even as it became abundantly clear that under his watch Citigroup enabled some of the bubble's most scandal-ridden companies, and maybe its most conflicted analysts.

Others, however, were less fortunate. This book opened with portraits of the superstar analysts at the height of their power. But by the time the research settlement was complete, each had been reduced to shells of their former selves. As part of his own settlement with the government, Grubman did not face criminal charges, but he was forced to pay a $15 million fine, and banned from the securities business without admitting or denying wrongdoing, the standard clause that goes with such settlements. He is now working as a consultant for a small telecom company.

After having gotten a pass by Spitzer, Blodget was subsequently charged by the NASD with securities fraud and forced to pay a $4 million fine also without admitting or denying wrongdoing. Like Grubman, Blodget has been banned from working in the securities business, but in early 2004, just two years after his emails became national news, Blodget returned to his first love as a writer for the online *Slate* magazine, covering the trial of Martha Stewart, who was charged and later convicted for obstruction of justice after lying to regulators about her suspicious sale of Imclone stock. Maybe the only thing worse than Blodget's coverage of the Stewart trial (he predicted throughout the case that she would be found not guilty) was his bizarre public disclosure, presumably to alert readers to his own travails on Wall Street, in which he compared Martha's legal travails to his own. Both of them, he wrote, had "bathed in the golden glow of prosperity, a symbol of American capitalism and the optimism of the Internet Age," only to be viewed much later in "the harsh light of the bust."

Like Blodget and Grubman, Mary Meeker continues to be viewed in the context of the Internet bubble as well. Meeker is the only one of the three not to be charged, but her reign as Queen of the Internet is long over. She no longer commands legions of followers who hang on her every word, the fans who stop her on the street, or the lucrative job offers that were an almost daily event during the bubble years. Meeker says she is happy with her new status—her stock picks have done well as the Internet has made a comeback—though she's also a changed woman. In the past Meeker seemed to blame investors for their massive losses. "Where is the personal responsibility?" she asked me in an interview about a year ago. More recently she's had a change of heart. "People did lose money on the stocks that I recommended," Meeker said, "and I'm sensitive to that. I wish we would have downgraded them, and I'll have to live with that the rest of my life."

There would be others living with much worse consequences from their actions. When they were finished with Blodget, Meeker, and Grubman, regulators began focusing on the guy who may be most responsible for the tech boom of the 1990s, investment banker Frank Quattrone. To refresh memories, Quattrone was the banker who gave Mary Meeker her start, and helped bring public some of the biggest technology companies in Silicon Valley as his career took him from Morgan Stanley to Credit Suisse First Boston several years later. But like the others, he now had a giant target on his head. The NASD and the Massachusetts Secretary of

State continued to investigate Quattrone well into 2003, focusing on spinning and a host of other alleged abuses. Quattrone told his boss, CSFB CEO John Mack that things were getting so bad that after a cop pulled him over and looked at his license, he let him go, remarking, "You've got enough problems already."

But, in fact, his problems were just beginning. In May 2004, Quattrone, was convicted of obstruction of justice after federal prosecutors found an email suggesting he wanted to destroy documents relating to one of the probes into his practices. A federal judge later sentenced him to eighteen months in jail. Quattrone, who once made more than $100 million in one year, has steadfastly maintained his innocence, but a jury of average New Yorkers, the kind of people who lost money during the Internet bubble, disagreed. Nearly three years after the Internet bubble burst, the little guys are still out for revenge.

After graduating from the 92nd Street Y, the Grubman twins paid the ultimate price for being the children of a disgraced corporate executive. For a time, they couldn't find a private school that would accept them. Grubman and his wife were spotted exploring a public school on the Upper West Side. According to one person who witnessed the event, LuAnn "wasn't a happy camper." Carol Cutler wasn't so happy either. She attempted to return to the telecom business, but as the contents of the emails began to make their way through the Wall Street gossip mill, Cutler's job prospects worsened. Her last known place of employment was in the interior design department at Calvin Klein's Fifth Avenue store helping rich Wall Street types, possibly future Jack Grubmans, decorate their apartments.

Sanford Weill faced another kind of embarrassment. As part of Citigroup's settlement with Spitzer and the SEC, Weill and other top officials at the firm were singled out; they could no longer meet with analysts, except with a lawyer present. The practical impact of this rule was unclear after Weill suddenly announced in mid 2003 that he was ready to step down as CEO in the coming months, handing the top job to Prince. (Maybe this is what Dinallo meant when he said, "It ain't over till it's over.") Nevertheless, Weill and various board members denied he was forced out of the job, though it seemed clear that the scandals had taken their toll. In May of 2004, Citigroup paid $2.65 billion to settle a class action suit with the New York State pension fund and other plaintiffs who lost money investing in WorldCom by listening to Grubman's advice, and the firm is bracing for similar rulings. Weill, meanwhile, is shopping his own book about his long and controversial career on Wall Street, to be coauthored, ironically, by a former securities analyst.

Only time will tell whether the reforms pushed by Spitzer have any teeth or have merely created another set of rules that Wall Street will figure out how to avoid. Wall Street is said to have found other ways to use analysts to win business, and no one believes that the quality of research has improved, as evidenced by the continued prevalence of positive ratings on banking clients. The IPO of Google, as Allan Sloan of *Newsweek* reported, received high ratings from all five underwriters of the deal (including Meeker) despite a sharp rise in the stock that suggested a new bubble was in the making and about to pop.

While Spitzer's investigation was said to be a boon for investors trying to get their money back, its record on that front appears to be mixed as well. Despite the mother lode of evidence, firms weren't required to admit "guilt," meaning that the settlement cannot be used as evidence of wrongdoing when investors try to recover some of their losses by filing arbitration cases. A federal judge, Milton Pollack, hurt investors even more by throwing out the research cases that have come his way, many of them involving Blodget's research, on the grounds that many investors were "high risk speculators" and that he was "utterly unconvinced" that Merrill was purposely attempting to mislead investors through Blodget's research.

Spitzer's office seemed to add to investors' pain. A spokesman for his office told *Forbes* that the AG's office didn't bring charges against Grubman for his WorldCom research because "we did not find Grubman's public and private views were divergent." That quote has turned out to be a powerful weapon for Citigroup's lawyers in their efforts to defeat scores of investors filing arbitrations over Grubman's WorldCom research. Plaintiffs' attorneys regularly complain that the quote is used by Citigroup to show that the firm is on the same side of this issue as Spitzer.

None of this, however, has stopped Spitzer and his people from proclaiming "victory" over fraudulent stock research. Members of his staff have used their newfound fame to score lucrative jobs in the private sector. Dinallo, for one, took a job working for Don Kempf at Morgan Stanley while Beth Golden took a position in Bear Stearns's legal department. One reason these people are in such hot demand is because Spitzer has anointed himself Wall Street's new top cop, demonstrating the continued inability of the Securities and Exchange Commission to protect small investors.

It's hard to argue with Spitzer's results. Through 2004, Spitzer racked up an impressive record, charging some of the biggest names in the mutual fund business—and later, the insurance industry—with fraud over conflicts of interest that put consumers at a disadvantage. In both cases, Spitzer followed the same recipe that proved so successful during the research investigation: Threaten criminal charges, settle for something less, and declare victory while showing up allegedly incompetent federal regulatory authorities, a point Spitzer loves to drive home. "I wouldn't let the SEC's lawyers do a house closing for me," he said at one conference attended by several former SEC officials. But Spitzer's ultimate ambition is not to become SEC chairman. Some say he's a shoo-in for New York State governor in 2006, though at one point Senator Chuck Schumer looked like he might have something to say about that. Schumer, who sparred with Spitzer during the research probe, weighed giving up his Senate seat to challenge the man who made his biggest campaign contributors squirm. He later backed down.

Spitzer, for his part, has vowed to keep up his fight against Wall Street abuse, and by the spring of 2004, he had even found a new target, his good friend Dick Grasso. For Spitzer, his imbroglio with Grasso can be traced back to the spring of 2003, just after Weill decided to throw a huge birthday party for himself at Carnegie Hall, inviting every major player in New York State politics, except Spitzer. Publicly Spitzer said he was unfazed. But privately, aides said he was seething. A few weeks later, when Spitzer learned that Grasso had nominated Weill as a member of the NYSE board to represent, of all things, small investors, he hit the ceiling. "First the birthday party and now this!" he boomed in a telephone call to Grasso just moments after he read about the move, both an aide to Spitzer and Grasso confirm. "I'm not going to be part of the rehabilitation of Sandy Weill!"

He gave Grasso twenty-four hours to remove Weill from consideration or he would go public with his opposition. By the next evening, Weill was no longer on the list.

Grasso's misstep would be the start of his own long, slow decline and eventual court battle with the New York attorney general. After Spitzer crowned him the single most important person in the research settlement, Grasso's conduct at the NYSE came under increasing scrutiny. Despite his overall popularity Grasso had created his fair share of enemies inside the Big Board. Some firms were still seething that he forced them into the global settlement to appease Spitzer. One top Wall Street executive called him a "star fucker" for his huge public profile and frequent dinners and meetings with politicians like the Reverend Jesse Jackson and the junior Senator from New York, Hillary Rodham Clinton.

Others like Goldman Sachs CEO Hank Paulson apparently wanted Grasso out for purely business reasons. For years, Paulson had advocated slowly replacing specialists on the floor of the exchange with computers, arguing that traders would receive better pricing under a computerized model. Grasso had beaten back the effort every time, and told anyone who would listen that Goldman had much to gain by ditching the specialist system, namely keeping all its customer orders in-house, rather than sending to the exchange.

Grasso won that battle with Paulson, but ultimately lost the war. His downfall started to take shape after it was reported that the NYSE had launched an investigation into several specialist firms, underscoring the need to reform a system Grasso so vigorously defended over the years. But Grasso's real problem surfaced a little later, after *The Wall Street Journal* reported that the big firms on the NYSE board were paying Grasso a salary of more than $10 million a year, and that his huge salary had helped him stash away around $100 million in his NYSE retirement account—an unheard-of sum for someone who was supposed to be regulating the same outfits. Soon, stories began to leak, one after the other, that Grasso's pay was actually higher, closer to $25 million a year, and that he had saved $130 million in a retirement account. By now, William Donaldson, a former NYSE chairman in the early 1990s, had replaced Pitt as SEC chief. Donaldson and Grasso were mortal enemies when they worked together, and for Donaldson it was payback time. Donaldson publicly announced he wanted a full accounting of Grasso's pay package, guaranteeing the "scandal" would continue.

With his pay package under scrutiny, Grasso was in a box, not for anything he did, but for how much money he made. Ironically, it was Paulson who came to him with a solution: Release the full details of the pay package as close to the Labor Day weekend as possible. The press, he guaranteed, would be doing other things.

Grasso agreed. On August 27, he announced that he had deferred compensation of close to $140 million based on a contract approved by the various compensation committees of the NYSE's board of directors. Grasso declared that he agreed to give up another $48 million as a show of good will when the new NYSE board members granted him an extension on his contract and allowed him to take the money out of his retirement account. Even Spitzer seemed to be pleased. Grasso called him with the news, and Spitzer said he was glad to have Grasso around for a few more years.

But on the floor of the exchange, where the traders and salesmen historically found a comrade in their working-class chairman, Grasso had lost control. As the stock market crash lowered profits at the exchange, Grasso began increasing the fees paid by some of the people who supported him the most over the years—floor traders and specialists. It was a huge mistake. Most of these people pull down salaries of around $200,000 a year; they couldn't understand how anyone, much less some guy from Queens, could make that much money while they were fighting for survival. Paulson, meanwhile, assured Grasso the entire mess would blow over, and that he was in Grasso's corner. Grasso didn't trust Paulson, but he had some reason to believe him on this issue. After all, the Goldman CEO sat on the board that approved Grasso's $30 million salary for 2001 as well as several of his other massive yearly pay deals.

But behind the scenes, several Wall Street CEOs say, Paulson was moving in a different direction, looking to drum up support for Grasso's execution. Jimmy Cayne, the street-smart CEO of Bear Stearns, and NYSE board member, was one of the first NYSE board members to hear from Paulson about his plan to fire Grasso. Cayne, having just come on the NYSE board, wasn't crazy about Grasso's pay deal, but he didn't trust Paulson's motives either. "A contract is a contract," he replied before ending the conversation. Paulson moved on, successfully convincing other board members to join his effort. Paulson's rationale was simple: Grasso had not fully disclosed the size of his pay and given the public outrage over executive compensation, Grasso must go. It was, of course, an absurd charge for someone in Paulson's position. First, Grasso wasn't the only highly paid executive on Wall Street. Second, the board of directors had approved many of Grasso's huge yearly bonuses; if added together, they easily approached $100 million. Third, and perhaps most galling, as board members, the NYSE board had a "fiduciary responsibility" to know exactly how much Grasso was earning.

With the increasing press frenzy surrounding Grasso's salary, Paulson soon found support even among people who Grasso once counted as friends. Watching his position weaken, Grasso turned for advice to one of his oldest friends and mentors, former NYSE chairman and Merrill board member John Phelan. When he had been at the NYSE, Phelan witnessed Grasso's transformation from a street-smart kid to a polished executive who could hold his own with the best Wall Street had to offer. Now all he could do is sit back and watch one of the greatest careers on Wall Street evaporate before his eyes.

Grasso himself appeared ready to call it quits. "I think I should resign," he said. Phelan told him not to give his enemies the satisfaction. "You never resign, let them fire you first," he said, before adding with disgust: "They always eat their own."

By now, Grasso knew what he was up against. Paulson's effort was gathering steam. Grasso decided to make one of his last "listing calls," dialing John Chambers, the CEO of Cisco, the big Silicon Valley computer company. For years, Grasso had tried to bring Cisco from the NASDAQ to the NYSE without success. "You could be the difference, John, between me staying or going," Grasso said with a laugh. Chambers laughed as well, but said there was nothing he could do.

Nor was there anything Grasso could do. By the end of the week, a majority of the board wanted him out, asking for his resignation. When he refused, they fired him.

The day that Grasso resigned, his good friend, Joe Grano, the former brokerage chief of UBS Paine Webber, recalls meeting with President Bush at a cocktail reception for large contributors. Grano, a Republican, had been chosen to head the president's council on homeland security, but this evening the conversation quickly turned to the events on Wall Street. Grano first spoke about Harvey Pitt, the former SEC chairman who was forced to resign not because of scandal, but because he bungled an appointment to an accounting oversight board. "He's a good man, but the beltway is unforgiving," the president said.

Then the subject turned to Grasso. "You know, Mr. President, today we lost another good man by the name of Dick Grasso," Grano said. "It will be difficult to replace him." The president acknowledged that he read many of the press accounts of Grasso's travails, as well as his triumphs, and agreed he was a good man, but added with a whiff of sarcasm: "I'm sure you can find someone to replace him for $70 million."

The president ended the conversation, Grano recalls, by suggesting that Grano seek the post himself. "No, sir," Grano replied. "It would be like dating his wife the first day after a divorce."

The Grasso saga continued. After his "execution," as Grasso likes to call his firing, Paulson arranged for a new leader to run the NYSE. His choice was John Reed, who had been spending most of his time lounging around his villa in France.

Reed, the former co-CEO of Citigroup, had surfaced throughout the research probe in name only, as the person Grubman helped "nuke" for Weill in his famous boardroom showdown. Now Reed was ready to nuke Grasso. He immediately demanded that Grasso return a chunk of his $139.5 million pay deal, and when Grasso declined, Reed called on Spitzer to recoup the money under an obscure state law (sound familiar?) that gives the New York attorney general oversight of nonprofits, like the New York Stock Exchange.

Spitzer attacked the Grasso case with about as much gusto as he did with conflicted research, initially seeking a settlement demanding that Grasso return about $50 million of the money he received. When Grasso refused, Spitzer went on the warpath, filing a civil case against Grasso, holding press conferences to announce his charges, much the same way he did against Merrill over Blodget's research. As this book goes to press, the case has yet to go to court, but when it does Spitzer will be in for one of the toughest battles in his career. Part of Spitzer's suit suggests that the stock exchange's board was misled, not by Grasso, but by his good friend and board member, financier Ken Langone, who as chairman of the NYSE compensation committee helped push through some of Grasso's biggest paydays.

Langone was the only board member charged by Spitzer, and has vowed to fight the case "to my last dying breath." His defense is simple: Board members like Paulson were fully aware of Grasso's package, and used the controversy over his pay merely as a weapon to get Grasso fired and remake the exchange in their own image. As for Spitzer, Langone says he's going to be the AG's "worst nightmare." Langone is planning to support any of his political opponents with a massive net worth, estimated at more than $1 billion. It should come as no surprise that Langone has already reached out to Schumer and told him he would back his efforts to keep Spitzer out of the governor's mansion.

Meanwhile, the street kid from Queens, the man who gave Spitzer his greatest victory, has vowed to fight as well. Despite Spitzer's impressive record over his Wall Street targets, no one is counting Grasso out. Unlike the celebrated analyst investigations, Spitzer has failed to produce "smoking gun" emails like the ones he found on Blodget and Grubman. The lawsuit is filled with accusations about conflicts of interest (Grasso was paid by people he was regulating), but the case itself is fairly straightforward: Grasso made too much money, Spitzer alleges, a violation of New York's not-for-profit laws.

The law in question says the salaries of executives who run such entities must be "reasonable" and "commensurate with services performed." Grasso plans to show how all his hard work during his thirty-five years at the exchange met those parameters. He has hired a tough defense attorney, Brendan Sullivan, who made a name successfully defending Oliver North during the Iran-Contra scandal, and even plans to call Spitzer as a character witness. Grasso has also launched an aggressive PR campaign, firing back at Spitzer as a political opportunist (Spitzer did not charge NYSE board member H. Carl McCall, a prominent New York State Democrat, as Grasso is quick to point out), and vows to drag every major Wall Street executive, including Paulson, into court to explain what they knew and didn't know. "I'm not going to stop until I win," Grasso said. "As far as I'm concerned this is about something bigger than money, it's about my integrity."

When was the last time you heard of a Wall Street executive putting integrity above money?

Acknowledgments

I could never have written this book without the support of some key people, first and foremost, my wife Virginia Juliano, who was there every step of the way, giving me encouragement through my many bouts with self-doubt, and serving as an editor through much of the writing process. This book is as much hers as it is mine. Todd Shuster, my agent, was instrumental in pushing me to take on this ambitious effort, believing that a major book on Wall Street research needed to be written and I was the right person to do it. Fred Hills, my editor at Simon & Schuster, didn't ask for the difficult assignment of editing my copy, but he provided valuable guidance and insight during those long months of writing and rewriting. I also would like to thank Dominick Anfuso, editorial director of Simon & Schuster's Free Press imprint, for continuing to believe in this story even as many of the subjects faded from the news pages, and Michele Jacob, Simon & Schuster's associate director of publicity, for her enthusiastic and intelligent promotion of *Blood on the Street*.

My brother-in-law, Joseph DiSalvo, has been among my most trusted advisers since the first day I undertook this book. He provided counsel regarding the various legal issues that confront first-time authors and many of the difficult editorial decisions I needed to make along the way. Likewise, I couldn't have asked for two better friends than Eric Starkman and Mark Schwartz, who were always there to listen to my problems during the course of this project. My old *Wall Street Journal* colleague Leslie Cauley, the tough and talented author and reporter for *USA Today*, did much to prepare me for the idiosyncrasies of the book world, while assuring me it would be worth it in the end. She was right.

I couldn't have completed this book without the assistance of my new employer, *Newsweek* magazine. For that, I must thank *Newsweek* editor Mark Whitaker, assistant managing editor Kathleen Deveny, as well as

Adam Bryant, *Newsweek*'s business editor and one of the most talented people I have worked with in journalism. My assistant, Susan A. Smith, worked under tight deadlines to help get the final manuscript into shape. I have always sought to emulate the journalism of James Stewart and Bob Woodward, and both were kind enough to take my telephone calls and share some of their thoughts about book writing. Andy Kessler, author of *Wall Street Meat,* and Dick Jenrette, who wrote an insightful account of his days as one of the founders of independent research at Donaldson Lufkin & Jenrette Securities, were invaluable resources about the history of stock research, while the various books and articles by my former *Journal* colleague Roger Lowenstein served as a constant standard of excellence during my reporting and writing. It was also very important to me to have the support of my brother, Dr. James Gasparino, and my mother-in-law, Angela Juliano, who is also my biggest fan.

Lastly, I'd like to thank the gang at Campagnola, Ian Carson, Ana, Sal, Frankie "D," Nicola G, Renato, Etienne, Murray, and Frankie Grimes, who helped me survive the ups and downs of this project through a combination of great food and lots of booze.

Notes

Much of the research in this book was completed during my years at *The Wall Street Journal*, and I utilized some of the notes of several *Journal* reporters who worked with me on various stories, including Anita Raghavan, Rebecca Blumenstein, and Michael Schroeder. I also reviewed the work of several journalists and authors who covered the research scandals during the 1990s bubble, and I have done my best to note places where I relied on their published work. They include John Cassidy, who wrote a profile on Eliot Spitzer for *The New Yorker* magazine, Gretchen Morgenson, the investigative reporter for *The New York Times*, Peter Elstrom of *BusinessWeek*, Peter Elkind of *Fortune*, and Andy Kessler, the author of *Wall Street Meat: Jack Grubman, Frank Quattrone, Mary Meeker and Me*, a timely and hilarious account of his years as a research analyst. I also benefited from the knowledge of Richard Jenrette and used his book *The Contrarian Manager* for much of the background information on the creation of Donaldson Lufkin & Jenrette securities. Joseph Stiglitz's book *The Roaring Nineties* was a valuable resource for facts and figures about the 1990s stock-market bubble and its impact on small investors. Although John Connor, the Washington bureau chief for Dow Jones newswires, didn't provide information for this book, he deserves recognition as well. Throughout my career, I have turned to John for advice and wisdom on how to cover tough stories. More than anything else, he demonstrated that the best journalism is fair, honest and above all, unrelenting

One question I often receive from people who have read my work in the *Journal* and now at *Newsweek* is how I get some of the information that appears in print. Here's some background: Much of the information that appears in this book comes from emails and other documents, such as depositions and internal company memos. Many of these documents were released by the New York State attorney general's office, the Securities and Exchange Commission, and other regulatory agencies as part of their investigations into Wall Street research. I have also been able to obtain some other key documents independently from various sources, and have cross-checked their validity with the people involved to confirm their authenticity. Like all investigative reporters, I used anonymous sources to provide information about the central characters appearing in this book. There are, however, very few unattributed quotes, and in those instances where they are necessary, I have done my best to contact the individuals involved to give them a chance to respond and check facts. These calls were placed to the individuals themselves or through their company's public relations office.

As I noted in the Prologue, of the three analysts, only Mary Meeker has agreed to cooperate fully, providing on-the-record interviews about the facts and circumstances surrounding her research. Blodget spoke only about his pre–Merrill Lynch record, and Grubman declined repeated requests for an interview. Even so, I have given both lawyers and press officials representing Blodget and Grubman a detailed account of what I have written, going so far as to read portions of the book back to them to ensure accuracy. Like most journalists, I have attempted to provide a truthful account of events, but where differing opinions make it impossible to come up with a single story line, I have tried to provide both sides of the story.

Prologue

Page 2   Ted Turner, now the vice chairman of TimeWarner, announced during one session that in his company's recent merger with AOL (a deal completed by Grubman's mentor, investment banker Eduardo Mestre), he had increased his net worth by another $2.5 billion—a feeling he compared to having sex for the first time. Various people who attended the event and various news accounts agree about his comment.

Page 2   Grubman's workout of 100 push-ups and 100 sit-ups from May 15, 2000 *BusinessWeek* article, "The Power Broker: From His Wall Street Perch, Jack Grubman Is Reshaping Telecom and Stirring Up Controversy" by Peter Elstrom.

Page 4   Grubman assists Joe Nacchio win CEO job at Qwest from March 25, 1997 *Wall Street Journal* article, "Jack of All Trades: How One Top Analyst Vaults 'Chinese Wall' to Do Deals for Firm" by Anita Raghavan.

Chapter 1. The Seeds of the Scandal

Page 11   Background on the creation of Donaldson Lufkin & Jenrette Securities gleaned from interviews with the three partners and with former company officials and from Richard Jenrette's book *The Contrarian Manager* (New York: McGraw-Hill, 1997)

Chapter 2. "This Guy's Going to Be Trouble"

Page 25   "I believed capitalism was evil," from interview with Henry Blodget.

Page 34   Description of Blodget's thinking before issuing $400 price target on Amazon.com is from an interview with Blodget and from Maggie Mahar's book *Bull!: A History of the Boom, 1982–1999: What Drove the Breakneck Market—and What Every Investor Needs to Know About Financial Cycles* (New York: HarperBusiness, 2003).

Page 36   Transcript of David Faber's CNBC reporting on Blodget's Amazon call published by Dow Jones News Service.

Page 38   Data on Blodget's newspaper citations and television appearances from a March 12, 2001 *Washington Post* article, "Who Blew the Dot-Com Bubble? The Cautionary Tale of Henry Blodget" by Howard Kurtz, and documents from the New York State attorney general's office.

Chapter 3. "Aren't You the Internet Lady?"

Page 47   Description of *Institutional Investor* magazine creating new analyst category for Internet research from author interviews with Meeker and May 14, 2001 *Fortune* article, "Where Mary Meeker Went Wrong" by Peter Elkind.

Page 49   Description of Mary Meeker's childhood gleaned from interview with Meeker and from April 30, 2001 *BusinessWeek* article, "Resume: Mary Meeker."

Page 66   Descriptions of eBay research from Meeker interview and various news accounts, including May 14, 2001 *Fortune* article, "Where Mary Meeker Went Wrong" by Peter Elkind.

Chapter 4. The Bloviator

Page 75   Description of Jack Grubman's childhood from various sources, including August 11, 2002 article in the *Newark Star-Ledger*: "High-Risk Life: From Cheerleader to Scapegoat—Telecom Analyst Has Become Symbol of All That's Wrong with the Industry" by Michael Rubinkam.

Page 81   Description of Eduardo Mestre's background from colleagues and from Nina Munk's book, *Fools Rush In: Steve Case, Jerry Levin, and the Unmaking of AOL Time Warner* (New York: HarperCollins, 2004).

Page 91   Information on interest expense and debt from various news sources including July 6, 1998 *Forbes* article, "Grand Illusions: World-Com's Bernie Ebbers Has Convinced Wall Street He Can Work Wonders with MCI. It Will Be a Wonder if He Can Make the Deal Pay Off" by Toni Mack.

Page 95   Description of Sandy Weill's removing plants to save money from past and present Citigroup executives and Monica Langley's book *Tearing Down the Walls: How Sandy Weill Fought His Way to the Top of the Financial World . . . and Then Nearly Lost It All* (New York: Simon & Schuster, 2003).

Chapter 5. Sucker Money

Page 97   Data on the stock market ownership comes from the Securities Industry Association, citing, among other sources, data from the Federal Reserve.

Page 103   Information about how Meeker measured Internet stocks comes from interview with Meeker and March 18, 2001 article in *The New York Times*: "How Did They Value Stocks? Count the Absurd Ways" by Gretchen Morgenson.

Page 104   Meeker's comparison of Steve Case to Henry Luce is from an interview with her and from Kara Swisher's book *There Must Be a Pony in Here Somewhere: The AOL Time Warner Debacle and the Quest for a Digital Future* (New York: Crown Business, 2003).

Page 106   Goldman's stock allocation to Meg Whitman—information from people at firm as well as from an October 3, 2004 article in *USA Today*: "Some Execs Dispute Claim of IPO Access; House Panel Says Shares Used to Woo Business" by Matt Krantz and Noelle Knox.

Page 106 Goldman's dealings with AOL from former Goldman executives and July 30, 2004 *BusinessWeek* article, "Is AOL's '1% Solution' 100% Legal? Time Warner Is Now Internally Probing Controversial 2001 Accounting at AOL Europe. More Shoes Could Soon Drop" by Paula Dwyer.

Page 108 Volcker's description of the modern financial supermarkets as "bundles of conflicts" from Francis Wheen's book *Idiot Proof: Deluded Celebrities, Irrational Power Brokers, Media Morons, and the Erosion of Common Sense* (New York: Public Affairs, 2004).

Page 110 Jesse Jackson's involvement from author interviews and Monica Langley's book *Tearing Down the Walls: How Sandy Weill Fought His Way to the Top of the Financial World . . . and Then Nearly Lost It All* (New York: Simon & Schuster, 2003).

Chapter 6. Oh, Henry

Page 114 Chapter title from March 2, 2001 *Wall Street Journal* article, "All Star Analyst Faces Arbitration After Internet Picks Hit the Skids" by Charles Gasparino.

Page 118 Blodget's television appearances from Howard Kurtz's book *The Fortune Tellers: Inside Wall Street's Game of Money, Media, and Manipulation* (New York: Free Press, 2001).

Chapter 7. The Queen Falls

Page 129 Meeker's description of Steve Case and Jeff Bezos as "wicked smart dudes" from an August 17, 1999 *SmartMoney* article, "Power Brokers—The SmartMoney 30: Who Are the 30 Most Influential People in Mutual Funds? The Answer Says a Lot About How the Industry Has Changed over the Past Year—For Better and for Worse" by Jeff Garigliano, Emily Harrison Ginsburg, Amy Gunderson, Danny Hakim, Tom Lauricella, David B. Lipschultz, Christopher Oster, Jackie Day Packel, Landon Thomas Jr., Richard ten Wolde, and Lauren Young.

Page 129 Faber's description of Meeker's discussion about Internet stocks from May 26, 1999 CNBC transcript.

Page 140 Description of Meeker's discussion about the Internet bubble at Stanford Business School from a May 13, 2001 article in *Straits Times*, "Mary Meeker's Fall from Grace" by Zuraidah Ibrahim and confirmed by author interview with Meeker.

Chapter 8. Jack in a Box

Page 152   Description of Michael Armstrong's background from a December 24, 1998 *Wall Street Journal* article, "Naughty or Nice—A New CEO's Choice: Keep the Old Team or Bring Your Own—AT&T's Mike Armstrong Is No 'Chainsaw Al'; At Least He Isn't Yet—Hiring Through Acquisitions" by Rebecca Blumenstein.

Page 183   Description of Grubman coaching Ebbers on how to answer analysts' questions from people with knowledge of the issue and from February 27, 2003 *New York Times* article, "Analyst Coached WorldCom Chief on His Script" by Gretchen Morgenson.

Page 184   Description of Grubman's WorldCom downgrade from April 23, 2002 *Financial Post* article, "WorldCom: Even Grubman Drops 'Buy,' " by Paul Haavardsrud.

Chapter 9. Keystone Cops

Page 188   Information about Ed Wolfe from author interviews with Wolfe; his attorney, Jake Zamansky; and from a February 9, 2003 *New York Times* article, "An Iceberg of Irate Investors" by Gretchen Morgenson.

Page 188   Information about Joel Cessna from Merrill Lynch public relations department confirming a June 20, 2004 article in the *Wall Street Letter,* "Merrill Terminates Broker With 25 Complaints," by Evelyn Juan.

Page 191   Levitt's fundraising for Clinton from March 15, 1993 *Wall Street Journal* article, "Levitt Helped Raise $3.5 Million During Clinton Campaign" by Christi Harlan and Michael K. Frisby.

Page 191   Description of SEC's enforcement record gleaned from data provided in SEC's annual reports.

Page 193   Description of Marvin Roffman's dealings with Donald Trump from author interviews with Roffman and James Meyer, and from Roffman's book, *Take Charge of Your Financial Future* (Secaucus: Birch Lane Press, 1994.)

Page 195   Quotes of Levitt's speeches and public discussions from October 18, 1999 article on Dow Jones Business News service, "SEC Chairman Calls Analysts' Relations with Firms 'Dysfunctional,' " and author interview with Levitt.

Page 195   Description of SEC case against Jonathan Lebed from September 21, 2000 *Wall Street Journal* article, "Teenage Trader Runs Afoul of the SEC as Stock Touting Draws Charges of Fraud" by Michael Schroeder, Ruth Simon, and Aaron Elstein.

Page 195   Richard Walker's comments about Jonathan Lebed from October 25, 2000 speech at the Bond Market Association's Sixth Annual Legal and Compliance Seminar.

Page 198   Information about Levitt's conversation with Mary Schapiro from Levitt's book *Take On the Street* (New York: Random House, 2002) and author interviews with Levitt and Schapiro.

Page 202   U. S. Senator Charles Schumer's position on financial issues and his fundraising from author interviews and two news stories: a July 15, 2002 article in *Barron's*, "Review and Preview," edited by Jay Palmer, and a March 10, 2002 article in *Newsday*, "Taking Schumer to Account: Critics Wonder What Happened to Once-Tough Stance on Audit Rules" by John Riley.

Page 202   Description of Arthur Levitt's last town hall meeting from a January 17, 2001 *Wall Street Journal* article, "SEC Chief's Valediction: Beware of the Investment World's Pitfalls" by Michael Schroeder.

Chapter 10. The Accidental Attorney General

Page 214   Spitzer's description as the "accidental attorney general" and criticisms by minority politicians confirmed by people involved in New York State Democratic Party politics.

Page 217   Dinallo's discussion with his father from author interview and an April 7, 2003 article in *The New Yorker*, "The Investigation: How Eliot Spitzer Humbled Wall Street" by John Cassidy.

Page 226   U.S. Senator Charles Schumer's description of Harvey Pitt as "the Zeus in his field," from a July 19, 2001 article in *CongressDaily*, "Banking Panel Gushes over Bush's SEC Chairman Pick."

Page 232   Wall Street analysts' explanation for missing Enron's financial demise from February 27, 2002 article in Forbes.com, "Congressional Hearings; Enron Analysts: We Was Duped" by Dan Ackman.

Page 233   Information about John Olson's experience at Merrill from author interviews with Olson as well as Roger Lowenstein's book, *Origins of the Crash: The Great Bubble and Its Undoing* (New York: Penguin, 2004).

Chapter 11. And the Walls Come Tumbling Down

Page 245   Spitzer's description of Rudy Giuliani as a "dictator" from an October 21, 2002 *New York Observer* article, "El-iot! Can Spitzer Go to 1600?" by Greg Sargent and Josh Benson; Spitzer's animosity toward Giuliani from author interview with Spitzer press officials.

Page 249   The sharp decline in Merrill's market value from various news accounts including an April 7, 2003 article in *The New Yorker*, "The Investigation: How Eliot Spitzer Humbled Wall Street" by John Cassidy.

Page 258   Spitzer's background from a December 22, 2002 *Time* magazine article, "Wall Street's Top Cop: In a Year When Business Let So Many Down, Eliot Spitzer Fought Back. How a Rich Kid from the Bronx Became the People's Champion" by Adi Ignatius.

Page 259   Spitzer's statement announcing the Merrill Lynch settlement from a May 21, 2002 CNNfn transcript of Spitzer's press conference.

Page 260   Spitzer's description as "The Enforcer" from a September 16, 2002 *Fortune* article, "Eliot Spitzer, The Enforcer. Forget the Perp Walks: What He Wants Is Change—Top to Bottom" by Mark Gimein.

Chapter 12. Jack on the Stand

Page 270   Description of Mike Huckman's interview with Grubman from author interview and videotape of event.

Page 274   Jack Grubman's statements before congressional committee and statements from members of Congress from transcript of hearings.

Chapter 13. Upgrades and Preschools

Page 306   Quotes from Eliot Spitzer and other regulators gleaned from author interviews and various news accounts, including a December 21, 2002 *Washington Post* article, "Wall Street Agrees to Mend Its Ways" by Ben White and a transcript of a December 20, 2002 press conference supplied by CNNfn.

Epilogue

Page 311   Description of Judge Pollack's ruling from July 2, 2003 *Wall Street Journal* article, "Judge Jeers at Stock-Hype Cases" by Randall Smith.

Index

329

About the Author

Charles Gasparino is a senior writer at *Newsweek* magazine. A former writer for *The Wall Street Journal*, he graduated from the University of Missouri School of Journalism. Gasparino was nominated for the Pulitzer Prize in beat reporting in 2002 and won the New York Press Club award for best continuing coverage of the Wall Street research scandals. He lives with his wife in New York City.